KYOTO CSEAS SERIES ON ASIAN STUDIES 14
Center for Southeast Asian Studies, Kyoto University

INDONESIAN WOMEN AND LOCAL POLITICS

KYOTO CSEAS SERIES ON ASIAN STUDIES
Center for Southeast Asian Studies, Kyoto University

The Economic Transition in Myanmar after 1988: Market Economy versus State Control, edited by Koichi Fujita, Fumiharu Mieno, and Ikuko Okamoto, 2009

Populism in Asia, edited by Kosuke Mizuno and Pasuk Phongpaichit, 2009

Traveling Nation-Makers: Transnational Flows and Movements in the Making of Modern Southeast Asia, edited by Caroline S. Hau and Kasian Tejapira, 2011

China and the Shaping of Indonesia, 1949–1965, by Hong Liu, 2011

Questioning Modernity in Indonesia and Malaysia, edited by Wendy Mee and Joel S. Kahn, 2012

Industrialization with a Weak State: Thailand's Development in Historical Perspective, by Somboon Siriprachai, edited by Kaoru Sugihara, Pasuk Phongpaichit, and Chris Baker, 2012

Popular Culture Co-productions and Collaborations in East and Southeast Asia, edited by Nissim Otmazgin and Eyal Ben-Ari, 2012

Strong Soldiers, Failed Revolution: The State and Military in Burma, 1962–88, by Yoshihiro Nakanishi, 2013

Organising Under the Revolution: Unions and the State in Java, 1945–48, by Jafar Suryomenggolo, 2013

Living with Risk: Precarity & Bangkok's Urban Poor, by Tamaki Endo, 2014

Migration Revolution: Philippine Nationhood and Class Relations in a Globalized Age, by Filomeno V. Aguilar Jr., 2014

The Chinese Question: Ethnicity, Nation, and Region in and Beyond the Philippines, by Caroline S. Hau, 2014

Identity and Pleasure: The Politics of Indonesian Screen Culture, by Ariel Heryanto, 2014

KYOTO CSEAS SERIES ON ASIAN STUDIES 14
Center for Southeast Asian Studies, Kyoto University

INDONESIAN WOMEN AND LOCAL POLITICS
Islam, Gender and Networks in Post-Suharto Indonesia

Kurniawati Hastuti Dewi

NUS PRESS
Singapore

in association with

KYOTO UNIVERSITY PRESS
Japan

The publication of this book is financially supported by the International Program of Collaborative Research at the Center for Southeast Asian Studies, Kyoto University, and the Kyoto University President's Special Fund.

© 2015 Kurniawati Hastuti Dewi

All rights reserved. This book, or parts thereof, may not be reproduced in any form or by any means, electronic or mechanical, including photocopying, recording or any information storage and retrieval system now known or to be invented, without written permission from the Publisher.

NUS Press
National University of Singapore
AS3-01-02, 3 Arts Link
Singapore 117569
www.nus.edu.sg/nuspress

ISBN 978-9971-69-842-3 (Paper)

Kyoto University Press
Yoshida-South Campus, Kyoto University
69 Yoshida-Konoe-Cho, Sakyo-ku
Kyoto 606-8315
Japan
www.kyoto.up.or.jp

ISBN 978-4-87698-363-6

National Library Board Singapore Cataloguing in Publication Data

Dewi, Kurniawati Hastuti, author.
    Indonesian women and local politics: Islam, gender and networks in post-Suharto Indonesia / Kurniawati Hastuti Dewi. – Singapore: NUS Press; Japan: in association with Kyoto University Press, [2015]
    pages cm – (Kyoto CSEAS series on Asian studies; 14)
    Includes bibliographical references and index.
    ISBN: 978-9971-69-842-3 (paperback)

    1. Muslim women – Political activity – Indonesia. 2. Indonesia – Politics and government – 1998–. I. Title. II. Series: Kyoto CSEAS series on Asian studies; 14.

HQ1236.5
305.4869709598 — dc23   OCN897086793

Cover image: Ratna Ani Lestari, Regent of Banyuwangi (2005–10), in an interview with journalists after attending a plenary session with the regional People's Representative Council (DPRD) of Banyuwangi on 29 July 2009. (Personal collection of Kurniawati Hastuti Dewi)

Printed by: Markono Print Media Pte Ltd

CONTENTS

List of Map vi
List of Figures vi
List of Tables vii
List of Graphs viii
Abbreviations ix
Acknowledgements xvii

1. Introduction 1
2. Impact of Islamization and Democratization in Expanding Indonesian Women's Roles in Politics 28
3. The Normative Expectation of Javanese Muslim Women and Islamic Perspectives on Female Leadership 50
4. Rustriningsih: Advantage of Familial Ties, Ability to Embrace Islamic Piety and Using Gender to Expand a Political Base 64
5. Siti Qomariyah: Using Islamic Piety and Gender and Securing Nahdlatul Ulama's Socio-political Base 108
6. Ratna Ani Lestari: Holding on to Familial Ties, Manipulating Islamic Piety and Using Gender to Attract Wider Support 141
7. Comparative Analysis and Conclusion 173

Appendix 196
Glossary 204
Bibliography 210
Index 235

LIST OF MAP

1. Location of Kebumen Regency, Pekalongan Regency and Banyuwangi Regency in Java   27

LIST OF FIGURES

1. Rustriningsih's New Style of Dress with the Headscarf   70
2. Bibit and Rustriningsih in a Pamphlet for the 2008 Central Java Gubernatorial Election   93
3. *Pengajian* for Women Every Tuesday Morning at *Kyai* Taufiq's *Pesantren*   120
4. Campaign Pamphlet for Siti Qomariyah and Pontjo in the 2006 Direct Election   126
5. Women's Networks behind Siti Qomariyah's Victory   129
6. Example of the *Mauluddan Pengajian* VCD and Promotion of Siti Qomariyah's Nomination   130
7. Example of Antono and Qurofi's Campaign Pamphlet   131
8. Gus Yus's Family Tree   152
9. Ratna and Gus Yus's Musical Media Campaign VCD for the 2005 Direct Election in Banyuwangi   158
10. Ratna and Gus Yus's Campaign Pamphlet   163

LIST OF TABLES

1. Female Politicians Elected in Direct Elections within and outside of Java (2005–08) — 21
2. Non-Elected Female Political Candidates in Direct Elections within and outside of Java (2005–06) — 24
3. Political Party Composition in Kebumen's People's Representative Council during the New Order and Post-Suharto Eras — 66
4. Profile of Regent and Vice-regent Candidates in the 2005 Direct Election in Kebumen — 76
5. Political Configuration in the Central Java DPRD in the 1992, 1999, 2004 and 2009 General Elections — 86
6. Profiles of Governor and Vice-governor Candidates in the 2008 Direct Gubernatorial Election in Central Java — 89
7. Political Party Composition in Pekalongan during the New Order and Post-Suharto — 109
8. Profile of Regent and Vice-regent Candidates in the 2006 Direct Election in Pekalongan — 123
9. Political Party Composition in Banyuwangi during the New Order and Post-Suharto Eras — 143
10. Profile of Regent and Vice-regent Candidates in the 2005 Direct Election in Banyuwangi — 150
11. Similarities and Differences of Factors Behind the Rise and Victory of Three Muslim Female Javanese Political Leaders — 173
12. Female Leaders Elected in Direct Elections (2010–14) — 190

LIST OF GRAPHS

1. Distribution of Votes across Districts as a Result of the 2005 Direct Election in Kebumen — 84
2. Distribution of Votes across Regencies/Municipalities as a Result of the 2008 Central Java Direct Gubernatorial Election — 91
3. Distribution of Votes across Districts as a Result of the 2006 Direct Election in Pekalongan — 133
4. Distribution of Votes across Districts as a Result of the 2005 Direct Election in Banyuwangi — 165

ABBREVIATIONS

AD	Anggaran Dasar, Basic Organizational Platform
ABIM	Angkatan Belia Islam Malaysia, Youth Islamic Group of Malaysia
ANRI	Arsip Nasional Republik Indonesia, National Archive of the Republic of Indonesia
ANSIPOL	Aliansi Masyarakat Sipil untuk Revisi UU Politik, the Alliance of Civil Society for Revision of Political Legislation
APBD	Anggaran Pendapatan dan Belanja Daerah, Local Government Revenue and Expenditure Budget
APBN	Anggaran Pendapatan dan Belanja Negara, State Revenue and Expenditure Budget
APPNP	Aliansi Partai Politik Non-Parlemen, Alliance of Non-Parliamentary Political Parties. This was intended to be the political vehicle of Ratna Ani Lestari in the 2010 direct elections in Banyuwangi
ART	Anggaran Rumah Tangga, Operational Organizational Platform
BARNAS	Partai Barisan Nasional, National Front Party
BLT	Bantuan Langsung Tunai, direct financial assistance for poor families
BPP	Bilangan Pembagi Pemilih, the Vote Division Number
BPUPKI	Badan Penyelidik untuk Persiapan Kemerdekaan Indonesia, the Investigative Body for the Preparation of Indonesian Independence, founded by the Japanese colonial government and responsible for drafting the Constitution for the newly independent Indonesia
BUMD	Badan Usaha Milik Daerah, Local Government Enterprises
CEDAW	The Convention on the Elimination of All Forms of Discrimination Against Women

CETRO	Centre for Electoral Reform
CLD	Counter Legal Draft, to counter the Compilation of Islamic Law (KHI)
DAU	Dana Alokasi Umum, General Allocation Fund from the Central Government
DDII	Dewan Dakwah Islam Indonesia, Indonesian Islamic Propagation Council
DI/TII	Darul Islam/Tentara Islam Indonesia, rebel group led by Kartosuwiryo in West Java that declared the establishment of an Islamic state in Indonesia
DI/NII	Darul Islam/Negara Islam Indonesia, Darul Islam/Indonesian Islamic State
DPR	Dewan Perwakilan Rakyat, People's Representative Council
DPRD	Dewan Perwakilan Rakyat Daerah, the regional People's Representative Council
FK3	Forum Kajian Kitab Kuning, Yellow Book (*pesantren* texts) Learning Forum
FPI	Front Pembela Islam, Islamic Defenders Front
FPIS	Front Pemuda Islam Surakarta, Surakarta Youth Islamic Front
FUUI	Forum Ulama Ummat Islam, the Islamic Religious Scholars Forum
GBHN	Garis-Garis Besar Haluan Negara, the Broad Guidelines on State Policy
Gerwani	Gerakan Wanita Indonesia, the Indonesian Women's Movement, a women's organization affiliated with the Indonesian Communist Party (PKI)
Gerwis	Gerakan Wanita Indonesia Sedar, the Conscious Indonesian Women's Movement, an embryo of Gerwani
GOLKAR	Golongan Karya, a confederation of functional groups created by Suharto in the 1970s which became his political party and vehicle
GPPNP	Gabungan Partai-Partai Politik Non Parlemen, Coalition of Non-Parliamentary Political Parties. The political vehicle of Tri Ratna Ani Lestari in the 2005 direct elections in Banyuwangi
GPSP	Gerakan Perempuan Sadar Pemilu, the Movement for Educating Female Voters

H.	Haji, special title for Muslim men who have made the pilgrimage to Mecca
Hj.	Hajjah, special title for Muslim women who have made the pilgrimage to Mecca
HTI	Hizbut Tahrir Indonesia, Indonesian Islamic Party of Liberation
IAIN	Institute Agama Islam Negeri, the State Institute of Islamic Studies
ICIP	International Center for Islam and Pluralism
ICMI	Ikatan Cendikiawan Muslim Indonesia, Indonesian Muslim Intellectual Association
ICRP	Indonesian Conference on Religion and Peace
IKIP	Institut Keguruan dan Ilmu Pendidikan, Teaching and Education Institute
IPNU	Ikatan Pelajar Nahdlatul Ulama, Nadlatul Ulama Student Association (NU)
IPPNU	Ikatan Pelajar Putri Nahdlatul Ulama, Nahdlatul Ulama Female Student Association (NU)
ITB	Institute Teknologi Bandung, Bandung Institute of Technology
JICA	Japan International Cooperation Agency
JIL	Jaringan Islam Liberal, Liberal Islamic Network
JIMM	Jaringan Intelektual Muda Muhammadiyah, the Muhammadiyah Intellectual Youth Network
JPPOL	Jaringan Perempuan dan Politik, the Network for Women and Politics
JPPR	Jaringan Pendidikan Pemilih untuk Rakyat, the Peoples' Voter Education Network
KAMMI	Kesatuan Aksi Mahasiswa Muslim Indonesia, the United Action of Indonesian Muslim Students
KPPSI	Komite Persiapan Penegakan Syariat Islam, Committee for Preparation of Syari'ah Implementation
KB	Keluarga Berencana, Family Planning Program
KH.	*Kyai* Haji, title for a religious scholar who has made the pilgrimage to Mecca (the *haj*)
KHI	*Kompilasi Hukum Islam*, Compilation of Islamic Law
KOWANI	Kongres Wanita Indonesia, the Indonesian Women's Congress, established in 1945. The umbrella for Indonesian women's organizations

KPI	Kongres Perempuan Indonesia, Indonesian Women's Congress, established in 1935
KPP	Kaukus Perempuan Parlemen, the Women's Parliamentary Caucus inside parliament
KPPI	Kaukus Perempuan dan Politik Indonesia, the Caucus for Women and Indonesian Politics outside of parliament
KPU	Komisi Pemilihan Umum, General Election Commission
KPUD	Komisi Pemilihan Umum Daerah, Local General Election Commission
KSF	Kartika Soekarno Foundation
LBH APIK	Lembaga Batuan Hukum Asosiasi Perempuan Indonesia untuk Keadilan, the Legal Aid Foundation of the Indonesian Women's Association for Justice
LIPI	Lembaga Ilmu Pengetahuan Indonesia, the Indonesian Institute of Sciences
LKAJ	Lembaga Kajian Agama dan Jender, Institute for Religion and Gender Studies
LKJ HAM	Lembaga Kajian Jender dan Hak Asasi Manusia, Institute for Gender and Human Rights Studies, in Semarang, Central Java
LKiS	Lembaga Kajian Islam dan Sosial, Institute for Islam and Social Studies
LP3ES	Lembaga Penelitian, Pendidikan dan Penerangan Ekonomi dan Sosial, the Institute for Economic and Social Research, Education and Analysis
MIAI	Majelis Islam 'Ala Indonesia, a federation of Islamic organizations and political parties initially founded in 1935
MASYUMI	Majelis Syuro Muslimin Indonesia, the evolution of MIAI from 1943
MMI	Majelis Mujahidin Indonesia, the Indonesian Mujahideen Council
MPR	Majelis Permusyawaratan Rakyat, Indonesian People's Consultative Assembly
MUI	Majelis Ulama Indonesia, Indonesian Council of Ulama
NU	Nahdhlatul Ulama
PIS	Partai Indonesia Sejahtera, Indonesia Welfare Party

P. PELOPOR	Partai Pelopor, Pioneer's Party
P.P. Pancasila	Partai Patriot Pancasila, Pancasila Patriotic Party
PPRN	Partai Peduli Rakyat Nasional, Concern for the People National Party
PAD	Pendapatan Asli Daerah, Regional Revenue
PAN	Partai Amanat Nasional, National Mandate Party
PANGKOSTRAD	Panglima Komando Strategis Angkatan Darat, Commander of the Army's Strategic Command
PAS	Partai Islam se-Malaysia, the Pan Malaysian Islamic Party
P. Buruh	Partai Buruh, Labor Party
PBB	Partai Bulan Bintang, the Star and Crescent Party
PBR	Partai Bintang Reformasi, the Reform Star Party
PBSD	Partai Buruh Sosial Demokrat, Social Democrat Labour Party
PCNU	Pengurus Cabang Nahdlatul Ulama, Regional Branch of Nahdlatul Ulama
PD	Partai Demokrat, Democrat Party
PD Politik	Pusat Pemberdayaan Perempuan dalam Politik, Center for Empowering Women in Politics
PDI	Partai Demokrasi Indonesia, the Indonesian Democratic Party
PDIP	Partai Demokrasi Indonesia Perjungan, the Indonesian Democratic Party of Struggle. New form of PDI under Megawati Sukarnoputri's leadership since 1997
PDK	Partai Demokrasi Kebangsaan, National Democratic Party
PDS	Partai Damai Sejahtera, Prosperous Peace Party
PERDA	Peraturan Daerah, local government regulation
PERSIS	Persatuan Islam, the Islamic Union
PERWAMU	Persatuan Wanita Murba, the Proletarian or Murba Women's Union
PGRI	Partnership for Governance Reform in Indonesia

PILKADA	Pemilihan Kepala Daerah, Election of Local Government Heads
PILKADA LANGSUNG	Pemilihan Kepala Daerah Langsung, Direct Elections
PK	Partai Keadilan, Justice Party
PKB	Partai Kebangkitan Bangsa, National Awakening Party
PKDI	Partai Kasih Demokrasi Indonesia, Indonesian Love Democracy Party
P. Kedaulatan	Partai Kedaulatan, Sovereignty Party
PKI	Partai Komunis Indonesia, Indonesian Communist Party
PKK	Pembinaan Kesejahteraan Keluarga, Family Welfare Guidance. After 1998, its name was changed to Pemberdayaan dan Kesejahteraan Keluarga (Family Welfare and Empowerment)
PKKPA	Tim Penanganan Korban Kekerasan terhadap Perempuan dan Anak, Team Advocating for Victims of Violence against Women and Children
PKNU	Partai Kebangkitan Nasional Ulama Indonesia, the Indonesian Ulama's National Awakening Party
PKPB	Partai Karya Peduli Bangsa, Concern for the Nation Functional Party
PKPI	Partai Keadilan dan Persatuan Indonesia, Indonesian Unity and Justice Party
PKS	Partai Keadilan Sejahtera, Prosperous Justice Party, evolution of Partai Keadilan (PK)
PKP	Partai Karya Perjuangan, Functional Party of Struggle
PM	Partai Matahari Bangsa, National Sun Party
P. Merdeka	Partai Merdeka, Freedom Party
PNBK	Partai Nasional Banteng Kemerdakaan, Freedom Bull National Party
PNI	Partai Nasionalis Indonesia, Indonesian Nationalist Party
PNIM	Partai Nasional Indonesia-Marhaenis, Indonesian National Party-Marhaenist Front
PP	Partai Patriot, Patriotic Party

PPD	Partai Persatuan Daerah, Regional Unity Party
PPDI	Partai Penegak Demokrasi Indonesia, Indonesian Democratic Vanguard Party
PPDK	Partai Persatuan Demokrasi Kebangsaan, National Democratic Unity Party
PPI	Partai Pemuda Indonesia, Indonesia Youth Party
PPPI	Partai Pengusaha dan Pekerja Indonesia, Indonesian Workers and Employers Party
PPPI	Perikatan Perkumpulan Perempuan Indonesia, the Indonesian Women's Association. A women's organization created in the first Indonesian Women's Congress in Yogyakarta on 22 December 1928
PPII	Perikatan Perkumpulan Istri Indonesia, the Indonesian Wives Association, formed in 1929. Evolution of PPPI
PPKB	Perempuan Partai Kebangkitan Bangsa, Women of the National Awakening Party
PPNUI	Partai Persatuan Nahdlatul Ulama Indonesia, the Indonesian Nahdlatul Ulama Unity Party
PPP	Partai Persatuan Pembangunan, the United Development Party
PROPENAS	Program Pembangunan Nasional, National Development Program
PSI	Partai Sarikat Indonesia, Indonesian Unity Party
PSII	Partai Sarikat Islam Indonesia, Indonesian Islamic Unity Party
PUSKESMAS	Pusat Kesehatan Masyarakat, Community Health Center
RAKERDASUS	Rapat Kerja Daerah Khusus, special meeting of PDIP branches in which a minimum of two pairs of candidates are chosen and whose names are then sent to the PDIP Central Board
RENSTRA	Rencana Strategis Daerah, Local Strategic Development Plan
RKPD	Rencana Kerja Pemerintah Daerah, Local Government Development Plan
RPJMD	Rencana Pembangunan Jangka Menengah Daerah, Local Government Mid-Term Development Plan
RRI	Radio Republik Indonesia, Indonesian Radio Broadcasting Company

SBMI	Serikat Buruh Migran Indonesia, Indonesian Migrant Workers Association
SDI	Sekolah Dasar Inpres, Presidential Instruction primary schools
SIP	Suara Ibu Peduli, the Voice of Concerned Mothers
STAIN	Sekolah Tinggi Agama Islam Negeri, Indonesian State College of Islamic Religion
SUPERSEMAR	Surat Perintah Sebelas Maret, Letter of 11 March
UGM	Universitas Gadjah Mada, Gadjah Mada University
UI	Universitas Indonesia, University of Indonesia
UIN	Universitas Islam Negeri, State Islamic University
UMY	Universitas Muhammadiyah Yogyakarta, Muhammadiyah University of Yogyakarta
UN ESCAP	United Nations Economic and Social Commission for Asia and the Pacific
UN	United Nations
UNDIP	Universitas Diponegoro, University of Diponegoro
USAID	United States Agency for International Development

ACKNOWLEDGEMENTS

I owe a great deal to Benedict R.O'G. Anderson's books *The Idea of Power in Javanese Culture* (1972) and *Language and Power: Exploring Political Culture in Indonesia* (1990). The embryo of this book originated from my critical reading of Anderson's book. As a Javanese Muslim woman raised with strong Javanese values in Yogyakarta, it is fascinating to read about ways in which outsiders, including Anderson, view and comprehend Javanese society. While fascinated by Anderson's book, I was left unsatisfied because the various examples he cited included only powerful male figures in Java, in fact, many Javanese noble women with super-abundant power played crucial roles throughout the Javanese history. Besides that, I was also curious to know how the idea of power in Javanese culture has become transformed in contemporary Indonesia. Anderson's work mainly encompasses the dynamics over ideas of power in Javanese culture and its manifestation in the Old Order and the early New Order Indonesian political context. I question the basic premise he offers on the quest for and the signs of power, as this question may reveal different features when considered from a woman's perspective in the changing social context of Islamization and democratization in Indonesia now. This is the initial research topic that I wanted to write for my PhD thesis at Kyoto University. However, I quickly realized my own limitations. I had not yet mastered the Old Javanese language that would be crucial for this kind of research. Ideally, I needed more years to learn, but my scholarship scheme was only for three and half years. I left the topic. But, the critical question is still stuck in my mind, about how Javanese women viewed and exercised power in contemporary Indonesia. From there, I turned to the very interesting phenomenon of the increasing success of Muslim women in local politics.

 I must admit that this book owes its spirit to many women friends of mine across Indonesia whom I met doing research from 2001 until 2014. Throughout years of research and personal interactions, I have learnt a number of values and insights that helped me to expand my personal, religious and intellectual frontiers. As young researcher with passion for gender and women's studies, I sometimes felt helpless about the many challenges that women face, and worried that I could not make a significant difference in their lives. As I have continued on this path of scholarship, I promised myself that I would make it my goal to honour the women that I have met by choosing to work on projects that contribute to the enhancement of Indonesian women. This present book is one of my ways, as a researcher and Indonesian woman, to fulfil my promise and at the same time contribute to scholarly work.

The bulk of this book, with some revision and updating, is from my doctoral dissertation for the Department of Southeast Asian Studies, Graduate School of Asian and African Area Studies (ASAFAS) of Kyoto University in 2012. A three and a half year scholarship (October 2008–March 2012) from Japan's Ministry of Education, Culture, Sports, Science and Technology (MEXT) made it possible for me to finish my doctoral degree at Kyoto University. I would like to thank Kyoto University-Global COE Program for sponsoring my fieldworks in Java. Although I spent a lot of time on the manuscript in Indonesia, in its final stages JASSO (Japan Student Services Organization) granted me a Follow-Up Research Fellowship at the Center for Southeast Asian Studies (CSEAS), Kyoto University, Japan, from September through October 2013, which greatly enabled me to prepare for the publication process.

I gratefully acknowledge that the publication of this book was made possible with financial support from the International Program of Collaborative Research at the Center for Southeast Asian Studies, Kyoto University, as well as the Kyoto University President's Special Fund. I am indebted to Professor Hayami Yoko, Chairperson of the Publications Committee of CSEAS Kyoto University, and Shitara Narumi who have helped me since the initial stage of acceptance of the manuscript as part of the Kyoto CSEAS Series on Asian Studies. I thank Rebecca Christine Lunnon for her kindness in carefully editing an early version of the manuscript for the refereeing process. I would also like to thank the three anonymous referees who thoughtfully read my manuscript and provided critical questions, details and important comments. I am indebted to Paul Kratoska of NUS Press for accepting the manuscript for publication. I thank Lena Qua, the Managing Editor of NUS Press, who oversaw the production of this book, Danielle McClellan for carefully editing it, and Charles Wheeler for compiling the index.

My life and intellectual endeavour in Kyoto has been fruitful. I would like to thank my main supervisor, Associate Professor Okamoto

Masaaki for his warm friendship, encouragement and significant support for my research as I completed this book. I would also like to thank my supervisors Professor Hayami Yoko and Associate Professor Caroline Sy Hau for the knowledge that they shared, as well as their motivation and inspiration. My deepest thanks to Professor Mizuno Kosuke for his critical comments and support, and to Professor Shimizu Hiromu for his encouragement.

I would like to acknowledge the help I received from my colleagues at the Research Center for Politics at the Indonesian Institute of Sciences (LIPI) Jakarta: Prof. Dr. Ikrar Nusa Bhakti for encouragement to pursue my PhD in Japan and to publish this book, Prof. Dr. Syamsuddin Haris, (the late) Dr. Muridan Satrio Widjojo, Dr Dhuroruddin Mashad and Dr. Rifqi Muna for support and inspiration. I owe thanks to several fellows at the Center for Southeast Asian Studies (CSEAS) who I met when I studied at Kyoto University: Dr. Tatik Hafidz, Dr. Tung Ju Lan, Prof. Oekan Abdullah, Prof. Mochtar Pabottingi, Prof. Dewi Fortuna Anwar, Drs. Ahmad Suaedy, George Wibisono and Prof. Ukrist Pathmanand. I thank Prof. Anthony Reid, for his insight, kindness and generously shared articles on female leadership in Southeast Asia. I thank Prof. Benedict Anderson whom I met when I was a student at Kyoto University for his encouragement when I shared my story and discussed this study. I thank Prof. Kathryn Robinson, Prof. Virginia Hooker and Dr. Sally White for their tremendous contribution in the initial stage of my intellectual endeavour as a master's degree student at the Faculty of Asian Studies, Australian National University (ANU).

The fieldwork in Indonesia would not have been possible without help from many people. I have limited space to name each of them, but here I mention several names. In Jakarta, I thank Mbak Yuniar Prastuti for giving me access to the data I needed from the Ministry of Home Affairs Republic of Indonesia; Mbak Yuni Zamhari for the excellent contacts to Nahdlatul Ulama's elites and information. In Canberra, I thank Mas Zahrul and Mbak Mei for their hospitality and Safira Machrusah for meeting with me in 2010. In preparation for my visit to Pekalongan, I thank my colleague Dr. Hamdan Basyar who provided me with important contacts. I am thankful to Kusmiyati, of Nasyiatul 'Aisyiyah, who assisted me in Pekalongan. I am thankful to the family of Mbak Wahidah Zein Siregar in Surabaya for providing a comfortable transit for me before I went to Banyuwangi. My thanks to my younger brother-in-law Taufiqul Mujib who has many connections among NU youth including in Banyuwangi. He introduced me to Gus Endy in Pesantren Bustanul

Makmur Genteng, and Ning Wafiroh in Pesantren Darussalam Blok Agung, both in Banyuwangi. It was due to their help that I was able to meet other *gus* and *kyai* in Banyuwangi. I thank Ramang, who assisted me in Banyuwangi for his excellent links to people from different social classes and ideologies. In preparation for my work in Kebumen, again I am thankful to my younger brother-in-law Taufiqul Mujib who introduced me to the Murtajib Director of INDIPT Kebumen which expanded my network in the region. I am also thankful to Irma and Rimba for their assistance with connections and interviews. In Semarang, I thank Masathosi Sakurai who introduced me to Andi Kristianto, chief of the Department of Communication and Information of the Provincial Board of PDIP Central Java who helped with my research inside PDIP. Ibu Fitriyah, Bapak Muhammad Adnan and Teguh Yuwono, my former lecturers when I was studying for my bachelor's degree at the Faculty of Social and Political Sciences, University of Diponegoro in Semarang, helped me with my research in Semarang. Thanks as well to the family of Mbak Neneng and Mistri Handayani in Semarang who helped me in many ways to make my stay in Semarang enjoyable. And of course, I am deeply thankful to Rustriningsih, vice-governor of Central Java (2008–13); Siti Qomariyah, regent of Pekalongan (2006–11); and Ratna Ani Lestari, regent of Banyuwangi (2005–10), who agreed to be observed and interviewed for this study.

I would also like to thank my friends in Okamoto's Discussion Groups during my study in Kyoto (2009–12) for their warm friendship and teamwork: Cherry, Kayane, Tetsu, Asegawa, Jen, and especially Mayumi for her sincere friendship in Kyoto. My fellow Indonesian friends in ASAFAS, Retno Kusumaningtyas, Syafwina, and especially Jafar Suryomenggolo who kindly shared his experience and helped me in many ways in publishing this book. I would also like to acknowledge the help I received from the staff of numerous libraries I visited: Arsip Nasional Republik Indonesia, Perpustakaan Nasional, Pusat Dokumentasi dan Informasi Ilmiah LIPI, RAHIMA, Center for Study of Religious and Culture Syarif Hidyatullah State Islamic University (all in Jakarta), the Main Library of Kyoto University, Center for Southeast Asian Studies, and the Graduate School of Human and Environmental Studies, Faculty of Integrated Human Studies, Graduate School of Letters and Faculty of Letters, Graduate School of Education and Faculty of Education Library, Faculty of Law Library, Graduate School of Economics and Faculty of Economics (all in Kyoto University). Some materials in this study have been published elsewhere: *Southeast Asian Studies* 1, no. 1 (April 2012): 109–40; *Jurnal Masyarakat Indonesia* 38, no. 2 (December 2012): 329–50.

I feel blessed by Allah SWT to have been raised by a compassionate and encouraging mother, Hj. Supeni. Under her guardianship, I have learnt and gained the value of giving, love, hard work, persistence, *syukur* and *shabar*. This book would not be possible without the abundant help, encouragement and prayers of my mother. I am deeply thankful to my late father Sudirjo for the inspiration to pursue my education to the limit; to my older sister Astin Hestining Wijayanti and my younger brother Didik Joko Nugroho for their abundant support and love throughout my life. Thank you to my mother-in-law, Hj. Hani'atien, and father-in-law, the late H. Subekti, for their support and prayer. Thanks to my big family in Yogyakarta, Tuban and Jakarta who always give me support in every tough situation. My special thanks to my beloved husband Ahmad Helmy Fuady for his continuous love, patience, help and encouragement. I owe a great deal to my two lovely daughters Aksari Sekar Fuady and Aaliyah Nimas Fuady for their understanding and patience as I had to travel away from home to Kyoto for two months to prepare the final manuscript for publication. The final stage of producing this book has been especially meaningful to me as I was pregnant and finally gave birth to my third child Akira Dewi Fuady at the end of November 2014. Let all my lovely children gain from and continue in the spirit of this book as members of the future generation of Indonesia.

Kurniawati Hastuti Dewi
South Tangerang, November 2014

CHAPTER 1

Introduction

Indonesian Muslim Women and Local Politics

There is a general perception, as noted by the prominent Indonesian Muslim activist the late Lili Zakiyah Munir, that Islam is a source of discrimination and oppression against women; this results in a common belief that as a religion Islam hinders the promotion of women's rights.[1] This widespread misconception about Islam's treatment of women has also been addressed by western scholars, such as Susan Blackburn, who specialize in researching Indonesian women. In one of her edited books, Blackburn notes that while there is an increase in interest in Islam around the world, "unfortunately, the interest of many people in Islam relates not just to its current connection with terrorism, but also to its perceived ill-treatment of women".[2] In this book, I seek to counter the general misconception by presenting an account of contemporary Indonesian Muslim women who, since the introduction of direct elections in 2005, have actively taken part in local politics and have secured leadership positions.

The rising number of Indonesian Muslim women taking part in political leadership on the local level has been made possible within a new political context of democratization that followed the overthrow of Suharto (the authoritarian Indonesian president during the New Order era, 1967–98). As part of a post-Suharto democratization movement, Law No. 5/1974, which had supported an authoritarian, centralized government during the New Order era, was replaced by Law No. 22/1999 on Regional Government, which contained a strong spirit of decentralization and provided for local autonomy. Several years later, Law No. 22/1999

---

[1] Lili Zakiyah Munir, "Islam, Gender and Equal Rights for Women", *The Jakarta Post*, 10 December 2002, p. 6.
[2] Blackburn et al., "Introduction", in *Indonesian Islam in A New Era*, p. 1.

was replaced by Law No. 32/2004, which introduced direct elections of governors (provincial heads) and regents (regency heads). The number of female leaders elected in local politics increased significantly after the introduction of direct elections in 2005. From 2005 through 2008, under Law No. 32/2004, 466 direct elections were held, consisting of 355 elections outside Java and 111 elections in Java (Central Java, East Java, West Java, Banten, Jakarta and Yogyakarta).[3] The percentage of pairs elected including at least one female (either as regents or vice-regents) in Java was higher (11 pairs or 9.91 per cent, with all female politicians being Muslim) compared to those elected outside of Java (15 pairs or 4.22 per cent).[4] This data indicates that initially, most of the Muslim female leaders elected in the direct election are from Java. The growth in Muslim female political leaders in Indonesia since 2005 has developed in tandem with a growing engagement of Muslims with Islamic principles and norms in the democratic atmosphere that began to develop after 1998.[5] It is generally understood that contemporary Indonesian Islam in the post-Suharto era shows a waning in the power of political Islam (as indicated by the weakening of Islamic political parties), but a deepening of—to borrow from Okamoto Masaaki, Ota Atsushi and Ahmad Suaedy —"social Islamization", as indicated by phenomena such as the increasing publication of Islamic books, the growing popularity of veiling, attention to Muslim women's rights, emergence of a new generation of Islamic preachers, or growing attention to Islamic banking systems.[6] This development indicates a growing influence of Islam in shaping the social,

---

[3] I compiled these figures based on data from the Ministry of Home Affairs, Republic of Indonesia, "Daftar Kepala Daerah dan Wakil Kepala Daerah Yang Telah Diterbitkan Keputusannya Presiden Republik Indonesia Hasil Pemilihan Kepala Daerah Secara Langsung Tahun 2005, 2006, 2007, dan Tahun 2008". The data from the Ministry of Home Affairs does not use the common geographical distinction between Java (Pulau Jawa) and outside Java (Luar Pulau Jawa). I created my own classification based on this common geographical distinction. For detailed information, see Tables 1 and 2 at the end of this chapter.

[4] Ibid.

[5] For an important book that signifies the increasing role of Islamic principles and norms, the tension surrounding the debate, and appropriate Islamic gender relations within Indonesian Muslim society including a section on Muslim women during the Reform period, see Robinson, *Gender, Islam and Democracy in Indonesia*.

[6] The decline of political Islam can be seen from the fact that Islamic political parties did not gain much support from voters and their electorate declined steadily, despite the participation of more than 40 Islamic political parties in the 1999 General Election. While Islamic political parties gained around 39 per cent of the vote in the 1999

economic and political dynamics of Indonesian society.⁷ Given this phenomenon in which Islam has gradually moved into the centre of Indonesian society and is shaping the Indonesian public sphere, this book investigates the roles of Islam and gender in the political rise of Indonesian Muslim women, particularly Javanese Muslim women, since 2005. I believe that the increasing number of female Muslim leaders elected through direct elections indicates that important changes and developments have taken place in Indonesia in relation to Islam, gender and politics. This interesting phenomenon will be explored deeply in this book.

Islam and Gender in Local Politics: A Different View

While the increase in the number of Indonesian Muslim women who are actively taking part in local politics since the introduction of direct elections has been significant, this phenomenon has rarely been studied, as the following review of relevant scholarly works demonstrates.

Studies on Islam in post-Suharto Indonesia can be divided into five themes: the dynamic of Islamic political parties in general elections during the Reform Era, Islamic thought and politics, "social Islamization", Islamic radicalism and Muslim women's roles in contemporary Indonesia.⁸

---

and 2004 general elections, their percentage of the votes fell to about 29 per cent in the 2009 election. See Masaaki et al., *Islam in Contention*, pp. 3, 5. According to Bahtiar Effendy, the rise of many Islamic political parties following the resignation of Suharto in 1998 seems to indicate political Islam's continuity with the past in aspects such as its formalistic and legalistic character. But, he further suggested that the defeat of Islamic political parties in the 1999 and the 2004 general elections "strengthened the thought that political Islam has substantially changed". See Effendy, "What is Political Islam?".

⁷ For deeper elaboration of practices that indicate the spreading influence of Islam in various aspects of Indonesian society and the public sphere, especially in post-Suharto Indonesia, see Hasan, "The Making of Public Islam".

⁸ Platzdasch, *Islamism in Indonesia*; Baswedan, "Political Islam in Indonesia", p. 670; Liddle and Mujani, "Leadership, Party, and Religion"; Hilmy, *Islamism and Democracy in Indonesia*; Assyaukanie, *Islam and the Secular State in Indonesia*; Zamhari, *Rituals of Islamic Spirituality*; Fealy and White, eds., *Expressing Islam*; Bamualim et al., eds., *Islamic Philanthropy and Social Development in Contemporary Indonesia*; Afadlal et al., *Islam Dan Radikalisme di Indonesia*; Bruinessen, "Genealogies of Islamic Radicalism in post-Suharto Indonesia"; Wichelen, "Embodied Contestations"; Syamsiyatun, "A Daughter in the Indonesian Muhammadiyah"; Nurmila, "Negotiating Polygamy in Indonesia"; and Adamson, "Globalization, Islam and the Idea of 'Woman' in Post-New Order Java".

Within the theme of Muslim women's role in contemporary Indonesia, Muslim women's leadership has not yet been given serious attention.[9] This is surprising considering the current trend of Indonesian Muslim women, especially (but not exclusively) in Java, who have actively taken part in securing political leadership positions. So far, no studies have been devoted to presenting and assessing this phenomenon, while at the same time recognizing the importance of Islam and gender in their trajectories.

Studies on gender in Java mainly reveal gender relations among women, or between women and men in different classes or geographical settings. None have addressed gender relations in the political setting.[10] On the other hand, studies on local politics in Java reveal the changing structures and functions of political institutions following the decentralization policy transition from Law No. 22/1999 to Law No. 32/2004. In the context of Law No. 22/1999, Vedi R. Hadiz offers a comparative perspective on the dynamics of power contestation among local elites in local politics of decentralized Indonesia, the Philippines and Thailand, and suggests that local politics in post-Suharto Indonesia should be seen as an important "arena of contestation".[11] This present book will take this focus a step farther by critically examining the impact of direct elections, under the Law No. 32/2004, on the political roles of Indonesian women, especially Muslim women in local politics.

Some studies have assessed the rise of female leaders in direct elections, yet they are lacking in gender perspectives.[12] Satriyo proposes a pessimistic argument about the prospect of female leaders in direct elections because she believes that male domination inside political parties remains the biggest barrier preventing female politicians' candidacy in local politics.[13] Satriyo's position contradicts my position, as I believe

---

[9] There are a few exceptions, such as Kurniawati Hastuti Dewi's studies of Muslim women's leadership in Muhammadiyah. See Dewi, "Women's Leadership in Muhammadiyah"; and Dewi, "Perspective Versus Practices".

[10] Stoler, "Changing Modes of Production", pp. 76–8, 78–84; Lont, "More Money, More Autonomy?"; Brenner, "Why Women Rule the Roost"; Sullivan, *Masters and Managers*; Hull, "Women in Java's Rural Middle Class"; Jay, *Javanese Villagers*; Koentjaraningrat, review of Geertz, *The Javanese Family*; Geertz, *The Javanese Family*; and Vreede-De Stuers, *The Indonesian Woman*.

[11] Hadiz, *Localising Power in Post-Authoritarian Indonesia*, p. 3.

[12] Examples include Tri Ratnawati, "Gender and Reform in Indonesian Politics"; and Satriyo, "Pushing the Boundaries".

[13] Satriyo, "Pushing the Boundaries", p. 251.

that direct elections have expanded structural opportunities for women to take greater political roles in local politics. In addition, as I will show throughout this book, gender is in fact an important variable used in political branding and in political campaigns to form a distinct political identity meant to attract voters. In this, as we shall see, this book challenges Satriyo's earlier conclusion that gender has not been used by female political candidates to mobilize voters in direct local elections since 2005.[14]

Thus to date, we can see that no comprehensive study has been conducted on the rise and victory of Muslim women in local politics that involves the intersection between Islam, gender and politics in post-Suharto Indonesia. This book fills this scholarly gap. It is the first to address the factors behind the rise and victory of female Muslim political leaders, especially Javanese, in direct elections by assessing the interplay of Islam, gender and networking.

In contrast to the recent outburst of field-based research on Indonesian local politics that has focused on the experiences of male politicians, this study primarily explores the rarely studied experiences of female politicians in their quest to power in direct elections. It bases its premises on reading the socio-political phenomenon of the rise of female political leaders in local politics by incorporation of gender analysis within political analysis. While scholarship concerned with the absence of gender analysis in studies of Southeast Asian politics emerged in the 1990s, its absence continues to persist today as observed and concluded by Susan Blackburn.[15] Thus, this study is in line with other scholarly efforts to incorporate gender analysis and political analysis. This has enabled me to understand the contribution of gender and Islam to the changing role Indonesian Muslim women are playing in politics, as well

---

[14] Satriyo states: "these women did not use their gender to mobilise voters. In Indonesia, candidates for local executive positions often appeal to ethnic and religious identities to attract voters. Gender identity cannot be used in the same way." ("Pushing the Boundaries", p. 260.)

[15] Errington notes the absence of gender analysis in writings on Southeast Asian politics, which according to her might be due to the relative economic equality between men and women in Southeast Asia that has caused a paucity of symbolic expression of gender differences in the region ("Recasting Sex, Gender, and Power"). Blackburn discovered that general books on Southeast Asian politics (Indonesia, Malaysia and Vietnam) since the mid-1990s have shown a disappointing level of gender analysis. See Stivens, ed., *Why Gender Matters*; and Blackburn, "Has Gender Analysis Been Mainstreamed in the Study of Southeast Asian Politics?".

as to see how far Indonesian women are able to shape the growth and direction of Indonesian democratization, especially in local politics.

Direct Elections: Widening Structural Opportunities for Women in Local Politics

The decentralization policy became an important political agenda signifying the period of reform in Indonesia, and often had positive impacts on the political role of women. This has also occurred in several other countries in Southeast Asia, such as the Philippines and Thailand, where decentralization has been implemented as part of democratic reform.[16]

In the Philippines, under the influence of international development organizations, the decentralization agenda was forged in the late 1980s, whereas in Thailand it started in late 1990s and was driven by powerful national technocrats, who were the primary forces behind its implementation.[17] In both countries, direct elections have been introduced as a component of the move toward the decentralization of political power. In Filipino politics, according to Mina Roces, while men exercise official power, women are ascribed significant kinship roles, which can include exercising power in support of their husbands.[18] Furthermore, Roces states that "the distinctive system of kinship politics has empowered women in post-war Philippines", because even women who do not hold official power can have access to real power by means of kinship alliances.[19] Lourdes Veneracion-Rallonza similarly notes that familial/kinship politics and patron-client networks have enabled Filipino women to negotiate their inclusion in politics either through informal or formal power.[20] Filipino women also occupy significant positions in local politics. In 2010, the Philippines had 18 female governors (22.5 per cent), 13 female vice-governors (16.25 per cent), 274 female mayors (15.76 per cent) and 230 female vice-mayors (14.41 per cent).[21] In the 13 May 2013 Philippines election, there were 35 female candidates for governor (17 per cent), 26 female candidates for vice-governor (14 per

---

[16] For similar phenomenon in South America, please see Macaulay, "Localities of Power", p. 87.
[17] Hadiz, *Localising Power in Post-Authoritarian Indonesia*, p. 23.
[18] Roces, "Negotiating Modernities".
[19] Roces, *Women, Power, and Kinship Politics*, p. 2.
[20] Veneracion-Rallonza, "Women and the Democracy Project", p. 215.
[21] "Updates on Women and Men in the Philippines".

cent), 749 female candidates for mayor (19 per cent) and 609 female candidates for vice mayor (16 per cent).[22]

Similarly to the Philippines, personal ties and patron-client relationships colour contemporary Thai politics,[23] but the political position of women is more peripheral in Thailand than in the Philippines. However, there have been some changes that have expanded the political roles available to Thai women. For example, since the 1982 annulment of the Interior Ministry's regulation that allowed only men to be village and sub-district heads, women have filled approximately 2 to 3 per cent of these positions.[24] In addition, in 1995, administrative power was decentralized down to the level of sub-district, and, in the 1997 Constitution this was extended down to the level of *tambon* (the lowest administrative unit in Thailand), which meant that after 1997 *tambon* councils and executive committees were directly elected by the people.[25] By 2005, women made up 12 per cent of elected provincial council presidents, 2.4 per cent of elected sub-district heads, and 3.3 per cent of elected village heads.[26]

In Indonesia, the Reform Era that began in 1998 and promoted freedom and autonomy replaced the centralized approach of the New Order's Law No. 5/1974 with Law No. 22/1999 on Regional Government. The new act was issued during President B.J. Habibie's term and gave considerable authority to regencies (*kabupaten*) and municipalities (*kota*, or *kotamadya* during Suharto's regime). Scholars like Edward Aspinall and Greg Fealy believe that Law No. 22/1999 was "one of the most radical decentralization programs attempted anywhere in the world".[27] Many international organizations such as the World Bank and the Asia Foundation vigorously supported the 1999 Act and its subsequent regulations, which have had mixed results. While it raised accountability in public service and bolstered public participation, there were

---

[22] "Number of Candidates by Elective Positions and Gender".
[23] Vichit-Vadakan, "Women in Politics and Women and Politics", p. 29.
[24] Vichitranonda and Bhongsvej, "NGO Advocacy for Women in Politics in Thailand", p. 64.
[25] Juree Vichit-Vadakan, "A Glimpse of Women Leaders in Thai Politics", p. 133.
[26] Data from the Department of Local Administration, Ministry of Interior, Bangkok, as cited in Vichitranonda and Bhongsvej, "NGO Advocacy for Women in Politics in Thailand", p. 61.
[27] Aspinall and Fealy, "Introduction", p. 3. For a comparative reading see also Michael Buehler, "The Rising Importance of Personal Networks in Indonesian Local Politics", p. 102; Mboi, "*Pilkada Langsung*", p. 45.

cases of misbehaviour by local government officials and members of the Regional People's Representative Councils (Dewan Perwakilan Rakyat Daerah, DPRD).[28] Several years later, Law No. 22/1999 was replaced by Law No. 32/2004. Some scholars have suggested that Law No. 32/2004 was a move towards "recentralization" in the sense that it strengthened the central government by giving it a degree of control over administrative and fiscal matters.[29]

In particular relation to women's roles in local politics, I argue that the introduction of direct elections under Law No. 32/2004 has had a positive impact. I suggest—borrowing Pippa Noris's idea about "the structure of opportunities" as one component in legislative recruitment[30]—that structural opportunities for women to be recruited into politics have increased under the new conditions for direct elections. Today, female politicians can move freely among voters without running into barriers set up by oligarchies and male-dominated political parties. This is because direct elections have lessened if not removed the institutional barriers of oligarchic, male-dominated political parties, including inside DPRD, which had been the mechanism through which local government heads were elected. It is now the voters who decide who wins, and not the male-dominated political elites inside DPRD, who formerly elected local leaders. Before 2005, under the former election mechanism, only five female leaders were ever elected to office by the members of the regional People's Representative Council under Law No. 22/1999. Of these, four were regents—Rustriningsih, regent of Kebumen (2000–05); Haeny Relawati Rini Widyastuti, regent of Tuban (2001–06); Rina Iriani, regent of Karanganyar (2003–08); Tutty Hayati Anwar, regent of Majalengka (2003–08)—and one was a vice-governor: Atut Chosiyah, vice-governor of Banten (2001–06).[31] Whereas after direct elections were

---

[28] See for example Suharyo, "Indonesia's Transition to Decentralized Governance", p. 96.

[29] See Pratikno, "Political Parties in *Pilkada*", p. 57; and Buehler, "The Rising Importance of Personal Networks in Indonesian Local Politics", p. 102.

[30] Norris, "Introduction: Theories of Recruitment", p. 11.

[31] There were only two female leaders ever elected under the Law No. 5/1974 (1974–98), in which local government heads were elected by the regional People's Representative Council with strong intervention from President (Suharto). They were Tutty Hayati Anwar as regent of Majalengka (1998–2003) and Molly Mulyahati Djubaedi as Mayor of Sukabumi (1998–2003).

introduced in 2005, the number of women elected (either as regents or vice-regents, governors or vice-governors) increased significantly as explained earlier in this chapter.

Moreover, on 22 March 2005, the Constitutional Court approved the judicial review of the North Sulawesi Branch of the National Awakening Party (Partai Kebangkitan Bangsa, PKB) on article 59 of Law No. 32/2004. As per the judicial review, coalitions of political parties, which do not have seats in DPRD but together have at least 15 per cent of the total number of votes approved in the electorate, can nominate a candidate in direct elections.[32] This regulation later proved to open up a critical opportunity for female leaders to proceed with their candidacies in local elections. While female candidates formerly had difficulty breaking into the oligarchic male-dominated atmosphere, direct elections have given female candidates wider opportunities to participate in, and win, elections by using various strategies, including their gender, against predominantly male candidates. Given this political development, the role of political parties and coalitions in combination with the use of individual capital, gender, Islam and networks cannot be underestimated in facilitating the rise and victory of female Muslim leaders in local politics.

Islam, Gender, Networks, Familial Ties: Assessing Interplays and Roles in Local Politics

In examining the factors behind the rise and victory of Muslim Javanese women in direct elections, this book's analysis is guided by four aspects that are considered significant: the roles of Islam, gender, networks and familial ties.

Islam

Scholars have addressed the topic of gender and religiosity across regions; there is a body of work devoted to understanding the impact of religiosity on gender equality and its role in cultural change worldwide. For example, for South and Southeast Asia, Claudia Derichs and Andrea Fleschenberg's edited volume investigates the influence of religious fundamentalisms on gender and women's rights, including in the political realm, as in the case of Catholic fundamentalism in the Philippines,

---

[32] "Partai Gurem Bisa Usung Calon".

Buddhist fundamentalism in Sri Lanka and conservative Muslims in Malaysia and Indonesia; where they found the commonality that women were often the first target of fundamentalist forces in any religion.[33]

Using a quantitative method that utilized multivariate regression to analyze the impact of eight major religions—Roman Catholic, Muslim, Protestant, Orthodox, Buddhist, Hindu, Jewish, other—on 190 nations, Ronald Inglehart and Pippa Norris have identified contrasts in attitudes about appropriate sex roles for men and women. They point out that Western Christian and non-denominational populations living in affluent post-industrial societies adhere to the most egalitarian beliefs about family, whereas Muslims living in poorer, agrarian nations are the most "traditional" in terms of attitudes toward gender equality.[34] Further research by Pippa Norris and Ronald Inglehart on religion and politics worldwide revealed even more interesting findings. After dividing societies worldwide by religious cultures—Protestant, Catholic, Islamic,[35] Orthodox, Central Europe, Latin America, Sinic/Confucian, Sub-Saharan Africa—they measured positions on political and social values, one of which was attitudes toward political leadership, and concluded that "Muslim publics do display greater support for a strong societal role by religious authorities than do Western publics."[36] Although Norris and Inglehart note that other societies, such as Sub-Saharan African countries and Catholic nations in Latin America, also support an active role for religious leaders in public life, their research pointed out the strong influence of religious beliefs on political behaviour in Muslim societies. Matthew Carlson and Ola Listhaug's research also concluded that Islamic and Sub-Saharan African civilizations, including Indonesia, see religion as an important consideration in recruiting and selecting political leaders.[37]

This book takes Norris and Inglehart's note that in Muslim societies religious belief has significant influence on political behaviour, as well as Carlson and Listhaug's note that Indonesia, a country with a dominant

---

[33] Derichs and Fleschenberg, eds., *Religious Fundamentalism and Their Gendered Impacts in Asia*, p. 5.
[34] Inglehart and Norris, *Rising Tide*, p. 68.
[35] Including Albania, Algeria, Azerbaijan, Bangladesh, Egypt, Indonesia, Iran, Jordan, Morocco, Pakistan and Turkey.
[36] Norris and Inglehart, *Sacred and Secular*, p. 147.
[37] Carlson and Listhaug, "Public Opinion on the Role of Religion in Political Leadership", p. 256.

Muslim population, sees religion as an important consideration in recruiting and selecting political leaders.[38] With these points in mind, this book will critically assess the role of Islam, namely perceptions of mainstream Indonesian Islam (Nahdlatul Ulama, NU)[39] and Muhammadiyah,[40] toward female leadership, especially in local politics. Such an understanding is necessary considering the fact that each of the three female Javanese office holders who won the direct elections and are thus observed in this book is Muslim. As we shall see, both groups have Islamic perspectives that support female leadership in local politics, thus serving as a strong religious foundation for these Muslim women to run for political leadership in direct elections.

Gender

Alice Schlegel defines gender as the way society "perceives, evaluates, and expects" the two sexes (male and female) to behave, and as a cultural construct which varies across cultures.[41] Similarly, Henrietta L. Moore sees gender as a social construction based on the obvious difference between the two biological sexes.[42] Michael S. Kimmel also defines gender as "the meanings that are attached to those differences within a culture".[43] However, Connel criticizes these common definitions of gender and suggests a shift in focus from gender difference to gender relations, arguing that gender is a matter of the social relations within which individuals and groups act.[44] He asserts that "gender relations" are the direct or

---

[38] Norris and Inglehart, *Sacred and Secular*, p. 147; and Carlson and Listhaug, "Public Opinion on the Role of Religion in Political Leadership", p. 256.
[39] Nahdlatul Ulama (NU) is Indonesia's traditionalist Islamic organization, founded by Hasyim Asy'ari and Wahab Chasbullah in 1926.
[40] Muhammadiyah is the largest Islamic reformist movement in Indonesia and was founded by K.H. Ahmad Dahlan in Kauman, Yogyakarta, in 1912. Other reformist movements include Persatuan Islam (Persis) which was established in Bandung in the early 1920s, and organizations for Arab Muslims such as Djamiat Chair, established in Jakarta on 17 July 1905, and Al-Irsjad, established in 1913. See Deliar Noer, *The Modernist Muslim Movement in Indonesia 1900–1942*, pp. 58–92; see also White, "Reformist Islam, Gender and Marriage in Late Colonial Dutch East Indies, 1900–1942", pp. 10–1.
[41] Schlegel, "Gender Meanings: General and Specific", p. 23.
[42] Moore, *A Passion for Difference*, p. 12.
[43] Kimmel, *The Gendered Society*, p. 3.
[44] Connel, *Gender*, pp. 9–10.

indirect interactions between women and men, or among men, or among women in everyday life, surrounding the gender arrangement in social structures (religious, political, kinship and cultural).[45] In this book, I am most interested in Schlegel, Moore and Kimmel's conceptions of gender as a culturally constructed difference between males and females. However, Connel's definition is also helpful, particularly when Connel focuses on gender as it is manifested through social relationships, where men and women interact either through thoughts or actions that constantly produce, reproduce, change and modify the concept of gender.

In this book, I initially observe the normative expectations or ideal gender norms of Javanese Muslim women, which infuses the everyday lives of the female Javanese Muslim leaders observed, and then assess the changes these have undergone in contemporary Java. I was inspired by one of the research findings in Claudia Derichs, Andrea Fleschenberg and Momoyo Hustebeck's study on the strategy of top female leaders in Asia. One important point they make is that female leaders in Asia are able to take advantage of the traditional images of women in their societies to win voters' hearts, rather than challenging the established gender norms. For example, in Japan, Tanaka Makiko, the former Japanese Foreign Minister, appeared to conform to traditional gender stereotypes and the role model of a "good housewife", while Park Geun-hye, leader of the South Korean Grand National Party, conformed to ideas of a "loyal daughter".[46] Here, I examine the way the female Javanese Muslim leaders play with the idealized gender norms in Javanese society in their exercise of power.

Networking

In exploring the tactics taken by Indonesian women to win direct elections, I have also considered the networking strategies that they have used. There are various studies on networks of women in politics in different societies. Women's solidarity in politics is, for example, a decisive factor among Igbo women in Northern Nigeria, Africa who have traditionally played considerable political roles.[47] In Western democracies such

---

[45] Ibid., pp. 54–5. See also Connel's standpoint in Connel, *Gender and Power*; and *The Men and the Boys*.
[46] Derichs, Fleschenberg and Hustebeck, "Gendering Moral Capital", p. 253.
[47] Van Allen, "Sitting on a Man".

as Canada, women's networks have also had a profound impact. Elisabeth Gidengil, Alison Harell and Bonnie H. Erickson studied data from the 2000 Canadian Election Study and concluded that women with more diverse ties to other women contributed more significantly to enhancing the scope for autonomy and independent political decisions.[48] However, R.W. Connel, who has primarily studied Western female politicians, has argued that female leaders are recruited into and assume political positions through male rather than female networks.[49]

In the context of my study in Java, most of the research on Javanese women's networks has focused on everyday life as it affects topics such as family businesses or childcare.[50] This book will specifically investigate the networking strategy used or created by Javanese Muslim women in politics. Albert-Laszlo Barabasi's concept is helpful in this book. Drawing from mathematical formulations, Barabasi noted that a network comprises of links and nodes where "hubs", namely, nodes with a large number of links, dominate the structure of networks.[51] Throughout this book, I have identified important figures, such as prominent Islamic leaders (both male and female) and prominent political actors, who hold key societal positions and have diverse connections and thus function as important "hubs" used by female Javanese Muslim leaders to generate their own networks of political support.

Familial Ties

The growing number of these leaders in Indonesian local politics is part of a global phenomenon that has seen an increase in the numbers of female national leaders worldwide since the 1990s. While female national leaders were rare in the 1960s through the 1980s, the 1990s brought dramatic change, and during that decade 26 women obtained positions of top executive leadership, followed by 29 more women from 2000 to 2009.[52] In total, 71 women from 52 countries have been elected as national female leaders, with the largest proportion being from Europe; 16 have been elected presidents and prime ministers in 5 regions (Asia,

---

[48] Gidengil, Harell and Erickson, "Network Diversity and Vote Choice".
[49] Connel, *Masculinities*, p. 204.
[50] Weix, "Hidden Managers at Home"; and Saptari, "Networks of Reproduction Among Cigarette Factory Women in East Java".
[51] Barabasi, *Linked*, pp. 16, 58–64.
[52] Jalalzai and Krook, "Beyond Hillary and Benazir", p. 6.

Africa, Europe, Latin America, Oceania).[53] Many factors have contributed to the rising number of female leaders worldwide, including the following: in some regions, including Southeast Asia, there are political structures in place that rely on familial ties or kinship politics and these are considered an important path to political office; in some regions, high levels of political instability have provided female leaders with opportunities to present themselves as alternative leaders; and, specific features of some political systems, such as some parliamentary systems, make it more possible for women to serve as prime ministers than as presidents under different political systems.[54]

This book is focused on Indonesian women, who, similar to Southeast Asian women in general, hold a relatively high position in society as can be seen in the complementarity of men and women's work and in the existence of leadership positions for women,[55] where familial ties are often seen as important factors facilitating their rise in politics. In South Asia, Rounaq Jahan, who analyzed cases of prominent female political leaders in India (Indira Ghandi), Bangladesh (Hasina Wazed, Khaleda Zia), Pakistan (Benazir Bhutto) and Sri Lanka (Sirimavo Bandaranaike), offers an interesting explanation of how these female leaders obtained political leadership due to their strong connections with male relatives (husbands or fathers) who were prominent and powerful politicians themselves. Jahan argues that "family connections" were central to their rise because "family connections" enabled the women to overcome obstacles generally faced in politics (such as lack of money, skills, experience, contacts, information), and helped them to decrease cultural constraints from *purdah*[56] because they could seek patrons from within their family circles.[57] In the case of kinship (relationships between individuals/groups which are constructed due to the sharing of family, marriage or genealogical relationships), Kathleen Fordham Norr notes that in India kinship ties shape cohesion or conflict in daily lives and even more so in politics.[58]

---

[53] Ibid., p. 7.
[54] Ibid., p. 9.
[55] For further reading, see Andaya, *The Flaming Womb*; Reid, "Females Roles in Pre-Colonial Southeast Asia"; Ward, *Women in the New Asia*; and Errington, "Recasting Sex, Gender, and Power", pp. 1–4.
[56] Gender separation and restrictions on women's physical mobility are present mainly in South Asian Muslim societies.
[57] Jahan, "Women in South Asian Politics", pp. 852–3.
[58] Norr, "Faction and Kinship".

Similarly, in East Asia, familial ties are considered to be a strong factor behind the political rise of female leaders such as in Japan (Tanaka Makiko, former Japanese foreign minister and daughter of former prime minister Tanaka Kakuei) or in Korea (Park Geun-hye, the current president of South Korea and the daughter of the former president Park Chung-hee).[59]

On a broader scope, Linda K. Richter analyzed the political experiences of female political leaders in national politics both from South and Southeast Asian countries and concluded that familial ties to prominent male politicians (husbands or fathers) was a very important factor behind their emergence.[60] Mark R. Thompson also assessed the political histories of popular female national leaders in Asia and boldly used the term "political dynasties" rather than familial ties as a key variable for female politicians in assuming political leadership.[61]

I prefer Richter's use of "familial ties" to express the influence of male relatives, who are also prominent politicians, toward developing and achieving political leadership roles for women.[62] "Political dynasty" applies specifically to families that continuously maintain political and economic power over generations, such as Indira Gandhi's family in India, Benazir Buttho's family in Pakistan, the Marcos family in the Philippines and Megawati Sukarnoputri in Indonesia. In the context of my study on Indonesian local politics, I explore "familial ties", specifically as they apply to those cases where Javanese Muslim women are related either as wife or daughter to prominent male politicians, and investigate how these ties may exert a strong influence on their political emergence.

---

[59] Derichs et al., "Gendering Moral Capital", p. 246.

[60] In developing the argument about what he called "familial ties", namely the strong influence of and role played by prominent male politicians in the rise of female politicians, Richter started with an elaboration of previous studies on female political leaders in the United States. Richter's elaboration shows that in the United States, most female politicians in the legislative body from the 1920s to 1970s assumed political roles after the deaths of their husbands, and very few prominent female leaders lacked links to politically prominent male relatives. See Linda K. Richter, "Exploring Theories of Female Leadership in South and Southeast Asia", pp. 525–8.

[61] Thompson, "Female Leadership of Democratic Transition in Asia", p. 538.

[62] Familial ties were also an important factor behind the rise of women in local politics (as city council members) in Norway in the 1960s. Although the author does not use the word "familial ties", the research points to the significant influence of two politically active parents as role models in women's exposure to politics, as well as the influence of having a brother or uncle involved in politics. See Means, "Women in Local Politics", p. 380.

There are established normative expectations about the role of women in politics that are primarily drawn from western democracies. This book will assess the normative expectations projected in regards to female political leadership. For example, in light of the increasing number of female parliamentarian members in the British House of Commons in 1997, Joni Lovenduski has examined the impact of having more women in British politics, including the extent to which policy might conform to women's perspectives.[63] Similar expectations also persist in the Muslim world. For example, Haleh Afshar, examining Syrian and Iranian female politicians who fought for women's rights, has suggested an ideal portrait of female politicians as political actors/agents who support and advocate policy on women's issues.[64] In examining normative expectations, I investigate and present the initial expectations of Javanese Muslim women as they consider what it would be like to be in power, their possible engagement with local women's groups in their pursuit of political power, their leadership characteristics and their policies on women's issues, if any.

Given the above analytical framework, this book attempts to answer several important questions: What role has Islam and gender played in the emergence and victory of female Javanese Muslim political leaders in direct elections? Has that role generally been positive or negative? What kind of networking was utilized to secure victory in direct elections? How have women drawn on familial ties in gaining access to political positions? Do women bring and advocate women's issues to the political process? How is the situation of Indonesian Muslim women (especially Javanese) in politics different from or similar to the political situation of women in Southeast Asia, and Muslim women elsewhere?

The emergence of female Javanese Muslim political leaders in local politics has been possible due to Muslim willingness to accept female leadership that is strongly justified by Islamic belief supporting female leadership in local politics. Female Javanese Muslim politicians' ability to use the idea and norm of Islamic piety in combination with gender in political campaigns, and to tap into religio-political support and networks is decisive to their political victory. While it is difficult to conclude that familial ties are a common factor behind the rise and victory of female

---

[63] Lovenduski, "Gender Politics", pp. 708–9.
[64] Afshar, "Introduction: Women and Empowerment-Some Illustrative Studies".

political leaders (including the three female Javanese Muslim leaders examined in this book) in the first term of direct elections (2005–10),[65] the influence of familial ties becomes strongly apparent behind the rise and victory of female political leaders in the second term of direct elections (2010–15).

The aim of this book is thus twofold. By presenting materials obtained from fieldwork and assessing factors behind the rise of Muslim female Javanese political leaders, I wish to contribute to providing a current understanding of the dynamic interplays between gender, politics and Islam in local politics that have been increasingly prominent in post-Suharto Indonesia. The second aim is to contribute to theoretical understanding of the agency of Indonesian Muslim women in politics. Susan Blackburn, Bianca J. Smith and Siti Syamsiyatun's edited book provides interesting analysis of the agency of Indonesian Muslim women in various aspects in post-Suharto Indonesia.[66] However, the book overlooked the very important development of Indonesian Muslim women's endeavours to gain political leadership in direct elections since 2005. Thus, my study provides an important portrait of Muslim women's agency in local politics that has not yet been addressed. I show the particular agency of Muslim female Javanese political leaders, namely their ability as subjects to engage with the dominant cultural concepts of gender and Islam in their quest for power, and at the same time use these concepts to expand the space and boundaries of their identity in contemporary Java.

---

[65] The service period for elected leaders in direct elections is five years; it is usually called one term (*satu periode*). Therefore, since the enactment of direct elections in 2005, their implementation can be divided into two terms (*dua periode*), namely 2005–10 and 2010–15. This study focuses primarily on three female Javanese Muslim political leaders who served during the first term of direct elections, between 2005 and 2010. However, especially for assessing the factor of familial ties, my analysis goes beyond the first term of direct elections, in which few female political leaders were victorious, and assesses the present influence of familial ties in the rise of female political leaders during the second term of direct elections between 2010 and 2015, in which many more women emerged and were victorious. This direct comparison is intended to create a clear picture of the different degrees of influence that familial ties have exerted since the initial implementation of direct elections.

[66] See Blackburn, Smith and Syamsiyatun, "Introduction", in *Indonesian Islam in a New Era*, p. 3.

Fieldwork

This book is based primarily on interviews and materials collected during fieldwork conducted between February 2009 and August 2010. Prior to my fieldwork, I reviewed contemporary published material in the Center for Southeast Asian Studies (CSEAS), Kyoto University, Japan. These written materials provided the background and context for this study.

According to the data I obtained from the Ministry of Home Affairs of the Republic of Indonesia, five Javanese Muslim women were elected as regents in the first implementation of direct elections in 2005 (2005–10). Three were elected in Central Java, namely Siti Qomariyah as regent of Pekalongan (2006–11); Rustriningsih as regent of Kebumen (elected under a mechanism inside DPRD, 2000–05; re-elected under direct elections, 2005–10), vice-governor of Central Java (2008–13); and Rina Iriani as regent of Karanganyar (elected under a mechanism inside DPRD, 2003–08; re-elected under direct elections, 2008–13). The other two were elected in East Java, namely Haeny Relawati Rini Widyastuti as regent of Tuban (elected under a mechanism inside DPRD, 2001–06; re-elected under direct elections, 2006–11) and Ratna Ani Lestari as regent of Banyuwangi (2005–10).

Considering the importance in Java of the social organization Nahdlatul Ulama (NU) and the nationalist-based political party the Indonesian Democrat Party of Struggle (Partai Demokrasi Indonesia Perjuangan, PDIP), I decided to observe three Javanese women in politics: Siti Qomariyah (Pekalongan), Ratna Ani Lestari (Banyuwangi) and Rustriningsih (Kebumen). The regions location of each of their regions (Kebumen, Pekalongan, Banyuwangi) in Java can be seen in Map 1 at the end of this chapter.

More specifically, I chose these three Muslim female Javanese leaders in Pekalongan, Banyuwangi and Kebumen because there are interesting points of comparison between the three. For example, although there are similarities in the religious orientation of residents in Pekalongan and Banyuwangi, in that they both tend towards the traditionalist religious organization NU, the two regions show contrasts in the cohesion between NU-affiliated political parties and NU *kyai* (religious teachers) which has resulted in different political configurations for each region. Siti Qomariyah was affiliated with the National Awakening Party (Partai Kebangkitan Bangsa, PKB) which has a strong connection with NU, and PKB gained the majority of seats in the Regional People's Representative Council (DPRD) of Pekalongan in the 2004 General Election which then nominated Siti Qomariyah as regent candidate in the 2006 direct election. However, Ratna Ani Lestari was nominated by a coalition of 18 political parties that did not hold any seats in the Banyuwangi DPRD yet she won the direct election and defeated the candidate from the NU-affiliated party, PKB, which had gained the majority of seats in the Banyuwangi DPRD in the 2004 General Election. The contrasting elements in this preliminary picture were fascinating and spurred me to further investigation. In addition, according to my preliminary understanding, Siti Qomariyah and Ratna Ani Lestari had contrasting political profiles: while Siti Qomariyah's husband was not a politician, Ratna Ani Lestari is married to the former regent of Jembrana, WS (2000–10), which indicates a presence of familial ties behind her political victory. Therefore, assessing these two leaders will help form a more complete picture of the various paths to power for women in Java.

Rustriningsih was the first female regent elected after direct elections were introduced in 2005, and she has become a role model for other female politicians who aspire to be regents. As an incumbent previously elected under the former election system inside the DPRD (2000–05), Rustriningsih successfully won the direct election in Kebumen in 2005, which bolstered her ability to run for Vice-Governor of Central Java in 2008. Eventually, she and her running partner (Bibit Waluyo, candidate for Governor of Central Java) successfully won the Central Java Gubernatorial Election in 2008. A survey by the Indonesian Survey Circle (Lingkaran Survey Indonesia, LSI) in 2008 on the success of the Bibit-Rustriningsih partnership identified the "Rustriningsih factor" as being prominent, from the fact that the PDIP voter preference gradually increased in favour of the Bibit-Rustriningsih partnership after the Central Board of PDIP announced that its official candidate, Bibit Waluyo, would run with Rustriningsih. Rustriningsih was a well-known and successful PDIP cadre, and her presence consolidated a swing in public interest.[67]

In addition to the three politicians studied, I was able to interview 163 respondents including their family members, friends, election teams, loyalists, opponents, NGO activists, religious leaders from Nahdlatul Ulama and Muhammadiyah, bureaucrats, activists from Muslimat NU (the women's wing of NU founded in 1926) and 'Aisyiyah (the women's

---

[67] Lingkaran Survey Indonesia (LSI), "Mesin Partai Dalam Pilkada", p. 12.

wing of Muhammadiyah founded in 1917), other female politicians, local journalists, local parliamentarians, and elite members of political parties, in Jakarta, Pekalongan, Kebumen, Banyuwangi and Semarang. Some of the attributions in the book are pseudonyms for the sake of confidentiality. These many in-depth interviews helped me to form a picture of the personal and political experiences of the three politicians studied. This allowed me to capture their personal experiences, family lives, the motives for their political stands, and it also illuminated the wider social, political, cultural and historical factors surrounding their political emergence, and later, victory in their respective electorates. All interviews were conducted on a one-on-one basis. A general interview guide approach was used for consistency.[68] In addition, the general interview guide approach was accompanied by informal discussion.

Book Outline

This book contains seven chapters. Chapter 2 provides an explanation of the context behind the emergence of female Javanese Muslim politicians in local politics in post-Suharto Indonesia. I show the impact of Islamization, since the 1980s, and democratization, since the late 1990s, in expanding the options for women in Indonesian politics.

Chapter 3 explores normative expectation about Javanese Muslim women and their everyday lives. As my study deals with female leadership within Islam, one section is devoted to exploring the current position of mainstream Indonesian Islam, as exemplified by Muhammadiyah and Nahdlatul Ulama, in dealing with the issue of female leadership. Here, as I will show, we can see that both Muhammadiyah and Nahdlatul Ulama have similar opinions in support of female leadership in local politics, though there is yet to be clear consensus in regards to female leadership as head of state.

Chapters 4, 5 and 6 present case studies of Rustriningsih, Siti Qomariyah and Ratna Ani Lestari, respectively. Each chapter is written in a similar pattern to ease the reader to gain a general understanding of the important aspects that contributed significantly to each woman's rise and victory. The case studies are presented separately rather than collapsed into one chapter, because each leader emerged under a specific

---

[68] Patton, *Qualitative Evaluation and Research Methods*, p. 280.

set of circumstances and their differences are as important as their similarities. The chapters provide a profile of each female leader, the sociopolitical landscape of their region, their political emergence, where I highlight the presence or absence of familial ties, an analysis of their political campaign and strategies to use Islam, gender, and networking to win the direct election, and, lastly, an assessment of their policy on women's issues.

Chapter 7 provides a comparative analysis and conclusion. The comparative analysis section presents a table summarizing the factors encompassing Islam, gender, networking and familial ties behind the rise and victory of female Muslim Javanese political leaders. This is will help the reader gain understanding of the general pattern, similarities and differences among the three case studies. The conclusion section then sums up the findings of this book.

Table 1 Female Politicians Elected in Direct Elections within and outside of Java (2005–08)

	Java (Central Java, East Java, West Java, Banten, Jakarta, Yogyakarta)				Outside Java		
No.	Name	Position	Party	No.	Name	Position	Party
1	**Hj. Rustriningsih, (incumbent)** and KH.M. Nashiruddin	Regent of Kebumen (2000–10), Vice-governor of Central Java (2008–13)	PDIP	1	Jefferson Rumajar and Linneke S. Watoelangkow	Vice-mayor of Tomohon (2005–10)	PNBK, PKPB, PP, PNIM, PPD
2	**Ratna Ani Lestari** and Yusuf Nuris	Regent of Banyuwangi (2005–10)	Coalition of 18 small political parties (PNIM, PBSD, PBB, PM, PDK, PNBK, PKPI, P. PELOPOR, PPDI, PNUI, PAN, PKPB, PKS, PBR, PDS, PSI, PPD, P. PANCASILA)	2	**Vonny Anneke Panambunan (Christian)** and Sompie S.F. Singal	Regent of North Minahasa (2005–10)	PP, PKPI, PPD

continued overleaf

Table 1 continued

		Java (Central Java, East Java, West Java, Banten, Jakarta, Yogyakarta)			Outside Java		
No.	Name	Position	Party	No.	Name	Position	Party
3	**Hj. Haeny Relawati Rini Widyastuti (incumbent)** and Lilik Soehardjono	Regent of Tuban (2001–11)	Golkar Faction (2000–2005), and Golkar + 16 small political parties (2006–11)	3	Abdullah Vanath and Sitti Umuria Suruwaky	Vice-regent of East Seram (2005–10)	PSI, PKS, PKPB
4	**Hj. Siti Qomariyah** and Ir. Wahyudi PontjoNugroho	Regent of Pekalongan (2006–11)	PKB	4	H. Ridwan Mukti and Hj. Ratnawati Ibnu Amin	Vice-regent of Musi Rawas (2005–10)	PDIP
5	**Rina Iriani Sri Ratnaningsih, (incumbent)** and Paryono	Regent of Karanganyar (2003–13)	*Pembaruan* Faction (no information of the political parties inside this group) in DPRD (2002–07); later PDIP (2008–13)	5	Drs. H. Syahrir Wahab and Hj. Nursyamsina Aroepalla	Vice-regent of Selayar (2005–10)	PKB, PPP, PBB
6	**Hj. Atut Chosiyah (incumbent)** and H. Masduki	Governor of Banten (2006–12)	Golkar, PDIP, PBB, PBR, PDS, PPI	6	Alberth H. Torey and Marice Pesurnay Kaikatuy (Christian)	Vice-regent of Teluk Wondama (2005–10)	Golkar, PBB
7	Suharto and Hj. Badingan	Vice-regent of Gunung Kidul (2005–10)	PAN	7	**Hj. Marlina Moha Siahaan** and Mokoagow Sehan	Regent of Bolaang Mongondow (2006–11)	Golkar
8	H. Hendy Boendoro and Hj. Siti Nurmakesi	Vice-regent of Kendal (2005–10)	PDIP, Golkar	8	H. Burhanuddin A. Rasyid and dr. Juliarti Djuhardi Alwi	Vice-regent of Sambas (2006–11)	PPP, PAN, PBR, PD, PBB
9	H. Bambang Guritno and Hj. Siti Ambar Fathonah	Vice-regent of Semarang (2005–10)	PKB, PKPI	9	Marcus Jacob Papilaja and Ny. Olivia CH. Latuconsina	Vice-mayor of Ambon (2006–11)	PDIP

Table 1 continued

	Java (Central Java, East Java, West Java, Banten, Jakarta, Yogyakarta)				Outside Java		
No.	Name	Position	Party	No.	Name	Position	Party
10	H. Tasman (incumbent) and Kartina Sukawati	Vice-regent of Pati (2006–11)	PDIP, PD	10	H. Mawardy Nurdin and Hj. Illiza Sa'aduddin Djamal	Vice-mayor of Banda Aceh (2007–12)	PPP, PBR, PD
11	H. Dadang S. Muchtar (incumbent) and Hj. Eli Amalia Priatna	Vice-regent of Karawang (2005–10)	Golkar	11	J.A. Yumame and Hj. Baisara Wael	Vice-mayor of Sorong (2007–12)	Golkar, PD, PKS, PBSD
				12	Rusda Mahmud and Hj. Suhariah Mu'in	Vice-regent of North Kolaka (2007–12)	PNBK
				13	**Hj. Suryatati A. Manan** and H. Edward Mushalli	Mayor of Tanjung Pinang (2008–13)	PDIP, Golkar
				14	H. Djazuli Kuris and Dr. Hj. Ida Fitriati	Vice-mayor of Pagar Alam (2008–13)	Golkar, PPP, PKB
				15	**Telly Tjanggulung (Christian)** and Josef Jermia Soleman Damongilala	Regent of Minahasa Tenggara (2008–13)	Golkar

Note: Names in bold represent the candidates for regent/mayor/governor. All of the female political leaders are Muslim, except those noted as Christian outside Java.

Source: Ministry of Home Affairs, Republic of Indonesia, "Daftar Kepala Daerah dan Wakil Kepala Daerah Yang Telah Diterbitkan Keputusannya Presiden Republik Indonesia Hasil Pemilihan Kepala Daerah Secara Langsung Tahun 2005, 2006, 2007, dan Tahun 2008".

Table 2 Non-Elected Female Political Candidates in Direct Elections within and outside of Java (2005–06)

\multicolumn{4}{c}{Java (Central Java, East Java, West Java, Banten, Jakarta, Yogyakarta)}	\multicolumn{4}{c}{Outside Java}
No.	Name	Position	Party	No.	Name	Position	Party
1	**Khofifah Indar Parawansa (2008)**	Governor of East Java	PPP, 12 small political parties	1	**Atien Suyati**	Mayor of Lampung	PDIP
2	**Amelia Ahmad Yani**	Regent of Purworejo	Democrat Party (PD), PBB	2	**Johana Jenny Tumbuan**	Regent of South Minahasa	Golkar
3	**Endang Setyaningdyah**	Regent of Demak	PDIP	3	**Mercy Bareds**	Regent of Kepulauan Aru	PDIP
4	Fatimah Toha Assegaf	Vice-regent of Sidorajo	Golkar and PDIP	4	**Reina Usman Ahmadi**	Regent of Pahuwato	Golkar
5	Ismawati	Vice-regent of Kendal	PKB	5	**Sri Indraningsih Lalusu**	Regent of Luwuk	PDIP
6	Nunik Tasnim	Vice-regent of Gunung Kidul	No Information	6	**Hariyanti Syafrin**	Mayor of Bandar Lampung	Coalition of 13 political parties
7	Siti Aisah	Vice-regent of Sumenep	Coalition of 14 political parties	7	**Risnawaty Dartatik Damanik**	Mayor of Pematang Siantar	PPP, PAN
8	Siti Chomsiyati	Vice-mayor of Semarang	Golkar, PDS	8	**Suryatinah**	Regent of Kotabaru	PPP
9	Endang Widayati Budirini	Vice-regent of Mojokerto	Democrat Party and PPDI	9	Aryanti Baramuli	Vice-governor of North Sulawesi	Golkar
10	Airin Rachmi Diany (2008)	Vice-regent of Tangerang	PKS, PKB	10	Dewa Ayu Putu Sri Wigunawan	Vice-regent of Jembrana	Golkar
				11	Emi Sunarsih	Vice-regent of South Lampung	PDIP
				12	Emma Yohana	Vice-regent of West Pasaman	Golkar

Table 2 continued

Java (Central Java, East Java, West Java, Banten, Jakarta, Yogyakarta)				Outside Java			
No.	Name	Position	Party	No.	Name	Position	Party
				13	Fatimah Siregar	Vice-mayor of Pematang Siantar	No information
				14	Fatimah Siregar	Vice-regent of Simalungun	PDS, PBSD, 9 non-parliamentary political parties
				15	Inggrid Sondakh	Vice-regent of North Minahasa	Golkar
				16	Lindawati MZ	Vice-regent of OKU	No information
				17	Muflikhah Ibrahim	Vice-regent of Serang	PDIP, PBR
				18	Mulyani Tiangso Ladwan	Vice-regent of Toli-Toli	Golkar, PKPB, PBR
				19	Pdt. Lis Sigilipu	Vice-regent of Poso	Coalition of *Partai Poso Bersatu*
				20	Rahanum	Vice-regent of Pasaman	PPP
				21	Rosavella Y.D.	Vice-mayor of Solok	No information
				22	St. Suhariah Muin	Vice-regent of North Kolaka	Golkar
				23	Suryawati Br Sebayang	Vice-regent of Karo	No information
				24	Susana Regina	Vice-regent of Sekadau	No information
				25	Theresia Jita	Vice-regent of Sintang	P Merdeka, PPD, P Patriot

continued overleaf

Table 2 continued

Java (Central Java, East Java, West Java, Banten, Jakarta, Yogyakarta)				Outside Java			
No.	*Name*	*Position*	*Party*	*No.*	*Name*	*Position*	*Party*
				26	Titin Suastini	Vice-regent of Cianjur	PPP
				27	Zus Sualang Pangemanan	Vice-regent of Minahasa Utara	PDIP
				28	Noorsinah	Vice-regent of Pasir	No Information

Note: Names in bold represent the candidates for regent/mayor/governor.

Source: CETRO, "Daftar Kandidat Perempuan Dalam Pilkada" and "Data Perempuan Terpilih Pilkada 2005", available at <http://www.cetro.or.id/> [accessed 19 January 2009], with the addition of Khofifah Indar Parawansa and Airin Rachmi Diany for 2008.

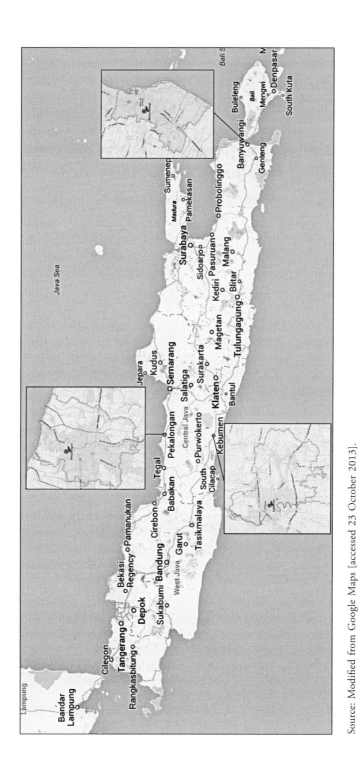

Source: Modified from Google Maps [accessed 23 October 2013].

Map 1 Location of Kebumen Regency, Pekalongan Regency and Banyuwangi Regency in Java

CHAPTER 2

Impact of Islamization and Democratization in Expanding Indonesian Women's Roles in Politics

The emergence of Indonesian Muslim women in local politics did not just suddenly occur. While the post-Suharto transformation of the vision and mission of official state women's organizations played an important role in facilitating the awakening of Indonesian women's roles in politics, a more significant catalyst was the rise of progressive Islam, which sought to promote greater participation of women in politics including in positions of leadership. At the same time, there was an accompanying growth in conservative Islamist groups, which took a more formalistic approach to Islam including more traditional definitions of women's roles and status. Surrounded by the tension between progressive and conservative Islam, which has continued to colour the everyday lives of Indonesians in post-Suharto Indonesia, Indonesian Muslim women hit the ground running towards political leadership once direct elections were introduced in 2005. In this chapter, we will explore the history of women and politics in Indonesia, beginning in the late 19th century, through to the Sukarno and Suharto periods, and then look at the major changes that occurred in post-Suharto Java. Two major trends, the Islamization that began in the 1980s and the embryonic emergence of democratization since the mid-1990s, have accelerated the expansion of the roles Indonesian Muslim women play in politics in the post-Suharto period, as evident by the participation of the female Javanese Muslims in direct elections observed in this book.

Late 19th Century to the New Order: The Beginning of Political Roles for Indonesian Women

Indonesian women's effort to elevate their positions and redefine their roles began in the late 19th century and continued into both Dutch and Japanese colonial rule. While rising awareness of the importance of women's dignity and education became a focus of the late 19th century and in the early 20th century Indonesian women's movement, it gradually moved into wider issues such as polygamy, child marriage, etc. Although women's groups have always had diverse ideologies and positions in response to particular problems, their discourse and actions since the late 19th century up to Indonesian independence made a significant contribution to the beginning of women's roles in politics, as I will present below.

Late 19th-century Indonesia saw the emergence of pioneering women who, either individually or collectively, sought to raise women's dignity by means of education and breaking free of discriminatory *adat* (customary or traditional laws), striving for progress (*kemajuan*) which then developed further under the rise of Indonesian nationalism. Most of the individual initiators of this early enlightenment came from royal families, such as Kartini, a daughter of the regent of Jepara Central Java, who was born of a mother trapped in a polygamous marriage. In 1892, when she turned twelve years old, Kartini was forced to undergo the isolation of *pingitan* (a period of time before marriage in which adolescent girls were kept at home, secluded from the public sphere) for six years.[1] She wrote in a letter to her Dutch friend, Stella Zeehandelaar, that she would be more than willing to end the unfair *adat* [such as *pingitan* and having *selir* (co-wives) or concubines] and challenge the narrow interpretation and practice of Islam.[2] Scholar Takashi Shiraishi sees Kartini's letters that criticize unfair *adat* and the narrow practice of Islam as important to the beginning of the movement (*pergerakan*) by natives who had developed a political consciousness and started to spread ideas of modernity during the "age of motion" in the first quarter of the 20th century.[3] Inspired by her own harsh experience, in the late 1890s, Kartini opened a girl's school in her home initially for daughters of the upperclass. Other noble women followed her steps: Dewi Sartika founded a girl's school in Bandung in 1904, Kartini's Dutch association under the initiative of Van Deventer in 1912 founded a number of Kartini schools in Semarang, Jakarta, Malang, Madiun, Solo and Bandung, and Rahma

---

[1] Zainu'ddin, "Kartini, Her Life, Work and Influence", p. 4; and Kartinah, "Kartini Penundjuk Djalan Kahidupan Baru".
[2] See Kartini's letters to Stella, entitled "To Stella Zeehandelaar", in *Letters of A Javanese Princess*, pp. 81–2.
[3] Shiraishi, *An Age in Motion*, p. xi.

El Junisia founded a school in Padang Panjang in 1922.[4] By 1910, there were at least 280 female pupils in Java, and there were 12,276 female pupils outside Java and Madura in 1908.[5]

The schooling of girls helped to spread the idea of progress for Indonesian women. Print media further facilitated the spread of the idea of progress across Indonesia. For example, Kartini and her relatives, as well as a female journalist, Siti Soendari, were able to publish their work on women and progress in the newspapers *De Locomotief* and *Wanita Swara*.[6] Similar attention was given to ideas about women and progress in magazines such as *Poeteri Mardika* (Jakarta 1914), *Wanita Swara* (Pacitan 1913), *Panoentoen Isteri* (Bandung 1918), *Esteri Oetomo* (Solo 1918) and *Soeara Perempoean Bergerak* (Medan).[7] For Muslims, Islamic organizations like 'Aisyiyah (the women's wing of Muhammadiyah, founded in 1917) promoted the enhancement of women's social status. For instance, K.H. Ahmad Dahlan (the founder of Muhammadiyah and 'Aisyiyah), together with his wife Siti Walidah, developed a religious consciousness among Muslim women and sent girls in Kauman, Yogyakarta, to formal schools.[8] Their ideas were later transmitted outside Yogyakarta by means of the *Suara 'Aisyiyah* magazine, which began publishing in 1926.[9] The early 20th century was thus a time in which education for girls in Indonesia was promoted as a way of raising girls' dignity and enabling them to progress.

---

[4] Vreede-De Stuers, *The Indonesian Woman*, pp. 58–9. Other in-depth historical accounts of women's education in West Sumatra focus on the tension between matriarchate and Islamic law, including cultural change and continuity after the Padri War and the formation of the Dutch colonial state when women in Minangkabau participated actively in education, politics and journalism, and took part in the male out-migration tradition of *rantau*. See Hadler, *Muslims and Matriarchs*.
[5] Suryochondro, *Potret Pergerakan Wanita di Indonesia*, p. 81.
[6] Ibid., p. 84.
[7] Ibid., p. 87.
[8] Alfian, "Islamic Modernism in Indonesian Politics", p. 272.
[9] The idea of developing a religious consciousness among Muslim women by sending girls in Kauman, Yogyakarta, to formal schools was an important stage in the early development of 'Aisyiyah. There were two important stages in the early development of 'Aisyiyah that provided a foundation for understanding the likely pattern of 'Aisyiyah's future development, namely the development of religious and organizational consciousness. For deeper analysis see Dewi, "Women's Leadership in Muhammadiyah", pp. 32–52.

Ideas about women's progress inspired the nationalist organization Budi Utomo (founded in 1908) to establish Putri Mardika, the first women's association in Indonesia, in Jakarta in 1912. The aim of Putri Mardika was to provide assistance to indigenous girls for schooling, to facilitate greater involvement of women in the public sphere and to elevate the status and dignity of women to a level equal to that of men.[10] Around the same time, several other women's organizations of various backgrounds (Islamic, Catholic and non-religious affiliations) were also established.[11] It was also during this period that a number of Indonesian women became interested in nationalism and established the Indonesian Women's Association (Perikatan Perkumpulan Perempuan Indonesia, PPPI) during the first Indonesian Women's Congress in Yogyakarta on 22 December 1928.[12] The active participation of Indonesian women in the struggle for progress and their engagement with nationalism declined under Japanese Occupation (1942–45). The Japanese colonial government did not approve of any individual or collective activities. There was only one approved women's organization, Fujinkai, but its sole purpose was supporting the Japanese army. Joining Fujinkai was compulsory for the wives of government officials such as regents or district heads, but voluntary for the public.[13] The members of Fujinkai functioned within a hierarchy that ran parallel to that of their husbands, and they were expected to propagate among women the Japanese view of a "Greater Asia" under Nippon leadership.[14]

---

[10] Suryochondro, *Potret Pergerakan Wanita di Indonesia*, p. 85.

[11] Ibid., pp. 207–11. Those with Islamic backgrounds include Serekat Siti Fatimah, established in Garut in 1918 (under Partai Sarekat Islam Indonesia); Wanodyo Oetomo in Yogyakarta, established in 1920 (under Sarekat Islam); Damesafdeeling Jong Islamieten Bond, established in Yogyakarta in 1925 (under Jong Islamieten Bond); Wanita Pertiwi (Persatuan Tarbiyah Islamiyah), established in 1928 (affiliated with Partai Islam Perti); and Nahdatoel Faat, established in Yogyakarta in 1920 (Walfadjrie). One specifically for Catholics was Wanita Katolik, established in Yogyakarta in 1924. Those without an official religious connection include Jong Java Meisjekring, established in 1915; Purborini, established in Tegal in 1917; Wanito Soesilo, established in Pemalang in 1918; Wanito Hadi, established in Jepara in 1919; Poetri Boedi Sedjati, established in Surabaya in 1919; Wanito Oetomo, established in Yogyakarta in 1920; Wanita Taman Siswa, established in Yogyakarta in 1922; and Ina Toeni, established in Ambon in 1927.

[12] Ibid., pp. 89–90.

[13] Ibid., p. 181.

[14] Wieringa, "Aborted Feminisms in Indonesia", p. 75.

After the harsh, but relatively short, Japanese Occupation, Indonesian women took further political action in the period (1945–59) following Indonesian Independence in August 1945. The return of the Dutch Army resulted in a revolutionary battle and many Indonesian women defended their national sovereignty alongside Indonesian men. Under this condition, various female *laskar* (groups or militias that support war) were established, such as the Indonesian Women's Union of Struggle (Persatuan Perjuangan Wanita Indonesia).[15] When the revolutionary war ended in 1949 and a liberal political system was founded, Indonesian women began to associate themselves with newly formed political parties. For the socialists of this period we shall note the presence of Gerwani (Gerakan Wanita Indonesia, Indonesian Women's Movement), founded in 1954 as the successor to the earlier movement, Gerwis, established in Semarang on 4 June 1950.[16] Gerwani shifted from a non-aligned position in 1954, to become a part of the Indonesian Communist Party (Partai Komunis Indonesia, PKI) in 1964.[17] Sukarno classified Gerwani as a progressive women's organization compared to other genteel women's organizations, because it had a more aggressive programme, and attempted to fight imperialism.[18] Although Gerwani was extremely influential in enforcing democratic marriage laws and vocal in its strict disapproval of polygamous marriage, the group did not publicly respond to Sukarno's polygamous marriage to Hartini because it did not want to undermine the President, who was an important ally of the socialists.[19]

Other women's groups offered diverse responses to Sukarno's endorsement of polygamy through his introduction of Government Regulation No. 19/1952, which allowed for the provision of government pensions to multiple widows of polygamous civil servants.[20] While 'Aisyiyah[21] and other Islamic women's organizations defended the regulation,[22] Catholic[23] and socialist women's organizations, including Isteri Sedar,

---

[15] Suryochondro, *Potret Pergerakan Wanita di Indonesia*, p. 135.
[16] Wieringa, *Sexual Politics in Indonesia*, p. 151.
[17] Ibid., p. 178.
[18] Ibid., p. 212.
[19] Wieringa, "Aborted Feminisms in Indonesia", p. 82; and Wieringa, *Sexual Politics in Indonesia*, p. 157.
[20] Blackburn, *Women and State in Modern Indonesia*, p. 129.
[21] Ibid., p. 129.
[22] "Indonesia Sudah Kaja Djanda", p. 1.
[23] "Wanita Katholik Tantang P.P. 19 Tjela Polygamie dan Tuntut Pembrantasan Tukang2 Riba", p. 2.

were against it.²⁴ By the first election in 1955, many women were affiliated with women's wings of political parties such as Gerwis (Gerakan Wanita Indonesia Sedar, or Movement of Conscious Indonesian Women) established in Semarang on 4 June 1950 of the PKI, Wanita Nasional of the Great Indonesia Party (Partai Indonesia Raya), and Murba Women's Union (Persatuan Wanita Murba, PERWAMU) of the Murba Party (Partai Murba).²⁵

In 1959, under President Sukarno's leadership, Indonesia entered the phase of Guided Democracy²⁶ (1959–66). When the Konstituante²⁷ failed to deliver a draft of a permanent constitution for Indonesia, Sukarno instituted the political system of Guided Democracy which consisted of two vital elements: a return to the 1945 Constitution,²⁸ and the formalization of Sukarno's position as the central power holder within the new system.²⁹ There were three influential political powers during Guided Democracy namely, Sukarno, PKI, and the Army. The period was also coloured by tension between PKI, Islamic groups and the Army. In turn, this tension affected women's groups, particularly between those founded on socialist and Islamic ideologies.

---

²⁴ Si De, "Isteri Sedar Tjoekoep Oemoernja 10 Tahoen", pp. 21–2.
²⁵ Suryochondro, *Potret Pergerakan Wanita di Indonesia*, pp. 138–9.
²⁶ This particular system of governance was called Guided Democracy because Sukarno had absolute power over the function of the government. He introduced and insisted on Guided Democracy because the parliamentary democracy implemented between 1950 and 1959 failed to establish stability in Indonesia. See Crouch, "The Trend to Authoritarianism", p. 179.
²⁷ The Konstituante was the constitutional assembly, the body set up to draft a permanent constitution for Indonesia after independence. Assembly members were elected in 1955, but by July 1959 they had yet to draft a permanent constitution due to ideological conflict between Nationalist, Islamic, Communist and other parties. See Schwarz, *A Nation in Waiting*, pp. 12–6.
²⁸ Indonesia has had three constitutions. The 1945 Constitution was announced on 18 August 1945, the day after Sukarno and Hatta proclaimed independence. The Federal Constitution replaced it on 27 December 1949; this new constitution was strongly influenced by the Dutch and called for the "Republic of the United States of Indonesia". Indonesians drafted another constitution a year later, one that implemented a parliamentary system. In 1955 elections were held for both the House of Representatives and the Constitutional Assembly (Konstituante) that would draft a definitive constitution. However, many disputes erupted between nationalists and Islamists over the role of Islam in the new nation. Finally, in 1959, President Sukarno issued a decree dissolving the assembly and restoring the 1945 Constitution. See Schwarz, *A Nation in Waiting*, p. 7.
²⁹ Ibid., pp. 12–6.

In 1966, Sukarno lost power after a failed coup,[30] and was replaced by Suharto and his New Order. Suharto, with his authoritarian style of leadership, constrained political Islam and the role of women in politics. Suharto's severe policy on Islam was due partly to the underlying fear of the idea of formalistic Islam, which sought the creation of an Islamic state and was largely proposed by the Islamic political parties during the Parliamentary Democracy period (1950–59).[31] Hence, once in power,

---

[30] The coup was triggered by the General Council, which consisted of some Army generals, was sponsored by the CIA, and forced Sukarno to resign. See Crouch, "The Trend to Authoritarianism", p. 188. In order to prevent a military coup from taking place, a group including DN Aidit, head of the PKI and closely affiliated with President Sukarno, and members of the PKI special bureau such as Syam, Pono and Walujo, planned the operation (see *Dokumen Terpilih Sekitar G.30S/THE PKI*, p. 35). Lieutenant Colonel Untung, a PKI member who also commanded one of the three battalions of President Sukarno's "Cakrabirawa" palace guard, led the operation. They kidnapped six generals on the night of 30 September and 1 October 1965. They took the kidnapped generals to Halim Air Force Base, called Lobang Buaya. They assumed that kidnapping and killing the generals would save President Sukarno from a military coup and ensure the PKI's continued existence in Indonesia. The coup failed, however, and the Army responded with force. Led by Major General Suharto as commander of KOSTRAD (the Army's Strategic Command), the Army searched for and killed members of the PKI and affiliated groups throughout Java. After the coup, Suharto and the Army played a significant role in Indonesian politics. On 11 March 1966, Sukarno signed SUPERSEMAR (*Surat Perintah Sebelas Maret*, the order of 11 March), which Suharto gave a mandate to manage the post-coup situation. SUPERSEMAR symbolically shifted political power from Sukarno to Suharto's New Order Indonesia. On 12 March 1965, Suharto banned the PKI and all of its followers. For an analysis of the mystery surrounding the coup, including detailed autopsy reports that address the rumours about the mutilation of the generals, see Anderson, "How Did the Generals Die?", pp. 109–34; Anderson and McVey, *A Preliminary Analysis of the October 1, 1965, Coup in Indonesia*.

[31] During the Japanese Occupation, the Japanese colonial government allowed room for the establishment of MIAI (Majelis Islam 'Ala Indonesia), a federation of Islamic organizations and political parties, which was initially founded in 1935 and later reestablished in Jakarta on 5 September 1942. Afraid of a possible revolt, the Japanese colonial government dismissed MIAI and replaced it with Masyumi (Majelis Syuro Muslimin Indonesia) in late 1943. In turn, Masyumi, PSII, NU and Perti served as the main vehicles through which Islamic activists could promote the idea of an Islamic state vis-à-vis the secular nationalist activists who dominated the Investigative Body for the Preparation for Indonesian Independence (Badan Penyelidik untuk Persiapan Kemerdekaan Indonesia, BPUPKI, which was founded by the Japanese colonial government and responsible for drafting the constitution of newly independent Indonesia). Eventually, the struggle between the Islamists and secular nationalists resulted in the

Suharto depoliticized Islam[32] by discouraging the practice of Islamic politics seeking the formation of an Islamic state. This was possible, according to Karl D. Jackson, because Suharto came to power assisted by the officer corps, the bureaucracy, technocrats and the military, all of whom were associated largely with a Hindu-Javanese identity and were thus not likely to favour formalistic Islam.[33] Depoliticizing Islam included, for example, Suharto's decision to continue the prohibition on Masyumi, the Islamic political party that had been banned by Sukarno in 1960.[34] Furthermore, Suharto commenced "departyization" to steadily reduce the influence of political parties in the lead up to the 1971 General Election.[35] He promoted a confederation of functional groups, the so-called Golkar,[36] to challenge existing political parties. Suharto then launched a policy to amalgamate political parties in 1973, under which the four existing Islamic political parties were amalgamated into a single party called the United Development Party (Partai Persatuan Pembangunan, PPP) while the nationalist, Protestant and Catholic parties were merged into the Indonesian Democratic Party (Partai Demokrasi Indonesia, PDI).[37]

Suharto also extended strong control over Indonesian women. Suharto styled himself as the "Father of Development" (Bapak Pembangunan), and developed what Julia Suryakusuma calls "state ibuism",

---

political compromise in the "Jakarta Charter" issued on 22 June 1945, which became the official philosophical foundation of the Indonesian state (Pancasila). In the initial version, the first principle of the Jakarta Charter read, "Belief in one God, with the obligation to implement Islamic Syariah for those who adhere to Islam". The second part of this phrase was later omitted from the final version, which disappointed Islamic activists. Some even took radical action, such as Kartosuwiryo's DI/TII rebellion in West Java, which declared the establishment of an Islamic State in Indonesia. See Noer, *Partai Islam Di Pentas Nasional*, p. 17; Maarif, *Islam Dan Politik Teori Belah Bambu Masa Demokrasi Terpimpin (1959–1965)*, p. 27. For comparative perspectives of the rationale behind the rise of Kartosuwiryo's DI/TII, see Jackson, *Kewibawaan Tradisional, Islam dan Pemberontakan*; and Dengel, *Darul Islam Dan Kartosuwiryo*.

[32] Hefner, *Civil Islam*, p. 72.
[33] Jackson, "A Bureaucratic Polity", p. 3.
[34] Noer, *Partai Islam di Pentas Nasional 1945–1966*, p. 367.
[35] Emmerson, "The Bureaucracy in Political Context: Weakness in Strength", p. 99.
[36] Golkar was established by the Army with the initial aim to coordinate anti-communist organizations in 1964, see Karim, *Negara dan Peminggiran Islam Politik*, p. 75; Ricklefs, *A History of Modern Indonesia since c.1200*, p. 360.
[37] Ricklefs, *A History of Modern Indonesia since c.1200*, p. 361; Karim, *Islam dan Konflik Politik Era Orde Baru*, p. 4.

a gender ideology that demanded total devotion from Indonesian women and expected them to focus on their roles as wives and mothers (*ibu*) in developing Indonesia.[38] In applying gender ideology within development, the New Order government largely focused on women's practical gender interests rather than strategic gender interests.[39] There were two different programmes according to its focus and aims: firstly, a programme which focused on women's roles as "mothers and wives" with the aim of controlling women's positions in the state. In this process, the loyalty of urban middle-class women to Suharto was channelled via Dharma Wanita, a compulsory women's organization founded in 1974 for the wives of all civil servants, and the Indonesian Women's Congress (Kongres Wanita Indonesia, KOWANI), an umbrella for all women's organizations.[40] Here, Suharto's wife, Madame Tien Suharto, played a crucial role as initiator of Dharma Wanita and as the patron of army wives in ensuring the political loyalty of Indonesian women.[41] Meanwhile, the Family Welfare Guidance (Pembinaan Kesejahteraan Keluarga, PKK) was founded in 1972 for lower-class urban and rural women.[42] Other programmes focused on women's reproductive roles, aiming to foster family ties and institute a state programme of population reduction. This was achieved

---

[38] Suryakusuma, "The State and Sexuality in New Order Indonesia", p. 96. Although Suryakusuma is the first scholar to call the gender ideology of the New Order "state ibuism", the term "*ibuism*" was not new when she coined the phrase. In 1987, Madelon Nieuwenhuis was suspicious of the practice of what she called "*ibuism*" ideology, which marked a change in the role and position of women in post-colonial Indonesia. In the mid-1980s, Nieuwenhuis described how upper-class women (wives of bureaucrats) were expected to safeguard the family and the nation by becoming good mothers and wives, while actual power remained in the hands of males. See Nieuwenhuis, "Ibuism and Priyayization: Path to Power?".

[39] There are two gender interests: first, "strategic gender interest", which comes from the analysis of women's subordination in society and resulted in the creation of a structural pattern that featured more equal relationships between women and men; secondly, "practical gender interest", which addresses women's obstacles so that they can optimize their functions within specific contexts and goals. See Blackburn, "Gender Interest and Indonesian Democracy", p. 174. For a basic elaboration on "strategic gender interest" and "practical gender interest", see Molyneux, "Mobilization Without Emancipation?", pp. 232–3; Moser, "Gender Planning in the Third World", pp. 89–90.

[40] KOWANI, *Sejarah Sentengah Abad Pergerakan Wanita Indonesia*, p. 279.

[41] "Riwayat Singkat Dharma Wanita"; Department of Information, *The Indonesian Women's Movement*, p. 61.

[42] Tim Penggerak PKK Pusat, *Sejarah Singkat Gerakan PKK*, p. 1.

by introducing a family planning programme (*Keluarga berencana*, KB) in 1970, which distributed modern contraception to the village level. The family planning programme was successful in that the rate of contraception use rose from 47.7 per cent in 1987 to 57.7 per cent in 1997,[43] and the total fertility rate declined from 5.61 per cent in the 1970s to 2.78 per cent in 1997.[44] Additionally, in order to promote a stable family, Suharto, with strong support from his wife, introduced the new Marriage Act in 1974, which promoted monogamy.[45] Overall, borrowing Saptari's term "Java-centric bias",[46] the politically active husband (Suharto) and his faithful companion-wife (Tien Suharto) were the bedrock of a stable family that served as the foundation of a strong state.

The vibrant atmosphere, in which Indonesian women had sought to elevate their position and role in politics since the late 19th century, changed considerably under the Sukarno's Guided Democracy regime and then Suharto's authoritarian New Order. However, significant development would soon begin in the 1980s and especially in the mid-1990s that would contribute to strengthening Indonesian women's role in politics. And, as we shall see in the next section, circumstances in the 1980s would see Muslim women, initially concentrated in Java, lead socio-religious movements that encouraged the implementation of Islam in everyday life and empowered women to create broader social and political actions.

Islamization and the Early Stages of Democratization: Strengthening Indonesian Women's Roles in Politics

The period from the 1980s until the late 1990s was pivotal for the social transformation of Indonesian women. While Indonesian women had surrendered any political autonomy they had once held and were encouraged only to be loyal to their husbands and the state during the period of the New Order, in the 1980s Islamization, embraced by various actors and including the university-centred *tarbiyah* movement, began to create new

---

[43] Robinson, "Indonesian Women—from *Orde Baru* to *Reformasi*", p. 150.
[44] Khofifah Indar Parawansa, "Institution Building", p. 72.
[45] Blackburn, *Women and State in Modern Indonesia*, pp. 130–4.
[46] Saptari, "Women, Family and Household", p. 19. Saptari used term "Java-centric" to address Sylvia Tiwon's notion of the centrality of the Javanese ideology of womanhood in the New Order's policy on women. See Tiwon, "Reconstructing Boundaries and Beyond", pp. 71–4.

arenas of engagement for Muslim women. By embracing Islamic principles such as wearing the veil, interacting intensively in religious learning groups and participating in discussions and social activities at various universities, Muslim women could maintain their own collective social existence. Additionally, the spread of Islamic feminism in the mid-1990s was a further catalyst for young female Muslim activists and intellectuals based in Java to promote progressive ideas in Indonesian Islamic thought, which further strengthened Indonesian women's roles in politics.

The New Order's severe stance on political Islam had generally made Indonesian Muslims politically powerless and alienated. Feeling politically alienated, Muslims in Indonesia had adopted the new spirit of Islamic revival in the 1970s,[47] which was inspiring many Muslim countries in Southeast Asia at the time. As part of the Islamic revival, there was an awakening interest in acts of piety; as defined by Joy Kooi-Chin Tong and Bryan S. Turner, acts of piety usually involve self-control and bodily practices concerning diet, attitude, clothing and bodily discipline.[48]

In Malaysia, the revival of Islam inspired the rise of the *dakwah* movement, propagated by Youth Islamic Group of Malaysia (Angkatan Belia Islam Malaysia, ABIM) since the 1970s in various universities, which called for the revitalization of the faith at a time when the government (under Prime Minister Mahathir Mohamad, 1981–2003) sought to produce a non-western modernity in Malaysia.[49] While the *dakwah* movement increased religious consciousness among the youth in Malaysia,[50] as manifested in the choice of many modern Malay women to wear the veil and practice their faith in an openly devout manner,[51] in the 1990s, the

---

[47] During this period, the so-called "Muslim world" experienced a political resurgence that was marked by a number of events, including the President General Zia-ul-Haq's move to make Pakistan an Islamic state in 1978, the American-backed *jihad* to liberate Afghanistan from the Soviet Union in 1979, and the Iranian Revolution led by Ayatullah Khomeini in 1979. This political upheaval soon spread to other Muslim-majority countries.

[48] Tong and Turner, "Women, Piety and Practice", p. 43.

[49] Saravanamuttu, "Introduction", p. 2. Malaysia consists of multiple ethnic groups; the Malays make up around 50 per cent of the total population, followed by the Chinese and Indians. The Malays are closely associated with Islam, because Article 160 of the Malaysian constitution considers all Malay citizens as Muslims. As the largest ethnic and religious community, Malays have dominated state political processes since Malaysia gained independence from the British Empire in 1957.

[50] Nagata, "Religious Ideology and Social Change", p. 415.

[51] Stivens, "Becoming Modern in Malaysia", p. 19.

government imposed strict rules to ensure Malay women's modernization accorded with Islamic values. For example it imposed laws and regulations to control women's dress and behaviour such as the *fatwa* banning Muslim women from taking part in beauty contests,[52] or the ruling by Terengganu State, which was strongly influenced by the conservative Islamic political party Partai Islam se Malaysia (PAS), before the 2004 General Election, that Muslim women should wear the *tudung* (Muslim headscarf).[53] Malaysia's official Islam is concerned about promoting an ideal Islamic norm of pious Muslim women as wives and mothers. Interestingly, the Islam promoted by the Malaysian state corresponds with ordinary pious Muslim Malay women's expectations. Sylva Frisk's research in urban Malaysia from the mid-1990s to around 2009 shows that for the majority of ordinary pious Malay women who were raised within Malaysia, Islamization has become conventional: they do not want to challenge or resist male authority because their desire to submit to their perception of God's will is more important than their need to resist a patriarchal norm,[54] a perspective in line with the state ideal. Now, the state in Malaysia continues to develop what Maila Stiven calls "family values" to strengthen the family in order to heal the social ills of the society, a position that asks women to bear the primary responsibility for the care of the home in contemporary Malaysia.[55]

Similarly, in Indonesia the revival of Islam brought with it Islamization, a socio-religious movement encouraging internalization of Islamic principles within society since the 1980s. Some features of Islamization in Indonesia were similar to those in Malaysia. For example, since the 1980s, the movement has been centred in universities and has been followed by the gradual adoption of veiling among young Muslim women. However, in Indonesia Islamization was initiated and spread by various actors rather than largely by state and university-based actors. As we shall see, Islamization in Indonesia was promoted by Muslim intellectuals and religious leaders of the two mainstream Islamic organizations, namely Muhammadiyah and Nahdlatul Ulama, as well as by the *tarbiyah* movement (urban-based Islamic education movement) in various universities across Java. In my opinion, the vibrant role of Islamic organizations in bringing Islamization to Indonesia resulted in a more plural form of

---

[52] Shuib, "Speaking with a New Voice", pp. 179–99.
[53] Ibid., p. 197.
[54] Frisk, *Submitting to God*, p. 190.
[55] Stivens, "Family Values and Islamic Revival", pp. 154–9.

Islam, which allowed it to welcome ideas about Islamic feminism in the mid-1990s.

In Indonesia, one Muslim intellectual that pioneered the socio-religious movement was Nurcholis Madjid; he advocated unity between Indonesia and Islam citing the basic Islamic principles of universality, openness and inclusiveness.[56] Similarly, Abdurrahman Wahid (Gus Dur) also saw Islam as complementary to Indonesian nation-building.[57] The socio-religious movement was also promoted by the two biggest Indonesian Islamic organizations, Muhammadiyah[58] and Nahdlatul Ulama.[59] Both encouraged Muslims to strengthen their individual and collective capacity and avoid political praxis. Islamization also took place among Muslim students in the form of the *tarbiyah* movement (*gerakan tarbiyah*, an urban-based Islamic education movement) in universities mainly centred in Java,[60] such as the Bandung Institute of Technology (Institut

---

[56] See Madjid, *Islam Doktrin Dan Peradaban*.

[57] For deeper elaboration of the thought of both Nurcholis Madjid and Abdurrahman Wahid, see Feener, *Muslim Legal Thought in Modern Indonesia*.

[58] The Muhammadiyah congress in Ujung Pandang in 1971 declared that it would not affiliate with political parties, and would promote economic, education and religious development in order to achieve a blessed society (*masyarakat utama*). For more on the high politics of Muhammadiyah, see Rais, *Moralitas Politik Muhammdiyah*; and Rais, *Tauhid Sosial*.

[59] The Nadhlatul Ulama congress in Situbondo in 1984 declared the return to the "*khittah 1926*", marking its withdrawal from political practice and focus on strengthening individuals and society in order to develop civic culture as a basis for democracy. Hikam, "Wacana Intelektualisme Tentang *Civil Society* di Indonesia", p. 40.

[60] Why mainly in Java? We must consider the socio-historical facts that contributed to the rapid development there. Figures from the Ministry of Home Affairs in 1952 show that Java and Madura were the most densely populated areas in Indonesia; this can be attributed to natural factors such as soil fertility, amount of rainfall and development initiatives by the former Dutch administration. See Ministry of Social Affairs, *Towards Social Welfare in Indonesia*, p. 11. This situation persists to this day: for example, 63.83 per cent of the Indonesian population lived in Java in 1971, and declined to 60.12 per cent in 2000. See Suryadinata, Arifin and Ananta, *Penduduk Indonesia*, p. 4. Moreover, in 1995, 59.32 per cent of all women lived inside Java, while only 40.68 per cent lived elsewhere (see Biro Pusat Statistik, *Indikator Sosial Wanita Indonesia*, p. 11). This unequal population distribution is attributed to education, health facilities and employment opportunities. Javanese women's better access to education, as a result, can be seen in the percentage of illiterate women between the ages of 10 and 19: in 1980, the lowest percentage (4.11 per cent) was found in Yogyakarta province, while the highest (32.12 per cent) was found in West Kalimantan (*Indikator Sosial*, p. 102). Javanese women, therefore, had better opportunities to intersect with both progressive and conservative Islamic ideas through higher learning.

Teknologi Bandung, ITB), University of Indonesia (Universitas Indonesia, UI), Gadjah Mada University (Universitas Gadjah Mada, UGM), the Education and Teaching Institute (IKIP) and the Islamic State Institute (IAIN).

Suharto's ban on political activity on university campuses in the early 1980s[61] also motivated students to develop socio-religious movements inspired by the revival of Islam in the 1970s. The *tarbiyah* movement was later institutionalized as the United Action of Indonesian Muslim Students (Komite Aksi Mahasiswa Muslim Indonesia, KAMMI) in the late 1990s, which further evolved into the Islamic party known as the Justice Party (Partai Keadilan, PK), which was the predecessor of today's Prosperous Justice Party (Partai Keadilan Sejahtera, PKS).[62] One of the vivid changes brought by the *tarbiyah* movement was the spread and adoption of veiling among young Muslim students at universities and schools throughout Java. Since then, scholars such as Suzanne Brenner,[63] Andree Feillard[64] and Nancy J. Smith-Hefner[65] have posited various theories for the reasons behind the adoption of veiling among young women in universities and schools in Java.

A rather different expression of the Islamic resurgence, as noted by Sita van Bemmelen and Mies Grijns, was the emergence of a new generation of female activists based largely in Java, who wanted to promote an alternative understanding of women's roles in Indonesian Islam. Van Bemmelen and Mies Grijns suggest that although the "general 'emergence' of more confident Muslim female identities was not an exclusively Javanese affair, the most influential traditional and modernist centres of Islamic learning and education could be found in Java and the majority of those taking part in the Muslim gender discourse were Javanese".[66] Thus, since the mid-1990s female Muslim activists in Jakarta, such as Wardah Hafidz, spread ideas about Islamic feminism via *Ulumul Qur'an* (a respected Indonesian journal on civil Islam) by presenting the writings of Ashgar Ali Engineer, Riffat Hasan and Fatima Mernissi. This was followed by the subsequent endorsement of Islamic feminism and gender equality within Indonesian Islam by figures such as Wardah Hafidz,

---

[61] Masaaki, "The Rise of the 'Realistic' Islamist Party", p. 221.
[62] Ibid.
[63] Brenner, "Reconstructing Self and Society", pp. 673–97.
[64] Feillard, "The Veil and Polygamy", n.p.
[65] Smith-Hefner, "Javanese Women and the Veil in Post-Soeharto Indonesia", pp. 389–420.
[66] Van Bemmelen and Grijns, "What Has Become of The Slendang?", p. 115.

Siti Musdah Mulia, Lili Zakiyah Munir, Farha Ciciek, Siti Ruhaini Dzuhayatin, Lies-Marcos Natsir, Nasaruddin Umar and K.H. Husein Muhammad. Through discourse and action, they encouraged the incorporation of a contextual approach[67] in line with the effort to promote feminism and gender discourse in Indonesian Islamic thinking. Today, there is a young generation of Muslims who propose a critical interpretation of Islam. Their work can be found in Nahdlatul Ulama-affiliated organizations such as the Liberal Islam Network (Jaringan Islam Liberal, JIL), or in Muhammadiyah-affiliated organizations such as the Muhammadiyah Intellectual Youth Network (Jaringan Intelektual Muda Muhammadiyah, JIMM).

All of these developments were accelerated when at the end of the 1980s and in the early 1990s, Suharto changed his stance toward political Islam. He started to embrace Muslim leaders and the Muslim community, and began to accommodate their interests as a way of tempering their criticism of the government.[68] Suharto began to demonstrate his public piety: he performed the *hajj* in 1991, established the Indonesian Muslim Intellectual Association (Ikatan Cendikiawan Muslim Indonesia, ICMI), and recruited more Muslim intellectuals into his political party, Golkar, and put resources into the development of thousands of mosques across Indonesia.[69] As Suharto gradually embraced Islamic values and attracted wider sympathy from Muslims, the spread of Islamic feminism continued to serve as a catalyst for young female Muslim activists and intellectuals based in Java to promote progressive ideas in Indonesian

---

[67] The contextual approach emphasizes the importance of context and insight in interpreting the Qur'an and Hadith by exercising human reason to capture the true wisdom rather than relying literally on the text. This approach is primarily used to understand and interpret the divine message on non-religious issues. In contrast to the contextual approach is the textual approach, which relies on the literal interpretation of texts (the Qur'an and Hadith) and is primarily used for interpreting the divine message of religious rituals (*ibadah*, such as prayer and fasting). However, some scholars also use the textual approach to understand social issues, including the role of women in society. As a result, scholars such as Ziba Mir-Hosseini have described the textual approach as one of the factors responsible for the practice of gender inequality in Islam. See Mir-Hosseini, "The Construction of Gender in Islamic Legal Thought", in *Islamic Family Law and Justice for Muslim Women*.
[68] Politically, since the early 1990s, Suharto changed the New Order's approach toward Islam and started to court the Muslim community and its leaders and tried to accommodate their interests as a way of tempering their criticism of the government. See Schwarz, *A Nation in Waiting*, p. 38.
[69] Hasan, "The Making of Public Islam", pp. 235–6.

Islamic thought. This would provide an important foundation for the expansion of Indonesian Muslim women's roles in politics in the post-Suharto era (after 1998).

Democratization in the Post-Suharto Period: Expanding Women's Roles in Politics

Within the democratized atmosphere of the post-Suharto era, we witnessed the transformation of the visions and missions of official state women's organizations as they began to embrace a spirit of gender equality in order to facilitate further expansion of Indonesian women's domestic and political roles. At the same time, the growing engagement of the young Muslim generation with Islamic principles and Islamic feminism was also deepening. However, in addition to these positive signs, there has also been a resurgence in practices commonly associated with a particular brand of Islam, such as polygamy and child marriage. Despite such paradoxical developments, democratization in post-Suharto Indonesia had provided wider room for Indonesian women to expand their political role in a number of ways, including participating in direct elections and securing leadership positions.

Carla Bianpoen described the year of 1998 as having provided the momentum for the enhancement of the role of women in politics.[70] While I agree, I would add that the expansion of women's roles in politics was possible due to transformation of the state ibuism gender ideology in the post-Suharto period. The initial challenge to the New Order's state ibuism gender ideology was, though in a very polite way, propagated by the Voice of Concerned Mothers (Suara Ibu Peduli, SIP) which was set up by feminists in Jakarta in response to the 1997 economic crisis. Besides morally encouraging the government to put into place responsive policies to tackle the rising price of basic food staples and formula milk for babies, SIP also played a crucial role in supporting a peace demonstration with students around February 1998, prior to the political turmoil of May 1998. As Doxey explains, even the name *Suara Ibu Peduli* had an effect on women's identity, as it was a strategic move that used the New Order's method of using the hegemonic identity of *"ibu"* (mother) to unify a heterogeneous country, in which SIP smartly played on the subject of *"ibu"* in their demonstrations.[71]

---

[70] Bianpoen, "Women's Political Call", p. 283.
[71] See Doxey, "Indonesian Feminist Movement".

A further sign of the transformation of the state ibuism gender ideology can be seen in the changes to the platforms, visions and structures of particular state women's organizations that had formerly been used by Suharto to control women's roles. For example, comparing three versions of Dharma Wanita's organizational platform (*Anggaran Dasar dan Anggaran Rumah Tangga*, AD/ART) from 1993, 2001, and 2008 reveals dramatic transformations in its vision and structure. During the New Order, the 1993 AD/ART of Dharma Wanita was aimed at guiding Indonesian women to fulfil their *kodrat* (ability to do a particular thing, appropriateness and boundary) as wives, mothers, and community members; and structurally was not neutral due to the intervention of the Supervisory Board (*Dewan Pembina*) from *Korpri*.[72] However, in response to political democratization since 1998, Dharma Wanita held a Special National Meeting on 6–7 December 1999 that resulted in a name change to Dharma Wanita Persatuan, as well as a reconfiguration of the organization's structure and goals.[73]

The 2001 AD/ART produced at the 1999 meeting clearly reflected a new spirit: it placed emphasis on the protection of human rights, maintaining a non-political position but no longer focusing on women's domestic roles, and it introduced a democratic mechanism by which the chief would be elected in a national meeting.[74] While these points remain in the latest edition of the 2008 AD/ART, article 3 (2), further emphasizes its non-affiliation to any political party, including Golkar.[75] This point of non-affiliation to any political party was also emphasized by Lies Luluk, Secretary General of the Central Board of Dharma Wanita Persatuan (2004–09).[76]

PKK also responded to the Reform Era by conducting a special National Meeting in 2000 which resulted in changing its name from Pembinaan Kesejahteraan Keluarga (Family Welfare Guidance) to

---

[72] The official organization of civil servants was closely linked to *Golkar*, Suharto's political machine. Sekretaris Jenderal Dharma Wanita, *Keputusan Musyawarah Nasional IV Dharma Wanita nomor*, pp. 9–31.

[73] For special coverage related to the 1999 national meeting of the Dharma Wanita, see "Dharma Wanita Persatuan" and "Kebijaksanaan tentang Hari Ulang Tahun Dharma Wanita Persatuan dan Seragam Organisasi".

[74] Sekretaris Jenderal Dharma Wanita Persatuan, *Dharma Wanita*, pp. 17–45.

[75] Sekretaris Jenderal Dharma Wanita, *Dharma Wanita Persatuan*, p. 23.

[76] Interview with Lies Luluk, Secretary General of the *Dharma Wanita Persatuan Pusat* (2004–09), 25 Jan. 2010.

Pemberdayaan dan Kesejahteraan Keluarga (Family Welfare and Empowerment), although the structure of PKK remains under the Ministry of Home Affairs.[77] PKK's National Meeting in 2005 also adopted a progressive agenda and targeted programmes such as gender equality, advocacy of human rights and raising awareness to prevent trafficking and violence against women and children.[78] These institutional changes show that transformation of the state ibuism gender ideology, which has taken place under democratization since 1998, has helped facilitate women's engagement with progressive agendas in support of greater roles for women in politics.

A significant event that inspired more Indonesian women to pursue roles in politics was the nomination of Megawati Sukarnoputri (chairman of PDIP) as the presidential candidate in the 1999 Presidential Election. Although she was defeated by Abdurrahman Wahid and only became his vice-president [though later Megawati took over the Indonesian presidency from Abdurrahman Wahid, who was removed from office due to impeachment by the Indonesian's People Consultative Assembly (Majelis Permusyawaratan Rakyat, MPR), in July 2001], her position as the first female presidential candidate and later the first female President of Indonesia in 2001–04, marked a new frontier in women's roles in politics. Since then, Indonesia has witnessed a number of initiatives in support of women's political rights. For example, the Women's Parliamentary Caucus inside parliament (Kaukus Perempuan Parlemen, KPP) and the Caucus for Women and Indonesian Politics outside of parliament (Kaukus Perempuan Politik Indonesia, KPPI) in collaboration with NGOs in Jakarta such as the Movement for Educating Female Voters (Gerakan Perempuan Sadar Pemilu, GPSP), the Center for Empowering Women in Politics (Pusat Pemberdayaan Perempuan dalam Politik, PD Politik) and the Network for Women and Politics (Jaringan Perempuan dan Politik,

---

[77] This means that the chief of the PKK's Central Board (*ketua PKK Pusat*) is the wife of the Minister of Home Affairs; the chiefs of provincial PKK branches are the wives of governors; those of regencial PKK branches are the wives of regents; those of municipal PKK branches are wives of mayors; those of district PKK branches are the wives of district heads; and those of village PKK branches are the wives of village heads. Interview with Arolis, Secretary IV of the PKK Central Board, 25 Jan. 2010; and Tim Penggerak PKK Pusat, *Sejarah Singkat Gerakan PKK*, p. 2.

[78] Tim Penggerak PKK Pusat, *Hasil Rapat Kerja Nasional VI PKK Tahun 2005*, p. 5; PKK Pusat, *Rencana Kerja Lima Tahun PKK Tahun 2005–2009*, pp. 3–9.

JPPOL) in 2000[79] have all been active in furthering options for women. Since 2002, JPPOL continuously demanded an affirmative action rule in the drafting process of the General Election Law for the 2004 General Election. Its persistent pressure resulted in the incorporation, though relatively weak, of the affirmative action rule in article 65 (1) of the General Election Law No. 12/2003.[80]

Similarly, in mid-2007, women from various NGOs in Jakarta (former members of GPSP, PD Politik, Koalisi Perempuan, and *Jurnal Perempuan*) united under the Alliance of Civil Society for Revision of Political Legislation (Aliansi Masyarakat Sipil untuk Revisi Undang-Undang Politik, ANSIPOL).[81] Although the two women's caucuses could no longer participate in the network, ANSIPOL progressively lobbied male and female politicians in parliament and collaborated with the Ministry of Women's Empowerment under Meutia Hatta (2004–09) to pass a new affirmative action rule in the drafting process of the General Election Act in 2007. As a result, a firmer affirmative action rule was enacted both in Law No. 2/2008 on Political Parties and Law No. 10/2008 on General Elections for the 2009 General Election. It was later made irrelevant by a Supreme Court Decree on "*suara terbanyak/* the majority vote".[82] In the 2014 General Election, a firmer affirmative

---

[79] Jaringan Perempuan dan Politik, *Tata Laksana Jaringan Perempuan dan Politik* (Jakarta: JPPOL, 2002), p. 1.

[80] Article 65 (1) of the General Election Law No. 12/2003 states: "Every political party that participates in the general elections can nominate its candidates (*dapat mengajukan calon*) for membership in the DPR (National House of Representatives), membership in the Regional Representative Council in the province/Regency/Municipality of each electorate by taking into account (*dengan memperhatikan*) female representation at a minimum of 30 percent". The affirmative action rule in Indonesia's national legislation is weak. The words *dapat* and *dengan memperhatikan* mean that the affirmative action rule is merely a suggestion, not a mandatory measure and there is no obligation to follow it.

[81] Testimony from the meeting of Jaringan Perempuan dan Politik in Jakarta, 6 Feb. 2008.

[82] Initially, Article 214 of Law No. 10/2008 stipulated that the 2009 General Election would be conducted through a "restricted open proportional system" (*proporsional terbuka terbatas*), in which the winner was the individual who gained a number of votes equal to or more than the Vote Division Number (Bilangan Pembagi Pemilih, BPP) within each electorate (Daerah Pemilihan, Dapil). However, the Indonesian Constitutional Court (Mahkamah Konstitusi, MK) declared that the system would no longer be used and would be replaced with a majority vote system (*sistim suara terbanyak*) in which the winner would be the individual who gained the majority of votes. See *SUARA KPU*, Jan. 2009, p. 3.

action rule was enacted with Law No. 2/2011 on Political Parties, which enforces the rule that political parties must include a minimum of 30 per cent women in the recruitment process of their legislative candidates at the local and national levels. This was strengthened with Law No. 8/2012 on the Election of Members of the People's Representative Council and Regional People's Representative Councils, which also enforced the rule that political parties must include a minimum of 30 per cent women in their list of candidates, and states that should they fail to do so the General Election Commission will not approve their list of candidates.

These positive trends have also been encouraged by the post-Suharto government support of gender equality. Official support can be seen in Indonesia's ratification of the Beijing Platform for Action to incorporate gender in development (Gender and Development, GAD), as a result of the Fourth United Nations World Conference on Women in Beijing in 1995. It was ratified in Law No. 25/2000 on the National Development Program 2000–04 (Program Pembangunan Nasional, PROPENAS). This was followed by introducing the term "gender" in the 1999–2004 Broad Guidelines on State Policy (Garis Besar Haluan Negara, GBHN) and implementation of Presidential Instruction No. 9/2000 on Gender Mainstreaming. These basic regulations were issued when Khofifah Indar Parawansa was the Minister for Empowerment of Women (1999–2001) under Abdurrahman Wahid's Presidency.[83] Khofifah Indar Parawansa's background as woman activist namely chief of Muslimat NU (2000–05) (2006–11) clearly affected her progressive effort to support women's role in Indonesian politics. By this point, gender equality and greater political rights for women were gradually being taken into account and were seen as an important aspect of national development in the post-Suharto era.

In everyday life, the debate over sexuality and expression of female bodies in writings, public spaces, performances, as well as the voices of the lesbian, gay, bisexual and transgender (LGBT) communities, are growing.[84] At the same time, there is a visibly growing attachment to Islamic principles, such as wearing the veil. According to Rachmah Ida, wearing the veil has now become part of contemporary fashion, with

---

[83] See her progressive approach for advancing the role and position of Indonesian women after the New Order, see Parawansa, "Institution Building", in *Women in Indonesia*, pp. 68–77.
[84] For further exploration see Schroter, "Gender and Islam in Southeast Asia", pp. 38–42; and Arnez, "A Dialogue With God?", pp. 73–94.

little association to the significance of veiling in the 1980s.⁸⁵ In addition, Islamic practises that amplify conservative Islamic agendas have made a public stand in the post-Suharto period. Polygamy, previously restricted, has been openly practised by Muslim public figures. The polygamous marriage of the former Vice President Hamzah Haz and the introduction of the Polygamy Award initiated by Puspo Wardoyo in 2003 has captured wide public attention.⁸⁶ The decision by Aa Gym (a famous preacher from Bandung, West Java) to take a second wife in 2006 reveals just how popular the practice of polygamy has become.⁸⁷ Another emerging phenomenon is the practice of child marriage, as in the case of Syaik Puji, a rich businessman and prominent *kyai* in Salatiga, Central Java, who took Lutfiana Ulfa, a 12-year-old female student, as his second wife, with, according to him, the consent of his first wife. In November 2010, Syaik Puji was eventually sentenced to four years in prison for violation of children's rights according to Law No. 23/2002 on Children's Protection.⁸⁸ There was also a gradual emergence of radical Islamic groups demanding implementation of an Islamic state following the Reform Era in 1998,⁸⁹ and a rising practice in the *perda sha'riah* (local government regulations based on Islamic law), which often disadvantage and victimize women. The Indonesian Women's Commission on Human Rights noted that in 2010 there were 154 local regulations that discriminated against women in 16 regencies in the provinces of Aceh, West Java, East Nusa Tenggara, South Sulawesi, South Kalimantan, Yogyakarta and Banten.⁹⁰ Last but not least, concerning Muslim women's roles, Islamic conservative

---

⁸⁵ Ida, "Muslim Women and Contemporary Veiling in Indonesia", pp. 63–5.

⁸⁶ For an understanding of the current practice of polygamy in ordinary households after the New Order, see Nurmila, "Negotiating Polygamy in Indonesia", pp. 23–46.

⁸⁷ Watson, "A Popular Indonesian Preacher", pp. 773–9; Fealy and White, ed., *Expressing Islam*, p. 107.

⁸⁸ "Syekh Puji Divonis Empat Tahun, Dua Istrinya Menangis", 24 Nov. 2010, at <http://www.tempointeraktif.com/hg/jogja/2010/11/24/brk,20101124-294259,id.html> [accessed 21 Dec. 2010].

⁸⁹ Islamic paramilitaries that emerged after the fall of Suharto include the Islamic Defenders Front (Front Pembela Islam, FPI), the Jihad Militia (Laskar Jihad) and the Mujahedeen Militia (Laskar Mujahidin). For further elaboration see Hefner, "Muslim Democrats and Islamist Violence in Post-Suharto Indonesia", pp. 284–98.

⁹⁰ "Konstituti: Mengupayakan Demokrasi Substansial". For detailed examples and an exploration of cases in which Islamic local regulations victimize women, see Noerdin et al., *Representasi Perempuan dalam Kebijakan Publik di Era Otonomi Daerah*.

interpretations of traditional gender relations driven by Islamist groups have gained influence.[91]

Throughout this chapter, we can track the history behind the rise of Indonesian Muslim women's role in local politics in contemporary Indonesia. While on the one hand conservative Islam painted a bleak picture for women's opportunities, on the other hand the growth of progressive Islam and the greater commitment of government in the post-Suharto period have accelerated the expansion of Indonesian women's political roles. This was further strengthened in local politics when direct elections were introduced in 2005 and many Indonesian Muslim women began to take greater leadership roles. Overall, the Islamization that has been taken place since the 1980s, followed by the rise of progressive Islam since the mid-1990s and a turn toward democratization where post-Suharto government shows greater commitment on gender equality, have all had a direct positive effect on the expansion of Indonesian women's roles in local politics in post-Suharto Indonesia.

---

[91] Robinson, *Gender, Islam and Democracy in Indonesia*, p. 192.

CHAPTER 3

The Normative Expectation of Javanese Muslim Women and Islamic Perspectives on Female Leadership

As the three case studies observed in this book are on Javanese Muslim women,[1] it is necessary to establish a basic understanding of the normative expectation of Javanese Muslim women, as the primary subject of this study. I examine how the Javanese community has expected women to behave within their families and in the public sphere, and the possible changes this expectation is now undergoing. Subsequently, I explore the perspectives of Indonesian Islam on female leadership. Understanding the Islamic perspective is important because this study deals with Indonesian Muslim women, and I believe that an Islamic perspective that supports female leadership in local politics serves as a strong religious foundation for them.

The Normative Expectation of Javanese Muslim Women: Across Social Classes

Although upper-class and lower-class Javanese women have experienced different degrees of freedom and autonomy in their daily lives, both have

---

[1] Rustriningsih, Siti Qomariyah, and Ratna Ani Lestari were elected to positions in Central and East Java. Anthropologically speaking, according to Koentjaraningrat, the two regions are home to the Javanese people, who maintained a culture and language that differentiated them from the Sundanese in West Java. Koentjaraningrat, *Javanese Culture*, p. 2. Statistically, Central Java, East Java and Yogyakarta had the three highest concentrations of Javanese among all of Indonesia's 30 provinces in 2000, at 97.96, 78.35, and 96.82 per cent respectively. See Ananta, Arifin and Suryadinata, *Indonesian Electoral Behaviour*, p. 61.

lived under similar normative expectations in Java.[2] In Javanese culture, men are perceived as the core of the Javanese family, and women come second. The Javanese proverb, *konco wingking* ("the friend in the back", literally the kitchen, which is usually at the back of the house) typically illustrates this subordinate role of Javanese women.[3] For the sake of her husband's dignity, a Javanese woman is expected to undertake *cancut tali wanda* (take the initiative to do everything necessary, particularly when her family is facing trouble) and to protect and provide a foundation for her husband's accomplishments.[4] A true woman (*wanita sejati*) is one who serves well at home as mother and wife, either in the kitchen or bedroom, and plays no public role because a public role or position might undermine her husband's dignity.[5]

This normative expectation is further reinforced by Islam, which colours the everyday life of Javanese Muslim women. Interaction between Javanese women and Islam happened throughout centuries in several phases and various forms.[6] Generally, in Islamic teachings, as the head of the family, the husband is obliged to give *nafaka* (money for living) to his wife.[7] In return, a wife performs her primary duties of taking care of the family, educating any children and managing the household as a manifestation of her role as a wife, mother and member of the community.[8] A husband and wife must complement each other for the sake of family harmony. This is regulated under Law No. 1/1974 of the Marriage Code. The major intention of the act was to unify Indonesian marriage codes. Previously marriage codes varied according to religion and ethnicity, with *adat* (customary) law for indigenous Indonesians, Islamic law for Muslims and yet a different law for Christians.[9]

---

[2] For example, upper-class Javanese women often experienced *pingitan*, a period of seclusion in which women remained at home, secluded from the public sphere, as happened in the case of R.A. Kartini, as discussed in Chapter 2. In places like Solo and Yogyakarta, lower-class or ordinary women enjoyed wider mobility in certain areas, such as trade and agricultural activities. See Brenner, "Why Women Rule the Roost", Keeler, "Speaking Gender in Java"; and Vreede-De Stuers, *The Indonesian Woman*.
[3] Handayani and Novianto, *Kuasa Wanita Jawa*, pp. 117–8.
[4] Ibid., p. 139.
[5] Ibid., p. 143.
[6] To see the interaction between Javanese women and Islam in the identity formation of Javanese Muslim women, see my paper, "Javanese Women and Islam".
[7] Huzaemah, "Konsep Wanita Menurut Qur'an, Sunah, Dan Fikih".
[8] Saefuddin, "Kiprah dan Perjuangan Perempuan Salihat".
[9] Blackburn, *Women and State in Modern Indonesia*, pp. 75–80.

There are some critical points in Law No. 1/1974 that triggered controversy, namely:

- article 7 (1) on the minimum age of a couple who wants to get married. It stipulates that men must be 19 years old while women must be 16 years old;
- articles 3, 4, and 5 address polygamy and permit men to take up to four wives if one of the following three reasons is satisfied: his wife cannot fulfil her duties, his wife has a physical disability, or his wife cannot bear children;
- article 31 (3) on the position of husband and wife states *"suami adalah kepala keluarga dan istri ibu rumah tangga"* (the husband is the head of the family while the wife should take care of the household).[10] This indicates a strict division of labour in the family and normatively constrains women from playing public roles.

In addition to the act, there is a special regulation for Muslim marriages enacted in the Compilation of Islamic Law (*Kompilasi Hukum Islam*, KHI), which is based on Presidential Instruction No. 1/1991. This law has become the primary reference for the Indonesian Religious Court on matters pertaining to marriage (*perkawinan*) and inheritance (*kewarisan*).

In 2004, Siti Musdah Mulia, a leading Indonesian Muslim feminist, challenged the 1974 Marriage Law and the Compilation of Islamic Law and urged reform of both, as they no longer met the spirit of gender equality and they violated children's rights.[11] Based on this rationale, Mulia and Marzuki Wahid of the Working Group for Gender Mainstreaming in the Ministry of Religious Affairs launched the Counter Legal Draft (CLD) to counter the Compilation of Islamic Law on 4 October 2004; this action was supported by various NGOs.[12] The debate resulted

---

[10] "Undang-Undang Republik Indonesia No. 1/1974 tentang Perkawinan".

[11] *Islam dan Inspirasi Kesetaraan Gender*, pp. 131–49.

[12] The Counter Legal Draft was primarily supported by NGOs advocating gender equality and plurality such as *Komnas Perempuan*, the Fahmina Institute, Lembaga Kajian Agama dan Jender (LKAJ), Rahima, Puan Amal Hayati, *Jurnal Perempuan*, PSW, Kalyana Mitra, Kapal Perempuan, Solidaritas Perempuan, LBH Apik, Fatayat NU, Rifka An-Nisa, the International Center for Islam and Pluralism (ICIP), the Indonesian Conference on Religion and Peace (ICRP), the Wahid Institute, Jaringan Islam Liberal (JIL), Lakpesdam NU and Lembaga Kajian Islam dan Sosial (LKiS). Conversely, radical Islamic organizations widely rejected the CLD, such as Hizbut Tahrir Indonesia (HTI), Front Pembela Islam (FPI), Dewan Dakwah Islam Indonesia (DDII), Majelis Mujahidin Indonesia (MMI) and Forum Ulama Ummat Islam

in an official ban of the CLD by the Minister of Religious Affairs, Muhammad Maftuh Basyuni, in February 2005.[13] This ban was followed by a *fatwa* from the Indonesian Council of Ulama (Majelis Ulama Indonesia, MUI) on 29 July 2005, stating that pluralism, liberalism and secularism, as manifested in the CLD, were contradictory to Islamic teachings, and Muslims were thus forbidden (*haram*) from following them.[14] Progressive efforts were also made by the NU-based NGO advocating women's rights in Islam namely the Yellow Book Learning Forum (Forum Kajian Kitab Kuning, FK3). One of FK3's primary actions was to promote critical thinking in scrutinizing the Yellow Books (literal translation of *Kitab Kuning*, the classical texts on which the views of NU on social and religious worship are based) used by NU followers for religious guidance. Led by Sinta Nuriyah Abdurrahmad Wahid, wife of Abdurrahman Wahid (Gus Dur), FK3 scrutinized *Uqud Al-Lujjayn*, a prominent *pesantren* text which regulated the relationship of husband and wife (written by Syeikh Nawawi al-Jawi al-Bantani asy-Syafi'i, who was born in Banten 1813 and died in Mecca 1898), and urged people not to follow the text blindly as it contains misogynous teachings including violence against wives by husbands.[15]

Besides these progressive efforts by Muslims, there have also been positive health, education and economic development since the 1970s, which have improved conditions for women. As noted in Chapter 2, the New Order tried to enforce absolute adherence to women's conventional roles as mother and wife. Even though New Order programmes were firmly committed to reinforcing women's conventional roles, development programmes had some unintentional positive effects in their addressing of women's basic needs. This can be seen in the case of the family planning programme (*Keluarga Berencana*, KB); as the average number of children per family dropped, women experienced better health and

---

(FUUI). Mainstream Indonesian Islamic groups like Muhammadiyah and NU did not publically take a formal position, although their members split between being pro- and anti-CLD. See Marzuki Wahid, "Pembaruan Hukum Keluarga Islam di Indonesia Paska Orde Baru".

[13] Ibid., p. 19.
[14] "MUI Keluarkan 11 Fatwa".
[15] See Forum Kajian Kitab Kuning, *Kembang Setaman Perkawinan*.

their life expectancy rose from 63 years in 1990 to 67 years in 1998.[16] Moreover, women benefited from education programmes launched in the mid-1970s when Presidential Instruction Primary Schools (Sekolah Dasar Inpres, SDI) were built in remote areas, and a minimum of six years of compulsory schooling was introduced in 1973. As a result, the primary school participation rate of boys and girls aged 7–12 increased from 83 per cent in 1980 to 94 per cent in 1995.[17] Moreover, the industrial sector grew rapidly in the 1970s, and new employment opportunities opened for women as factories producing clothing, textiles and footwear were built. As a result, women acquired better skills and incomes, which led to more confidence to expand their roles as well as positions. Here we can see that the level of socioeconomic development in Indonesia affected the structure of society in such a way that more women were able to get out of their homes to fill available jobs in the new industrialized era. This boosted women's status and later facilitated the expansion of their opportunities in the public sphere including in politics, both in Java and throughout Indonesia.

Due to these gradual developments, Indonesian women in general and Javanese Muslim women in particular have now become able to manoeuvre around traditional normative expectations. For example, Winarto and Utami's research in the rural agricultural areas of southern Yogyakarta in the 2000s suggests that rural Javanese women have gradually expanded their role and status from "*konco wingking*" wives to equal partners with their husbands, and even to the extent of being leaders (*panutan*) in their communities, though they persistently identify their husbands as being the heads of the family.[18] Further evidence can be found in the current trend of Javanese Muslim women initiating and taking leadership roles in local politics. Previously, it would have been considered inappropriate for a Javanese woman to hold a higher public position than her husband. The phenomenon whereby Javanese Muslim women are gradually claiming a greater political space has also been accelerated by the changing perspectives of mainstream Indonesian Islam which have become increasingly open to and supportive of female leadership in Indonesia.

---

[16] Parawansa, "Institution Building: An Effort to Improve Indonesian Women's Role and Status", in Blackburn, *Women in Modern Indonesia*, p. 72.
[17] Robinson, "Indonesian Women—from *Orde Baru* to *Reformasi*", p. 149.
[18] Winarto and Utami, "The Persisting and Changing 'Family' in Java".

Perspectives on Female Leadership in Indonesian Islam: Muhammadiyah and Nahdlatul Ulama

In order to understand Islamic perspectives on female leadership in Indonesia, I will compare the positions of the two mainstream Indonesian Islamic organizations, namely Muhammadiyah, the Islamic reformist movement and the second largest Islamic religious organization in Indonesia, and Nahdlatul Ulama (NU), the Islamic traditionalist movement and the largest Islamic religious organization in Indonesia. For some time, beginning in the 1930s, Muhammadiyah and NU held similar perspectives that emphasized Muslim women's roles inside the family (as pious mothers and wives). However, their positions have gradually evolved since the 1950s, and now both support women who take on political roles to meet contemporary socio-historical challenges. Muhammadiyah and NU have different positions on the idea of a female president: NU made its position on possibility of a female president clear in its 1999 *fatwa*, whereas Muhammadiyah has not produced a clear decision on the issue to date. Both Muhammadiyah and NU support women's leadership positions at the governor or regent level.

Muhammadiyah's position on women's roles and female leadership is evident from the writing and publications produced by Muhammadiyah's Central Board, the Majlis Tarjih, and 'Aisyiyah. The Majlis Tarjih is one of Muhammadiyah's divisions that have the authority to perform *ijtihad* (independent judgment, based on the recognized sources of the Qur'an and Hadith). In performing *ijtihad*, the Majlis Tarjih utilizes *ijtihad jama'iy*, that is, collective decision making in which *ulama* gather to discuss matters and formulate a final decision based on the strongest *dalil* (reasoning).[19]

In 1937, 'Aisyiyah and Muhammadiyah's Central Board published the book entitled *Tuntunan Menjadi Isteri Islam Yang Berarti* (Guidance for becoming a truly Islamic wife), based on recommendations from the 26th 'Aisyiyah Muktamar (general meeting) in Yogyakarta in 1937.[20] Although the book positioned women as equal to men (*kawan laki-laki*, literally friends of men), the latter part of the text noted the expectation that women should be "*isteri Islam yang berarti*" (the truly Islamic wife) and presented 12 normative guidelines that mainly focused on women's

---

[19] Basyir, "Mekanisme Ijtihad di Kalangan Muhammadiyah", p. 31.
[20] PP Muhammadiyah Majlis Tarjih 'Aisyiyah, *Tuntunan Menjadi Isteri Islam Yang Berarti*, p. 5.

private roles as wives and mothers.[21] The book reflects the early spirit of the development of religious consciousness within 'Aisyiyah, which endorsed the equal religious rights of men and women in implementing religious deeds, along with the expectation that women would perform religious obligations as pious women.[22]

Female leadership in Muhammadiyah was not an issue that was addressed until the 1970s. One of the recommendations produced during the 40th 'Aisyiyah Muktamar in Surabaya in 1978 proposed that 'Aisyiyah women be included on the Muhammadiyah Central Board or in the Majlis Tarjih to redress the male domination of these two strategic bodies.[23] At almost the same time, the discourse on female leadership in Muhammadiyah was endorsed in *Adabul Mar'ah Fil Islam* (Pious women in Islam), an influential book published by Muhammadiyah's Majlis Tarjih in 1977. The book addresses nine aspects of women's rights and obligations ranging from: women and socialization, clothing according to Islamic norms, public art carnivals and demonstrations, women and art, women and science, women and *jihad*, Muslim women in the political arena, whether a woman is permitted to become a judge and women as role models in history.[24] These last three sections deal specifically with women's leadership, and are elaborated below.

In the section on Muslim women in the political arena, the book asserts that the role of Muslim women in the political arena is underpinned in the Qur'an, in verse 71 of *At-Taubah* which says "the believers, men and women, are protectors of one another: they enjoin what is just, and forbid what is evil: they observe regular prayers, practice regular charity, and obey God and His Apostle. On them will God bestow His Mercy: for God is exalted in power, wise."[25] Muslim women and men are, therefore, expected to contribute to *amar ma'ruf nahi munkar* (doing good deeds and preventing bad or evil deeds) even in the arena of politics and state administration.[26] Muslim women's roles in the

---

[21] Ibid., pp. 19–35.
[22] For historical changes and a detailed explanation of the view of *Majlis Tarjih* or *Muhammadiyah* on the role, status, and leadership of Muslim women in the 1930s, 1970s, 1980s, 1990s and 2000s, see my Master's thesis, "Women's Leadership in Muhammadiyah", pp. 55–77.
[23] "Keputusan Muktamar 'Aisyiyah ke-40", p. 18.
[24] Majlis Tarjih Pimpinan Pusat Muhammadiyah, *Adabul Mar'ah Fil Islam*.
[25] Ibid., p. 54.
[26] Ibid., p. 55.

political arena, according to this book, can be specified into two categories: first, direct roles such as participating in representative bodies (parliament); and second, indirect roles such as participating in organizations or public meetings (as they are not directly connected with parliament).[27]

Another interesting aspect is the Majlis Tarjih's response to the religious question about whether women are permitted to be judges. The response to this question begins by quoting the Qur'an, verse 124 of *An Nisa* that says "whosoever does a virtuous deed, be it male or female in believing, they will be in heaven and they will not be dreadful whatsoever".[28] The Majlis Tarjih argues that every human being, either man or woman, is responsible for their own deeds, including the responsibility to contribute to *amar ma'ruf nahi munkar* in order to achieve justice and avoid crime.[29] In addition, the Majlis Tarjih boldly reviewed verse 34 of *An Nisa* particularly on *ar-rijalu qawwamuna 'ala al-nisa'*, which is usually cited as a counter argument in discussions of women's progress and leadership. This verse commonly translates as "men are the leaders of women" (*laki-laki adalah pemimpin perempuan*) which makes it problematic for women to progress beyond men. Interestingly, the Majlis Tarjih review is not in accordance with the conventional understanding. Instead, it provides an alternative interpretation of *ar-rijalu qawwamuna 'ala al-nisa'* as "men are to take care of and be responsible for women" (*laki-laki adalah penegak tanggung jawab atas wanita*).[30] The Majlis Tarjih concluded that there are no fundamental religious reasons to reject the leadership of women as judges, school directors, company directors, regents, heads of villages (*lurah*) and ministers.[31] Young Muhammadiyah scholars such as M. Amin Abdullah,[32] Agus Purwadi,[33] Syamsul Anwar[34] and Wawan G.A. Wahid,[35] refer to this book when talking about Muhammadiyah's perspective on female leadership.[36]

---

[27] Ibid., p. 55.
[28] Ibid., p. 56.
[29] Ibid., p. 56.
[30] Ibid., p. 57.
[31] Ibid., p. 57.
[32] Abdullah, "Perlu Rekonstruksi Pembacaan Teks", pp. 37–45.
[33] Purwadi, "Militerisme dan Tradisi Islam Ihwal Kepemimpinan Wanita", pp. 135–44.
[34] Anwar, "Kepemimpinan Perempuan Dalam Islam", pp. 47–76.
[35] Wahid, "Kepemimpinan Perempuan Dalam Kajian Majlis Tarjih Muhammadiyah".
[36] See, for example, Anwar, "Kepemimpinan Perempuan Dalam Islam", pp. 47–76; and Wahid, "Kepemimpinan Perempuan Dalam Kajian Majlis Tarjih Muhammadiyah".

'Aisyiyah is blazing the trail in promoting women's leadership in Muhammadiyah. In 1978, 'Aisyiyah began to ask for greater opportunities for women's leadership, and this was long before the lively discourse on female leadership hit Indonesia in the late 1990s. It was again pursued at the 41st Muhammadiyah Muktamar in Surakarta in 1985, and then again at the 43rd Muhammadiyah Muktamar in Aceh in 1995. In the post-Suharto era, in 1999, 'Aisyiyah again addressed the question of female leadership in Islam and concluded that "there is no objection for women to become a leader, from the level of household to the level of head of the country, as long as she possesses the capacities to complete her task in a faithful way, using her knowledge, while at the same time not ignoring her main duty, that is a housewife".[37] 'Aisyiyah's systemic effort to foster women's leadership inside Muhammadiyah was continued in the 44th Muhammadiyah Muktamar in Jakarta in 2000 and was reinforced in the 45th Muhammadiyah Muktamar in Malang in July 2005, where 'Aisyiyah demanded a minimum of 2 seats for women among the 13 positions on the Muhammadiyah Central Board (Pimpinan Pusat Muhammdiyah). Although initially there were 11 women among the 126 contenders, none were elected to the Muhammadiyah Central Board.[38] My assessment of the 45th Muhammadiyah Muktamar indicates that while most of the Muhammadiyah and 'Aisyiyah elite supported women's leadership on the Muhammadiyah Central Board, this was not supported by Muhammadiyah and 'Aisyiyah followers from *wilayah* (provincial) and *daerah* (regency) regions who make up the largest representative group in the Muktamar; these groups still hold the textual approach in their interpretation of the religious texts on women's leadership (verse 34 of An Nisa) and therefore hinder the effort to enhance women's position inside Muhammadiyah.[39]

So, as we have seen, since 1978 groups within Muhammadiyah and 'Aisyiyah have put forth progressive perspectives to support women's leadership at least in levels below that of president (though in practice it is difficult for female leaders to take key positions in the Muhammadiyah

---

[37] Pimpinan Pusat 'Aisyiyah, *Kepemipinan Wanita Menurut Ajaran Islam* (Yogyakarta: PP 'Aisyiyah, 1999), cited in Van Doorn-Harder, *Women Shaping Islam*, p. 80.
[38] "Perempuan Minta Dua Kursi di Keanggotaan PP Muhammadiyah", *Jawa Pos*, 2 July 2005, at <http://www.jawapos.co.id/index.php?act=detail_c&id=178651> [accessed 16 July 2005].
[39] For a detailed analysis of this historical event and an explanation of the failure to place female leaders on the Muhammadiyah Central Board, see Dewi, "Perspective Versus Practices", pp. 161–85.

Central Board). However, Muhammadiyah as an organization, as reflected in the Majlis Tarjih decision, has given no clear explanation to date on its stance pertaining to women and the presidency. Since 1999 'Aisyiyah has shown a progressive standpoint in endorsing female leadership at every level (as the head of local government, or as the head of the country).

Similarly, NU has also produced certain legal opinions (*fatwa*), which are only advisory and yet are often used by members as guidelines in solving problems. In NU, *fatwa* on various issues are produced in Bahtsul Masa'il. Bahtsul Masa'il are held at every NU event from the village levels to the central levels. Ordinary Muslims first approach *kyai* who provide informal replies to their queries; the *kyai* then submit the problems to Bahtsul Masa'il forums in search of a solution, and the queries may even proceed up to the highest level of Bahtsul Masa'il, held during the NU Muktamar (NU National Congress).[40] There are two types of decisions made in Bahtsul Masa'il, namely decisions pertaining to *masail waqi'iyyah* (practical/factual matters) and to *masail maudhu'iyyah* (conceptual/thematic problems).[41] According to the observation by Kobayashi Yasuko on the compilation book of Bahtsul Masa'il decisions (1926–2004), there were 84 decisions pertaining to *masail waqi'iyyah* concerning women's issues such as family law (marriage, divorce, inheritance, gender).[42] Here, I would like to focus on decisions related to women's political roles and leadership.

Until the early 1940s, NU *fatwa* primarily suggested that women stay at home, with *fatwa* no. 133 (1933), stating that it was considered *haram* (forbidden) for women to leave home to attend meetings for religious activities "if she is sure that she will get slanders although she is not dressed up, nor uses perfumes, and does not obtain permission from her husband or *sayyid* (community leader), it is a big sin...."[43] The *fatwa* changed slowly to accommodate women's public roles, with *fatwa* no. 273 (1946) stating that women were permitted to wear the military uniform as men do, and participate in battles, although these should take place in isolation from men.[44] Eventually, in the atmosphere of a newly independent Indonesia where women were actively involved in

---

[40] Yasuko, "Ulama's Changing Perspectives on Women's Social Status", p. 289.
[41] Ibid., p. 293.
[42] Ibid., pp. 297–98.
[43] Ibid., p. 301.
[44] Ibid., p. 302.

politics, there was a particular inquiry asking for a legal opinion about women becoming members of parliament. *Fatwa* no. 281 (1957) ruled that women were permitted to become parliament members as long as six conditions were fulfilled (one of the conditions was to obtain permission from their husband, or father if they were not married).[45]

Interestingly, according to Safira Machrusah, it was Muslimat NU's (the women's wing of NU, established in 1946) persistence in lobbying the NU Central Board that led to progressive development for NU women. For example, NU supported Muslimat's NU 1954 proposal that women be eligible to become members of religious courts,[46] which in 1957 resulted in the more affirmative decision to support positions for women in parliament.[47] Muslimat NU's political activities were prominent, though, even before the 1957 decision. For instance, Muslimat NU successfully secured 10 per cent of seats for women in the House of Representatives (at that time NU was a political party) in the September 1955 General Election, and placed six Muslimat NU women as members of the Constituent Assembly in December 1955.[48]

In 1997, NU began to respond to the issue of women's leadership. As a result of *bahtsul masail maudhu'iyyah*, during an NU national meeting of *ulama* in Lombok, NTB, in 1997, a *fatwa* was produced, titled "The Thoughts of *Alim Ulama* on a Female President" (Pendapat Alim Ulama tentang Presiden Wanita, Fatwa no. 004/MN-NU/11/1997). In short, the decision stated that in accordance with the divine message of the Qur'an, such as verse 71 of *At-Taubah*, NU would encourage and support women taking on roles in the public sphere to serve society, for those women who had the quality, capacity, capability and acceptability and who did not forget their *kodrat* as mothers (becoming pregnant, delivering babies, breastfeeding, being the primary educator of any children and other family roles). This was part of NU's responsibility to promote cultural transformation.[49] For some people, this *fatwa* was triggered by

---

[45] Ibid., p. 302.
[46] However, no. 309 (1961) did not permit a woman to become a judge; instead, it permitted a woman to become a village head only in the case of an emergency. See Yasuko, "Ulama's Changing Perspectives on Women's Social Status", p. 306. Thus, compared to Muhammadiyah as stated in *Adabul Mar'ah Fil Islam*, Muhammadiyah was more progressive since it supported women becoming judges or village heads. The Indonesian government has allowed women to become judges since the late 1970s.
[47] Machrusah, "Muslimat and Nahdlatul Ulama", pp. 46–52.
[48] Ibid., pp. 48–9.
[49] PBNU, *Pendapat Alim Ulama Tentang Presiden Wanita*.

the political movement of Siti Hardijanti Rukmana, Suharto's daughter, who sought to be nominated as a vice-presidential candidate following the 1997 General Election.[50] However, this positive beginning did not translate into changes in the composition of the Central Board of NU with NU Central Board members remaining predominantly male as a result of the 30th NU Muktamar in Kediri in 1999.[51]

In the meantime, the debate over a female president intensified when Megawati Sukarnoputri announced her nomination as a female presidential candidate in the 1999 Presidential Election. Islamic scholars began to look for possible justification in support of a female presidential candidate, as it was a striking issue not only for the Islamic community, but also for society in general. It was the Congress of Indonesian Muslims (*Kongres Umat Islam Indonesia*, KUI) on 3–7 November 1998 that recommended that the MUI publish a *fatwa* on female leadership as "Perempuan Untuk Sementara Tidak Dibenarkan Jadi Presiden" (For the time being, women are not allowed to be presidents).[52] In response to the discourse and possibility of a female president, conservative Muslims often made reference to the Qur'an and *hadith* (sayings of the Prophet) to support their view that a woman could not be the head of a nation. For example, the Indonesian Mujahedeen Council (Majelis Mujahidin Indonesia, MMI) often cited passages from the Qur'an which were interpreted as prohibiting women from assuming positions of leadership namely "men are *qawwamun* of women" (Q 4:34); here MMI translated *qawwamun* as "leader" and as such that the right to lead was only for men.[53] In addition, the Indonesian Islamic Party of Liberation (Hizbut

---

[50] In the lead-up to the 1997 General Election, Suharto was determined to reverse the decrease in the vote seen in the votes Golkar received in the 1992 General Election. He was helped by Abdurrahman Wahid (Gus Dur), who had shifted his political stance vis-à-vis Suharto's presidential renomination from opposition to support, abandoning his previous alliance with Megawati. In the months preceding the 1997 General Election, Indonesia witnessed a harmonious political affiliation develop between Gus Dur and Siti Hardijanti Rukmana, when he took the daughter of Suharto on a tour of *pesantren* (traditional boarding schools) in Central and East Java. As interaction between Siti Hardijanti Rukmana, as the vice-chairperson of Golkar's executive board, and NU *kyai* became inevitable, the discourse turned to the possibilities and religious justification for Siti's vice-presidential candidacy. See McIntyre, *The Indonesian Presidency*, pp. 172–3; and Ricklefs, *A History of Modern Indonesia Since c. 1200*, p. 404.
[51] See Mulia, *Muslimah Reformis*.
[52] Wahid, "Merumuskan Kembali Agenda Perjuangan Perempuan Dalam Konteks Perubahan Sosial Budaya Islam di Indonesia", p. 16.
[53] Machrusah, "Islam and Women's Political Participation in Indonesia", p. 70.

Tahrir Indonesia, HTI) cited a famous *hadith*: "A nation which makes a woman its ruler will never succeed"; thus, according to HTI, the *hadith* explains clearly that women are prohibited from leading a state.[54] Here we can see how a distinct identity as a female candidate became a critical point to attack women to seek positions as the head of state (president) in response to Megawati Sukarnoputi's nomination in 1999.[55]

Interestingly, NU delivered a rather progressive *fatwa* just one month after Megawati Sukarnoputri was defeated by Abdurrahman Wahid in the 1999 Presidential Election. The *fatwa*, no. 419 (1999), on "A woman president can become a wali" explained that following the 1999 General Election, PBNU would need to formulate a definite concept dealing with the important problem for Muslims in regards to *wali hakim* in case the presidency was occupied by a woman. The official statement and *fatwa* read:

> At this point NU has already determined since Bung Karno (Sukarno) that the president of the Republic of Indonesia is *waliyul amril al-syaukah* (interim holder of full power) with the authority to validate a marriage concluded by *wali hakim*.
>
> Sa [*soal*, question]: In whose hand does the authority of *wali hakim* fall, the president or the minister of Religious Affairs?
>
> J [*jawab*, answer]: The President has jurisdiction over *wali's* authority in marriage, or an official appointed by the president can manage it.
>
> Sb: If (*wali's* authority in marriage) is in the hand of the president, can a woman legally become *wali hakim*?
>
> J: It is legal, because the institution of presidency is recognized as *wilayah amanah* (trust territory/jurisdiction).[56]

From this, it is clear that NU was anticipating the possibility that Indonesia could have a female president in the future and that NU would support a female president.

From the above exploration, we can see that, by active participation of their women's wings ('Aisyiyah and Muslimat NU), Muhammadiyah and NU have gradually been able to embrace progressive perspectives

---

[54] Ibid., p. 70.
[55] See also White and Anshor, "Islam and Gender in Contemporary Indonesia", p. 138.
[56] Cited in Yasuko, "Ulama's Changing Perspectives on Women's Social Status", p. 305 (brackets added).

supporting women's political roles to meet contemporary socio-historical challenges. Although initially, in the 1930s, Muhammadiyah and NU had similar perspectives that emphasized Muslim women's roles inside the family (as pious mothers and wives) and not in the public sphere, they gradually changed. Although both now support women's roles in local politics, NU has seemingly led the way ahead, compared to Muhammadiyah. NU has a clearer position on endorsing the possibility of a female president as evident in the 1999 *fatwa*, while Muhammadiyah has not produced a clear decision on the issue to date. One explanation of this, according to Pieternella Van Doorn-Harder, is due to the methodology of interpreting Islamic sources. Muhammadiyah promotes direct reading of the Qur'an and Hadith, which allows the use of independent reasoning (*ijtihad*) in shaping opinion about texts and strives to cleanse Islam of non-Islamic ritual and beliefs; whereas NU relies on the Qu'ran, *hadith* and an entire body of *fiqh* (Islamic jurisprudence), which has been affected by the influential development of the Social *Fiqh* School led by Abdurrahman Wahid and Sahal Mahfudh since the end of the 1970s and that urged people to reinterpret the *fiqh* texts on gender issues according to contemporary conditions and actual needs.[57] As a result NU has become more progressive in response to and engaged with women's issues in contemporary Indonesia, while Muhammadiyah have lagged behind.

In sum, we can see the two mainstream Indonesian Islamic organizations Muhammadiyah and NU have similar perspectives and attitudes in supporting women's leadership, at least at the level below president including as regents or governors, the locus where the three female Javanese Muslim political leaders exercise power. These progressive changes in Islamic perspectives and attitudes concerning women's roles and leadership in local politics have helped accelerate Javanese Muslim women's expansion in politics, as exemplified by the three women in this study. In practice, these three female Javanese Muslim political leaders have adopted particular strategies to take advantage of the Islamic perspective on female leadership, particularly that held by NU, as NU is the dominant religious orientation in the regions where they exercise power. In combination with that, these three politicians have tried to maximize their distinct individual capital in seeking greater political leadership at the same time as manoeuvring between their multiple roles as wives and mothers, as we shall see in the following case studies.

---

[57] Van Doorn-Harder, *Women Shaping Islam*, pp. 2, 9–11.

CHAPTER 4

Rustriningsih: Advantage of Familial Ties, Ability to Embrace Islamic Piety and Using Gender to Expand a Political Base

This chapter, the first of three case studies, will focus on how Rustriningsih, the first female regent elected in direct elections in Java, developed her political career initially as the regent of Kebumen and later as a candidate for vice-governor of Central Java in 2008. While strong familial ties and individual capital (such as her education and entrepreneurial background) were significant factors behind Rustriningsih's political emergence, her ability to create a political strategy that embraced both her Islamic piety and her gender became a vital element in her political victory. We will first address the social and political landscape of Kebumen Regency, where Rustriningsih initially spread her political influence and developed her political career.

Kebumen Regency: The Social and Political Landscape

The regency of Kebumen, which shares its south border with the Indian Ocean, is one of 29 regencies in the province of Central Java (comprises 29 regencies and 6 cities) and, in 2008, consisted of 26 districts (*kecamatan*), 11 administrative villages (*kelurahan*) and 449 villages (*desa*).[1] In that year, the region was home to 1,241,437 inhabitants (626,923 male, 614,514 female).[2] Islam is the religion of the majority, and most Muslims are affiliated with NU as reflected by the 130 *pesantren* (traditional boarding schools, commonly associated with NU) with 15,011

---

[1] Badan Pusat Statistik Kabupaten Kebumen, *Kebumen Dalam Angka 2008*, pp. 5, 23.
[2] Ibid., pp. 5, 53.

santri (*santri* can refer to devout Muslims according to Clifford Geertz's concept of cultural type of Javanese society, see footnote 5 below). And yet, particularly in context of this sentence *santri* also means religious students studying in *pesantren*) in Kebumen.[3] According to data of the NU branch (*pengurus cabang* NU) in Kebumen, there were 26 NU vice-branches (*majelis wakil cabang*) in districts (*kecamatan*) and 347 NU village branches (*ranting*) in 2003.[4] NU followers are mainly concentrated in the eastern part of Kebumen ("*wetan kali*") such as Prembun, Ambal, Mirit, Kutowinangun, Kebumen and Alian, while the western part ("*kulon kali*") is populated with *abangan*[5] or nationalists (including Petanahan, Pejagon, Kuwarasan, Sempor, Gombong and Rowokele).[6]

Table 3 shows the domination of Suharto's political party, FKP/Golkar, in the 1992 General Election. Golkar was followed by PPP, the only Islamic party, and then PDI. PDIP, under the new leadership of Megawati, strengthened its grip and gained the majority of seats in the 1999, 2004 and 2009 General Elections though the exact number of seats it held fluctuated. PKB, the new NU-affiliated political party, succeeded in obtaining nine and seven seats respectively in the 1999 and 2004 General Elections, which made it the second biggest political party in the region in 1999, and equal second with Golkar in 2004. The Democrat

---

[3] Ibid., p. 88.

[4] PCNU Kebumen 2003, cited in Jatmiko, "Kiai dan Politik Lokal", p. 79.

[5] *Abangan* refers to nominal Muslims, strongly influenced by the Hindu-Buddhist practices of Javanese syncretism. *Santri* refers to a religious class of devout Muslims, *priyayi* the white-collar elite rooted in Hindu-Javanese courts and ethic. Clifford Geertz introduced these three cultural types of Javanese society in his pioneering study in Modjokuto, *The Religion of Java* (see p. 5). Since then, Geertz's concepts have sparked wide debate and influenced Indonesianists. My research respondents used the term *abangan* to explain the political geography of Kebumen. See interview with IS, a prominent INDIPT NGO activist, Kebumen, 27 July 2010.

[6] Respondents in Kebumen used the terms *wetan kali* and *kulon kali* to explain the place's political geography of the regency, based on the distribution of *santri* and *abangan* followers throughout the region. Interview with IS, a prominent INDIPT NGO activist, in Kebumen, 27 July 2010, and interview with SW, vice-chief of the Regional Board of PKB in Kebumen between 2007 and 2013, 28 July 2010. Another source reported something similar. The term also refers to the physical demarcation of Kebumen by the Luk Ulo River, a river that divides Kebumen into East and West. *Wetan kali* refers to the area located to the east of Luk Ulo River (Ambal, Mirit, Kutowinangun, Kebumen and Alian), while *kulon kali* refers to the area located to the west of Luk Ulo River (Petanahan, Pejagon, Kuwarasan, Gombong and Sempor). See Jatmiko, "Kiai dan Politik Lokal", p. 143.

Table 3 Political Party Composition in Kebumen's People's Representative Council during the New Order and Post-Suharto Eras

Political Party	The New Order	Post-Suharto		
	1992	1999	2004	2009
PDI	8	–	–	–
PDIP	–	16	19	15
FKP/Golkar	17	5	7	7
PKB	–	9	7	4
PPP	11	5	5	6
PAN	–	2	4	5
PBB	–	1	–	–
PNU	–	1	–	–
PKP	–	1	–	–
TNI/Polri	9	5	–	–
Democrat Party	–	–	3	7
PKNU	–	–	–	3
PKS	–	–	–	2
GERINDRA	–	–	–	1
Total	45	45	45	50

Note: I was not able to obtain figures from the 1997 General Election. This is because there is no archival record of the election in the documents I collected.

Source: Figures from the 1992 General Election were obtained from *Memori Pengabdian DPRD Kabupaten Dati II Kebumen Masa Bhakti Tahun 1992–1997*, pp. 15–25. Figures from the 1999 General Election were obtained from *Buku Lampiran Penyelenggaraan Pemilihan Umum Tahun 1999 Kabupaten Dati II Kebumen*, pp. 485–9. Figures from the 2004 and 2009 General Elections were obtained from Sekretaris DPRD Kebumen, "Daftar Nama Anggota DPRD Kabupaten Kebumen Periode Tahun 2004–2009" and "Daftar Anggota DPRD Masa Bakti 2009–2014".

Party, a new and rising political party, successfully won seven seats in the 2009 General Election.

These political figures reflect the socio-political nature of Kebumen as a largely *abangan*-based (nationalist) region, as evident from PDIP's significant victories in the three consecutive elections after the fall of Suharto (after 1998). Considering the fact that both PKB and PPP are NU-affiliated political parties proven to be the second or the third most popular parties in Kebumen, it is not an exaggeration to say that Kebumen is also home to a significant *santri* population (devout Muslims). That Kebumen has a strong base of *abangan* and *santri* voters is an important factor that Rustriningsih considered when creating a political strategy to win the 2000 in-direct election and the 2005 direct election in Kebumen, as well as the 2008 Central Java Gubernatorial Election.

Rustriningsih: An *Abangan* Woman with Strong Individual Capital

Rustriningsih, who was born in Kedungampel village, Wonokriyo, Gombong (located in the western part, or nationalist pocket, of Kebumen) on 3 July 1967, is a charismatic politician. She is a mother of five children, one of whom is adopted. She was five months pregnant when I met her in February 2010. Rustriningsih does not come from a strong Islamic background and fits more into an *abangan* milieu.[7] Her father, Sukamto, was a prominent activist of Sukarno's Indonesian Nationalist Party (Partai Nationalis Indonesia, PNI) during the Old Order. Rustri, as she is commonly called, is the eighth of ten children (four boys and six girls). According to Rustri, her father never discriminated between them according to their gender. Her grandfather, grandmother, father and mother were originally traders from Kotagede, Yogyakarta. After Rustri's third eldest sibling was born, her parents moved from Kotagede to Gombong, where Rustri was eventually born. While Sukamto ran various small businesses, her mother was a typical housewife who had considerable influence on Rustri's emotional development.

Rustriningsih's encounter with politics was facilitated by her father's political activities as a nationalist in Kebumen. Sukamto was the former treasurer of PNI in Kebumen and later a PDI activist until 1987. Since elementary school, after breakfast Sukamto often discussed socio-political

---

[7] Although Clifford Geertz's categorization of Javanese society and political orientations as *abangan*, *santri* and *priyayi* has provoked debates and questions about the reliability of Geertz's findings in contexts other than Modjokuto and contemporary Indonesia. I use Geertz's categorization because it is a useful analytical tool to define and understand the three female Javanese Muslim leaders I observed in this study. For example, Rustriningsih's life history does not show a strong connection to Islamic traditions, such as the *pesantren* tradition, even though she was born into a Muslim family and is officially Muslim. Thus, I define Rustriningsih as *abangan*, which is also consistent with her political affiliation to PDIP, originally an *abangan-* or nationalist-based political party. However, as we shall see in this chapter, Rustriningsih's personal orientation has changed since 2004 as she has become more pious, undertook the pilgrimage and donned the veil. This is how Geertz's categorization helps to explain Rustriningsih's change from a relatively nominal Muslim (*abangan*) into a more devout Muslim, which I believe is an important factor contributing to her current success in expanding her political support base and acceptability beyond the loyal voters within the nationalist circle.

issues (such as land disputes or corruption) with Rustriningsih and her younger brother RS as her other siblings were not interested. Because Sukamto was an influential PNI activist, the family home was often the centre of PNI, and later PDI, activities. For instance, Sukamto would provide equipment for making T-shirts for campaign purposes while Rustriningsih's mother opened a public kitchen (*dapur umum*) to feed everyone. Sukamto had the courage to increase PDI's base across the region, despite strong intimidation from the New Order apparatus (under Suharto's rule) which sought to counter any political movement other than *kuningisasi*.[8]

Rustri, who liked reading books and comics since childhood, had read various autobiographies of outstanding politicians in the United States such as Woodrow Wilson, Abraham Lincoln and Richard Nixon, which were precious books from her father's collection. She recalled how, before reading these books, her father would warn her to wash her hands first to ensure she would not dirty the books. This caused Rustri to suspect that her father loved the books more than her. Young Rustri also learnt about various political intrigues by watching Indian movies that were screened in her father's small cinema (*bioskop*).[9] Rustri adored her father because of his idealism, discipline and honesty.

Rustriningsih also has an entrepreneurial spirit and much experience. After completing her schooling in Gombong, she enrolled at Jenderal Sudirman University in Purwokerto in the State Administration Department, Faculty of Social and Political Science. Rustri was asked to be a trainer at the PDI cadre training which gave her the opportunity to meet Megawati Sukarnoputri, the head of PDI, for the first time in 1988. After receiving her bachelor's degree in 1991, she initially wanted to apply to become a civil servant. However, she changed her mind and decided to run a newspaper agency in front of her parents' house in Gombong and a food catering business in the back of the house. By earning her own money, she believed she would no longer be a burden on her parents and, more importantly, would be an independent person.

As the first news agency in the area, Rustri's business gradually grew bigger and allowed her to easily make friends among local journalists.

---

[8] *Kuning* is the Indonesian word for yellow, which in this case refers to Suharto's New Order vision to strengthen Golkar's power (the party's official flag is yellow) and counter the influence of the other two political parties, namely the PDI (nationalist party, symbolized by red) and PPP (Islamic Party, symbolized by green).
[9] Interview with Rustriningsih in the office of the vice-governor of Central Java, Semarang, 3 Feb. 2010.

As her agency developed, she was able to open a bigger news agency with 28 employees including street children as vendors and distributors. At this stage, I believe Rustri's successful entrepreneurship laid a vital foundation for a future political career, because not only was she financially independent and able to contribute funds for the operation of a political party, but she had also created close connections with lower-class society in Gombong, which was an important PDI pocket in western Kebumen. Young Rustriningsih was able to garner a rare and significant individual capital, namely the combination of being an educated woman and successful entrepreneur from a well-known political family.

Another interesting story is of Rustri's personal transformation. While conducting the Haj in 2004 she met, and later married, Soni Achmad Saleh Ashar, a businessman from Makassar who owns a company in Jakarta. Since then, Rustri has worn a headscarf and Muslim clothing in her everyday life and at the office (see Figure 1). This interesting aspect of Rustriningsih's personal story, including her marriage, has attracted public attention and discourse.[10] The tendency of media coverage of female political candidates to include explicit references to their marital status and children has also been observed in the cases of Australian female members of parliament as noted by Margaret Fitzherbert,[11] and Hillary Clinton in the 2008 US presidential election as observed by Eileen L. Zurbriggen and Aurora M. Sherman.[12]

Rustri's gradual embracing of the idea and practice of Islamic piety proved to not only be a private matter, but also an important political strategy in the 2005 direct election for regent of Kebumen and the 2008 direct election for governor and vice-governor of Central Java, as I will explore in this chapter. Figure 1 depicts Rustri's new style of dress with her adoption of the headscarf.

Political Emergence: Familial Ties and Support from *Santri*

One important factor behind Rustriningsih's political emergence was her familial ties. Rustri's father provided advice and support for her early political career as a member of the regional board of PDI in Kebumen. Rustriningsih has acknowledged her father's political mentorship and

---

[10] See, for example, "Dra Rustriningsih Msi".
[11] See Fitzherbert, "The Politics of Political Mothers and Wives", p. 39.
[12] See Zurbriggen and Sherman, "Race and Gender in the 2008 U.S. Presidential Election", p. 241.

Source: Reproduced by author from picture in the office of vice-regent Kebumen, 9 Feb. 2010 (Rustriningsih was regent of Kebumen from 2005 to 2010.)

Figure 1 Rustriningsih's New Style of Dress with the Headscarf

encouragement in her early political career.[13] Rustri had only recently gained her bachelor's degree when, with a recommendation from her father's friend, she was accepted as vice-secretary of the Regional Board of PDI in Kebumen in 1993. At the time, it was rare for women with bachelor's degrees to join PDI due to its harsh, alienated and lower-class imagery politics,[14] as the majority of PDI followers were often perceived as lower-class people (*wong cilik*) with poor education.

However, Rustriningsih was an exception and proved her determination when in 1996 she was elected chief of the Regional Board (Dewan Pimpinan Cabang, DPC) of PDI in Kebumen, and she bravely led a demonstration to defend Megawati against Suryadi following the 1996 PDI internal conflict. Although the New Order regime under Suharto officially approved of Suryadi's leadership of PDI, Rustriningsih supported Megawati and throughout 1997 tried to consolidate Megawati loyalists by forming sub-branches (Pengurus Anak Cabang, PAC at the district

---

[13] Interview with Rustriningsih in the office of the vice-governor of Central Java, Semarang, 3 Feb. 2010.
[14] Ibid.

level) of PDI loyal to Megawati across the region. This made her a figure of interest to the military apparatus and she was often arrested, though later released.[15] Thanks to Rustriningsih, 24 sub-branches were established in Kebumen, according to HU, the former coordinator of the sub-branches.[16] He added that Rustriningsih was very brave to publicize the existence of the Pro-Mega PDI and talked about one successful occasion that Megawati attended in Gombong without the military's knowledge. All these actions led the Kebumen Pro-Mega PDI together with the Pro-Mega PDI branches in Magelang and Semarang to become known as the *segitiga emas* (golden triangle) in the region due to the strong constituency of pro-Megawati PDI supporters.[17]

In fact, Rustriningsih's confrontational approach to Suryadi, and her gradual rise as a female leader within Pro-Mega PDI was not universally supported by the *kaum tua* (old cadre) inside Pro-Mega PDI in Kebumen.[18] However, the small team of Rustriningsih and her fellow loyalists (the so-called Team 9 or Team 11) continued its fight to publicize the existence of the Pro-Mega PDI force in Kebumen, which later attracted mass support and social solidarity.[19] According to CA, the

---

[15] "Mengenal Wakil Gubernur Jateng Terpilih Rustriningsih".
[16] Interview with HU in Kebumen, 28 July 2010. HU was coordinator under Rustriningsih for establishing Pro-Mega PDI sub-branches in Kebumen since 1998, secretary of Pro-Mega PDI in Pejagon district Kebumen (1998–99); secretary of the PDIP faction in the Kebumen DPRD (1999–2004); chief of PDIP of Kebumen DRPD (2004–09); chief of PDIP's successful campaign team for the 2008 Central Java Gubernatorial Election.
[17] Ibid.
[18] Interview with AP, former member of the Team 9 Pro-Mega PDI loyalists in Kebumen, 28 July 2010. AP shared an interesting story about how Rustriningsih and friends of the progressive Pro-Mega PDI Team 9 went about winning the hearts of the *kaum tua*. In order to convince the *kaum tua* that Rustriningsih, though female, was the "chosen" leader, they made up the rumour that Rustriningsih was granted a special blessing from the Imogiri Cemetery (special cemetery for the noble families of the Yogyakarta Court located in the southern part of Yogyakarta) and was told that she would be the future leader in Kebumen and beyond. The story was circulated widely in Kebumen via the *Wawasan* newspaper (strongly affiliated with PDI) and people believed it. AP later stated that due to the rumour, Rustriningsih gained strong cultural legitimacy from the *kaum tua*, and they gradually approved of her political emergence as a female leader from the Pro-Mega PDI faction in Kebumen. CA, the *Wawasan* correspondent in Kebumen, also mentioned this story in an interview, but did not explain that the rumour was false.
[19] Interview with AP, former member of Kebumen's Team 9 Pro-Mega PDI loyalists, Kebumen, 28 July 2010.

former correspondent of *Wawasan*, a nationalist newspaper during the New Order, Rustriningsih was the only "icon" in Central Java who bravely fought against Suryadi's PDI faction.[20] From Rustriningsih's political career in Kebumen, we can see that her strong, brave, and persistent leadership character had enabled her to overcome various political challenges, and to become a successful female leader who broke the conventional norm of politics as a man's world. This kind of political breakthrough and achievement was still very rare in newly democratized Indonesia at the end of the 1990s.

When the New Order finally collapsed in 1998, Rustriningsih's strong political record brought her into an important position as chief of the General Election Commission in Kebumen (Komisi Pemilihan Umum, KPU) responsible for conducting the 1999 General Election, the first election in the post-Suharto era (after 1998). The holding of two strategic positions, chief of the Regional Board of PDIP in Kebumen and chief of the General Election Commission in Kebumen, not only elevated Rustri's popularity but also increased her ability to negotiate power with other political actors in the region. Rustri's political achievement climaxed when she was elected to the People's Consultative Assembly (Majelis Permusyawaratan Rakyat, MPR) in the 1999 general election from the Kebumen PDIP electorate, though she resigned due to her candidacy for regent of Kebumen in the 2000 local government election.

In the lead up to the 2000 election for regent, the Regional Board of PDIP in Kebumen held an internal meeting to choose which candidate it wanted to run for the position of regent. It was this meeting that opened the way for Rustri to become regent of Kebumen. According to some versions, Rustri did not initially run in the primary election to select the PDIP candidate. However, there was a group opposed to the fact that a number of PDIP candidates were former members of Golkar, which changed her mind and she decided to run as a candidate.[21] Eventually, according to RS, Rustriningsih's younger brother and chief of the PDIP campaign team in the 2005 and 2008 direct election and vice-regent of Kebumen (2008–10) of around 20 nominees, Rustriningsih

---

[20] Interview with CA in Kebumen, 27 July 2010. CA was former correspondent of *Wawasan*, a nationalist newspaper published during the New Order, and a close friend of KH. Nashiruddin Al Mansyur and member of the General Election Commission in Kebumen (2003–09).

[21] Institute for International Cooperation, Japan International Cooperation Agency, "Government Decentralization Reforms in Developing Countries" (Report), IFIC/JICA, Mar. 2001, p. 30.

gained the highest number of votes from 26 PDIP sub-branches and was officially nominated as the PDIP candidate for regent.[22] Given her *abangan* background, as well as the nature of Kebumen as base of both *abangan* and *santri*, Rustri needed a balancing figure to appeal to the *santri* element.

She approached and recruited KH. Nashiruddin Al-Mansyur, an influential *kyai* who lead the At-Taqwa *pesantren* and about a thousand *santri*, to be the PDIP candidate for vice-regent. KH. Nashiruddin was born on 10 October 1961 into a famous NU family as his father, *Kyai* Sururuddin, was a prominent NU *kyai* and a former leader of AUI (Angkatan Umat Islam, during the Old Order) who initially struggled to establish NU in Kebumen.[23] KH. Nashiruddin Al-Mansyur, who studied in a *pesantren* in Ploso, Kediri (1981–83), was not only the leader (*mursyid*) of the Syadziliyah *tarekat* or Sufi Order with nearly 3,000 followers, mainly businessmen and civil servants, but is also the leader of the Dzikrul Ghafilin *majelis mujahadah akbar* (mass religious propagation council) that has nearly 14,000 followers in Kebumen.[24] In around 2000, KH. Nashiruddin was the most popular and sought-after preacher (*kyai panggung*) in Kebumen due to his handsome look, charisma and down-to-earth approach.[25] Therefore, it is understandable that Rustriningsih chose him as her running partner. She explained:

> I looked for someone who was clean and didn't have any problems. I had to ensure the community's trust by responding to and reassuring society's uncertainties at the time (*nutup apa yang menjadi keraguan masyarakat waktu itu*), by showing that there were *kyai* who supported *me* [female candidate, emphasis added] and wanted to be my vice-regent. This was part of my strategy.[26]

---

[22] Interview with RS, Rustriningsih's younger brother, chief of the PDIP campaign team in the 2005 and 2008 direct elections, and vice-regent of Kebumen (2008–10), in the office of the vice-regent of Kebumen, 9 Feb. 2010.
[23] Interview with CA in Kebumen, 27 July 2010. KH. Nashiruddin took several key socio-political positions such as chief of the Nadlatul Ulama Students Association (Ikatan Pelajar Nahdlatul Ulama, IPNU) in Kebumen (1972–82), member of the NU board in Kebumen, secretary of the Kebumen PPP branch (1996), and vice-chief of the Regional Board of PKB in Kebumen (1998–2000). In 2003 he split from the PKB and in 2010 became chief of the Democrat Party in Kebumen (2010–15).
[24] Jatmiko, "Kiai dan Politik Lokal", p. 117.
[25] Ibid., p. 118.
[26] Interview with Rustriningsih, office of the vice-governor of Central Java, Semarang, 3 Feb. 2010.

Here we can see that Rustriningsih tried to win the peoples' hearts by securing society's trust, especially the majority NU *santri* element, by recruiting someone prominent, who would be a vivid example and provide religious support to the proposal of having a female leader in Kebumen. KH. Nashiruddin Al-Mansyur also confirmed that Rustriningsih had approached him and that he agreed to her proposal after initially refusing.[27]

Rustriningsih's strategy in breaking up NU solidarity inside the DPRD by picking KH. Nashiruddin as her partner was smart, and it contributed to the defeat of the PKB and PPP candidates. Prior to 2005 mechanisms to select local government heads such as regents, including in Kebumen, were conducted inside DPRD. There were 45 members of Kebumen DPRD who voted on 15 March 2000. The two pairs with the highest votes were Rustriningsih and KH. Nashiruddin (PDI) with 17 votes, and Rahardjo Mocharor and Faried Subagyo (official PKB) with 12 votes.[28] As no pair gained more than the minimum 50 per cent plus one of the total vote, there was a second round of elections for the two most popular pairs.[29] The second round of elections was held immediately on the same day and Rustriningsih and Nashiruddin won the election with 22 votes, while Rahardjo Mocharor and Farid Subagyo obtained 20 votes, with one voter abstaining.[30] Thus, eventually on 23 March 2000, Rustriningsih and Nashiruddin officially became the regent and vice-regent of Kebumen.

The 2005 Direct Election in Kebumen: Candidates

Initially, Rustriningsih served as regent of Kebumen from 2000 to 2005. When Rustriningsih finished her term in 2005, she gained advantage from the political momentum in the implementation of the first direct

---

[27] Interview with KH. Nashiruddin Al-Mansyur, vice-regent of Kebumen (2000–08) and regent of Kebumen (2008–10), in the office of the regent of Kebumen, 12 Feb. 2010.
[28] DPRD Kabupaten Kebumen, "Berita Acara Pemilihan Bupati dan Wakil Bupati Kebumen Masa Jabatan 2000–2005".
[29] Keputusan DPRD Kabupaten Kebumen No. 19/KPTS-DPRD/2000, "Peraturan Tata Tertib Pencalonan Dan Pemilihan Bupati dan Wakil Bupati Kebumen Periode Tahun 2000–2005", 21 Feb. 2000.
[30] DPRD Kabupaten Kebumen, "Berita Acara Pemilihan Bupati dan Wakil Bupati Kebumen Masa Jabatan 2000–2005"; "Dra Rustriningsih MSi".

elections in Kebumen. For this event, the Regional Board of PDIP in Kebumen nominated its chief, Rustriningsih, as candidate for regent. The Central Board of PDIP's decision to nominate Rustriningsih as PDIP's candidate was due to the achievement of the Regional Board of PDIP in Kebumen in winning support for the presidential and vice presidential candidates from PDIP, namely Megawati and Hasyim Muzadi (PKB) in the Kebumen electorate, though nationally the pair lost the 2004 Presidential Election.[31]

In order to select one out of the nine people willing to run as vice-regent with Rustriningsih, the Regional Board of PDIP in Kebumen held a special meeting on April 2005. Again, Rustriningsih showed her political tactics in breaking up the solidity of PPP, one of the NU-based political parties, in the upcoming election. According to YC, who was allied with PPP, Rustri initially approached him to be her running partner. In response to her inquiry, YC registered his name with PDIP as a possible vice-regent candidate and followed all the necessary steps. However, YC, who claimed to have gained support from many PDIP sub-branches, lost to KH. Nashiruddin Al-Mansyur, who, YC believed, had never registered his name during PDIP's special meeting and had never presented his vision and mission for the position, and yet was appointed as PDIP's candidate.[32] When confronted by YC, KH. Nashiruddin Al-Mansyur also stated that Rustriningsih had asked him (KH. Nashiruddin) seriously to be her running partner in the 2005 election, which thus supported YC's allegation that Rustriningsih's move to ask him to be the candidate for vice-regent was only part of her political strategy.[33] In the end, Rustriningsih and KH. Nashiruddin Al-Mansyur were elected as the PDIP candidates for regent and vice-regent.[34] There were four pairs of candidates in the 2005 direct election for regent, in which their personal details can be seen in Table 4.

---

[31] Interview with HU, in Kebumen, 28 July 2010.
[32] Interview with YC, vice-secretary of the Regional Board of the PPP in Kebumen (1999–2000); chief of the Regional Board of the PPP in Kebumen (2005–10); and member of the Kebumen DPRD from PPP (1999–2014) in Kebumen DPRD, 12 Feb. 2010.
[33] Interview with KH. Nashiruddin Al-Mansyur, in the office of the regent of Kebumen, 12 Feb. 2010.
[34] Komisi Pemilihan Umum Kabupaten Kebumen, *Buku Laporan Pemilihan Bupati Dan Wakil Bupati Kebumen 5 Juni 2005*, p. 110.

Table 4 Profile of Regent and Vice-regent Candidates in the 2005 Direct Election in Kebumen

No. on Ballot Paper	Political Party	Name of Regent and Vice-regent Candidates	Profile
1	PDIP	**Rustriningsih**	Muslim, Regent of Kebumen (2000–05)
		KH. Nashiruddin Al-Mansyur	Muslim, vice-regent of Kebumen (2000–05)
2	PAN Democrat Party	**H.M. Zuhri Effendi**	Muslim, born 30 November 1942, Bachelor's Degree from the Islamic State Institute in Kalijaga, Yogyakarta, teacher and former member of Kebumen DPRD
		Agus Supriyanto	Muslim, born 11 August 1957, Master's Degree in Management, businessman
3	PKB	**Koesnanto Karsoprayitno**	Muslim, born 11 December 1947, Master's Degree, businessman
		KH. Imam Muzani Bunyamin	Muslim, born 18 September 1951, member of Regional Board of NU in Kebumen, chief of the Dewan Syuro of PKB in Kebumen, leader of Darussa'adah pesantren, Petanahan
4	Golkar	**Ananto Tri Sasongko**	Muslim, born 10 May 1966, Bachelor's Degree, businessman
		Suprapto	Muslim, born 7 July 1957, chief of Regional Board of Golkar in Kebumen, member of Kebumen DPRD (1997–2004), vice-chief of Kebumen DPRD (2004–05)

Note: Names in bold represent the candidates for regent.
Source: Komisi Pemilihan Umum Kabupaten Kebumen, *Buku Laporan Pemilihan Bupati dan Wakil Bupati Kebumen 5 Juni 2005*, pp. 74–8.

Strategy to Win: Countering Religious Opposition

Once Rustriningsih and KH. Nashiruddin Al-Mansyur officially ran as candidates for regent and vice-regent in the 2005 direct election in Kebumen, they had to overcome basic problems such as religious opposition. As the first Muslim female regent candidate in Java, Rustriningsih faced religious opposition from opponents early in her career. This also occurred during her political nomination in 2005 when some NU *kyai* opposed her.

However, opposition from PPP *kyai* was not strong because an NU *fatwa* allowed female leaders to occupy the position of regent.[35] There were also *kyai* from PKB who opposed Rustriningsih, such as the prominent preacher Syarif Hidayat.[36] In 2000 Rustriningsih had overcome the opposition by using overt action as seen in her orchestration of *becak* drivers to counter the *kyai* demonstration in front of the Kebumen DPRD, but in 2005 Rustriningsih used a soft approach, responded calmly to criticism and turned to KH. Nashiruddin to provide necessary religious explanations.[37] In order to ease the tension, Rustri often visited important *kyai* homes in a practice known as *sowan*, including the home of *Kyai* Wahib Mahfudz, chief of the *Syuriah* of the Regional Board of NU in Kebumen, who is from Jetis in Kutosari Kebumen, and the home of KH. Muhammad Afif Sulchan (*Gus* Afif), Rustri's competitor in the 2000 election for regent, who is from Sumolangu.[38] However, the opposition seemed mainly centred at the elite level, while local female activists shared high expectations of Rustri as a female leader.[39]

In the cases where NU *kyai* in Kebumen opposed Rustriningsih, according to *Kyai* MSKB, chief of Kebumen NU's Tanfidziah (1994–2002), it was mainly due to political interests,[40] and not religious rationale which

---

[35] Interview with LM, former member of the Kebumen DPRD from PPP (1997–99) and chief of Fatayat NU in Kebumen (1995–2005), 29 July 2010.
[36] Interview with CA, close friend of KH. Nashiruddin Al-Mansyur and former member of Kebumen KPUD (2003–09), 27 July 2010.
[37] Interview with Rustriningsih, Semarang, 3 Feb. 2010.
[38] Interview with SW, Kebumen, 28 July 2010.
[39] Interview with DL, member of Fatayat NU, Muslimat NU, and member of Kebumen DPRD from PDIP (2004–14), Kebumen, 10 Feb. 2010.
[40] Interview with KH. Muhammad MSKB, chief of the Tanfidziah of NU in Kebumen (1994–2002), Kebumen, 28 July 2010. My effort to understand and contact the important *kyai* within Kebumen NU basically developed from my conversation with HMR, an activist in a prominent NGO in Kebumen, INDIPT and MTJ, the director of INDIPT, 27 and 28 July 2010 respectively.

was in line with the NU's position to support female leadership in local elections. This is further affirmed by a statement by *Gus* TH, chief of the Dewan Syuro of the Regional Board of PKB in Kebumen (2007–13):

> In NU there is not a problem over women's leadership. Women do not only have a domestic role to play in the kitchen, at the well, or in bed (*dapur, sumur, kasur*). As long as they have the capability, capacity, etc. If we talk about gender equality, men and women are equal except in things of *kodrati*.... However, I do not deny that there are *kyai* who oppose women's leadership because the issue is *khilafiah* (uncertain). However, after the NU Central Board issued a decision on gender [the 1997 *fatwa* in Lombok], NU circles were more comfortable in their responses to the issue of women's leadership.[41]

When I confronted KH. Nashiruddin, as Rustriningsih's vice-regent, one of the reasons he accepted Rustri's leadership since 2000 was because of his religious belief:

> I relied on the divine message of the Qur'an, verse 97 of *An-Nahl*, which says, "whosoever does a virtuous deed, be it male or female in believing, Allah will surely give them a goodly life".... So it is clear that it refers to anyone who does a virtuous deed, whether they are man or woman. In other words, men and women are the same in the sense that they shall deliver progress that is underpinned by *iman* [belief in One God] and that aims for good outcomes. Therefore we cannot discriminate [against women].[42]

At this stage, we can see that while there was religio-political opposition to Rustriningsih's nomination, the opposition seemed mainly centred at the elite level. Moreover, as shown above, PKB and NU in Kebumen supported female leadership for Rustriningsih as regent based on the NU central board's decision and position which supports female leadership in local politics.

Campaigning Strategy: Using Islamic Piety in Political Branding

Rustriningsih's campaign to win voters' hearts in the 2005 direct elections began when she was regent of Kebumen. Initially, Rustriningsih

---

[41] Interview with *Gus* TH, chief of the Dewan Syuro of the PKB, Kebumen (2007–13), 28 July 2010.
[42] Interview with KH. Nashiruddin Al-Mansyur in the office of the regent of Kebumen, 12 Feb. 2010. See also his similar statement in an interview with *Tempo* Magazine, "Bupati Kebumen M. Nashiruddin Al Mansyur", p. 78.

developed a political brand as "a reformist and trusted female leader" by promoting transparency and opening wider communication channels with grassroots society. In so doing, Rustriningsih, helped by the late Ken Sudarto, Kebumen's media advertising expert who owned an advertising company in Jakarta (Matari Advertising), developed RATIH TV, a private TV station, in Kebumen in 2002.[43] The station's leading programme was called *Selamat Pagi Bupati* (Good morning regent, *SPB*) and its format had Rustri answer direct calls from viewers at home who questioned her about various problems in the region. A similar programme was also launched on the government's Radio IN FM. This interactive programming, in which the *Bupati* talked directly to the people, was very new in Indonesian local politics. Since its introduction, *SPB* has become a famous programme in Kebumen and it even drew recognition to Kebumen by CNN, which highlighted it as one of the nine best examples of local autonomy, according to *Tempo* magazine in August 2009.[44]

Rustriningsih's effort to create a new government that was reformist, accountable, transparent and closer to the people impressed elites and the public in Kebumen. Rustriningsih was well known as a reformist and trusted female leader, and she inspired other regents to adopt similar programmes. In the language of Derichs, Fleschenberg and Hustebeck, Rustriningsih's reputation and standing can be categorized as important "moral capital" in terms of being a core asset for female politicians in Asia on their way to power (excellent examples of this kind of moral capital are Aung San Suu Kyi in authoritarian isolation in Burma, the moral campaigning of Wan Azizah in the semi-authoritarian setting in Malaysia, and Park Geun-hye in South Korea and Tanaka Makiko in Japan, all cases of moral capital in consolidated democracies).[45]

---

[43] Winarno, *Rumah Iklan*, pp. 140–1.

[44] *Tempo* magazine highlighted the success of the *SPB* programme, which continued to be broadcast even after Rustriningsih became vice-governor of Central Java in 2008 (see "Kabupaten Kebumen", pp. 75–6). News information on CNN, obtained from Dinas Informasi Komunikasi dan Telematika Kabupaten Kebumen.

[45] By using Kane's definition of moral capital as "a specific political value of virtue that inclines others, in particular the political public and followers, to bestow (ethical) prestige, respect, loyalty, and authority on a political actor or the representative of an institution that the actor herself/himself can use as a resource to mobilize for political goals, activities, or support", Derichs, Fleschenberg and Hustebeck have examined how female politicians in Asia use moral capital as a political strategy. For more exploration, see Derichs, Fleschenberg and Hustebeck, "Gendering Moral Capital", pp. 245–66.

Interestingly, since 2004, Rustriningsih has further developed her moral capital into a new political image in which she has incorporated the embodiment of Islamic piety to become "a reformist, trusted, pious-nationalist female leader". As such, 2004 was an important turning point in Rustriningsih's personal life and political carrier. After undertaking the pilgrimage in 2004, she donned the headscarf and then married. She not only began to gradually embrace Islamic piety but also entered a new phase in life as a married and mature woman. As noted in Chapter 3, the Javanese norm is that true women (*wanita sejati*) are those who serve well in the home as mother and wife,[46] which requires marriage. I believe that gaining the status of the ideal Javanese Muslim woman made Rustriningsih's individual capital even stronger. In a sense, her marriage status benefited her political image of a mature pious Javanese Muslim woman, and she also gained the additional advantage of her husband's economic capital. So, rather than challenging the established gender norm of how a true woman is construed in Javanese society, Rustriningsih took advantage of it, and she utilized her embodiment of the role to gain voters' political sympathy. This finding is similar to the finding of Derichs, Fleschenberg and Hustebeck in which female leaders in Asia have taken advantage of the traditional image of women in their societies to win voters' hearts.[47]

Rustri's decision to wear a headscarf, given that she had not originally been a strict Muslim and was relatively *abangan* (being raised in an *abangan* family and being politically affiliated with PNI, PDI and PDIP), reflects her political intuition in response to Indonesian Muslim society's growing attachment to Islamic principles since the late 1990s. I suspect that Rustri's decision to wear a veil since 2004 has not only attracted more Muslim voters from her nationalist base in *kulon kali* but has also won the hearts of NU *santri* based in *wetan kali*.[48] Robin T. Reid, who has observed the political strategies of women running for the U.S. Senate in the 1996 election, noted that appearance has become more important since the advent of television, as previously people saw politicians mainly via photographs in newspapers or magazines.[49] Further Reid

---

[46] Handayani and Novianto, *Kuasa Wanita Jawa*, p. 143.
[47] See Derichs, Fleschenberg and Hustebeck, "Gendering Moral Capital", p. 253.
[48] Similar views were also stated by SW, vice-chief of the Regional Board of PKB in Kebumen (2001–05); see interview with SW, 28 July 2010.
[49] Reid, "Appearances Do Matter", pp. 23–4.

has noted that as political campaigning becomes more visual, makeup and clothes play an increasingly important role in creating an ideal image to attract voters. This has also been the case for Rustriningsih. After she began to routinely appear on RATIH TV, she visibly changed her style of dress to that of a more "pious" Muslim around 2004. By doing so, she gradually gained wider sympathy from voters beyond her loyal nationalist base a long time before the official campaign for the 2005 direct election began.

Rustriningsih's tactic to boost her popularity and counter issues of corruption by organizing a mass fun bike event,[50] fit with her new political image as "reformist, trusted, pious-nationalist female leader". This is because being "pious" is often associated with being "clean" and not committing sins, including corruption. Interestingly, following Rustriningsih's nomination in the 2005 direct regent election, a group of nearly 75 people under the name ARAK (*Aliansi Rakyat Anti Korupsi*, Alliance of People Against Corruption) held a demonstration in early April 2005 asking the local police to take Rustriningsih to court because of suspicion that she had been involved in various corruption cases as regent of Kebumen from 2000–05.[51] ARAK pointed to at least 15 possible instances of corruption during Rustriningsih's term, ranging from infrastructure projects including construction of RATIH TV, IN FM, a press centre, a road in Karangsambung and a relief fund for natural disasters.[52] However, the local police and courts failed to respond to ARAK's political challenges and the group soon disappeared. This did not affect Rustriningsih's candidacy in the 2005 direct regent election.[53]

Compared to the other candidates in the 2005 election, I found that the incumbent Rustriningsih's campaign strategies were more attractive, pioneering, personal and marketable. The other three candidates relied mainly on their religious cultural bases and mass campaigning. For instance, H.M. Zuhri Effendi and Agus Supriyanto claimed to have a strong base of support in the eastern sections of Kebumen (such as Prembun, Ambal, Padureso and Mirit) as they were populated by NU

---

[50] For analysis regarding this event, see "Beruntungnya Kebumen Peroleh Penghargaan Muri".
[51] "ARAK Tuntut Korupsi Diusut Tuntas".
[52] "Disodori 15 Dugaan Korupsi".
[53] "Pencalonan Kembali Rustriningsih: Digoyang Dugaan Korupsi"; "Sujud Membantah Dibayar Rp 10 Jutan".

followers and *kyai*.[54] Koesnanto Karsoprayitno and KH. Imam Muzani Bunyamin ran an interactive campaign by visiting villagers or appearing on RATIH TV.[55] Meanwhile, Ananto Tri Sasongko and Suprapto ran an open campaign (*kampanye terbuka*).[56]

Penetrating and Using Women's Networks, Intensifying Influence Through *Mauluddan*

As the only female regent candidate, Rustriningsih gained support from local female activists who shared high expectations of Rustri as a female leader.[57] One of Rustriningsih's strategies to take advantage of the existing women's networks in Kebumen was to connect to Islamic-based voters such as those attending *pesantren* in Kebumen.[58] At almost the same time that she began to get closer to Muslim voters, in 2003 Rustri approached local female activists such as those in the Kebumen chapter of Koalisi Perempuan Indonesia (Coalition of Indonesian Women),[59] Muslimat NU and 'Aisyiyah in Kebumen, where she was gradually adopting the veil including for official activities. Due to her gradual adoption of the veil, Rustriningsih was perceived as a good role model for female Muslim politicians in Kebumen.[60] Here, I believe that by these actions, Rustriningsih, who was not a strict *santri* and culturally came from the *abangan* milieu, was able to increase her religious acceptability to Muslim women and Muslim adherents in general.

In addition, Rustriningsih, who had mainly until that point accessed nationalist networks, further developed connections to Islamic networks. The women's networks were made available through KH. Nashiruddin's wife's connections with other *nyai* (wives of *kyai*). Nashiruddin's wife, Nyai Hj. Nuryani, consolidated political support among *pesantren* in Kebumen by approaching Nyai Hj. Sakhiyah from Al Falah Pesantren

---

[54] "Di Balik Pilbub Kebumen (1)".
[55] "Calon Lain Pilih Dialogis".
[56] "Kampanye Sasongko-Suprapto Dipadati Pendukung".
[57] Interview with DL, member of the Fatayat NU and Muslimat NU, and a member of the Kebumen DPRD from PDIP (2004–14), Kebumen, 10 Feb. 2010.
[58] Interview with *Kyai* H. ABS, leader of Al-Hasani *pesantren*, Jatimulyo, Alian, Kebumen, 29 July 2010.
[59] Interview with KHS, member of the Kebumen KPI, Kebumen, 9 Feb. 2010.
[60] Interview with SHW, Secretary General of 'Aisyiyah, Kebumen (2000–05), Kebumen, 11 Feb. 2010.

in Sumolangu and Nyai Hj. Djurdjani from Riadlul 'Uqul Pesantren in Petanahan via the women's religious group Nasyi'atul Islamiyah.[61] This consolidation resulted in the gradual support of influential *kyai* such as *Kyai* Wahib Mahfudz (Gus Wahib, chief of the Syuriah of NU in Kebumen), KH. Musyafa Ali (Sumolangu), KH. Margono Rustam (Klirong), *Kyai* Masrur Rustam (Pejagon) and *Kyai* Masykur Rozaq (chief of the Regional Board of NU in Kebumen).[62] When the candidate favoured by Gus Wahib and *Kyai* Masykur Rozaq was not nominated by the Regional Board of PKB in Kebumen, both eventually supported Rustriningsih and KH. Nashiruddin by attending their campaigns, instead of supporting Koesnanto Karsoprayitno and Imam Muzani Bunyamin who were officially nominated by the Regional Board of PKB in Kebumen.[63] In addition, Rustriningsih and her team tried to win over Islamic followers by attending and donating money for various *Mauluddan* events as explained by her brother RS:

> So, when it was Mauluddan [celebration of the Prophet Muhammad's birthday]... we were invited to many events. The closer it got to Election Day the more intense it was. In any one day we would have forty [invitations], which meant forty million rupiah [spent by Rustri's team at the various Mauluddan events in one day]. *Alhamdulillah* we tried our best to attend the invitations we received, but if we could not we had a team who would attend as our representatives. All were attended.[64]

DL also talked about effectively using Islamic events to get closer to Muslim followers and consolidate their political support:[65]

> At the time it was nearly Mauluddan. Therefore, the campaign was during Mauluddan. Money given [for the sake of God's blessing] was *sadakah*. Other candidates also tried to replicate [her strategy of attending Mauluddan and giving money], but it was difficult [because other candidates did not get invitations, thus did not get such vast

---

[61] Jatmiko, "Kiai dan Politik Lokal", p. 210.
[62] Ibid., p. 210.
[63] Ibid., p. 213.
[64] Interview with RS, Rustriningsih's younger brother in the office of the vice-regent of Kebumen, 9 Feb. 2010.
[65] Interview with DL member of Fatayat NU, Muslimat NU, and member of Kebumen DPRD from PDIP (2004–14), in Kebumen, 10 Feb. 2010.

access to Mauluddan events as did Rustri's team]. *Ibu* received direct invitations. Other candidates did not. They tried to develop closer relationships so they would be invited.

The combination of her tactic to secure religious (Islamic) support from prominent NU *kyai*, her use of Islamic piety in political branding for campaigning and her use of Islamic men and women's networks particularly through *Mauluddan* events, resulted in Rustriningsih's tremendous victory in the 2005 election in Kebumen in almost all 26 districts as apparent in Graph 1.

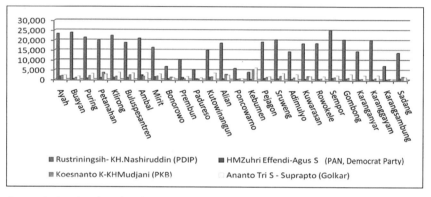

Source: Author, based on data from Komisi Pemilihan Umum Kabupaten Kebumen, *Buku Laporan Pemilihan Bupati dan Wakil Bupati Kebumen 5 Juni 2005*, p. 161.

Graph 1 Distribution of Votes across Districts as a Result of the 2005 Direct Election in Kebumen

There were 854,447 people registered to vote, while 241,450 (28.19 per cent) did not employ their right to vote on 5 June 2005.[66] As Graph 1 shows, Rustriningsih and KH. Nashiruddin (PDIP) overwhelmingly won in 25 of 26 districts in Kebumen. They successfully gained more than 15,000 votes in 17 districts mainly located in the north (Alian, Sruweng and Karanggayam), the west (Kuwarasan, Pejagon, Rowokele and Gombong) and the south (Ayah, Buayan, Puring, Petanahan, Klirong, Buluspesantren, Ambal and Mirit), with one in the east (Kutowinagun). It is clear that Rustriningsih and KH. Nashiruddin gained the

---

[66] Komisi Pemilihan Umum Kabupaten Kebumen, *Buku Laporan Pemilihan Bupati dan Wakil Bupati Kebumen*, 5 Juni 2005, p. 98.

majority of their votes from the *abangan*-based region in the western part (*"kulon kali"*) of Kebumen. In the other eight districts (Bonorowo, Prembun, Padureso, Poncowarno, Adimulyo, Karanganyar, Karangsambung and Sadang) they won with less than 15,000 votes. The pair lost only in Kebumen district, which is an important pocket of NU *santri* and is located in the eastern part of Kebumen or *"wetan kali"*. In Kebumen district, Ananto Tri. S and Suprapto (Golkar) won with 6,258 votes. Koesnanto and Imam Muzani (PKB) did not get a significant number of votes in any of the 26 districts, with their highest number being obtained in Kebumen district with 5,392 votes. HM. Zuhri Effendi and Agus S (PAN and Democrat Party) obtained the least number of votes in each district, with below 2,500 votes. In terms of percentages, Rustriningsih and KH. Nashiruddin won overwhelmingly with 77.48 per cent of votes and thus became regent and vice-regent of Kebumen (2005–10).

The 2008 Direct Election in Central Java: Candidates

Having a relatively solid power base as the regent of Kebumen for two terms (2000–05, 2005–10) set Rustriningsih up for higher political endeavours in the 2008 Direct Central Java Gubernatorial Election. In this election, Rustriningsih again became the only female politician to run as a vice-gubernatorial candidate within a male-dominated political candidacy. Recognizing the unique nature of this distinct condition, Rustriningsih continued to incorporate Islamic piety and gender as a key strategy in her campaign to attract Islamic-based voters. The province of Central Java in 2008 had a total population of 32,244,004 (15,959,945 males and 16,287,059 females).[67] Islam was the dominant religion, followed by Catholicism/Protestantism and Hinduism/Buddhism.[68] Central Java is well known as a PDIP base, especially post-Suharto (after 1998), as can be seen in Table 5.

From the table, we can see that PDIP was the dominant party in Central Java in the 1999, 2004 and 2009 general elections, replacing Golkar's domination during the New Order. While Golkar and PKB were the second and the third most popular parties in the 2004 General

---

[67] Badan Pusat Statistik Provinsi Jawa Tengah, *Statistik Sosial dan Kependudukan Jawa Tengah*, p. 9.
[68] Badan Pusat Statistik Provinsi Jawa Tengah, *Statistik Sosial dan Kependudukan Jawa Tengah: Hasil Susenas 2008*, p. 98.

Table 5 Political Configuration in the Central Java DPRD in the 1992, 1999, 2004 and 2009 General Elections

Political Party	The New Order	Post-Suharto		
	1992	1999	2004	2009
PDI	17	–	–	–
PDIP	–	39	31	23
Golkar	44	12	17	11
PKB	–	16	15	9
PPP	19	10	10	7
Democrat Party	–	–	10	16
PAN	–	6	10	10
PKS	–	–	7	10
GERINDRA	–	–	–	9
HANURA	–	–	–	4
PKNU	–	–	–	1
PNU	–	1	–	–
PNI	–	1	–	–
PKP	–	1	–	–
PK	–	1	–	–
PBB	–	1	–	–
PNI-FM	–	1	–	–
PNI-MM	–	1	–	–
TNI/POLRI	20	10	–	–
Total	100	100	100	100

Note: Results from the 1997 General Election were not available in the documents I was able to obtain.

Sources: Results from 1992 obtained from *Penyelenggaran Pemilihan Umum Tahun 1992 di Jawa Tengah*, p. 396. Results from 1999 obtained from *Buku Lampiran Penyelenggaraan Pemilihan Umum Tahun 1999 di Jawa Tengah*, p. 201. Results from the 2004 and 2009 General Elections obtained from Komisi Pemilihan Umum Provinsi Jawa Tengah, Feb. 2010.

Election, this was not the case in the 2009 General Election. The Democrat Party, which started to compete in elections in 2004, strengthened its grip and become the second most powerful party in the 2009 General Election. With only 10 seats left of the original 17 seats it secured in the 2004 General Election, Golkar ranked third in the 2009 General Election. While PAN and PKS came equal fourth, PKB and Gerindra took equal sixth. The table clearly indicates the nature of Central Java as an important national base for PDIP.

The 2008 Central Java Gubernatorial Election was held on 22 June 2008. Bibit Waluyo, a retired general,[69] and Rustriningsih had gained an official recommendation from the Central Board of PDIP to run as governor and vice-governor. Regardless of rumours that Megawati had told Bibit, who is not a PDIP cadre, not to run in the 2007 Jakarta Gubernatorial Election, in the 2008 Central Java election[70] both Bibit and Rustri successfully defeated other candidates[71] in a fit and proper test at the Central Board of PDIP in Jakarta on 14 February 2008.[72]

There is an interesting story behind Rustriningsih's political stand in 2008 that is related to her role as mother and politician. During the RAKERDASUS (Rapat Kerja Daerah Khusus, Special meeting of the PDIP branch) held by the Provincial Branch of PDIP in Central Java to select PDIP's candidates for governor and vice-governor in January 2008 in Semarang, Rustriningsih was hospitalized after undergoing a caesarean operation to deliver her second child in a hospital in Yogyakarta, and

---

[69] Bibit Waluyo was born in Klaten on 5 August 1949. He graduated from the military academy in Magelang, Central Java in 1972 and developed a bright military career in Banyumas, Cilacap. He accepted a key position as Panglima Angkatan Darat IV/Diponegoro (commander in chief of army command IV/Diponegoro) centred in Semarang, Central Java in 1999, and then as PANDAM JAYA (commander in chief of the central army command) in 2001, and occupied the highest position as PANGKOSTRAD (*Panglima Komando Strategis Angkatan Darat*, commander in chief of the strategic army command) in 2002 before he retired in 2004. As cited from Zubaidah, "Strategi Pemenangan Pasangan Bibit Waluyo-Rustriningsih Dalam Pemilihan Gubernur Jawa Tengah 2008".
[70] Interview with AK, Semarang, 28 Jan. 2010.
[71] The mechanism through which to select the candidates to run as governor and vice-governor from PDIP is regulated by Decree No. 428/DPP/KPTS/XII/2004. According to the decree, there are four steps to select candidates, namely gathering potential names, verifying, making a selection, and making a final decision. The names of candidates who pass verification proceed to a Rapat Kerja Daerah Khusus (RAKERDASUS, Special Meeting of the PDIP Branch), in which a minimum of two pairs of candidates are chosen and their names sent to the Central Board of the PDIP. The board then gives its recommendation as to who the official pair will be. The RAKERDASUS of the Provincial Board of PDIP in Central Java was held on 20 Jan. 2008, but instead of nominating only two pairs of candidates, the RAKERDASUS sent all the candidate names to the PDIP Central Board. See "Murdoko Mundur dari Bursa Cagub".
[72] Those involved in the fit and proper test at the PDIP Central Board who sought to become candidates for governor were: Ali Mufiz (incumbent, governor of Central Java, 2003–08), Bibit Waluyo, M. Tamzil, Imam Suroso, Sumaryoto, Chaerul Rasjid and Eko Budihardjo. Murdoko, chief of the Provincial Board of the PDIP in Central Java, cancelled his nomination. Those running to become candidates for vice-governor were Rustriningsih and Muji Utomo. See "Uji Kepatutan dan Kelayakan Cagub PDI-P".

thus could not attend the meeting.[73] Her loyal team suspected that Murdoko, chief of the Provincial Branch of PDIP in Central Java, would endanger Rustriningsih's candidacy by making a regulation requiring all candidates to attend the meeting. Murdoko was believed to have had a personal ambition to become the candidate for governor from PDIP, and yet he was aware that the Central Board of PDIP was likely to support Rustriningsih rather than him. The critical situation almost pushed Rustriningsih to attend the meeting in a wheelchair accompanied by her private doctor. However, this did not happen as the Central Board of PDIP stated that candidates did not need to attend the RAKERDASUS.[74] A similar battle to juggle her roles as mother of a nearly one-month-old baby and a politician occurred when Rustriningsih attended the fit and proper test at the Central Board of PDIP in February 2008. Rustriningsih explained that she does not have time to pump breast milk ("*meres saja gak sempat*") for her baby during the test as the process took the whole day.[75]

Rustriningsih's struggle to cope with her motherhood role while performing her political role is one that is also faced by female politicians in developed countries. Joanna Mckay's research on the experiences of female politicians in the UK and Germany and the challenges faced by women who combined political careers with motherhood is interesting. Mckay discovered that many female politicians had been burdened with family responsibilities that prevented them from reaching a top position, while they also found it difficult to break into the existing male-dominated political culture.[76] However, Rustriningsih's case also shows consistency in her ability to maintain, rather than abandon, her motherhood role while pursuing political activities. Rustriningsih's position is similar to that of Marina, a female politician in Mexico who strongly upholds the norm of ideal motherhood while taking an active political role, although the common understanding in Mexico is that female politicians may be liberated from motherhood.[77] Despite all the challenges, Rustriningsih successfully secured her position as a PDIP representative and became one of the five contending pairs in the 2008 Central Java Gubernatorial Election, in which the details of each pair profile can be seen in Table 6.

---

[73] "Usai Caesar, Nyaris Hadiri Rakerdasus Naik Ambulan".
[74] Interview with Rustriningsih in the office of the vice-governor of Central Java, 3 Feb. 2010.
[75] Ibid.
[76] Mckay, "Having it All?", p. 714.
[77] Davids, "The Micro Dynamics of Agency", pp. 163–4.

Table 6 Profiles of Governor and Vice-governor Candidates in the 2008 Direct Gubernatorial Election in Central Java

No. in Ballot Paper	Political Party	Name of Governor and Vice-governor Candidates	Profile
1	Golkar	**H. Bambang Sadono**	Muslim, born in Blora on 30 January 1957. Member of the National House of Representatives from Golkar. Chief of Indonesian Association of Journalists in Central Java (1992–98)
		H. Muhammad Adnan	Muslim, born in Semarang on 16 September 1960. Lecturer at Diponegoro University, secretary of NU in Central Java, chief of NU in Central Java (1999–2012)
2	PKB	**H. Agus Soeyitno**	Muslim, born in Bojonegoro on 23 March 1951. Retired Military Officer
		H. Abdul Kholiq Arif	Muslim, born in Wonosobo on 16 September 1968. Regent of Wonosobo. Vice-chief of the Dewan Syuro of PKB in Central Java (2005–10)
3	PKS Democrat Party	**H. Sukawi Sutarip**	Muslim, born in Pati on 27 January 1951. Mayor of Semarang
		H. Sudharto	Muslim, born in Semarang on 2 November 1941. Member of DPD (Provincial Representative Council)
4	PDIP	**H. Bibit Waluyo**	Muslim, born in Klaten on 5 August 1949. Retired Military General
		Hj. Rustriningsih	Muslim, born in Kebumen on 3 July 1967. Regent of Kebumen. Chief of PDIP in Kebumen (1996–present)

continued overleaf

Table 6 continued

No. in Ballot Paper	Political Party	Name of Governor and Vice-Governor Candidates	Profile
5	PPP PAN	**H. Muhammad Tamzil**	Muslim, born in Ujung Pandang on 16 August 1961. Regent of Kudus
		H. Abdul Rozaq Rais	Muslim, born in Surakarta on 5 May 1946. Lecturer at Muhammadiyah Nursing Academy in Surakarta. Vice-chief of Muhammadiyah in Central Java (2005–10)

Note: Names in bold are candidates for governor.
Source: Komisi Pemilihan Umum Provinsi Jawa Tengah, Feb. 2010.

Table 6 shows that the personal backgrounds of the candidates in the 2008 election were varied with various occupations such as lecturers, prominent activists of Islamic organizations, parliamentarian members, retired military personnel, regents and mayors. However, compared to the other candidates, Bibit Waluyo and Rustriningsih (PDIP) had stronger individual capital because Bibit Waluyo was the former commander in chief of the army in Central Java, which enabled him to draw on his old network of retired military figures, as well as his network of active military officers in Central Java. More importantly, his running partner Rustriningsih, who had an outstanding record as a successful PDIP politician and as regent of Kebumen for two periods (2000–05, 2005–10), was the only female candidate. The result of the election is depicted in Graph 2.

There were 25,855,542 registered voters, though only 15,116,390 (58.46 per cent) exercised their right to vote.[78] As shown in Graph 3, Bibit and Rustri (PDIP) won the election with 6,084,261 votes (43.44 per cent), with majorities in 29 of the 35 regencies/municipalities in Central Java. The pair only lost in Rembang, Pati, Kendal, Kudus, Blora

---

[78] Komisi Pemilihan Umum Provinsi Jawa Tengah, *Laporan Pelaksanaan Tugas KPU Provinsi Jawa Tengah Pada Pemilu Gubernur dan Wakil Gubernur Jawa Tengah 2008*, p. 138.

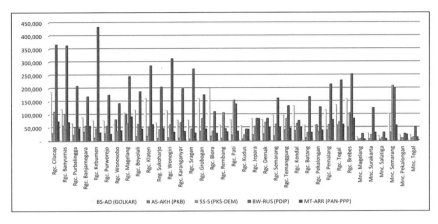

Notes: BS-AD (Bambang Sadono and Muhammad Adnan)
AS-AKH (Agus Soeyitno and Abdul Kholiq Arif)
SS-S (Sukawi Sutarip and Sudharto)
BW-RUS (Bibit Waluyo and Rustriningsih)
MT-ARR (Muhammad Tamzil and Abdul Rozaq Rais)

Source: Graph created by author based on data from Komisi Pemilihan Umum Provinsi Jawa Tengah, *"Rapat Pleno Terbuka Rekapitulasi Penghitungan Suara Pemilu Gubernur dan Wakil Gubernur Jawa Tengah Tahun 2008, Juli 1, 2008"*.

Graph 2 Distribution of Votes across Regencies/Municipalities as a Result of the 2008 Central Java Direct Gubernatorial Election

and Semarang. They were followed by Bambang Sadono and Adnan who won a majority of votes in Blora (where Bambang is originally from), Kendal and Kudus with a total of 3,192,093 votes; Sukawi Sutarip and Sudharto who won in Pati (where Sukawi is originally from) and Semarang (where Sukawi was Mayor at the time) with a total of 2,182,102 votes; Tamzil and Abdul RR who secured 1,591,243 votes; and lastly by Agus Soeyitno and Abdul Kholiq, who won 957,343 votes.[79]

The "Rustriningsih factor" is believed to have contributed significantly to Bibit and Rustri's victory. This is supported by the result of a Lingkaran Survey Indonesia (LSI) survey prior to the 2008 election. These results showed that voters' preference for PDIP gradually increased in favour of Bibit and Rustriningsih after the Central Board of PDIP announced that its official candidate Bibit Waluyo would run with

---

[79] Ibid., p. 136.

Rustriningsih.[80] A similar conclusion was expressed by TY, the former political consultant for Bambang Sadono and Muhammad Adnan (Golkar) and for Sukawi Sutarip and Sudharto (PKS, Democrat Party), who conducted a survey for the pairs prior to Election Day.[81] The significance of the Rustriningsih factor was also shown in LSI surveys: in March 2008 when Bibit and Rustriningsih were first introduced as PDIP candidates, they only gained 15 per cent of votes, far below Bambang Sadono and M. Adnan who gained 34.8 per cent of votes. However, in April 2008, preference for Bibit and Rustri increased dramatically to 29.5 per cent, and continued to increase to 30.9 per cent by June 2008. During this period preference for Bambang and M. Adnan declined to 27.5 per cent in April 2008 and remained relatively stable up to June 2008. In third position were Sukawi and Sudharto with 12.5 per cent of votes, followed by M. Tamzil and Rozak Rais with 5.5 per cent of votes and finally Agus and Kholiq with only 3 per cent of votes, all in June 2008.[82]

Despite the fact that Bibit Waluyo, according to the LSI survey, was the most recognizable and liked candidate among all candidates, Rustriningsih's presence was a key factor to the pair's victory. According to the LSI survey, in July 2007, only 4.8 per cent of PDIP voters voted for Bibit; this increased to 25 per cent in February 2008 when there was word that PDIP would support Bibit in partnership with Rustriningsih, and continued to increase to 62.2 per cent by June 2008.[83]

These figures strongly indicate that Rustriningsih's presence contributed significantly to the victory of Bibit and Rustri in the 2008 Gubernatorial Election. Rustriningsih confidently pointed to her contribution to the victory by referring to a district in Boyolali, where Bibit-Rustri won with 9,000 votes, with 7,000 of those voters punching a hole in her picture on the ballot paper.[84] The next section uncovers in detail the key

---

[80] Lingkaran Survey Indonesia (LSI), "Mesin Partai Dalam Pilkada: Kasus Pilkada Jawa Tengah dan Nusa Tenggara Barat", pp. 6–12.

[81] Interview with TY, lecturer in the Faculty of Social and Political Sciences, Diponegoro University, Central Java and former political consultant for Bambang Sadono and Muhammad Adnan (Golkar), as well as Sukawi Sutrip and Sudharto (PKS, Democrat Party), in the 2008 Central Java Gubernatorial Election, Semarang, 2 Feb. 2010.

[82] Lingkaran Survey Indonesia (LSI), "Grafik 3", p. 7.

[83] Lingkaran Survey Indonesia (LSI), "Mesin Partai Dalam Pilkada", p. 12.

[84] Interview with Rustriningsih in the office of the vice-governor of Central Java, Semarang, 3 Feb. 2010. Rustriningsih explained that she used AC Nielsen to undertake the survey for the purpose of the 2008 Direct Gubernatorial Election.

strategy used by Rustriningsih to optimize her individual and political capital in order to win the 2008 Central Java Gubernatorial Election.

Campaigning Strategy: Using Islamic Piety and Gender

Understanding that Central Java is a PDIP stronghold where loyalist voters could be relied on, Bibit and Rustriningsih concentrated on attracting non-PDIP voters, including Muslim women. The direct election system requires voters to choose one pair of candidates represented by their pictures on the ballot paper, so Rustriningsih prepared her ballot paper picture and relevant posters carefully. She sought to make them very attractive, and choose a picture where Bibit and herself were smiling, where their teeth were visible, they made eye contact and had a good background colour.[85] AP, a close friend and consultant for Rustriningsih who was also a member of the General Election Commission in Central Java (2003–13) agreed that "the ballot paper is really influential" and that Rustriningsih devoted serious effort to create a very good picture for the ballot itself.[86] Figure 2 shows Bibit and Rustri's picture in a campaign pamphlet.

Source: Pamphlet photograph taken by author, 4 Feb. 2010.

Figure 2 Bibit and Rustriningsih in a Pamphlet for the 2008 Central Java Gubernatorial Election

---

[85] Interview with Rustriningsih, Semarang, 3 Feb. 2010.
[86] Interview with AP, close friend of and consultant for Rustriningsih, and also a member of Central Java KPUD (2003–13), Semarang, 1 Feb. 2010.

Here we can see Rustriningsih's intelligence in choosing and creating an appropriate picture for use in the campaign pamphlets. The picture of Bibit and Rustri is attractive as both of them are smiling and their teeth are visible, while in their pictures that I saw in the ballot paper collection of the General Election Commission of Central Java Province the other four candidate pairs were not smiling. Rustriningsih was also skilled in the colours she used: while she used red (commonly associated with PDIP) for the background in the ballot paper I saw, she used green (commonly associated with the Islamic organization NU) as the background in the campaign pamphlet. It appears that her decision to use green in the background of the pamphlet was intended to create the impression that Rustriningsih, who was wearing a veil, was also an NU adherent, in order to attract wider sympathy and political support from Muslimat NU followers who knew little about the candidates. My suspicions were affirmed by Rustriningsih's further explanation of her tactics used in her campaign slogan, "Please vote for she who wears the veil! (*coblos kerudunge!*)", which was circulated through 20 radio stations in Central Java,[87] as also mentioned by AK, a volunteer on Rustriningsih's campaign team who arranged the slogan to be broadcast on RRI [Radio Republik Indonesia, Indonesia radio broadcasting company].[88]

In using Islamic symbols of piety such as veiling, Rustriningsih to some extent manipulated her image to appear as if she was a NU woman in order to increase her acceptability among Muslimat NU followers, as noted by SM, the chief of Muslimat NU in Kebumen (2005–10), and her husband TQ, a former PKB parliamentarian member in Kebumen (1999–2004).[89] In practice, Rustriningsih's *"coblos kerudunge"* campaign was effective in attracting political support from Muslimat NU followers as confirmed by FZ, a Central Java Muslimat NU activist and member of Bambang Sadono's (Golkar candidate for governor, in partnership with Muhammad Adnan) campaign team, who said "eventually, the villagers chose the only woman who wore a veil. Sometimes they did so because

---

[87] Interview with Rustriningsih, Semarang, 3 Feb. 2010.
[88] Interview with AK, Semarang, 28 Jan. 2010.
[89] Interview with SM, chief of Muslimat NU in Kebumen (2005–10), and her husband Taufiq, former PKB parliamentarian member in Kebumen (1999–2004), Kebumen, 27 July 2010.

they were confused".⁹⁰ It was also effective among housewives in Kauman [a Muslimat NU base] where they chose the woman who was wearing a veil.⁹¹

In addition to using Islamic symbols of piety to attract non-PDIP voters, Rustriningsih and her team strategically used her gender to take advantage of the fact that she was the only female candidate through the use of the slogans "*wadon milih wadon*" (women vote for women) in one of her campaigns as documented in the picture collection of the Press Centre of Kebumen Regency dated 2008 and "please choose our own people, please choose our own mother" (*wis milih wonge dewek, milih biyunge dewek*).⁹²

At this point, we can see from pictures, pamphlets and ballot papers, as well as the slogans "*coblos kerudunge*", "*wadon pilih wadon*" and "*milih biyunge dewek*",⁹³ that Rustriningsih was out to sell a distinct political identity as the only female Javanese Muslim candidate (wearing a veil) among a set of entirely male candidates. Rustriningsih highlighted the effectiveness of using identity politics as the only female Javanese Muslim candidate:

> I learnt that even just the appearance of a female figure was very communicative. We can see from the performance that I was very distinct compared to other pairs. And yet, I am sure it was not merely due to me being a woman (*tidak hanya sekedar perempuan*). Because in some *pilkada*, women do not always win though the number of women in politics continues to increase. I had already invested in my name during eight years as regent [of Kebumen]. In addition, in the lead up to the Reform Era [in 1998] I already had a political existence. Thus in combination with having been regent [of Kebumen] I had some other points working in my favour.⁹⁴

---

⁹⁰ Interview with FZ, a Central Java Muslimat NU activist and member of Bambang Sadono's (Golkar) campaign team, Semarang, 30 Jan. 2010.
⁹¹ Interview with FY, chief of KPU in Central Java (2003–08), Semarang, 28 Jan. 2010.
⁹² Interview with SW, Kebumen, 28 July 2010.
⁹³ *Biyung* is the Kebumen word for mother.
⁹⁴ Interview with Rustriningsih, Semarang, 3 Feb. 2010.

PDIP's Strategy and the Effectiveness of Its Political Machine[95]

Despite Rustriningsih's individual strategy, there was a specific strategy implemented by the Provincial Board of PDIP in Central Java to win the 2008 Direct Gubernatorial Election. According to Murdoko, chief of the Provincial Board of PDIP in Central Java and chief of the PDIP campaign team in the 2008 Gubernatorial Election, the strategy was called "Tri Pataka", which refers to the three steps to achieve political party credibility and consists of: mapping the region (*pemetaan wilayah*), appointment of party cadres (*penempatan kader partai*) and political action (*kerja politik partai*).[96] In accordance with the implementation of Tri Pataka, the Provincial Board of PDIP in Central Java issued a decree that instructed all PDIP cadres in the legislative branches (either at the provincial or regency level) and executive branches (regents or mayors) to secure support in their region for Bibit and Rustri in the 2008 Gubernatorial Election. For example, legislators from PDIP in the Central Java DPRD were responsible for making Bibit and Rustri win in their respective electorates. They also worked together with the coordinator of the electorate team in each district of all 35 regencies in Central Java.[97] PT, a volunteer on Rustriningsih's campaign team for the 2008 election and a former member of Central Java DPRD from PDIP (2004–09) also said similarly:

---

[95] Siti Zubaidah described this phenomenon with the phrase *"tim sukses yang solid"* (a solid campaign team), which she saw as one of the key factors for Bibit and Rustri's victory. However, her study does not provide any further gender analysis, which is the contribution my study seeks, although she mentioned the importance of popular figures. Nevertheless, I was thankful of Zubaidah's thesis, especially the appendix that provided detailed information useful to my study. See Zubaidah, "Strategi Pemenangan Pasangan Bibit Waluyo-Rustriningsih Dalam Pemilihan Gubernur Jawa Tengah 2008", pp. 143–59.

[96] Murdoko, *Selayang Pandang PDI Perjuangan Jawa Tengah*, pp. 8–19.

[97] The names of the coordinators in each district throughout the 35 regencies in Central Java were decided by the Provincial Board of the PDIP in Central Java based on decree no. 41/KPTS/DPD/III/2008, "Petugas Pengampu Kecamatan Dalam Rangka Pemenangan Pemilihan Gubernur dan Wakil Gubernur Jawa Tengah Periode 2008–2013" (District coordinators' duty to secure victory for the governor and vice-governor in the election in Central Java for the 2008–13 period). For details about these names see "Daftar Nama Petugas Pemenangan Pemilihan Gubernur", in the appendix of Zubaidah, "Strategi Pemenangan Pasangan Bibit Waluyo-Rustriningsih Dalam Pemilihan Gubernur Jawa Tengah 2008".

We, those of us who were in the legislative bodies, had the responsibility to secure support in our own regions. This was congruent with other functions. Therefore, DPRD members in regencies would also work in the province... the target was to win. How to do so was up to the parliamentarian members who were PDIP cadres.... For example, I had to control our activities in the regency, in districts, and in community association units [*RW, rukun warga*].... We contributed money, by taking a salary cut. This was the policy of our party [PDIP] and other political parties tried to copy it. They could imitate us but they did not have the complete infrastructure that we did. Our party structure extends down to RW units.[98]

To ensure all PDIP cadres and the PDIP structure would work well as a political machine, Megawati Sukarnoputri, chief of the Central Board of PDIP, said in a campaign in Solo and Banjarnegara that she would fired PDIP cadres who did not follow instructions to secure victory for Bibit and Rustri in the 2008 election.[99] Besides the official campaign team under the Provincial Board of PDIP in Central Java led by Murdoko as well as Rustriningsih's own campaign team, there was also Bibit Waluyo's campaign team, which concentrated on the north coast of Central Java (in areas such as Kedu, Banyumas, Pekalongan, Blora and Pati) and was led by Umar Dhanu.[100] Bibit Waluyo's main campaign slogan was "*Bali Deso Mbangun Deso*" (Return to the village and develop the village) as he was originally from a peasant family in a village, and thus he promised to increase peasants' welfare and the development of villages.[101] As a retired military officer, Bibit's team specifically used military networks (either active or retired)[102] as stated by Bibit Waluyo: "I have served quite a long military career in Central Java. Thus, I am quite famous within the big family of the army and *Isyaallah* they will support me."[103] Moreover, Bibit Waluyo was supported by the

---

[98] Interview with PT, a volunteer on Rustriningsih's campaign team and a former member of the Central Java DPRD from PDIP (2004–09), Semarang, 2 Feb. 2010.
[99] See "Mega Pecate Kader Mbalelo", *Seputar Indonesia*, 31 Mar. 2008; and "Megawati Tagih Komitmen".
[100] I could not interview Umar Dhanu because of the circumstances following the criminal case of bribery brought against him over the way he had recruited new bureaucrats was unclear. He was dismissed from his position as a staff member for Bibit Waluyo, governor of Central Java (2008–13).
[101] "Jika Terpilih Bibit Janji Keliling Desa".
[102] Interview with PT, Semarang, 2 Feb. 2010.
[103] Bibit Waluyo's statement, as cited in "Bibit Yakin Didukung Keluarga TNI".

Bumi Putera Insurance Company 1912 network (*Asuransi Jiwa Bersama Bumiputera 1912*, AJB Bumiputera) because he had close connections with its director SHS,[104] who also came from Klaten. Bibit approached SHS, who had supported Syahrul Yasin Limpo and Agus Arifin Nu'mang to win the 2007 South Sulawesi Gubernatorial Election, and asked SHS to support him in the 2008 Central Java Gubernatorial Election. Their emotional ties, as both men came from Klaten, meant SHS agreed that it was the right time to help Bibit.[105] SHS instructed all his employees and family members to support Bibit and Rustri: AJB Bumiputera has 35 main branches in Central Java, with nearly 2,600 employees across three main divisions in Purwokerto, Semarang and Yogyakarta.[106] In the end, Bibit and Rustri were also supported by a coalition of 53 social and professional organizations in Central Java,[107] the Christian Forum in Central Java[108] and the Provincial Board of the Prosperous Peace Party in Central Java (Partai Damai Sejahtera, PDS, a Christian-based political party),[109] while PDIP in Salatiga took the initiative to establish at least 150 campaign centres (*posko pemenangan*) to attract mass support.[110]

While Bibit and Rustri's victory could be explained by the combination between the effectiveness of the Central Java PDIP political machine in implementing instructions from the PDIP Central Board, the success of Rustriningsih's strategy and Bibit's military and personal networks, I believe the other candidates' weak strategies also contributed. In fact, according to Muhammad Adnan, Golkar wanted to follow the strategy of PDIP's Central Board and instruct all Golkar cadres, both legislative and executive, across Central Java to win support for Bambang and Adnan, but it failed.[111] While Golkar could not rely on its political machine, Muhammad Adnan, despite serving as the chief of NU in Central Java (1999–2012), also could not rely on NU's support. This was

---

[104] Interview with KRS, a volunteer on Rustriningsih's campaign team in the 2008 election and a businessman from Purbalingga, Semarang, 2 Feb. 2010.
[105] "Perjalanan Panjang Bibit Waluyo".
[106] "Dukungan ke Bibit dan Tamzil Mengalir".
[107] "Bibit Minta Dukungan Mengangi Pilgub".
[108] "Bibit Waluyo Diberkati".
[109] "PDS Merapat ke PDIP".
[110] "Pasangan Bibit-Rustri Dirikan Ratusan Posko".
[111] Interview with Muhammad Adnan, chief of NU in Central Java (1999–2012), and vice-gubernatorial candidate for Golkar, Semarang, 3 Feb. 2010.

because officially NU in Central Java was neutral and did not support Adnan's nomination.[112] Hoping to get the solid support of NU followers was difficult, because NU voters' support was divided across three candidates who had close affiliation to NU, namely: Bambang and Muhammad Adnan (chief of NU in Central Java), M. Tamzil (who had the support of NU *kyai* in PPP) and Rozaq Rais, and Agus and Kholiq (who had the support of NU *kyai* in PKB). In the end, Bambang Sadono and Adnan gained official support from the association of nearly 600 retired village chiefs in Central Java.[113]

Agus and Kholiq mainly relied on NU followers loyal to PKB by mobilizing 35 PKB branches across Central Java,[114] though this seemed ineffective due to the factors mentioned above. Meanwhile, the Provincial Board of the Democrat Party in Central Java promised a cow to each of the Party's village branches (*ranting*) in Central Java that won support for their candidates, Sukawi and Sudharto, with at least 60 per cent of votes, though the party gave no specific method through which the village branches could do so.[115] Muhammad Tamzil and Rozaq Rais (PPP, PAN) used the popularity of Amein Rais, the former chief of Muhammadiyah who campaigned for his younger brother, Rozaq Rais, though he stated that Muhammadiyah itself was neutral.[116] Despite support from PDIP followers who adopted the name "*naga merah*" (red dragon) after being disappointed by the PDIP Central Board's decision not to nominate Tamzil as the PDIP candidate for governor,[117] Tamzil and Rozaq Rais were defeated in the 2008 election by the mainstream majority of PDIP followers who favoured Rustriningsih as PDIP's most popular figure in partnership with Bibit.

Policies on Women's Issues

This section is devoted to assessing Rustriningsih's policies as a female leader, and examining whether she has met the normative expectation that female leaders pay more attention to women's issues and bring them into their political agendas to ensure women's perspectives in their

---

[112] Ibid., "PW NU Tegaskan Netral".
[113] "Mantan Kades Siap Dukung BS-Adnan".
[114] "PKB Garap Kultur NU".
[115] "Menangkan Sukawi Akan Mendapat Sapi".
[116] "Amien Kampanyekan Rozaq Rais", *Radar Kebumen*, 30 May 2008.
[117] "Deklarasi Bakal Dihadiri Naga Merah", *Suara Merdeka*, 14 Mar. 2008.

policies. We begin with a look at Rustriningsih's leadership style and her engagement with women's groups in her quest for power.

I have noted that Rustriningsih mainly relied on male-based political networks of the nationalist elite and their followers, rather than women's groups. This has had an impact on her stance concerning female perspectives. Rustriningsih's distinct leadership style saw her try to embrace various elements and political actors of different ideological orientations, though this was mainly underpinned by a strategy to consolidate political power. For example, her decision to recruit KH. Nashiruddin who was a prominent NU *kyai* as her running partner since the 2000 election was intended to create a balance of power between the nationalist and *santri* elements that supported her. In addition, when she served as regent, she often asked prominent local political actors such as SPR, and YC from PKB, Golkar and PPP to discuss serious matters, such as the local budget, in informal meetings at her home which created conducive relationships within the DPRD.[118] Rustriningsih had a strong determination to promote pluralism in politics. Being rooted in the nationalist party of PDIP, Rustriningsih engineered the appointment of BUS, a Chinese Christian, loyal PDIP cadre and member of Kebumen DPRD (2004–13), as the chief of Kebumen DPRD (2009–13). This unpopular decision provoked controversy in Islamic circles as Muslims feared that the appointment of BUS would endanger Islamic interests.[119]

In terms of her relationship with local women's groups in Kebumen, it is perhaps best described as "pragmatic-strategic". Rustriningsih did not specifically establish closer relationships with women's groups because she originally had no affiliation with religious women's groups and has also had negative experiences with some local female activists. She stated:

> For NGOs, I do not underestimate their active and passive roles. And yet from my experience, some female activists in Kebumen do not support me, or they underestimate me. They think that I am only an ordinary woman and what I now enjoy is pure luck....[120]

---

[118] Interview with SPR, chief of Golkar's Regional Board in Kebumen, 10 Feb. 2010; and interview with YC, vice-secretary of the PPP Regional Board in Kebumen (1999–2000), in the Kebumen DPRD, Kebumen, 12 Feb. 2010.

[119] Interview with BUS, treasurer of the PDIP Regional Board in Kebumen, member of the Kebumen DPRD from PDIP (2004–13) and chief of the Kebumen DPRD (2009–13), Kebumen, 10 Feb. 2010.

[120] Interview with Rustriningsih, 3 Feb. 2010.

Rustriningsih's minimal engagement with women's groups in her quest for power and her distinct leadership style has led her to take a unique political stand. Rustri expressed her original expectations as a female leader:

> I feel women preserve personal values more. I think they [female politicians] are more shy (*rasa malu*).... People often say that women are sensitive. They define sensitive as responsive, emotional, easily angered, and easy to influence. I think if we work seriously, responsiveness could be an extraordinary weapon....[121]

I had expected that her answer would reflect the normative notion that female leaders adopt female perspectives. Yet Rustri's answer touched on the quite important aspects often mentioned in reference to female leadership including the ideas that female leaders are sensitive and think more about values,[122] though she did not directly link these values to specific cases such as women's needs and problems. When I asked additional questions about the main problems women face in Kebumen, she gave the classic and diplomatic answer of "poverty" without providing a detailed exploration.[123] I got the impression that women's issues were not one of the priority areas for development in the region.

To test the validity of this assessment, I further examined local government documents on women and gender since Rustriningsih's first term in power (2000–05) and throughout her second term (2005–08). Although I could not obtain the Local Strategic Development Plan 2000–05 (*Rencana Strategis Daerah*, RENSTRA), I was able to obtain the Local Government Development Plan 2006–10 (*Rencana Kerja Pemerintah Daerah*, RKPD) which was based on the achievements of the 2000–05 development plan. The effort to implement gender equality in local development is mentioned in the 2006–11 RPKD of Kebumen under the programme to eradicate poverty and disparity.[124] However,

---

[121] Ibid.
[122] For example, see King, "Sex Role Identity and Decision Making Styles", pp. 72–86. Here, Simrell King defines two types of leadership, namely a masculinized image of leadership that displays the masculine qualities of assertiveness and aggression; and contrasts this with the feminine image of leadership that emphasizes cooperation and consensus.
[123] Interview with Rustriningsih, 3 Feb. 2010.
[124] Pemerintah Kabupaten Kebumen, *Rencana Kerja Pemerintah Daerah (RPKD) Kabupaten Kebumen Tahun 2006*, p. 73.

further scrutiny reveals that the document states that the government would merely focus on fulfilling women's basic needs and population control.[125] The document does not mention women's issues, such as violence against women and children, though it does seek to eliminate gender inequality in education.

Despite the weak policy statement, the local government is quite serious about improving women's conditions. For example, the maternal mortality rate in every 100,000 births has gradually declined from 122.57 in 2001 to 86.65 in 2002,[126] to 59.71 in 2005 and to 51.28 in 2007.[127] The gradual improvement of women's health is perhaps due to the local "making pregnancy safer" programme implemented since the turn of the century.[128]

Although the figures look better, gender disparity remains. For example, in education the literacy rate for women above 10 years of age is 99.16 per cent, which was slightly behind the literacy rate of 99.63 per cent in 2008 for men in the same age group.[129] Another striking problem is the increasing number of cases of violence against women and children in Kebumen: from 67 (2006), to 86 (2007), to 93 (2008).[130] This increase may be because the local government has not yet identified or addressed violence against women and children as a critical problem; there was no mention of violence against women in the 2006–11 RKPD. The national government did, however, institute the instalment of a team advocating for victims of violence against women and children (*Tim Penanganan Korban Kekerasan terhadap Perempuan dan Anak*, PKKPA) in each province and regency, and thus a Kebumen PKKPA branch was established in 2004. The effort to eradicate violence against women and children in Kebumen has been incorporated into the Mid-Term Development Plan of Kebumen (*Rencana Pembangunan Jangka Menengah Daerah*, RPJMD) for 2010–15. It is included as part of the women's empowerment programme as one of 26 compulsory sectors stipulated by the

---

[125] Ibid.
[126] Ibid., p. 58.
[127] Bappeda Kabupaten Kebumen, *Rencana Pembangunan Jangka Menengah Daerah (RPJMD) Kabupaten Kebumen Tahun 2011–2015*, p. 20.
[128] Badan Pemberdayaan Perempuan dan Keluarga Berencana, *Data Pilah Gender Statisik dan Analisis Kabupaten Kebumen 2008*, p. 27.
[129] Ibid., p. 91.
[130] Ibid., p. 46.

central government to be carried out under the authority of the local government.[131]

However, an interview with PR, chief of the Women's Empowerment and Family Planning Bureau in Kebumen, suggested that Rustriningsih is passive in taking the initiative to address local women's needs and problems, including violence. Rather, it was PR and other staff members who have proposed and initiated programmes to address local women's needs and problems.[132] IS, a female activist of INDIPT, a prominent and vocal NGO in Kebumen that promotes eradicating violence against women, also expressed her disappointment that although they have a female regent it has not made the local government more gender sensitive.[133]

Rustriningsih has had a similar attitude while serving as vice-governor of Central Java (2008–13). My observations and an interview with DW, the chief of the section on women's empowerment in the Women's Empowerment and Family Planning Bureau in Central Java, revealed similar features. According to DW, although Rustriningsih initially showed strong sympathy and support for the bureau she was passive.[134] DW and her staff continued to work in partnership with prominent women's NGOs such as the Institute for Gender and Human Rights Studies (Lembaga Kajian Jender dan Hak Asasi Manusia, LKJ HAM) and the Legal Aid Foundation of the Indonesian Women's Association for Justice (Lembaga Batuan Hukum Asosiasi Perempuan Indonesia untuk Keadilan, LBH APIK) to advocate various cases of violence against women and to develop capacity building.[135] DW told how it was because of her staff and their consistent partnerships with local NGOs that were established long before Rustriningsih came to be vice-governor, and that the Bureau of Women's Empowerment in Central Java twice

---

[131] Bappeda Kabupaten Kebumen, *Rencana Pembangunan Jangka Menengah Daerah (RPJMD) Kabupaten Kebumen Tahun 2011–2015*, p. 125.
[132] Interview with PR, chief of the Women's Empowerment and Family Planning Bureau of Kebumen, Kebumen, 10 Feb. 2010.
[133] Interview with IS, a prominent female activist at the NGO INDIPT, Kebumen, 27 July 2010. See also INDIPT's publication, "Menurunnya Komitmen Kesetaraan Gender Dalam Dokumen Pembangunan Pemerintah Kabupaten Kebumen".
[134] Interview with DW, chief of the women's empowerment section in the Women's Empowerment and Family Planning Bureau in Central Java, Semarang, 5 Feb. 2010.
[135] Interview with EV, chief of LKJ HAM, Semarang, 1 Feb. 2010; and SKH, chief of LBH APIK, Semarang, 29 Jan. 2010.

received the Parahita Eka Praya Utama award (2008, 2009) from the Indonesian government for being the province with the strongest commitment to and work on gender equality.[136]

Further interviews with prominent female activists in Semarang such as ML, the chief of the Indonesian Women's Coalition (Koalisi Perempuan Indonesia, KPI) in Central Java (2008–12), also revealed that Rustriningsih was passive and instead it was local female activists who always took the initiative to approach Rustriningsih and to push her to commit to addressing women's needs and problems.[137] AP, a close friend and consultant for Rustriningsih and a member of Central Java KPU (2003–13), further explained the dilemma faced by Rustriningsih due to her position as vice-regent, who does not have a key position in decision making, as well as her relatively weak access to women's networks in Central Java.[138]

To sum up, as a female leader who rose within the ranks of the nationalist party PDIP, Rustriningsih was able to develop pluralism politics in Kebumen. And yet, although she has acknowledged that responsiveness is an important characteristic of female leaders, she has not been able to put it into practice. She does not have a clear concept in her mind about local women's problems in Kebumen, is relatively passive and lets the staff at the Women's Empowerment Bureau initiate changes and build bridges with local women's NGOs. I suspect her gradual approach to some female activists from 'Aisyiyah and Muslimat NU in 2004 was heavily motivated by her desire to increase political support in the lead up to the 2005 direct election, as explored earlier. She has remained relatively passive even while serving as vice-governor of Central Java. One plausible explanation is perhaps due to her lack of connections with local women's networks, and yet she has not tried to embrace or actively approach them.

Conclusion

My analysis reveals that familial ties, namely the influence of Rustriningsih's father, Sukamto, were very important to Rustriningsih's political

---

[136] Interview with PR, Kebumen, 10 Feb. 2010.
[137] Interview with ML, chief of the Indonesian Women's Coalition in Central Java 2008–13, Semarang, 5 Feb. 2010.
[138] Interview with AP, member of the Central Java KPU (2003–13), Semarang, 1 Feb. 2010.

career in Kebumen especially since the mid-1990s. Rustriningsih was able to rise as a successful politician due to strong familial ties and strong individual capital (as an educated and entrepreneurial woman). Rustriningsih's political emergence as the first female candidate in Kebumen in the 2000s had been possible due to her good political career in PDI in Kebumen, which was facilitated by strong "familial ties" due to the prominence of her father, and strengthened by her ability to secure support from NU *santri* by recruiting KH. Nashiruddin Al-Mansyur as the vice-regent candidate. Then, after gaining valid religious legitimacy from the Islamic belief about female leadership as articulated by Kebumen NU's position, which was not opposed to female regents, Rustriningsih comfortably ran as a female candidate for regent, and later vice-governor.

In the lead up to the 2005 direct election in Kebumen, Rustriningsih had used Islamic piety and gender in her political branding as a "reformist, trusted, pious-nationalist female leader" which was developed since 2004 as part of her effort to move from being an originally *abangan* woman from *kulon kali*, to create balance with and gather the mass support of NU followers from *wetan kali*. Islamic piety and gender continued to be used as an important strategy in the 2008 Direct Gubernatorial Election in Central Java. Rustriningsih deliberately used the idea and practice of Islamic piety, such as wearing the veil, in combination with her gender to signify a distinct political identity as the only nationalist, pious female candidate among male candidates in the election. This was emphasized through her use of slogans such as *"coblos kerudunge*! (Please vote for she who wears the veil)", *"wadon pilih wadon* (Women vote for women)" and *"milih biyunge dewek* (Please choose our own mother)". While the slogan *"wadon pilih wadon"* was intended to specifically garner support from female voters, the slogans *"coblos kerudunge!"* and *"milih biyunge dewek"* were used to attract all voters, both men and women. Here, I want to highlight that gender was not a hindrance but instead an important selling point in the direct elections. Rustriningsih strategically used a combination of Islamic piety and gender to expand her political base beyond her *abangan*/nationalist-based voters, in particular to attract wider support from Islamic-based (NU) voters. Lastly, despite the significance of predominantly male networks of PDIP elites and followers, and to some extent Islamic women's networks, either via organizations (Islamic organizations and NGOs) or the network of *nyai* via KH. Nashiruddin's wife, to Rustriningsih's political career, I suggest her relative lack of cooperation with women's organizations was one of the factors that contributed to her weak policies on women's issues both as regent of Kebumen and as vice-governor of Central Java.

Rustriningsih continued to serve as vice-governor of Central Java (2008–13). However she failed to become chief of the PDIP Provincial Board in Central Java as she was defeated by the incumbent, Murdoko, in February 2010. Megawati's support of Rustriningsih gradually declined with the decrease in Rustriningsih's political popularity in Kebumen, due to her domination and greedy political ambitions. For example, Rustriningsih has persisted as chief of PDIP in Kebumen since 1996, during which she has tried to secure local power by installing family members such as her younger brother, RS as candidate for regent in the 2010 direct election in Kebumen, though she failed. This attitude decreased her popularity. Realizing her decreasing popularity in PDIP, including the weakening support from Megawati, Rustriningsih manoeuvred to join the National Democrats (NASDEM, a newly formed non-political party organization lead by Surya Paloh, which became a political party in the 2014 Election). Although she received a warning from the Central Board of PDIP, Rustriningsih agreed to be the chief of NASDEM in Central Java in January 2011.[139] In addition to that, Megawati's gradual withdrawal of support for Rustriningsih was because Megawati and (the late) Taufik Kiemas (Megawati's husband and important figure in the PDIP Central Board) wanted to promote Puan Maharani, their daughter who is currently chief of Political and Institutional Relations on the PDIP Central Board. As the promising female leader to continue the legacy of Megawati, Megawati and Taufik Kiemas made a strategic move inside PDIP to make sure that there were no other female PDIP cadres who would likely become potential rivals of Puan Maharani in the near future.[140]

Rustriningsih lost political support from Megawati in the 2013 Central Java Governor Election. Rustriningsih, who wanted to nominate herself as candidate for governor in the 2013 Central Java Governor Election, in fact did not gain a recommendation from Central Board of PDIP.[141] Conversely, the PDIP Central Board officially nominated

---

[139] "Sekjen PDIP Ingatkan Wagub Jateng yang Gabung Nasdem".
[140] Conversation with EK, female parliamentarian member from PDIP, Jakarta, 28 Nov. 2012.
[141] "Langkah Rustriningsih Setelah Gagal Dapat Rekomendasi PDIP".

Ganjar Pranowo, a prominent PDIP cadre and parliamentarian member, who originally comes from Karanganyar, Central Java, as the candidate for governor, in partnership with Heru Sujatmoko, PDIP cadre who is currently regent of Purbalingga (2010–15). The pair was officially declared by Puan Maharani in the RAKERDASUS of the Provincial Board of PDIP in Central Java in Solo on 9 March 2013, as the governor and vice-governor candidate from PDIP in the 2013 Gubernatorial Election in Central Java.[142] Ganjar Pranowo won the gubernatorial election and becomes governor of Central Java (2013–18). Rustriningsih, who could not compete in the election, evaluated her dedication to PDIP over 27 years, and is preparing to return to society with a social empowerment plan.[143]

---

[142] "Puan: Hanya Ganjar-Heru Representasi PDIP di Pilgub Jateng".
[143] "Langkah Rustriningsih Setelah Gagal Dapat Rekomendasi PDIP".

CHAPTER 5

Siti Qomariyah: Using Islamic Piety and Gender and Securing Nahdlatul Ulama's Socio-political Base

This chapter presents the case study on Siti Qomariyah, whose profile and background supported her 2006 political emergence and then later her victory in the 2006 direct election in Pekalongan. Her ability to secure the political support of Nahdlatul Ulama's and her political strategy that embraced her Islamic piety and gender were vital elements in her political victory in the 2006 direct election in Pekalongan.

Pekalongan Regency: The Social and Political Landscape

Pekalongan, which is situated on the north coast of Java, is one of 29 regencies in the province of Central Java (comprises 29 regencies and 6 cities) and in 2007 consisted of 19 districts, 13 administrative villages (*kelurahan*), 270 villages and 209 hamlets (*dusun*).[1] The region, known as the centre of Java's batik industry, was as of 2007 home to 912,365 inhabitants, the majority of whom were Muslim and NU followers,[2] and it contained 19 district (*kecamatan*) NU branches. The changes in the political situation in Pekalongan are reflected in Table 7.

From Table 7, we can see that during the 1992 and 1997 General Elections, Golkar was the dominant party in Pekalongan while the United Development Party (Partai Persatuan Pembangunan, PPP), the only Islamic-based political party allowed during the New Order, came in second.

---

[1] Pemerintah Kabupaten Pekalongan, *Profil, Potensi, Peluang Invenstasi dan Kebijakan Pembangunan Kabupaten Pekalongan Tahun 2007*, p. 25.
[2] Ibid.

Table 7 Political Party Composition in Pekalongan during the New Order and Post-Suharto Eras

The New Order			Post-Suharto			
Political Party	1992	1997	Political Party	1999	2004	2009
PPP	9	15	PPP	4	4	3
Golkar	18	20	Golkar	4	6	6
PDI	9	1	PDIP	17	13	10
TNI/Polri	9	9	TNI/Polri	5	–	–
			PKB	10	15	11
			PAN	4	5	6
			PNI Marhaen	1	–	–
			Democrat Party	–	1	3
			PBB	–	1	–
			HANURA	–	–	3
			PKNU	–	–	2
			Gerindra	–	–	1
Total	45	45	Total	45	45	45

Source: Political party composition following the 1992, 1997 and 1999 General Elections obtained from Basyar, "Peran Ulama Dalam Penyelesaian Kekerasan Politik Pada Pemilu Tahun 1997 dan tahun 1999 di Pekalongan", p. 91. Political party composition as a result of the 2004 General Election obtained from Komisi Pemilihan Umum Kabupaten Pekalongan, "Dokumentasi Penyelenggaraan Pemilu Anggota DPR, DPD, dan DPRD Serta Pemilu Presiden dan Wakil Presiden Tahun 2004 Di Kabupaten Pekalongan", pp. 168–9. Political party composition as a result of the 2009 General Election obtained from Komisi Pemilihan Umum Kabupaten Pekalongan, "Calon Terpilih DPRD Kabupaten Pekalongan Dalam Pemilu 2009", n.p.

PPP's weak position in Pekalongan can be attributed to Suharto's policy of eliminating the influence of all political parties except Golkar. In turn, Suharto used Golkar and its bureaucracy from the central to village levels to gain victory in every election and consolidate power under the New Order.[3]

Unlike the New Order period, when only three political parties were represented in elections, the general election of 1999, the first election of the Reform Era, saw 48 political parties contend. While Golkar was the dominant party in Pekalongan during the New Order, the

---

[3] See also M. Hamdan Basyar, "Peran Ulama Dalam Penyelesaian Kekerasan Politik Pada Pemilu Tahun 1997 dan tahun 1999 di Pekalongan", p. 92.

Indonesian Democratic Party of Struggle (Partai Demokrasi Indonesia Perjuangan, PDIP) under Megawati's leadership gained 17 seats and became the new dominant power. Interestingly, the number of seats held by PPP dropped dramatically to only four, far behind the new NU-based National Awakening Party (Partai Kebangkitan Bangsa, PKB) which became the second dominant party after PDIP. PKB consolidated its influence even further in the 2004 General Election by winning 15 seats and becoming the new power holder, with PDIP second and Golkar third. PKB's dominance in the region prevailed in the 2009 General Election, although it lost four seats due to the fragmentation of NU-based voters that followed the formation of NU splinter parties such as the National Ulama Awakening Party (Partai Kebangkitan Nasional Ulama Indonesia, PKNU). PDIP remained in second position. Table 7 shows the clear shift in configuration of power from Golkar during the New Order, to PDIP in 1999, and PKB since 2004. It indicates that while Golkar's domination was unavoidable during the New Order, in post-Suharto Pekalongan, NU *santri* and elites solidified their voice through PKB.

Siti Qomariyah: A Modern Female NU *Santri* with Distinct Individual Capital

Siti Qomariyah was born on 8 July 1967, and comes from a devout Islamic, or *santri*, NU family.[4] Her father is a *kampong* (village) *kyai* and runs the small Darul Hikmah *pesantren* in Wonoyoso, Buaran, Pekalongan, while her mother used to be a kindergarten teacher. Siti is the eldest of nine (three girls, six boys). Her father studied at Lirboyo Pesantren in Kediri, one of the most influential NU traditional boarding schools in Java, but he has no political experience like the rest of Siti's family. According to Siti, her father is very disciplined in teaching Islamic doctrine. For instance Siti chants verses of the Qur'an every day after the *shubuh* prayer (the early morning prayer). Meanwhile, Siti's mother has always urged her to be brave and not shy. Siti was raised with NU's strong religious doctrine. She attended junior high school (1980–83) in Madrasah Tsanawiyah Maarif in Buaran, Pekalongan, and senior high

---

[4] As noted in Chapter 4, *santri* refers to a religious class whose members are devout Muslims, according to Clifford Geertz's categorization (1960). Siti Qomariyah's origin from and strong connection to NU *pesantren*, including her consistency in veiling, places her in the *santri* category.

school (1983–86) at the Madrasah Aliyah Negeri in Denanyar, Jombang, East Java. Siti excelled as a student: she spoke and wrote in English fluently and often achieved the best grades in English, Math and Arabic.[5] From senior high school, Siti went on to study at IAIN (Institute Agama Islam Negeri, State Institute of Islamic Studies) in Walisongo, Pekalongan, which paved the way towards a Master's degree at McGill University in Canada and the PhD she was undertaking at the time of my research at Diponegoro University. In one of our interviews Siti explained the many benefits obtained from her diverse education: while in *pesantren* (Jombang) she learnt the essence of religion (Islam), and her experience at McGill University widened her perspective, provided academic networks and opened new methodologies of thinking.[6]

Siti married H. Rosikin, a batik trader/businessman in Pekalongan. They have two sons. Neither Siti's husband nor his family members have any experience in politics. Siti taught at Aliyah Syafii in Pekalongan and later became a lecturer at STAIN (Sekolah Tinggi Agama Islam Negeri, Indonesian State College of Islamic Religion) in Pekalongan (1992–present). While lecturing, Siti also actively took part on the board of Fatayat NU (NU women's youth organization). Although Siti has never officially joined Muslimat NU in Pekalongan, due to her prominence and experience she has been a member of the ethical board of Muslimat NU in Pekalongan since 1998. She was also a member of the *fatwa* commission of the Indonesian Council of Ulama (Majelis Ulama Indonesia) in Pekalongan since 1997.

Siti was thus naturally raised in a family with a strong NU religious tradition. Although she is a girl, her father and mother gave her many opportunities and encouraged her, due to her excellent academic achievements, to seek further Islamic education outside Pekalongan in Jombang. Because she was raised in a devout Islamic family with an Islamic education, it is not surprising that Siti consistently wears Islamic dress, such as long sleeved shirts and long skirts, and covers her hair with a veil. She did so back when she studied abroad at McGill University, and does so now as regent of Pekalongan. Siti's intellectual competency, nurtured through her various educational experiences, is a significant part of her life history. A combination of personal and family background as an NU

---

[5] Interview with Ibu AKH, Ibu ZLH and HSY, all of whom were Siti's friends at MTS Maarif, in Pekalongan, 19 June 2009.

[6] Interview with Siti Qomariyah, in the official house of the regent of Pekalongan, 21 June 2009.

santri and her impeccable educational record has made her famous in local history as the first young female NU *santri* in Pekalongan to successfully study abroad on a scholarship. This distinct individual capital has proven to be an important selling point which has paved her way into politics.

Political Emergence: Distinct Individual Capital Without Familial Ties

Siti's initial foray into politics in Pekalongan started in the lead-up to the 2001 local election in Pekalongan. Because PDIP was the strongest party in the region as a result of the 1999 General Election, PDIP fielded its cadre and bureaucrat Amat Antono as candidate for regent in the 2001 local election. Amat Antono had a strong PDIP family background as his father was a PDIP politician (his younger sister is currently chief of the Regional Board of PDIP in Pekalongan for 2009–14). Amat Antono had been a bureaucrat in Sambas, Kalimantan, but returned to Pekalongan because he was favoured by PDIP followers across districts (*ranting*) in Pekalongan to be their candidate for regent.[7] PDIP then approached PKB, the second strongest party as a result of the 1999 General Election. The Regional Board of PKB in Pekalongan nominated Siti as the candidate for vice-regent to partner up with Amat Antono. In fact, Siti was initially not interested in joining political activities, but the Regional Board invited and then eventually selected her as a candidate.[8]

An interview with AB, secretary of the *Tanfidz* of the Regional Board (Dewan Pimpinan Cabang, DPC) of PKB in Pekalongan (2002–07), revealed the rationale behind choosing Siti as the vice-regent candidate from PKB in the 2001 direct election of local government, regulated under the Law No. 22/1999, which was held inside and by the Regional People's Representative Councils election in Pekalongan:

> ...If we [PKB] took [a candidate] who was a politician, there would be political resistance. Therefore, we selected our cadres who were not politicians. Eventually, Qomariyah was one of those who were selected by the internal mechanism.... It was due to the simple consideration

---

[7] Interview with TH, Amat Antono's younger sister and chief of the Regional Board of PDIP in Pekalongan (2009–14), Pekalongan, 28 June 2009.

[8] Interview with Siti Qomariyah, in the official house of the regent of Pekalongan, 17 June 2009.

that she was a very young [NU] cadre with much potential, who was smart and was the daughter of a prominent NU figure (*anak tokoh*).... That's it. And because at the time we were allowed to allocate someone for the vice-regent position, where the candidate for regent was male, we therefore *chose a female* [emphasis added], besides considering her potential as I said earlier.[9]

Based on AB's explanation we notice clearly that her position as a female candidate was seen as a selling point to create an ideal team comprising of a male and female figure. Siti's distinct individual capital, as a smart, young, modern NU woman, who comes from a strong *santri* NU family on her father's side, was an important factor that facilitated Siti's involvement in politics. Although Siti's father was never involved in any formal political activities, it was his strong religious base (NU) that drove PKB Pekalongan to choose Siti as the most appropriate candidate for regent. If we stick to our working definition of "familial ties" as the case in which there are prominent male politicians in the family (either father or husband) of the Javanese Muslim women studied, and examine how these presences may exert a strong influence on a candidate's political emergence, it is clear that in the case of Siti Qomariyah there were no clear familial political ties behind her political emergence. However, Siti Qomariyah's emergence was strongly due to her father's prominent reputation as an influential local NU leader, though he had never been active in politics. It is important to note that this goes beyond the common understanding of "familial ties", so as to include the strong influence of prominent male relatives whose religious/cultural reputations facilitate the rise of female family members as politicians, though the male relatives are not involved in formal politics themselves.

Eventually, PKB nominated Siti as its candidate for vice-regent in coalition with Amat Antono as the candidate for regent from PDIP. The election was on 17 May 2001, and all 45 members of the Pekalongan DPRD attended. Two candidate pairs competed: Amat Antono and Siti Qomariyah (PDIP, PKB), and Yusuf Yahya and Dr. Muritno (chief of the Regional Board of PAN in Pekalongan and bureaucrat in Pekalongan from Golkar). Although the coalition of PDIP (17 seats) and

---

[9] Interview with AB, secretary of the *Tanfidz* of the Regional Board of the PKB in Pekalongan (2002–07), Pekalongan, 17 June 2009.

PKB (10 seats) gathered a total of 27 votes in the Pekalongan DPRD, the power contest was intense and it took two rounds for Amat Antono and Siti Qomariyah to win the election. The first round resulted in Antono and Qomariyah obtaining 21 votes, while Yusuf Yahya and Muritno won 18 votes.[10] As neither gained the minimum of 50 per cent plus one, a second election round was required. The second round was held on 23 May 2001 and Antono and Siti won the election with 27 votes to Yusuf Yahya and Muritno's 18 votes.[11] Antono and Siti thus became the regent and vice-regent of Pekalongan (2001–06), which marked a new political height for Siti.

The 2006 Direct Election: The Political Momentum, NU's Interests and Muslimat NU's Initiatives

AB, the chief of Siti Qomariyah's campaign team and secretary of the *Tanfidz* of the Regional Board of PKB in Pekalongan (2002–07), explained the rationale behind why NU in Pekalongan wanted political power in the 2006 direct election:

> And yet the problem is cultural as a result of colonialism...in the end, *santri* [NU] could not achieve sufficient formal education. Thus, when they became bureaucrats they were not competent. Then during the New Order it became worse [NU was in the periphery during the early years of the New Order, while Muhammadiyah was closer to the New Order regime]. Actually in the early years of independence, for example, when Pak Wahid Hasyim was a minister, we [NU] gained many positions. And yet, during the New Order this changed as *santri* were not interested in bureaucracy.... As a result Nahdhliyin [NU adherents] and Muslims in the bureaucracy were replaced by non-Muslims [Christians].[12]

---

[10] DPRD Kabupaten Pekalongan, "Risalah Rapat Paripurna Khusus DPRD Kabupaten Pekalongan Dalam Rangka Pemilihan Bupati Pekalongan Masa Bhakti 2001–2006 Tahap Pertama Tanggal 17 Mei 2001".

[11] DPRD Kabupaten Pekalongan, "Risalah Rapat Paripurna Khusus DPRD Kabupaten Pekalongan Dalam Rangka Pemilihan Bupati Pekalongan Masa Bhakti 2001–2006 Tahap Kedua Tanggal 23 Mei 2001"; and "Permohonan Pengesahan Pasangan Calon Terpilih Bupati dan Wakil Bupati Pekalongan Masa Bhakti 2001–06".

[12] Interview with AB, secretary of the *Tanfidz* of the Regional Board of PKB in Pekalongan (2002–07), in Pekalongan, 17 June 2009.

Siti Qomariyah provided more clarity on NU's relative alienation and its potential political power:

> It is a fact that bureaucracy makes the situation difficult. Since long ago *pondok pesantren* have never been considered. For many years *pondok pesantren* were suppressed... NU took control of education in *pondok pesantren*, while Muhammadiyah took control of formal education. Muhammadiyah had access to the central government, whereas NU did not have access to the state because it did not deal with the state, though it did gain a special place in, and trust from, society... Muhammadiyah is more formal or structural while NU is more cultural. Politically, NU is stronger because it has many links (*linknya itu banyak*)....[13]

These explanations clearly describe NU's political alienation during the New Order. Although Pekalongan had a strong base of NU followers, politically NU's interest was represented in PPP (the only Islamic party allowed during the New Order), which was defeated by Golkar in the 1992 and 1997 General Elections and by PDIP in the 1999 General Election. Ordinary NU followers and the NU elite hoped for the right political momentum to take political control in the region where the NU cultural tradition was at its strongest. The political momentum they sought emerged in 2004 when PKB won the highest number of seats in Pekalongan DPRD. PKB's newfound political power came at the right time for the first direct election to be held in Pekalongan in 2006. The right political momentum (PKB's strong power and the 2006 direct election) boosted PKB's confidence in its ability to claim power by fielding its own candidate for regent, and it selected Siti Qomariyah. AKB, a member of Siti Qomariyah's campaign team and chief of Pekalongan DPRD (2004–11) from PKB, explained the rationale behind choosing Siti as PKB's candidate for regent:

> First, she was a PKB cadre, an NU cadre, and a PKB member who had an excellent education... fortunately she was *female* [emphasis added] and was born of a prominent NU family. Her father is a *kyai*. The place where she was born is Buaran, an NU pocket.... Thus, at that time she was the best cadre who had served quite successfully as

---

[13] Interview with Siti Qomariyah in the official house of the regent of Pekalongan, 21 June 2009.

vice-regent. She had the potential to be elevated to regent. Therefore we elevated her and she was supported fully by all NU components in society. Thus, at the time NU was in total support of her.... So we chose her to fill the position in the executive body. There are strategies to secure [both] bodies of power, namely having people elected in the executive body and in the legislative body [AKB was in the legislative body as chief of Pekalongan DPRD for two periods].[14]

AKB's explanation does, to some extent, support Siti's statement that she actually did not want to run again in the 2006 direct election, but that NU elites, some from Muslimat NU, encouraged her re-nomination. She said:

> My first capital is because I am *female* [emphasis added] (*saya itu perempun*). Thus those who promoted and registered my name were women (*kaum perempuan*). Muslimat [NU] initially recommended my name to Pak *Kyai* [from an interview with the chief of Muslimat NU in Pekalongan, *kyai* here refers to Kyai Taufiq and Habib Lutfi]. We had a preliminary discussion with Muslimat...I had never joined Muslimat, maybe because of my family capital as I have a clear NU tradition, a clear affiliation with PKB...it is still difficult to imagine how a villager (*orang kampung*) can become *bupati*. [In the past it was impossible for NU followers, who were often considered *orang kampung*, to become *bupati*, but people wanted this change.][15]

As can be seen in these two interviews, to the strategists, Siti Qomariyah's gender as a female candidate was not a hindrance, but a political selling point. Siti later incorporated her gender into her political strategy to create distinct identity politics in the 2006 direct election.

Siti Qomariyah also explained that in mid-2005, long before PKB's official declaration, Muslimat NU under FA's leadership went to influential *kyai* such as *Kyai* Taufiq and Habib Lutfi, chief of the Indonesian Council of Ulama in Central Java, for permission to nominate Siti Qomariyah as the candidate for regent in the 2006 direct election.[16] Further

---

[14] Interview with AKB, member of Siti Qomariyah's campaign team and chief of Pekalongan DPRD (2004–11) from PKB, Pekalongan, 29 June 2009.
[15] Interview with Siti Qomariyah in the official house of the regent of Pekalongan, 17 June 2009.
[16] Interview with Siti Qomariyah in the official house of the regent of Pekalongan, 21 June 2009.

clarification with FA, chief of Muslimat NU in Pekalongan (2005–10), revealed other interesting facts. In one Muslimat NU meeting, FA urged Siti to run as the candidate for regent. FA recalled:

> It was around 2005, and she [Siti Qomariyah] had nearly finished her term. People started talking about who would be the next candidate. I made suggestions to Ibu [Siti Qomariyah] because she had experience as the vice-regent, and here [in Pekalongan] PKB won 15 seats as the majority [in the 2004 General Election]...I suggested that for the sake of Pekalongan's progress and to elevate women's dignity, that she was capable of being regent. And then Ibu [Siti Qomariyah] answered, "If the *kyai* agree, I will not refuse"....[17]

We can see that Siti Qomariyah's re-election in the 2006 election was possible because of the right political momentum—the NU elite in Pekalongan could maximize their political goals and interests via PKB, in combination with initiatives from Muslimat NU in Pekalongan, which wanted to make changes in Pekalongan. The leader of Muslimat NU, and Muslimat NU as an institution, played a significant role in promoting Siti Qomariyah as a promising leader for the 2006 direct election.

Siti's name was circulated among the NU elite in the region. *Kyai* MA, vice-chief of the Regional Board of PKB in Pekalongan (2002–08), explained that in the lead-up to the PKB internal meeting to decide on the candidate for regent, *Kyai* SB, chief of NU in Pekalongan (2007–12), favoured Siti and asked *Kyai* MA to invite Siti to the PKB meeting.[18] Politically, *Kyai* SB was in conflict with *Kyai* BR, chief of the Regional Board of PKB in Pekalongan (2002–08), because of the former's decision to run as chief of the Provincial Board of PKB in Central Java without permission from the latter. Therefore, when *Kyai* SB heard rumours that *Kyai* BR would run as a candidate for regent, he did not support him.

Further, in the special meeting of the Regional Board of PKB in Pekalongan held on 31 December 2005, two names appeared as the strongest candidates, namely Siti Qomariyah and *Kyai* BR. Siti gained more support from NU followers in the meeting, with at least 11 of the 19 sub-branches (Pengurus Anak Cabang, PAC, at the district level)

---

[17] Interview with FA, chief of Muslimat NU in Pekalongan (2005–10), Pekalongan, 22 June 2009.
[18] Interview with *Kyai* MA, vice-chief of the Regional Board of PKB in Pekalongan (2002–08), in Pekalongan, 22 June 2009.

of PKB voting for her.[19] Eventually, the Pekalongan Regional Board of PKB, based on the decree from the Central Board of PKB under the leadership of Abdurrahman Wahid (*Gus* Dur) No. 876/DPP-02/IV/A.I/II 2006, officially nominated Siti Qomariyah as PKB's candidate for regent in partnership with Wahyudi Pontjo Nugroho from Golkar.[20] Wahyudi Ponjto Nugroho was a bureaucrat in Pekalongan and an influential Golkar cadre who had very good social networks in the region. He is, for instance, chief of Pemuda Pancasila (2004–present) and chief of KONI (Komite Olahraga Nasional Indonesia, the Indonesian Sports Committee) in Pekalongan (2005–present). Pontjo Nugroho won nearly 90 per cent of the votes from the Regional Board of Golkar in Pekalongan, defeating the other two contenders, and thus was nominated as the vice-regent candidate from Golkar, in pair with Siti Qomariyah.[21]

Securing Religious Support from Prominent NU *Kyai*

Securing religious permission and support from prominent NU *kyai* in Pekalongan is a crucial aspect for those who want to make a political stand in the region because it is a strong pocket of NU *santri*. In this section, we will examine the ways in which Siti's re-election was made possible because of *restu* (religious permission) from two of the most influential *kyai* in the region, namely *Kyai* Taufiq and Habib Lutfi.

Kyai Taufiq (b. 1950) leads At-Taufiqy Pesantren which has more than 100 *santri*. His charisma has attracted many NU followers not only in Pekalongan but also outside the region. This is reflected in the millions of people who walk, ride bicycles or drive to attend the routine *pengajian* (religious propagation) led by *Kyai* Taufiq for women every Tuesday morning (7–10 am) and for men every Wednesday night (6–10 pm). People in Pekalongan are accustomed to the traffic and the appearance of informal markets (*pasar tiban*) selling Islamic items along the street near

---

[19] The 11 district branches of PKB that favoured Siti Qomariyah were Doro, Petungkriyono, Lebakbarang, Karanganyar, Kajen, Bojong, Kedungwuni, Wonopringgo, Buaran, Siwalan and Wonokerto. See *Data Rekapitulasi Form Penilain Calon Kepala Daerah PKB Kabupaten Pekalongan* (Pekalongan: DPC Partai Kebangkitan Bangsa Kabupaten Pekalongan, 2005).

[20] "Qomariyah-Pontjo Resmi Berpasangan", *Radar Pekalongan*, 22 Feb. 2006.

[21] Interview with MCH, chief of the Regional Board of Golkar in Pekalongan (1999–2009), in Pekalongan, 30 June 2009. See also "Pontjo Menang Konvensi", *Radar Pekalongan*, 6 Feb. 2006.

Kyai Taufiq's *pesantren*. With the help of Ibu FA, I was able to attend a *pengajian* on a Tuesday morning, which was attended by approximately 12,000 women, and then to go inside *Kyai* Taufiq's house and sit near him. *Kyai* Taufiq has never revealed his face to the women attending these *pengajian*, and always keeps a green curtain (*hijab*) to separate his *mimbar* (the area where he sits) in an inner room, which is encircled by a wooden bench to separate him from the women who sit in front of him. The *pengajian* start with chanting of the *Al-Fatihah* verse followed with *istighfar* (*astagfirullah*) and *tasbih* (*subhannallah*).[22] Once this is finished, *Kyai* Taufiq begins to talk in a very calm and soft voice, sometimes interspersed with humour, and finishes by chanting the *sholawat* for Prophet Mohammad. Those who ask questions cannot ask them directly to *Kyai* Taufiq. They write their question on a piece of paper and give it to his assistant, who sits inside the inner room, through a small window. It is forbidden to take any pictures or record the activities of the *pengajian*, yet I was able to take a few pictures depicting the surrounding *pengajian* atmosphere as can be seen in Figure 3.

Habib M. Lutfi Ali Bin Ayahya is the chief of the Indonesia Council of Ulama (Majelis Ulama Indonesia, MUI) in Central Java. He has a special *tareqah* group with millions of followers, including women. He usually holds *pengajian* for men on Wednesday or Thursday evenings. Sometimes, he gives talks on Sunday mornings (*pengajian ahad pagi*) with the location moving from one district to another throughout Pekalongan.

In order to obtain religious permission from *Kyai* Taufiq, Siti required assistance from Ibu FA, who is a close relative of *Kyai* Taufiq. In fact, it was Ibu FA who initially went to influential *kyai* such as *Kyai* Taufiq and Habib Lutfi to get permission to nominate Siti Qomariyah as a candidate for regent in the 2006 direct election. Long before the official nomination from PKB, according to FA, Habib Lutfi endorsed Siti Qomariyah and asked Muslimat NU to support her.[23] FA's account is similar to the one given by Wahyudi Pontjo Nugroho (Golkar). He said:

> Initially, Golkar and PKB would not fit together...while all the *kyai* failed to unite Golkar and PKB, to be honest it was Habib Lutfi who

---

[22] Both are special Islamic chants. *Astagfirullah* asks for forgiveness from God, while *subhannallah* gives praise to God.
[23] Interview with Ibu FA, chief of Muslimat NU in Pekalongan (2005–10), 22 June 2010.

Source: Photograph taken by author, 3 June 2009.

Figure 3 *Pengajian* for Women Every Tuesday Morning at *Kyai* Taufiq's *Pesantren*

succeeded. At the time, all the Dewan Syuro of PKB, the board of Golkar including its chief, myself and Bu Qom [Siti Qomariyah] were invited to his house in Pekalongan. He said "*pokoke Pilkada sesuk sing maju Qomariyah, titik!*" (It is instructed that Qomariyah will be nominated for the next election [2006 direct regent election]).[24]

When I interviewed Siti, she also said that while the internal recruitment process inside the Regional Board of PKB in Pekalongan was still underway, it was Habib Lutfi who urged her to go through with, and prepare quickly for, a nomination in the 2006 election.[25] Habib Lutfi claimed neutrality, so he did not publicly display his support for Siti.[26] Ibu FA

---

[24] Interview with Wahyudi Pontjo Nugroho, vice-regent of Pekalongan (2001–11), in the office of the vice-regent of Pekalongan, 23 July 2010.
[25] Interview with Siti Qomariyah at the official house of the regent of Pekalongan, 21 June 2009.
[26] "Ketua MUI Jateng Habib M Luthfy Ali Bin Yahya: Saya Bukan Milik Salah Satu Kelompok", *Koran Wawasan*, 31 March 2006.

further explained *Kyai* Taufiq rationale and the power of his *doa* (blessing, religious endorsement from a *kyai*) for Siti's success:

> Maybe because according to Kyai Taufiq, it was time to struggle so that the regent of Pekalongan would be in the hands of NU... Kyai are the most important thing, due to [the power of] their *doa*. I still believe in the power of [these blessings]. For example, when we conduct *pengajian* (religious gatherings) we hold *istighozah* (collective *doa*) where *kyai* deliver *doa*.[27]

Here we can see the centrality of *kyai* in the NU cultural and religious tradition in influencing the political behaviour of NU followers, including in supporting women such as Siti Qomariyah. It is clear that these two influential NU *kyai* in Pekalongan do not oppose women's leadership in local politics. My interview with *Kyai* SB confirmed this:

> We [NU in Pekalongan] are aware that the position of regent is not the highest leadership position in the state. There are also the positions of governor and president. Therefore it is okay.[28]

Similarly, *Kyai* MA, the vice-chief of the Regional Board of PKB in Pekalongan (2002–08), explained:

> I support women's leadership based on the decision of the *batsul matsail* in East Java maybe in 1982 [he was not sure about the year].... At that time, the NU Congress decided that women's leadership was allowed as long as it pertained to worldly matters (*urusan dunia*) and not religious matters... it means [women could not be] *syariah* leaders. It means they could be regents.... Yet, I am not sure about president because the position rules over everything... Kyai [in Pekalongan] have never discussed it. This is my own analysis according to my reading, including the result of the Muktamar in 1982.[29]

Clearly, Siti's political re-engagement in the 2006 direct election was strongly supported by religious legitimacy from the most influential NU

---

[27] Interview with FA, chief of Muslimat NU in Pekalongan (2005–10), 22 June 2010.
[28] Interview with *Kyai* SB, chief of the Regional Board of NU in Pekalongan (2007–11), Pekalongan, 20 June 2009.
[29] Interview with *Kyai* MA, vice-chief of the Regional Board of PKB in Pekalongan (2002–08), Pekalongan, 22 June 2010.

kyai, which later consolidated NU power in the 2006 direct election. The general public also knew that Siti Qomariyah and Pontjo gained support from the majority of NU *kyai* in Pekalongan,[30] which further strengthened their political acceptability.

Some people may argue that the prominent NU *kyai* in Pekalongan who supported Siti Qomariyah's nomination did so merely based on a political desire to support their favourite candidate. However, we cannot ignore the fact that NU *kyai*'s positions which support female leadership (at the levels below president) are always based on the decision of the *batsul matsail* on women's leadership, which, since the 1950s, has supported female leadership in political positions, and, in an even more progressive move, has supported female leadership as president since 1997, as I have explained in Chapter 3.

From the above story, we can see that Siti's political rise in the 2006 direct election through PKB was to some extent "orchestrated", and was strongly supported with religious legitimacy from the most influential NU *kyai*. The general public also knew that Siti Qomariyah and Pontjo were the pair which gained support from the majority of NU *kyai* in Pekalongan,[31] which even further strengthened their political acceptability. Here I note that for candidates from Islamic-based organization such as Siti Qomariyah, strong endorsement by the Islamic mass organization to which she was affiliated was crucial to generate political support. In this case, Siti Qomariyah as a female Muslim candidate gained strong support from NU Pekalongan and endorsement from NU *kyai*. In NU cultural and religious traditions, *kyai*'s support is central to influencing the political behaviour of NU followers including the support of Siti Qomariyah's nomination.

The 2006 Direct Election in Pekalongan: Contenders

There were two pairs of candidates who competed in the 2006 direct election, namely Siti Qomariyah and Wahyudi Pontjo Nugroho (PKB, Golkar), and Amat Antono and H.A. Qurofi Hajin (PDIP). Their profiles can be seen in Table 8.

---

[30] "Pasangan Siti Qomariyah dan H Wahyudi Pontjo Nugroho MT Dapat Simpati Rakyat", *Cakrawala*, no. 247: 2–6 May 2006.
[31] Ibid.

Table 8 Profile of Regent and Vice-regent Candidates in the 2006 Direct Election in Pekalongan

No. in Ballot Paper	Political Party	Name of Regent and Vice-regent Candidates	Profile
1	PDIP (supported by PPP,[32] PAN, PBB, and a coalition of 15 political parties)	**H. Amat Antono**	Born in Tegal Dowo, Tirto District, Pekalongan, 5 October 1958. Bureaucrat in Sambas, Kalimantan. Regent of Pekalongan (2001–06).
		H.A. Qurofi Hajin, BA	Teacher, activist with NU in Pekalongan, married to a prominent figure in 'Aisyiyah in Pekalongan.
2	PKB, Golkar	**Hj. Siti Qomariyah, MA**	Born in Pekalongan, 8 July 1967. Lecturer at STAIN Pekalongan (1992–present), vice-regent of Pekalongan (2001–06).
		Ir. H. Wahyudi Pontjo Nugroho, MT	Born in Magelang, 9 May 1957. Chief of the Bureau of Workers in Pekalongan (1997–2006).

Note: Names in bold represent the candidates for regent.

Source: Compiled by author from diverse sources including newspapers and the personal CVs of Siti Qomariyah and Wahyudi Pontjo Nugroho.

The table above shows that the former regent and vice-regent of Pekalongan competed against one another in the 2006 direct election. It is also obvious that Amat Antono, who comes from a nationalist background, sought Islamic support from both NU (because A. Qurofi Hajin comes from the NU tradition) or Muhammadiyah (because Qurofi's wife is a prominent activist of Muhammadiyah and 'Aisyiyah). Antono and

---

[32] According to the explanation by H. Mustain Huda, chief of the Regional Board of PPP in Pekalongan, PPP supported AQUR because they were being consistent with Islamic *syariah* which suggests electing male leaders, as he explained in the article "PPP Sasaran Selebaran Gelap", *Koran Wawasan*, 14 May 2006.

Qurofi's partnership was referred to with the acronym AQUR, while Siti Qomariyah and Pontjo were known as QONCO during the campaign.[33] Siti Qomariyah was quite confident of her support from the NU elite and followers in the region but also gained support from PKS and the Democratic Party,[34] and later PBB (Partai Bulan Bintang, the Star and Crescent Party), though some PBB district branches supported AQUR.[35]

On 3 May 2006, the two pairs presented their visions and missions to the Pekalongan DPRD. Antono and Qurofi promised to achieve a prosperous, productive society with sustainable development and Siti and Pontjo promised to create a democratized, progressive and prosperous society.[36] The two pairs launched open campaigns and gathered crowds of supporters in various districts during the six campaign rounds regulated by the General Election Commission in Pekalongan.[37] The next section will elaborate on the strategy used by Siti Qomariyah and her team to win the 2006 direct election.

Campaign Strategy: Selling Islamic Piety and Using Gender

In the NU cultural tradition, the position and respect of an individual is often determined by the family line and whether or not they are descendants of *kyai* and thus so-called *darah biru* (literally blue blood). Because Siti's father is a *kampong* or village *kyai*, Siti is considered to have *darah biru* and thus acquired quite a high level of respect among the NU elite in the region. This family background in combination with Siti's Islamic appearance and consistency in wearing a veil contributed to her image as a modern, pious NU woman, which made the NU elite proud of her. As Ibu FA stated, "Bu Qom is a person with a strong religious commitment."[38] Here we can see that, Siti Qomariyah's persistent

---

[33] "PPKB Alihkan Dukungan ke Qonco", *Suara Merdeka*, 3 May 2006; "PBB Alihkan Dukungan ke Qonco", *Suara Merdeka*, 5 May 2006.
[34] Interview with CS, chief of the Regional Board of PKS in Pekalongan, 24 June 2009.
[35] "12 PAC PBB Tetap Dukung AQUR", *Koran Wawasan*, 10 May 2006.
[36] See "2 Cabup Sampaikan Visi-Misi", *Koran Wawasan*, 4 May 2006.
[37] See media coverage related to their campaign in "Kirab Peserta Pilkada Disambut Hujan Lebat", *Suara Merdeka*, 4 May 2006; "Kampanye Putaran Pertama: AQUR Gelar Rapat Terbuka", *Suara Merdeka*, 5 May 2006; "Pendukung Qonco Penuhi Lapangan Wiradesa", *Suara Merdeka*, 8 May 2006.
[38] Interview with FA, chief of Muslimat NU in Pekalongan (2005–10), 22 June 2009.

piety served as—to borrow from Derichs, Fleschenberg and Hustebeck[39]—"moral capital".

Siti's pious image together with her thoughtful positioning of her gender helped her to win the 2006 direct election. For example, in her initial move to gain support from the Regional Board of PKB in Pekalongan and from Muslimat NU women, she attended the special meeting of the Regional Board of PKB in Pekalongan held on 31 December 2005 together with her husband, as I saw in a photographic collection of Dewan Pimpinan Cabang PKB Pekalongan, dated June 2009.

By attending the meeting with her husband, Siti demonstrated to the public that she had the support of her husband for her nomination as a female candidate for regent, and that although she would be exceeding her husband's public position it would not disrupt the primary relationship and authority in their family. In so doing, she gained wider sympathy from the majority of Muslim voters who were happy to see a smart, modern NU woman who maintained her piety by respecting and maintaining harmony in her family. Again, as did Rustriningsih, Siti Qomariyah utilized the idealized gender norms of *wanita sholehah* (pious women in Islam) and true women in Javanese society, rather than challenging them. In her wider campaign, Siti presented herself as a smart, pretty and down to earth (*pintar, cantik, merakyat*) female regent candidate.

Once Siti Qomariyah and Pontjo were officially nominated by the Regional Board of PKB in Pekalongan, AB and Siti's campaign team, with help from the Institute for Economic and Social Research, Education and Analysis (Lembaga Penelitian, Pendidikan dan Penerangan Ekonomi dan Sosial, LP3ES), conducted two surveys. In the first survey in March when the campaign began, Antono was more popular and won 40 per cent of votes while Siti Qomariyah only won 18 per cent of votes. However in the second survey, as Antono's popularity declined, Siti Qomariyah's increased.[40] According to AB, the rising popularity of Siti in the second survey was due to the campaign team's strategy in

---

[39] Derichs, Fleschenberg and Hustebeck, "Gendering Moral Capital: Morality as a Political Asset and Strategy of Top Female Politicians in Asia", in *Religious Fundamentalism and Their Gendered Impacts in Asia*, ed. Claudia Derichs and Andrea Fleschenberg, pp. 245–66 (Berlin: Friederich-Ebert-Stiftung, 2010).
[40] Interview with AB, secretary of the *Tanfidz* of the Regional Board of PKB in Pekalongan (2002–07), 17 June 2009.

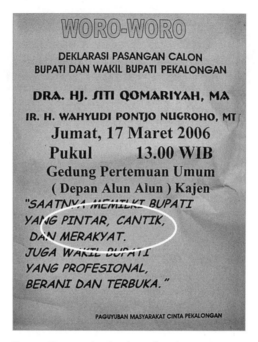

Source: Photograph taken by author, June 2009.

Figure 4 Campaign Pamphlet for Siti Qomariyah and Pontjo in the 2006 Direct Election

using the first campaign to effectively introduce their candidates (*pawai ta'aruf*). NU followers made a strong contribution by providing materials such as posters and pamphlets and penetrating Antono's voter base.[41]

The slogans "please choose a woman" (*pilih wadon bae*) and "please choose the only woman" (*wadon wae, wadon wae*) circulated during the campaign,[42] including one campaign in Sijambe, Sragi, Pekalongan, on 11 May 2006 where the crowds sang "*wadon bae, wadon bae, wadon bae bupatine*".[43] AKB, a member of Siti Qomariyah's election team and chief of Pekalongan DPRD (2004–11) from PKB, explained the effectiveness of this slogan:

---

[41] Ibid.
[42] Interview with AB, secretary of the *Tanfidz* of the Regional Board of PKB in Pekalongan (2002–07) and chief of Siti's campaign team, 17 June 2009.
[43] "Kampanye Qomariyah-Ponco: Massa Tertahan di Jalan Raya", *Suara Merdeka*, 12 May 2006.

At that time, there was an idiom "*wadon wae, wadon wae, wadon wae*". This became an important attraction for women to support Bu Qom and it occurred across political parties and ideologies.[44]

The slogan "*wadon bae*" continued to be used in rallies and campaigns as I had seen from the photographic collection of Komisi Pemilihan Umum Kabupaten Pekalongan, dated June 2009.

Through pamphlets and slogans we can see that Siti considerably emphasized her distinct gender identity as the only female Javanese Muslim NU candidate, pious, and modern. Another interesting feature of Siti's strategy in generating support among Muslimat NU women was through discussing her relative lack of power in her former position as vice-regent (2001–06) to create an image of being weak:

> At the time, the *bupati* [Amat Antono] rejected all of my aspirations.... He thought that if I could not propose my aspirations, I would withdraw [from the position of vice-regent of Pekalongan]. In fact, our spirit was raised yesterday because our effort had not yet succeeded.... The TPQ Program [Taman Pendidikan Al-Qur'an, The Qur'an Education Group] was opposed (*Dia pikirannya kalau saya menggoalkan aspirasi nggak bisa, pasti akan mundur, kita itu justru semangat karena kemarin kita belum berhasil... TPQ dihadang*). None of my suggestions had ever been accepted. Therefore, society felt that their aspirations had not been fulfilled.... And I never made any act of resistance. We created a sympathetic act as a kind of campaign.[45]

ZFR, Secretary General of the Regional Board of PKB in Pekalongan, noted the same feature:

> When she gave speeches in religious gatherings at Fatayat NU or Muslimat NU, she sometimes cried. It made people feel sympathy.... This was around 2005.... Even closer to the direct election day, in almost every speech she cried in front [of the audience as a way of expressing her sadness that as vice-regent of Pekalongan she was being alienated by Regent Amat Antono]....[46]

---

[44] Interview with AKB, member of Siti Qomariyah's campaign team and chief of Pekalongan DPRD (2004–11) from PKB, Pekalongan, 29 June 2009.
[45] Interview with Siti Qomariyah, in the official house of the regent of Pekalongan, 17 June 2009.
[46] Interview with ZFR, Secretary General of the Regional Board of PKB in Pekalongan, 26 June 2009.

This sort of strategy was intended to increase sympathy for and solidarity with Siti Qomariyah among female NU followers. And although at that time, they had Siti as vice-regent from NU it did not guarantee that their interests would be fulfilled unless Siti became regent. Interestingly, Siti's successful use of tears to gain political sympathy seems also in line with current findings in western campaigns. While previously there was a stereotype that female candidates who cried were at a disadvantage relative to male candidates, according to Deborah Jordan Brooks's research there is no longer truth to that perception. In a sample of US adults, Brooks discovered that crying increases perceptions of empathy in female candidates and thus does not disadvantage them.[47]

Intensifying Women's Networks and Using *Mauluddan* Events

Once Siti was officially declared the PKB candidate for regent, she did not have significant difficulties in gathering the support of female NU-based followers across social classes and geographic settings. Siti intensified women's networks via Muslimat NU and Fatayat NU. She was assisted mainly by FA, who used *pengajian* (religious propagation) of Muslimat NU held across villages that were attended by women and men and organized by the district branches of Muslimat NU.

There are 18 district branches and 312 sub-district branches (at the village level) of Muslimat NU across Pekalongan, and FA was convinced of the effectiveness of this Muslimat NU network, noting, "We [Muslimat NU in Pekalongan] are like bureaucrats. Just push the button and it will work all the way down."[48] Siti also owed much to women's networks in Fatayat NU and Women of the National Awakening Party (Perempuan Partai Kebangkitan Bangsa, PPKB). HD, chief of Fatayat NU in Pekalongan (2000–10) and chief of PPKB (2009–14), explained that in promoting Siti, she did not officially use Fatayat NU as an organization. Instead she and other Muslimat NU women and women in PPKB created the Team of Nine (*tim sembilan*) which, together with Siti Qomariyah, conducted *pengajian* in more than two hundred villages in the three months before the official campaign period.[49] Both FA and HD affirmed that they were also helped by *nyai* (wife of *kyai*) in various

---

[47] Brooks, "Testing the Double Standard for Candidate Emotionality", pp. 597–615.
[48] Interview with FA, chief of Muslimat NU in Pekalongan (2005–10), 22 June 2009.
[49] Interview with HD, chief of Fatayat NU in Pekalongan (2000–10) and chief of PPKB (2009–14), Pekalongan DPRD, 2 July 2009.

pesantren to promote Siti and influence NU followers to choose her. Siti did not have much money,[50] so Muslimat NU and Fatayat NU followers bore all the costs of the *pengajian* and socialization.[51] Their effort was supported by NU *kyai* such as the prominent businessman, *Kyai* MA, vice-chief of the Regional Board of PKB in Pekalongan (2002–08). He said, "…I created and gave out 1,600 *kerudung*. This was for people who attended the campaign…."[52] The illustration of the women's networks can be seen in Figure 5.

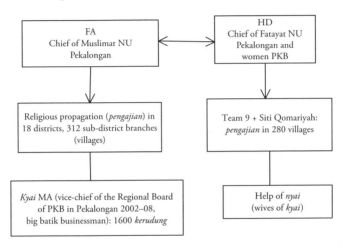

Source: Author, based on interviews.

Figure 5 Women's Networks behind Siti Qomariyah's Victory

---

[50] In one of my interviews with Siti Qomariyah, she said that she only had Rp 250,000,000 as primary capital with which to fund her election, a very small amount. She also acknowledged her strong reliance on her NU-based supporters. Interview with Siti Qomariyah, 17 June 2009. This reminded me of a comment that AB made in conversation before I met Siti Qomariyah. According to AB, someone who wants to compete in a direct election should have *jeneng* and *jenang*. *Jeneng* is the Javanese word for name, which refers to popularity, while *jenang* is money, literally a very sweet traditional Javanese food that ants are easily attracted to. In the context of politics, having *jenang* means having a lot of money. So, according to AB, Siti Qomariyah was not rich, but by implication, she did have a great deal of charisma and drew people's interest. Interview with AB, secretary of the *Tanfidz* of the Regional Board of PKB in Pekalongan (2002–07) and chief of Siti's campaign team, 17 June 2009.
[51] Interview with FA and HD on 22 June 2009 and 2 July 2009, respectively, in Pekalongan.
[52] Interview with *Kyai* MA, vice-chief of the Regional Board of PKB in Pekalongan (2002–08), Pekalongan, 22 June 2010.

Interestingly, FA was also approached by the wife of Qurofi, an NU figure who ran for vice-regent with Antono, to promote the Antono-Qurofi team through Muslimat NU. When Qurofi's wife attended *pengajian*, FA avoided endorsing any of the candidates. Yet, in other *pengajian*, FA explicitly asked NU followers to vote for Siti—NU's "strong cadre" —such as in the *pengajian* that was held in commemoration of the birth of Prophet Muhammad (*Mauluddan*).[53] FA gave out a VCD titled "*Pengajian Mauluddan*", which featured Siti attending the *pengajian* and aimed to promote Siti's nomination among NU-based voters with help from Muslimat NU. See Figure 6.

Source: Author, 22 June 2009.

Figure 6 Example of the *Mauluddan Pengajian* VCD and Promotion of Siti Qomariyah's Nomination

In order to consolidate NU followers across the region, Siti Qomariyah and her team held an *Istiqhotsah Kubro* (a mass *pengajian* where followers collectively chant verses from the Qur'an) on 28 April 2006 in Siti's official house as vice-regent of Pekalongan to also celebrate *Mauluddan*. The *istiqozah*, which was attended by thousand of NU followers, was led by many prominent *kyai* such as Habib Lutfi, *Kyai* Akrom Shofwan, *Kyai* Failasuf, *Kyai* Zuhdi Hariri, *Kyai* Ilyas Jaza, *Kyai*

---

[53] Interview with FA, chief of Muslimat NU in Pekalongan (2005–10), 22 June 2009.

Izzurahman, *Kyai* Abdullah and *Kyai* Imron Masyhadi.⁵⁴ During the event, Habib M. Lutfi, chief of the Indonesian Council of Ulama in Central Java, asked NU followers to follow Prophet Mohammad's teachings including the example of elevating women's dignity and thus supporting women in playing public roles, as Siti Qomariyah was doing.⁵⁵

Siti's victory was also aided by the weaknesses of Amat Antono's team due to fragmentation inside PDIP and the particular nature of Antono's support base, mainly public servants,⁵⁶ including the network of village heads,⁵⁷ and the perceived arrogant style of Antono's leadership.⁵⁸ Despite such circumstances, Antono's team kept promoting the pair as shown in the pamphlet below.

Source: Author, June 2009.

Figure 7 Example of Antono and Qurofi's Campaign Pamphlet

---

⁵⁴ "Ribuan Orang Ikuti Istighotsah Kubro".
⁵⁵ Ibid.
⁵⁶ Interview with SUR, volunteer on Antono's campaign team, 26 June 2009.
⁵⁷ Interview with KRM, board member of Muhammadiyah in Pekalongan, member of the Regional Board of PAN in Pekalongan and treasurer of Antono's campaign team, Pekalongan, 2 July 2009.
⁵⁸ Interview with MM, former vice-regent candidate from Golkar in the 2001 regent election in Pekalongan and chief of the Small to Medium Enterprises and Cooperatives Bureau in Pekalongan, 25 June 2009 and interview with AR, NGO activist in Pekalongan, 23 June 2009.

In addition to the network of village heads, Antono tried to generate support from Muhammadiyah's elite, for example by approaching FAK, chief of Muhammadiyah in Pekalongan, though FAK maintained the neutrality of Muhammadiyah.[59] Interestingly, 'Aisyiyah in Pekalongan deliberately supported Antono and Qurofi as stated by DRM, the vice-chief of 'Aisyiyah in Pekalongan:

> I am from 'Aisyiyah and I said to Muhammadiyah "I have asked my people ['Aisyiyah members] to vote for Pak Antono and his vice-regent partner, Pak Qurofi. Because the wife of Pak Qurofi is the chief of the Muhammadiyah Education Bureau [in Pekalongan].[60]

An additional factor that contributed to Siti Qomariyah's victory was due to a "black campaign" which concerned an alleged affair between Siti and Pontjo. Three days before the election day in 2006, some members of Antono's team published shocking pictures of Siti and Pontjo together supposedly displaying their intimacy.[61] The pictures caused uncertainty about the morality and trustworthiness of Siti among *kyai* and NU followers. From many interviews with NU *kyai* I found that initially they doubted Siti's trustworthiness. There was a series of religious meetings between Siti and NU *kyai* in response to the pictures and the *kyai* decided to believe in Siti.[62] Even Siti's campaign team believes that Siti benefited from the negative campaigning as she gained sympathy from swing voters who eventually voted for her.[63] Eventually, Siti Qomariyah and Pontjo won the election by gaining approximately 52 per cent of votes, as depicted in Graph 3.

---

[59] Siti Qomariyah also approached FAK. Interview with FAK, chief of Muhammadiyah in Pekalongan, 25 June 2009.

[60] Interview with DRM, vice-chief of 'Aisyiyah in Pekalongan, 25 June 2009.

[61] According to CKW, he actually warned his team not to publish the pictures as he thought it might be a blunder for Antono as the public would be more sympathetic towards Siti. Interview with CKW, chief of Antono's campaign team in the 2006 direct election in Pekalongan, 3 July 2009.

[62] Interview with *Kyai* MA, vice-chief of the Regional Board of PKB in Pekalongan (2002–08), 22 June 2010; interview with *Kyai* JA, vice-chief of the *Syuriah* of the Regional Board of PKB in Pekalongan, 22 June 2009; and with *Kyai* BR, chief of the Regional Board of PKB in Pekalongan (2002–08), 21 June 2009.

[63] Interview with AB, secretary of the *Tanfidz* of the Regional Board of PKB in Pekalongan (2002–07) and chief of Siti's campaign team, 17 June 2009.

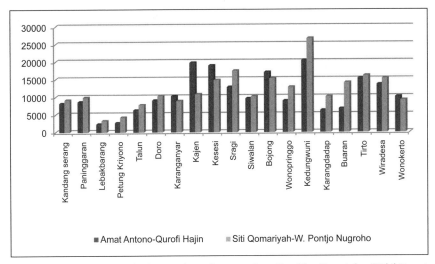

Source: Author, from "Rekapitulasi Hasil Penghitungan Suara PemilihanBupati dan Wakil Bupati Pekalongan Tahun 2006 di Tingkat Kabupaten", in *Dokumentasi Penyelenggaraan Pemilihan Bupati Dan Wakil Bupati Pekalongan Tahun 2006* (Pekalongan: Komisi Pemilihan Umum Kabupaten Pekalongan, 2006), p. 134.

Graph 3 Distribution of Votes across Districts as a Result of the 2006 Direct Election in Pekalongan

Graph 3 shows that Siti Qomariyah and Pontjo won the majority of votes in 14 districts and gained the highest number of votes in Kedungwuni, which is well known as the main pocket of Nahdlatul Ulama. They also secured three other known NU pockets, namely Wonopringgo, Karangdadap and Buaran. Antono and Qurofi, however, only won in five districts, namely Karanganyar, Kajen, Kesesi, Bojong and Wonokerto. Although there were a series of demonstrations by a group of people asking the Ministry of Home Affairs not to inaugurate Siti and Pontjo as the elected regent and vice-regent,[64] they officially became regent and vice-regent of Pekalongan (2006–11).

Policies on Women's Issues

This section is devoted to assessing Siti Qomariyah's policies as a leader and whether she has met the normative expectation that female leaders

---

[64] See for example "Kasus Foto Selingkuh, Goyang Qonco" and "Qonco Digoyang Foto Selingkuh", *Radar Pekalongan*, 26 May 2006.

pay more attention to women's issues and have women's perspectives in their policies. In regards to her leadership, Siti Qomariyah actually tried to embrace various entities, including Muhammadiyah and 'Aisyiyah and non-Muslim groups as well. Siti stated in one interview:

> ... Every Christmas I gave funds to all churches. There are 11 churches and each received two million rupiah ... I just wanted to ensure justice for everyone. I wanted to try to embrace every element and not to take sides with particular groups. And if we did defend [some groups] it was based on social awareness. For many years, NU was not supported by the government. They [NU] are the majority, yet they have never been considered so by the government. In fact, they should have gained rights proportional to their numbers. This is not because I have sided with NU, but because of proportions. For example, the number of TPQ [Taman Pendidikan Al-Qur'an, Quran Learning Group] associated with NU is higher than those associated with Muhammadiyah.... We [NU] and Muhammadiyah are complementary to each other. Muhammadiyah has a formal role, while NU has a cultural role. Who taught us this? It was our ancestors.... We are complementary. I respect Muhammadiyah. I also support NU.[65]

While Siti predominantly has a strong base in NU women's networks, she also maintains a good relationship with Muhammadiyah women and men. I spoke with RS, a prominent secretary of Muhammadiyah in Pekalongan; KU, a prominent member of Nasyiatul 'Aisyiyah; and SCH chief of Nasyiatul 'Aisyiyah in Pekalongan, and all of them confirmed Siti's effort to embrace various entities in the region including Muhammadiyah and its women's needs.[66] Siti's relatively neutral position, evident for example in her refusal to campaign for PKB national candidates in the 2009 legislative election, or for presidential candidates Susilo Bambang Yudhoyono and Boediono who were endorsed by PKB in the 2009 Presidential Election, caused disappointment among PKB elites in Pekalongan.[67]

Despite this, having a confident female *bupati* does not guarantee that women's needs and problems are better addressed in Pekalongan. In

---

[65] Interview with Siti Qomariyah in the official house of the vice-regent of Pekalongan, 21 June 2009.

[66] Interview with RS, secretary of Muhammadiyah in Pekalongan, 3 July 3009; and KU, prominent activist with Nasyiatul 'Aisyiyah in Pekalongan, 23 June 2009; and SCH, chief of Nasyiatul 'Aisyiyah in Pekalongan (2004–09), 25 June 2009.

[67] Interview with *Kyai* MA, vice-chief of the Regional Board of PKB in Pekalongan (2002–08), 22 June 2010.

one interview, when I asked Siti about her position as female regent and addressing women's problems in Pekalongan, she gave the general answer:

> I never promised anything. I avoided making any promises. The point is I want to guide Pekalongan (*mengarahkan* Pekalongan)... the important point is that I am communicative. I can meet people and I am willing to go to the grassroots.... Particularly to create democratic features which become a foundation to develop the community. We should treat all groups justly and all people should feel at home (*merasa punya tempat*)....[68]

A close look at the Mid-Term Development Plan (Rencana Pembangunan Jangka Menengah Daerah, RPJMD) of Pekalongan (2006–11) shows that women's empowerment was clearly not one of the eight priorities for local development, though the document acknowledges that there is a lack of awareness of women's rights, as well as violence against women and institutional weakness.[69] I gained the impression that the local government has not paid serious attention to local women's needs and problems, although women contribute considerably to local development. The industry sector, especially the manufacture sector, made the greatest contribution to the Gross Regional Domestic Product (Produk Domestik Regional Bruto, PDRB) of Pekalongan in 2005, 2006 and 2007.[70] The high contribution of the industry sector can be attributed to the *batik*-making industry where local women are involved as labourers. This can be seen from the fact that of the productive women, 47.94 per cent work, while 29.41 per cent manage their households.[71] However, the average wage of nearly 67 per cent of female workers was still below the minimum standard wage in Pekalongan (Rp 484,672/month) as they received an average of only Rp 322,326/month in 2007.[72] Women in the

---

[68] Interview with Siti Qomariyah in the office of the regent of Pekalongan, 25 June 2009.
[69] Pemerintah Kabupaten Pekalongan, *Rencana Pembangunan Jangka Menengah (RPJM) Daerah Kabupaten Pekalongan Tahun 2006–2011* (Pekalongan: Pemerintah Kabupaten Pekalongan, 2006), pp. 85–6.
[70] Ibid., p. 14.
[71] Bagian Sosial Setda Kabupaten Pekalongan, *Statistik dan Analisis Gender Kabupaten Pekalongan Tahun 2007* (Pekalongan: Bagian Sosial Detda Kabupaten Pekalongan, 2008), p. 49.
[72] Bagian Sosial Setda Kabupaten Pekalongan, *Statistik dan Analisis Gender Kabupaten Pekalongan Tahun 2007*, p. 57.

region also lag behind men in terms of education. This can be seen from percentages of the population above ten years of age who are illiterate. Women had higher illiteracy rates than men: with men at 8.75 (2002), 9.41 (2003), 8.61 (2004) and 6.53 per cent (2007), and women at 17.70 (2002), 17.69 (2003), 16.07 (2004) and 16.48 per cent (2007).[73] The health sector is also an important indicator of women's development. The maternal mortality rate increased in Pekalongan from 2005 to 2008: from 85/100,000 births (2005), to 149 (2006), 176 (2007) and 173 (2008).[74] Yet the baby mortality rate in Pekalongan gradually decreased from 92/100,000 births (2005), to 73 (2006), 76 (2007) and 72 (2008).[75]

The bleak condition of women in Pekalongan is made worse by the fact that Pekalongan is an important city in Central Java from which Indonesian migrant workers originate. This can be seen from the fact that female Indonesian migrant workers from Pekalongan outnumbered males from 2005 to 2008. For example, the number of female migrant workers from Pekalongan was 135 (2005), 298 (2006), 501 (2007) and 686 (2008) while the number of male migrant workers was only 14 (2005), 35 (2006), 103 (2007) and 44 (2008) with the destination countries in order of popularity being Saudi Arabia, Malaysia, Taiwan, Singapore, Hong Kong and South Korea.[76] These poor and lowly educated women experienced much abuse, violation of their working rights and illegal work. When I undertook observation in Pekalongan, I had the opportunity to attend Siti Qomariyah's official visit to Ida Aidha (17 years old, 2009), a female migrant worker from Buaran (an important pocket of female migrant workers in Pekalongan) who was forced to work overtime and was abused. She had wounds on many parts of her body.[77]

---

[73] Pemerintah Kabupaten Pekalongan, *Statistik Gender dan Analisis Kabupaten Pekalongan 2004* (Pekalongan: Pemerintah Kabupaten Pekalongan, 2005), p. 19; Bagian Sosial Setda Kabupaten Pekalongan, *Statistik dan Analisis Gender Kabupaten Pekalongan Tahun 2007*, 22.

[74] Pemerintah Kabupaten Pekalongan, "Outline Penulisan Statistik dan Analisis Gender, Anak dan Perempuan Tahun 2009", p. 28.

[75] Ibid.

[76] Ibid., p. 16.

[77] Although Siti Qomariyah could not meet Ida Aidha as she was in Jakarta for a medical examination, she met Ida's mother and gave her official support to the family, and said that local government would do its best to help Ida receive protection and her rights. Observation of Siti Qomariyah's visit to Ida Aidha in Kertijayan, Buaran district, Pekalongan, 26 June 2009.

Despite this, my observation of the way the local Bureau for Migrant Workers dealt with migrant workers revealed that the local government faces various difficulties in tackling the problem, though serious efforts to promote and uphold female workers rights have just began.[78] In addition, the region has only recently embraced efforts to combat violence against women, as I could not find any data of cases of violence against women both in the 2004 and 2007 gender statistics of Pekalongan. The effort to address violence against women began after the establishment of The Department for Women's Empowerment and Family Planning (Badan Pemberdayaan Perempuan and Keluarga Berencana) in 2008, which was based on the national and provincial regulation which placed women's empowerment as a compulsory sector in local government. The effort to inform society about standard operational procedures and to establish a structure for advocating violence against women in Pekalongan was only launched on 27 June 2009, the same day of my observation in Pekalongan.[79]

Conclusion

This chapter's assessment of Siti Qomariyah shows that familial political ties were not prominent in Siti Qomariyah's political emergence. It does, however, reveal the significance of Siti's father's prominent reputation as an NU *kyai*, in combination with Siti's educational achievement, which led PKB Pekalongan to select Siti as candidate for regent in the 2006 direct election in Pekalongan. Later, Siti's gender, being the only female Muslim NU candidate, became an important point and not a hindrance to her political stand in Pekalongan. Her political candidacy had been supported by religious endorsement from NU *kyai* in Pekalongan that supported women's leadership, at least at the level below president as in accordance with the decision of the NU Central Board in 1997.

---

[78] One problem is that female migrant workers make illegal documents without following the procedures initiated by the bureau. An example of the efforts made is the establishment of the association of PJTKI (agency for recruiting migrant workers), which has about nine branches in Pekalongan in order to ease communication and tackle any problems that arise. Interview with IN, chief of the Bureau for Migrant Workers in Pekalongan, 3 July 2009.

[79] Observation of the seminar for establishing and socializing standard operational procedures in advocating non-violence against women in Pekalongan on 27 June 2009 and interview with MG, chief of the Department for Women's Empowerment and Family Planning in Pekalongan, 27 June 2009.

I also highlighted how Siti's strong connections with Muslimat NU women's networks effectively provided women's solidarity along religious lines which contributed substantially to her political rise and victory in the 2006 direct election. Siti's quest to power shows the central role of Javanese women in handling, controlling and utilizing same-sex and intra-sex networks. As for Siti's political strategy, I have shown that Siti and her team strategically used and promoted her gender in combination with the Islamic norm of piety by use of the slogan "*wadon bae, wadon bae* (please choose the woman)". Again, gender was an important selling point rather than a hindrance to Siti Qomariyah's rise. In terms of her policy, Siti's intense interaction with particular women's groups, such as those from NU who sought greater power, and those from Muhammadiyah to some extent, contributed to Siti's cooperative and open leadership, and welcomed women's interests. However, it has not guaranteed the incorporation of women's empowerment in local development documents in Pekalongan because of Siti's low commitment to local women's issues.

At the end of her term in 2011, Siti Qomariyah sought re-election in the 2011 direct election in Pekalongan which was held on 1 May 2011. Interestingly, the election was coloured not only by both incumbents' (Siti Qomariyah and Wahyudi Pontjo Nugroho) efforts to maintain power, but also by the political comeback of Amat Antono, the former regent of Pekalongan (2001–06), who had been defeated by Siti Qomariyah in the 2006 direct election. In the 2011 election, four pairs of candidates competed, namely: (i) Imam Djamhuri and Cashuri (independents), (ii) Wahyudi Pontjo Nugroho and Broto Rahardjo (Golkar, PPRN, Barnas Party, PKP, PDK, Patriotic Party), (iii) Siti Qomariyah and Riswadi (PKB, PDIP and a coalition of 12 non-parliamentary political parties), and (iv) Amat Antono and Fadia A. Rafiq (Gerindra, PKNU, PPP, Democrat Party, PKS). Siti Qomariyah competed separately from her former vice-regent, Wahyudi Pontjo Nugroho (2006–11), a move which had been indicated by Pontjo Nugroho during an interview in July 2010.[80]

Siti Qomariyah, who has a strong NU background, tried to expand her political base and gain sympathy by recruiting Riswadi, a new figure in PDIP in Pekalongan. Wahyudi Pontjo Nugroho combined support

---

[80] Interview with Wahyudi Pontjo Nugroho in the office of the vice-regent of Pekalongan, 23 July 2010.

from Golkar and other small political parties. Interestingly, Wahyudi, who was officially nominated by the Regional Board of Golkar in Pekalongan, was challenged by the nomination of Fadia A. Rafiq, another Golkar cadre, who was in partnership with Amat Antono. Fadia A. Rafiq, daughter of the famous singer A. Rafiq, holds an important position in Golkar as the vice-chief of the Regional Board of Golkar in Depok, West Java, and as a member of the Youth Cadre of Golkar (Angkatan Muda Partai Golkar, AMPG). Although the Regional Board of Golkar in Pekalongan sent a protest letter to the Provincial Board of Golkar in Central Java to seek Fadia A. Rafiq's withdrawal,[81] Fadia continued as a vice-regent candidate in partnership with Amat Antono, though she was not officially nominated by Golkar. Here we can see how smart Amat Antono was in trying to divide the vote of Golkar's followers in Pekalongan by recruiting a fresh, young and pretty female Muslim cadre to attract voters' sympathy.

Aman Antono and Fadia A. Rafiq won the election by gaining 254,762 votes (54.75 per cent) and thus become regent and vice-regent of Pekalongan (2011–16), while the incumbent Siti Qomariyah won only 166,210 votes (35.72 per cent), followed by Wahyudi Pontjo Nugroho with 19,683 votes (4.23 per cent) and Imam Djamhuri with 8,395 votes (1.80 per cent).[82] Amat Antono won in 17 of the 19 districts in Pekalongan, mainly in the remote, hilly areas and the outskirts of Pekalongan such as Sragi, Bojong, Kesesi, Kandangserang, Paninggaran, Lebakbarang, Petungkriyono, Doro and Talun, where the infrastructure (roads) are in bad condition. Kajen was the only exception. Surprisingly, Amat Antono also won in two districts that have traditionally been NU bases, namely Kedungwuni and Wonopringgo, where Siti Qomariyah had formerly won (2006).[83] There were many factors behind Amat Antono's victory and Siti Qomariyah's failure. Some said it was because of Antono's smart promises and programmes: to develop better infrastructure using the slogan "*Sego Bungkus Sego Megono, Pingin Jalan Bagus Pilih Antono*" (Wrapped rice, *megono* rice, if you want good roads choose Antono)"

---

[81] "Golkar Pekalongan Meradang, Mucul Calon Ganda Pilkada", at <http://www.antarjateng.com> [accessed 24 June 2011].
[82] "KPU Serahkan Hasil Pilkada ke DPRD", at <http://www.radar-pekalongan.com> [accessed 24 June 2011].
[83] "Antono-Fadia Menang di 17 Kecamatan", at <http://www.suaramerdeka>; Ali Riza, "Di Balik Kemenangan Mantan", *Suara Merdeka*, 10 May 2011.

and to introduce a fairer mechanism in the selection of local public servants through the slogan "*Mengapa Pilih Antono, Jadi PNS tidak bayar* (Why Choose Antono, So Civil Servants Don't Pay [Bribes to Be Employed])".[84] Those two issues were significant problems during Siti Qomariyah's term, which Antono exploited to his benefit.

In addition, there was a spirit of solidarity among Antono's followers in the bureaucracy and the grassroots (nationalist followers), who had felt alienated by Siti Qomariyah's power and traditional networks (NU).[85] Siti Qomariyah, who only won in the two districts of Buaran and Karangdadap, had to deal with fragmentation in the Regional Board of PKB in Pekalongan and within NU in Pekalongan. Although the Regional Board of PKB in Pekalongan followed the official recommendation of the Central Board of PKB, in reality they did not support Siti Qomariyah, and some of the NU elite and followers gave their votes to Antono.[86] While the Regional Board of PKB in Pekalongan, the NU elite and NU followers were united in the 2006 direct election, they were not in the 2011 election, though Siti Qomariyah still secured support from Muslimat NU and two prominent *kyai* (Habib Lutfi and *Kyai* Taufiq).[87]

Although PKB and PDIP gained the majority of seats in Pekalongan DPRD as the two big parties in 2009, it did not necessarily make it easy to secure executive positions for their candidates, with Siti Qomariyah and Riswadi losing to Amat Antono, an old political player without the backing of a strong party in parliament but who had concrete programmes and a strong psychological connection to the disappointed grassroots followers.

---

[84] Ali Riza, "Di Balik Kemenangan Mantan", *Suara Merdeka*, 10 May 2011.
[85] Ibid.
[86] Telephone interview with FA, chief of Muslimat NU in Pekalongan (2005–10), 26 June 2011.
[87] Ibid.

CHAPTER 6

Ratna Ani Lestari: Holding on to Familial Ties, Manipulating Islamic Piety and Using Gender to Attract Wider Support

The third case study observed in this book is on Ratna Ani Lestari, the first female regent elected in Banyuwangi in the 2005 direct election. Ratna's profile, her social and family backgrounds, as well as the socio-political context in Banyuwangi provide a starting point to uncover the way she first developed social and political networks on the Regional Board of PDIP in Banyuwangi in the lead up to the 2005 election. Ratna Ani Lestari gained ground in her political career from her husband's influential political position as regent. As for her campaign strategy, this book reveals that she deliberately utilized her Islamic piety and gender to attract wider support especially from Islamic-based voters in Banyuwangi, while at the same time try to secure religious support from NU *kyai*.

Banyuwangi Regency: The Social and Political Landscape

Banyuwangi, one of 38 regencies in the province of East Java, lies in the south of the province. In 2007, it was home to around 1,580,441 inhabitants, most of whom were Muslim adherents,[1] followed by Hindus and Christians.[2]

---

[1] Bappeda Kabupaten Banyuwangi, *Kabupaten Banyuwangi Dalam Angka Tahun 2008*, p. 49.
[2] Bappeda Kabupaten Banyuwangi, *Selayang Pandang Kabupaten Banyuwangi Tahun 2005*, p. 21.

Banyuwangi, which consists of 24 districts, 217 administrative villages (*kelurahan*) and 825 hamlets (*dusun*),[3] is multiethnic. The three main ethnic groups are the Osing (original Banyuwangi inhabitants with a distinct Hindu culture) comprising 20 per cent of the total population of Banyuwangi, the Maduranese comprising 12 per cent of the population, and the Javanese as the majority ethnicity comprising 67 per cent of the total population in Banyuwangi.[4] The Osing are adaptive, open to other cultures, egalitarian and do not live isolated from other ethnic groups (those who isolate themselves include the Tengger community in Tengger near Mount Bromo or the Baduy community in Banten).[5] The Osing predominantly live in the central part of Banyuwangi, in places such as District (*kecamatan*) Rogojampi, Singojuruh, Kabat, Giri, Glagah and Songgon. The Javanese-Hindus who are commonly called the Mataraman live mainly in the central, southern and western parts of Banyuwangi such as District Gambiran, Pesanggrahan, Silir Agung, Bangorejo, Purwoharjo, Tegaldlimo and Tegalsari. Whereas those of Maduranese origin predominantly live in the coastal areas in the eastern part of Banyuwangi such as District Muncar, Kalibaru and Glenmore. Some areas such as Cluring, Srono and Genteng are inhibited by both Mataraman and Osing.[6] Banyuwangi (previously called Blambangan) was the second Hindu territory in Java conquered by the Islamic Mataram Kingdom in the 17th century after a series of military expeditions.[7] The changes in the political situation in the region are reflected in Table 9.

Table 9 shows that during the New Order, FKP/Golkar was the dominant party followed by PPP, as the only Islamic political party allowed, while PDI came last with only two seats. However, the configuration changed dramatically in the Reform Era (after 1998) in favour of Islamic-based political parties, with PKB, a new NU-based political party, being the dominant party followed by PDIP and Golkar in the 1999 General Election. The situation prevailed in the 2004 General Election. However, a new and popular party, the Democrat Party, gained

---

[3] Bappeda Kabupaten Banyuwangi, *Kabupaten Banyuwangi Dalam Angka Tahun 2008*, p. 25.
[4] Suwardiman, "Banyuwangi", p. 36.
[5] Ibid.
[6] The ethnic distribution in Banyuwangi and the term *Mataraman* comes from the explanation given by UD, an NGO activist in Banyuwangi (interview, 29 July 2009).
[7] Fransiscus Assisi Sutjipto Tjiptoatmodjo, "Kota-Kota Pantai Di Sekitar Selat Madura", pp. 169–78; and Robert R. Jay, *Religion and Politics in Rural Central Java*, p. 9.

Table 9 Political Party Composition in Banyuwangi during the New Order and Post-Suharto Eras

New Order		Post-Suharto			
Political Party	1987	Political Party	1999	2004	2009
FKP	25	Golkar	5	8	7
PPP	8	PDIP	13	12	12
PDI	2	PKB	17	16	6
TNI/Polri	9	PPP	2	4	2
		PAN	2	–	1
		TNI/Polri	5	–	–
		PKU	1	–	–
		Democrat Party	–	5	10
		PKNU	–	–	5
		HANURA	–	–	2
		PGRIR	–	–	4
		PRN	–	–	1
Total	44	Total	45	45	50

Note: I was not able to collect the composition of Banyuwangi DPRD as a result of the 1997 General Election, because neither the library nor archival bureau in Banyuwangi had the information.

Sources: The 1987 results are from *Kabupaten Banyuwang dalam Angka Tahun 1987*. The results from the 1999, 2004 and 2009 general elections were collected from Komisi Pemilihan Umum Kabupaten Banyuwangi, "Anggota Badan Perwakilan Rakyat Daerah Kabupaten Banyuwangi Masa Jabatan 1999–2004"; "Anggota Badan Perwakilan Rakyat Daerah Kabupaten Banyuwangi Masa Jabatan 2004–2009"; and "Anggota Badan Perwakilan Rakyat Daerah Kabupaten Banyuwangi Masa Jabatan 2009–2014".

five seats and ranked fourth after Golkar. Today the Democrat Party has consolidated its grip, emerging as the second major political party, while PDIP also emerged as a stronger political party in the 2009 General Election. The decrease in votes for PKB in the last election could also be attributed to the appearance of new NU-based political parties such as PKNU, which fragmented the NU voter base despite internal conflicts in the big family of PKB, namely the split between PKB under Gus Dur's leadership and Muhaimin Iskandar. Generally, the table describes the local characteristics of Banyuwangi: it is not only a base of faithful NU *santri* as reflected in PKB's strong performance in the 1999 and 2004 General Elections, but also a base of *abangan* followers, as can be seen from PDIP's gradual rise.

Ratna Ani Lestari: An *Abangan* Housewife with Strong Familial Ties

Ratna Ani Lestari, who was born on 6 December 1965, has a Master's degree in management from Udayana University, Denpasar, and received a doctoral degree in Public Administration in 2010 from the University of Brawijaya in Malang. Although Ratna said she was a descendent of a *kyai* grandfather in Kediri, her father, a contractor, comes from Bondowoso (and is perhaps Maduranese), and her mother comes from a wealthy business family of Javanese descent in Banyuwangi. Ratna has an older sister and a younger brother. She attended elementary school in Kediri, moved to Banyuwangi for junior high school, and moved back again to Bondowoso to attend senior high school. Ratna was not involved in Fatayat NU or Muslimat NU, even though Banyuwangi, Kediri and Bondowoso are relatively strong NU regions. She never attended a *pesantren*, and none of her family members has been involved in politics.

After high school, Ratna went to Denpasar to take up a course in economics at the National Education University (Universitas Pendidikan Nasional) where she met WS, a dentist who became the regent of Jembrana (2000–10) and who she later married after he divorced his first wife. The couple have a daughter together and WS has three children from his previous marriage. Ratna's decision to marry WS, who is of Hindu origin, is interesting. Mixed marriages between Muslim women and non-Muslim men have been a highly sensitive issue for *santri* and ordinary residents of Banyuwangi, which is widely known as a stronghold of NU ideology. Therefore, Ratna's decision to marry WS can be further seen as affirmation of Ratna's *abangan* leanings.

Ratna's initial involvement in politics began after her marriage to WS, who at that time was in power in Jembrana. WS, who was born on 9 March 1950 and raised in Jembrana, has had an interesting education. He graduated from the School of Dentistry at Airlangga University, Surabaya, in 1978 and accepted opportunities to pursue further studies in Dentistry in Japan at Hiroshima University and Tokushima University until 1993. After initially serving as a dentist in Banyuwangi, he moved to Bali in the late 1980s, but he continued to pay close attention to his hometown of Jembrana, for example by initiating the NGO called Jembrana Development Centre for which he is well known. In 1999, WS's name was circulated within Jembrana PDIP to be nominated as PDIP's candidate for regent in the 2000 regent election. However, the Central Board of PDIP did not approve his name. WS tried to proceed with his nomination through PPP, which supported him to become regent of Jembrana (2000–05).[8] Besides being regent of Jembrana, WS later became chief of the Regional Board of PDIP in Jembrana, but he left the party because it did not support his nomination for governor of Bali in 2008; he then joined the Democrat Party. As regent of Jembrana, WS was well known for his pioneering and successful programme of free education (from elementary to senior high school) and free health services via Puskesmas (Health Service Centres at the district level) for all Jembrana residents. These successful programmes won WS national and international acknowledgment for good local governance, and awards from the central government and MURI (Museum Rekor Indonesia, Indonesian Records Museum). However, now that he is no longer in power, WS is facing trial for corruption during his two terms as regent of Jembrana (2000–10).[9]

Ratna's political career in Banyuwangi began when WS was serving his second term as regent of Jembrana. As a regent's wife, Ratna was exposed to her husband's political activities, which familiarized her with the political scene, including encounters with PDIP. Because of WS's political power, Ratna was elected as member of Jembrana DPRD (2004–09) for PDIP, which was to later pave the way for her political career in Banyuwangi.

Here we can see that Ratna originally had good individual capital derived from her family's business background and her educational achievements, which to some extent eased her entry into politics. In addition, her husband's political power empowered Ratna to gain her own political standing, experience political power and gradually increase her opportunity to become known as the politically active wife of a prominent regent when she ran as regent candidate in Banyuwangi in the 2005 direct election. The next section will examine Ratna's political emergence in the lead up to the 2005 direct election in Banyuwangi.

Political Emergence: The New Political Opportunity and Influence of Familial Ties

In assessing the important factors behind Ratna's political emergence in Banyuwangi, I will show the significance of the direct election that facilitated Ratna's emergence and the influence of familial ties, particularly

---

[8] "Profil", at <http://voteforwinasa.wordpress.com/profil/> [accessed 10 February 2011]; Kansas, *Anak Desa Penantang Zaman*, pp. 63–7.
[9] "Terkait Korupsi, Mantan Bupati Jembrana Dilimpahkan ke Kejati Bali".

given WS's prominent role in politics, in supporting Ratna's success in Banyuwangi. Ratna who was at that time wife of WS, regent of Jembrana, returned to Banyuwangi just six months before Election Day in 2005. Given that this would be the first direct election in Banyuwangi in 2005, Ratna saw an opportunity to try her luck. She said:

> There was an opportunity, so we went for it. Particularly for *female candidates* [emphasis added]. And at that time, I was already in politics. So, we tried our luck (*coba*) and though people did not know me we sold a real program.[10]

According to STY, a former bureaucrat in Banyuwangi and once a close friend to Ratna, it was Ratna's husband's political intuition that assessed the situation in Banyuwangi and recognized that women candidates were becoming increasingly popular and that Banyuwangi at that time had never had a female *bupati*.[11] In paving her political career in Banyuwangi, Ratna, assisted by her husband's influence in the Banyuwangi PDIP, hit the ground running during the January 2005 convention of the Regional Board of PDIP in Banyuwangi, which met with the intention of gathering prospective names for the PDIP candidate for regent, which would then be proposed to the Central Board of PDIP (Dewan Pimpinan Pusat, DPP). Although Ratna gained the majority of votes from the sub-branches (Pengurus Anak Cabang, PAC, at the district level) of the Regional Board of PDIP in Banyuwangi due to the active lobbying of WS, who was also the chief of Ratna's campaign team,[12] she did not gain support from the chief of the Provincial Board of PDIP in East Java (Dewan Pimpinan Daerah PDIP, DPD PDIP). The chief of the Provincial Board of PDIP, due to recommendation from the East Java governor, Imam Utomo (2003–08), instead nominated Ali Sa'roni, a bureaucrat in East Java who was originally from Banyuwangi, as the candidate for regent from PDIP. Eventually, the Regional Board of PDIP in Banyuwangi officially declared Ali Sa'roni in partnership with Yusuf

---

[10] Interview with Ratna Ani Lestari in the office of the regent of Banyuwangi, 29 July 2009.

[11] Interview with STY, formerly a bureaucrat in Banyuwangi, businesswoman and close friend of Ratna, Banyuwangi, 9 Aug. 2009.

[12] "Ratna Kantongi 900 Suara", *Radar Banyuwangi*, 2 March 2005; and interview with YW, chief of Banyuwangi PDIP PDC (2000–05), Banyuwangi, 30 July 2009.

Widyatmoko PDIP's candidates for regent and vice-regent, instead of Ratna who had gained the majority of votes from the sub-branches of PDIP in Banyuwangi.

Meanwhile, on 22 March 2005, the Constitutional Court (Mahkamah Konstitusi, MK) approved the judicial review of the chief of the Provincial Board of PKB in North Sulawesi on the basis of Article 59 of Law No. 32/2004. That ruling stated that political parties and their coalitions, which do not have seats in DPRD but have at least 15 per cent of the total number of votes approved in the region, could nominate a candidate in direct elections.[13] The smaller political parties without seats in Banyuwangi DPRD saw the opportunity and, after several meetings, agreed to unite and nominate their own candidate. Eighteen political parties (PNIM, PBSD, PBB, PM, PDK, PNBK, PKPI, P. PELOPOR, PPDI, PNUI, PAN, PKPB, PKS, PBR, PDS, PSI, PPD, P. PANCASILA) under the name of the Coalition of Non-Parliamentary Political Parties (Gabungan Partai-Partai Politik Non Parlemen, GPPNP) held a convention open to anyone who wanted to be a candidate for regent on 27 March 2005.[14]

There were four pairs of candidates at the convention: Ratna Ani Lestari and Yusuf Nuris (Ratna's rationale in choosing Yusuf Nuris will be explained later), Dr. Sholohin MS (the former chief of Muhammadiyah in Banyuwangi) and A. Qusyairi, Samsul Hadi (the incumbent regent of Banyuwangi 2000–05, who had not secured a position with his party, PKB) and Effendi, and then Bambang and Gutomo. After lobbying and consolidating with at least seven political parties (PDS, PNIM, PBSD, PNBK, P. PELOPOR, PPDI, PPD) coordinated by RM from the National Indonesian Party-Marhaenist Front (Partai National Indonesia Marhaenisme, PNIM), Ratna won the convention with ten votes in her favour, while Sholihin MS won five votes, Samdul Hadi won two votes and Bambang won only one vote.[15] Some of the reasons for supporting

---

[13] "Partai Gurem Bisa Usung Calom".
[14] Gabungan Partai-Partai Politik Non Parlamen, "Kontrak Politik Pasangan Bakal Calon Kepala Daerah Dan Wakil Kepala Daerah Banyuwangi Tahun 2005–10 dengan Gabungan Partai-Partai Politik Non Parlemen". The full names of these political parties can be found in the Abbreviations section at the beginning of this book.
[15] Interview with RM, Secretary General of PNIM (Partai Nasional Indonesia Marhaenisme) in Banyuwangi and lobbyist for Ratna Ani Lestari in the GPPNP Convention, Banyuwangi, 26 July 2009. See also "Bupati Samsul Kembali Kalah".

Ratna, according to RM from PNIM, one of the 18 political parties that nominated her, were as follows:

> We thought like this, this was an opportunity for small parties to nominate their own regent candidate. Why shouldn't we be able to manage Banyuwangi by nominating our own regent…. The main issue was looking for a clean candidate. We considered that the other four candidates [the regent and vice-regent candidate pairs from other political parties] were not clean…. Therefore, we positioned Bu Ratna as an alternative figure who we thought was clean.[16]

There are two important points in RM's statement. First, he emphasizes looking for a clean (non-corrupt) candidate. RM's statement echoes a common positive stereotype regarding female candidates across societies, that they are less likely to be corrupt. The second point from RM's statement is that Ratna was perceived as an alternative figure. Ratna's position, as just an ordinary women who later became the wife of the regent of Jembrana, was attractive to the small alienated elites in Banyuwangi. Ratna's origin as a housewife with little professional involvement in political praxis became a strong consideration for them to choose her as they assumed that her leadership would bring a clean, trusted and more prosperous government, compared to the all male candidates who were already involved in politics in Banyuwangi.[17]

In fact, some members of the GPPNP did not thoroughly agree with the decision to support Ratna. There was friction, for example, within the National Mandate Party (Partai Amanat Nasional, PAN), as reported by IS, executive secretary of Muhammadiyah in Banyuwangi and activist for the Regional Board of PAN in Banyuwangi, because they were unclear about Ratna's religion as some believed that Ratna had converted from Islam to Hinduism.[18] Thus, while Islamic-based political parties such as the Star and Crescent Party (Partai Bulan Bintang, PBB), the Prosperous Justice Party (Partai Keadilan Sejahtera, PKS), PAN and the Concern for the Nation Functional Party (Partai Karya Peduli Bangsa,

---

[16] Interview with RM, 26 July 2009.

[17] Interestingly, the situation in which female candidates who were originally ordinary housewives are more likely to enjoy support and win elections than career politicians also occurs in the suburban towns and cities of Cook County, Illinois, USA, as studied by Sharyne Merrit (Merrit, "Winners and Losers", p. 739).

[18] Interview with IS, executive secretary of Muhammadiyah and activist of the Regional Board of PAN, both in Banyuwangi, 30 July 2009.

PKPB) gave their support to Dr. Solihin who gained five votes,[19] Ratna and Gus Yus won the majority of votes at the convention and were officially nominated as regent and vice-regent candidates from GPPNP. Interestingly, once Ratna's name was officially registered with the General Election Commission of Banyuwangi, GPPNP splintered as the Islamic-based political parties PKS, PBB and PAN once again questioned Ratna's religiosity as to whether she was truly Islamic.[20] In addition, Ratna did not include PKS members in her campaign team, which disappointed the party and resulted in its withdrawal from GPPNP.[21]

The 2005 Direct Election in Banyuwangi: Contenders

There were five contenders in the 2005 direct election: Ratna Ani Lestari and Yusuf Nuris (GPPNP),[22] Ali Sa'roni and Yusuf Widyatmoko (PDIP), Achmad Wahyudi and Eko Sukartono (PKB), Acmad Masduki and Syafii (PPP and Democrat Party), and Soesanto Soewandi and Abdul Kadir (Golkar). Their profiles can be seen in Table 10.

From the above profiles, we can see that Ratna Ani Lestari and Gus Yus (Yusuf Nuris) made an interesting pair compared to the other candidates. This is not only because they were nominated by the coalition of 18 small political parties who had no seats in the Banyuwangi DPRD, but also because of their strong profile as the only female candidate and wife of the successful regent of Jembrana in combination with Gus Yus,

---

[19] Interview with AI, chief of the Regional Board of PBB in Banyuwangi (2002–09), Banyuwangi, 29 July 2009; and interview with AM, chief of the Regional Board of PKS in Banyuwangi (2007–10), Banyuwangi, 3 Aug. 2009.
[20] Interview with SM, secretary of the Regional Board of PAN in Banyuwangi (2005–10), Banyuwangi, 28 July 2009.
[21] Interview with AM, 3 Aug. 2009.
[22] There was some controversy and suspicion surrounding Ratna's nomination, because some people believed that Ratna gave false personal information, including about her religion. DS, a journalist and the general manager of *DE*, a local newspaper in Banyuwangi, claims that he obtained data (which he allowed me to see) that shows that Ratna had converted from Islam to Hinduism in 1988 for the sake of her marriage to WS. However, on the form that Ratna submitted to the General Election Commission of Banyuwangi in 2005, she wrote that she was Muslim. The Banyuwangi public, the majority of whom are Muslim, believed that Ratna deceived them because she was a Hindu but claimed to be a Muslim for the sake of her nomination. Conversation with DS, Banyuwangi, 9 Aug. 2009. Some *kyai* and NU followers protested against Ratna, who according to them had degraded Islam because she converted to Islam for the sake of political interests only. See "Pelecehan Agama".

Table 10 Profile of Regent and Vice-regent Candidates in the 2005 Direct Election in Banyuwangi

No. in Ballot Paper	Political Party	Name of Regent and Vice-Regent Candidates	Profile
1	PKB	**Ir. Achmad Wahyudi**	Chief of Banyuwangi DPRD from PKB (1999–2004), member of Banyuwangi DPRD from PKB (2004–08). Chief of the Regional Board of PKB in Banyuwangi (2002–07).
		Ir. HM Eko Sukartono	Chief of Banyuwangi DPRD from Golkar (2004–09).
2	PPP, Democrat Party	**H. Achmad Masduki**	No information
		H. Syafi'i	Alumni of Darussalam Pesantren, Blok Agung, Banyuwangi
3	Golkar	**Ir. H. Soesanto Soewandi**	No information
		EC. H. Abdul Kadir	No information
4	GPPNP (coalition of 18 political parties)	**Ratna Ani Lestari**	Wife of the successful regent of Jembrana (2000–10), member of Jembrana DPRD from PDIP (2004–09).
		Yusuf Nuris	A *gus* (son of an NU *kyai*), activist of PMII (NU Youth organization) in Banyuwangi, member of the Regional Board of PKB in Banyuwangi (2000), branch secretary of NU in Banyuwangi (2003–08), member of Banyuwangi KPU (2005).
5	PDIP	**Ali Sa'roni**	Prominent NU figure from Banyuwangi, bureaucrat in East Java
		Yusuf Widyatmoko	Chief of the Regional Board Banyuwangi PDIP (2000–05)

Note: Names in bold represent the candidates for regent.
Source: Author, table assembled from various interviews and CVs.

a prominent young NU cadre. The other candidates were all bureaucrats and politicians. In the next section, I will elaborate on Ratna and Gus Yus's strategy to win the 2005 direct election.

Strategy to Win: Generating Support from Prominent NU *Kyai*[23]

As a female candidate in a predominantly NU-based region, Ratna was aware of her difficult position, which was not helped by the fact that she has an *abangan*, rather than a strong *santri*, background. However, she and her husband WS dutifully visited the influential *kyai* in Banyuwangi to seek permission and advice, including on the choice of her running partner. Ratna said:

> At the time, we approached some *kyai*. And because my family has a few *kyai* [kin] from Kediri, I asked my family to accompany me to see the *kyai* whom they were acquainted with. Some of the prominent *kyai* we met, those from Blok Agung [a highly influential *pesantren* in Banyuwangi] recommended three names [as candidates for vice-regent], namely Arifin Salam, Ustad Ghofar and Yusuf Nuris...Yusuf Nuris was the youngest and most organizationally active and was well-educated with a Master's degree. Therefore we chose him.... We only asked suggestions for names. We did not know any. Fortunately, the wife of a *kyai* in Blok Agung is friend with my aunt in Kediri, who also manages a *pesantren*....[24]

As she explained above, with help of her aunt, Ratna went to meet *Kyai* AHS, of the Rois Syuriah Branch of NU (Pengurus Cabang NU, PCNU) in Banyuwangi, in Blok Agung *pesantren*.[25] *Kyai* AHS eventually recommended three names of young NU cadres that could become Ratna's

---

[23] My effort to engage and understand local NU *kyai* in Banyuwangi largely developed from my initial contact and conversation with Gus EN, one of the grandsons of the late KH Zarkasyi, the most charismatic *kyai* in Banyuwangi. *Kyai* Zarkasyi was the owner of Bustanul Makmur Pesantren in Genteng Wetan, Banyuwangi, which has approximately 500 to 1,000 (male and female combined) *santri*. Gus EN's mother is the younger sister of the late *Kyai* Zarkasyi. Conversation with Gus EN, Bustanul Makmur Pesantren, 25 July 2009.
[24] Interview with Ratna Ani Lestari, 29 July 2009.
[25] Darussalam Pesantren was founded by *Kyai* Syafaat in 1951. Currently, it has approximately 1,000 female and 2,000 male *santri* from Java and outside of Java (Sumatra and Kalimantan) who study there. Explanation from NW, one of the granddaughters of *Kyai* Syafaat, the founder of Darussalam Pesantren, Blok Agung, Banyuwangi, in conversation with me at Darussalam Pesantren, Blok Agung, 1 Aug. 2009. NW also facilitated meetings and interviews with *Kyai* AHS.

running partner, but eventually chose Gus Yus (Yusuf Nuris), a 34-year-old with strong ties to *kyai* through both parents.²⁶ Below is an illustration of Gus Yus's family tree.

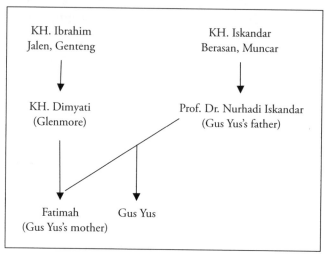

Source: Author, based on an interview with *Kyai* AHS in Darussalam Pesantren, Blok Agung, Banyuwangi, 1 August 2009.

Figure 8 Gus Yus's Family Tree

Gus Yus's mother (Fatimah) is the daughter of *Kyai* Haji Dimyati in Glenmore. *Kyai* Dimyati is the son of *Kyai* Haji Ibrahim from a *pesantren* in Jalen, Genteng, which is the oldest and the most prominent *pesantren* in Banyuwangi. Gus Yus's father is the son of *Kyai* Haji Iskandar from Berasan, Muncar. The late *Kyai* Syafaat (father of *Kyai* AHS) from Darussalam Pesantren in Blok Agung, the second most prominent *pesantren* in Banyuwangi, was the student of *Kyai* Ibrahim in Jalen (the grandfather of Gus Yus's mother). Moreover, *Kyai* Syafaat was also taught by *Kyai* Haji Iskandar (Gus Yus's grandfather).²⁷ Gus Yus is an activist in Banyuwangi PMII, and was a member of the Regional Board of PKB in Banyuwangi (2000), branch secretary of NU in Banyuwangi (2003–08) and member of Banyuwangi KPU (2005).²⁸

---

²⁶ Interview with *Kyai* AHS in Darussalam Pesantren, 1 Aug. 2009.
²⁷ Interview with Gus Yus in the official house of the vice-regent of Banyuwangi, 27 July 2009; and an explanation by *Kyai* AHS in Darussalam Pesantren, 1 Aug. 2009.
²⁸ Interview with Gus Yus, Banyuwangi, 27 July 2009.

Gus Yus indeed comes from a very strong *kyai* circle in Banyuwangi and has close connections with Blok Agung, which *Kyai* AHS, one of *Kyai* Syafaat's sons, controls. Ratna's decision to go initially to Blok Agung to seek religious justification from *Kyai* AHS and then choose Gus Yus is understandable. As matter of fact, it was not only Ratna who went to Blok Agung. Achmad Masduki and Syafi'i (PPP, Democrat Party) also went there to meet *Kyai* AHS in April 2005 to gain sympathy from the Rois Syuriah of the Regional Board of NU in Banyuwangi.[29] In an interview, Gus Yus spoke also of the central role that Ratna's husband, WS, played in their candidacy to recruit him to run with Ratna Ani Lestari. WS persuaded Gus Yus that prominent *kyai* in Banyuwangi such as *Kyai* Nur Muhammad and *Kyai* Sarbini (Berasan), and *Kyai* Hisyam and *Kyai* Abdullah (Glenmore) had all supported WS's move to put Ratna and Gus Yus as a pair in the 2005 direct election.[30] Eventually, Ratna successfully recruited Gus Yus, though the pair did not receive further endorsement from other NU *kyai*. NU *kyai* could not be united, having split into two factions.

For example, *Kyai* MAS, chief of the Syuriah of NU in Banyuwangi, and other *kyai* supported Achmad Masduki and Syafi'i (PPP and Democrat Party) because Masduki, the former secretary to the regent, was more experienced and more closely connected with *kyai* and had a low profile compared to Achmad Wahyudi, who was considered arrogant in the way he opposed Samsul Hadi, the former regent of Banyuwangi (2001–06).[31] Some NU followers and NU *kyai* supported Ali Sa'roni and Yusuf Widyatmoko (PDIP) because Ali Sa'roni comes from the oldest *pesantren*, Darulnajah, in Banyuwangi.[32] Achmad Wahyudi and Eko Sukartono

---

[29] "Masduki-Syafi'I Temui Hisyam", *Radar Banyuwangi*, 13 April 2005.
[30] Interview with Gus Yus in the official house of the vice-regent of Banyuwangi, 27 July 2009.
[31] Interview with *Kyai* MAS, chief of the Syuriah of NU in Banyuwangi, 1 Aug. 2009. In the NU tradition, if an individual wants to meet a *kyai* they should not go alone but instead should be accompanied by someone who is already familiar with the *kyai*. Thus, during the process of approaching and meeting *kyai* and *gus* in Banyuwangi I was assisted and accompanied by SG and MQ, both of whom are activists with the Indonesian Migrant Workers Association (Serikat Buruh Migran Indonesia, SBMI) branch in Banyuwangi and have very strong connections with many of the NU elite and *kyai* in Banyuwangi.
[32] Interview with Gus MK, vice-chief of the Tanfidziyah of NU in Banyuwangi, 25 July 2009.

(PKB and Golkar) did not receive support from the NU institution or NU *kyai* in Banyuwangi.[33]

Ratna and Gus Yus kept trying to obtain blessings from old charismatic NU *kyai* such as *Kyai* Haji HA from Asshidiqi Pesantren in Glenmore.[34] Ratna also gained advantage from Gus Yus's nature as a young NU cadre. Thus it was not surprising to see that the Nahdlatul Ulama Student Association (Ikatan Pelajar Nahdlatul Ulama, IPNU) and the Nahdlatul Ulama Female Student Association (Ikatan Pelajar Putri Nahdlatul Ulama, IPPNU) in Glenmore supported Ratna and Gus Yus in the election.[35]

Using Male Networks

One of Ratna's strategies was to intensify her male networks, which were mainly derived from her husband's connections. To some extent, this strategy was based on the fact that Ratna had no intersections with female activists and women's organizations throughout her personal life. She mainly relied on her husband's male networks, either political or religious in nature, and these networks were effective contributors to her political victory in the election.

With NU *kyai* distancing themselves from Ratna and Gus Yus, Ratna intensified contact with male networks along the lines of her husband's political connections in PDIP. WS's strong networks and influence among Banyuwangi PDIP can be seen from Ratna's success in gaining support from 14 of 21 sub-branches (Pengurus Anak Cabang, PAC) in the convention of the Banyuwangi PDIP in January 2005, though she did not receive approval from the PDIP Central Board,[36] as well as in the support Ratna received from the 18 small non-parliamentary political parties in March 2005, as noted earlier. Ratna did not have networks with Islamic women's organizations either in NU or Muhammadiyah, so she relied predominantly on her husband's political connections in PDIP.

WS, the husband of Ratna, played a dominant role in helping Ratna create a strategy. ES, Ratna's contender in the 2005 direct election

---

[33] Interview with ACW, chief of the PKB in Banyuwangi (2002–07), and member of Banyuwangi DPRD from PKB (1999–2008), 26 July 2009.

[34] Conversation with *Kyai* HA, Glenmore, 1 Aug. 2009. See also "Ratna Haul Syech Abdul Kadir Jailani".

[35] "IPNU-IPPNU Dukung Ratna".

[36] Interview with YD, former chief of the Songgon sub-branch of PDIP and coordinator of Ratna's campaign team, 4 Aug. 2009.

from Golkar, affirmed WS's strong role when he said "he [WS] had a dominant role...the actor was the male (*yang lakinya*)".[37] In turn, with the support of the majority of PDIP sub-branches in Banyuwangi who were disappointed with PDIP's decision not to nominate Ratna and Gus Yus, WS created a special campaign team outside the PDIP structure. The campaign team consisted of 15 people, mainly PDIP cadres, and was led by WS, while YD was assigned as coordinator. The team had branches in every district, village and neighbourhood association unit (Rukun Tetangga, RT), and at least two people in every election station (Tempat Pemungutan Suara, TPS), which were mainly organized by PDIP cadres.[38] In addition, Ratna also intensified her communication with the political party elite with nationalist ideologies, as shown by her decision to recruit RM, the Secretary General of PNIM in Banyuwangi, as her main lobbyist.

As her husband was originally from Bali and is Hindu, I also examined the possibility of Ratna utilizing the network of Hindu followers in Banyuwangi. It is important to note that there are more Hindus in Banyuwangi than in any other regency in the province of East Java throughout 23 branches of Parisada Hindu Dharma Indonesia (the official organization for Hindus, founded in Bali in 1959). The Hindu diaspora in Banyuwangi is mainly located in the southern parts of Banyuwangi such as District Rogojampi, Muncar, Tegaldlimo, Purwoharjo, Bangrejo, Pesanggaran, Kabat, Genteng and Glenmore. In an interview, Ketut SDR, a member of the Central Board of Parisada Hindu Dharma Indonesia (1966–present) and a prominent Hindu leader in Banyuwangi, explained that organizationally, Hindu Dharma and its structure in Banyuwangi did not support Ratna's nomination in 2005, although WS had asked for support from Parisada Hindu Dharma Banyuwangi. He did not deny the fact, however, that many prominent Hindus in the Hindu diaspora played a considerable role in supporting Ratna and Gus Yus's team, including as their coordinator and as members of their campaign team.[39] YD, coordinator of Ratna's campaign team, confirmed that Hindus definitely supported Ratna as some were also PDIP cadres.[40]

---

[37] Interview with ES, chief of Banyuwangi DPRD from Golkar (2004–09), Banyuwangi, 5 Aug. 2009.
[38] Interview with RM, 26 July 2009.
[39] Interview with Ketut SDR, prominent leader of Parisada Hindu Dharma in Banyuwangi, 8 Aug. 2009.
[40] Interview with YD, 4 Aug. 2009.

Ratna also tried to connect with the grassroots, such as the organization of parking service providers in Banyuwangi, led by JL. JL was a loyal follower of PKB's Samsul Hadi, the former regent of Banyuwangi. It is important to note that since 2004, internal conflict had been brewing in the Regional Board of PKB in Banyuwangi, which eventually split into two main factions: one behind PKB under the leadership of Samsul Hadi and another for PKB under the leadership of Achmad Wahyudi. Achmad Wahyudi was the official chief of the Regional Board of PKB in Banyuwangi (2000–07) and a member of Banyuwangi DPRD from PKB (1999–2008), though in 2008 he had a conflict with Gus Dur and moved to PKNU. The majority of NU *kyai* and NU followers, including JL, supported Samsul Hadi rather than Achmad Wahyudi. However, as Achmad Wahyudi held power in the Regional Board of PKB in Banyuwangi, he declared himself candidate for regent and left Samsul Hadi without any structural backup from PKB, hence Samsul Hadi's failure to run as a candidate for regent in the 2005 election. Samsul Hadi's loyal followers who were disappointed with the situation, such as JL, did not support any other NU candidate for regent. JL explained that it was RM who recruited him to join Ratna's team. He gave an example of his contribution to Ratna:

> The parking organization has approximately 300 members. The organization is easy to work with, as it interacts every day with the community. For example, to distribute pamphlets, I just needed to call a supervisor and ask for help. Only one supervisor did not cooperate with me... Bu Ratna promised to increase the welfare of parking service providers by means of a cooperative. However, we have not yet focused on that particular goal. We were focused on getting our salaries. *Alhamdulilah*, now all of my friends have been able to enjoy their salaries again, even though it's only Rp 400,000. Bu Ratna fulfilled her promise.[41]

Campaigning Strategy: Using Gender and Approaching the Grassroots Community

In this section, we will see how Ratna as the only female candidate used her distinct gender identity as an important selling point in her political

---

[41] Interview with JL, coordinator of the Parking Service Organization in Banyuwangi, 31 July 2009.

campaign. Understanding the fact that she was the first and only female regent candidate in Banyuwangi, she deliberately used gender, the local norms of an ideal women and a relatively feminine approach in dealing with the grassroots community to attract wider sympathy. AG, the chief of the Regional Board of the Indonesian Democratic Vanguard Party (Partai Penegak Demokrasi Indonesia, PPDI) in Banyuwangi and an important figure on Ratna's campaign team, stated:

> Yes, that is true. Because at that time we heard the voice of the grassroots. Bu Ratna was the right choice, because the male [candidates] were like that [the other three candidates in the coalition of small political parties, including Samsul Hadi, former Regent of Banyuwangi (2000–05), were corrupt], therefore we nominated the *female* [emphasis added] candidate.[42]

Here we can see that Ratna gained advantage from the fact that the other contenders were seen as relatively unclean (corrupt) whereas Ratna as a new player and as a female was expected to bring change. Ratna further promoted her gender and its positive stereotype in her campaign, which was made easier by the fact that she found no major obstacles in terms of the religious legitimacy for female leadership in Banyuwangi. She said in an interview:

> I did not find I had any disadvantage from religious aspects. NU did not issue any *fatwa* (religious edict) or *tausyiah* (religious teaching) banning people from voting for a female candidate. We gained the advantage. In addition, society really wanted a female candidate at that time. So, the political timing was really good…. There was no gender-based opposition. They opposed me based on the fact that my husband was from Bali and thus they questioned my religion… so, most of the opposition centered around issues of SARA (Indonesian abbreviation for *suku, agama, ras, antar golongan*; ethnicity, religion, race and class relation) and not gender.[43]

When I spoke to *Kyai* MAS, chief of the Tandfiziah of NU in Banyuwangi, he expressed a similar point:

---

[42] Interview with AG, chief of the Regional Board of PPDI in Banyuwangi and an important figure on Ratna's campaign team, Banyuwangi, 29 July 2009.

[43] Interview with Ratna Ani Lestari, 29 July 2009.

Demonstrations mainly questioned the rumor that administrative procedures [concerning Ratna and Gus Yus's nomination at the Banyuwangi KPU] had not yet been completed. Secondly, they were about her religious status. I was often asked... "so we will be led by a whore?" [Islam does not support the marriage of a Muslim woman to a non-Muslim man].[44]

There was a bit of dissent regarding Ratna's candidacy as a female regent, including from *Kyai* SY of Mansya'ul Huda Pesantren,[45] and *Kyai* DL chief of MUI in Banyuwangi said that *ulama* in Banyuwangi did not approve of women's leadership.[46] Yet Ratna's distinct identity as the only female candidate was not really a point of contention. In fact, Ratna was strategically able to use her gender identity as the only Banyuwangi woman among an entirely male slate of candidates by creating, for instance, musical VCDs that were distributed to her followers and the general public, and that promoted her distinct profile and policy for the future of Banyuwangi. See Figure 9.

Source: Photograph taken by author, August 2009.

Figure 9 Ratna and Gus Yus's Musical Media Campaign VCD for the 2005 Direct Election in Banyuwangi

---

[44] Interview with *Kyai* MAS, chief of the Tandfiziah of NU in Banyuwangi, 1 Aug. 2009.
[45] Ibid.
[46] Ibid.

The VCD lasts 7.06 minutes. One of my colleagues from Banyuwangi described the music as *"kendang kempul"* in which the Osing and Indonesian languages are used altogether, perhaps so as to address the different ethnicities in Banyuwangi.[47] Some important words in the campaign song on the VCD read:

> Han sing koyo han sing uwis-uwis...saiki muncul wanito Banyuwangi, calon bupati hanggede tekade lawan visi lan misine han jelas. Utamane bebasno biaya sekolahe kanggo murid-murid SD sampe SMA. Sopo ketiban loro bebas biayane nyang Puskesmas lan nyang dokter swasta, lan sing arep ningkatno wisatane. Ayo milih Ibu Ratna, calon <u>*bupati wanito Banyuwangi*</u>, ojo lali coblosen sing nomer papat. Kadung awake kepingin seger lan sehat [emphasis added].

The English translation reads:

> Unlike previously, a Banyuwangi woman has emerged as a candidate for regent with a strong commitment and a clear vision and mission. Her goal is free education for students from elementary to senior high school. Anyone ill will receive free treatment in hospital and a private doctor, and tourist attractions will be improved. Let's chose Ibu Ratna, *the female candidate for Regent of Banyuwangi*, do not forget to choose number four. If you want to feel fresh and healthy.

The above text shows that Ratna strategically promoted her distinct gender identity as a Banyuwangi woman who wanted to be seen as an alternative leader who would bring more prosperity and welfare to Banyuwangi by promising free health services and education. Although Ratna is not Osing, by using both the Osing language and Indonesian in her song, she created an impression that she could be part of the indigenous Banyuwangi people without forgetting the other ethnic communities such as the Javanese and Maduranese. Samsul Hadi, former regent of Banyuwangi (2000–05) and a contender in the convention of the 18 small political parties, stated that he was originally Maduranese, and yet due to a political deal he eventually supported Ratna. One of his strategies was to suggest to his loyal NU constituents that Ratna was Osing. He stated "I said to Ratna, everything can be arranged (*semua bisa diatur*), how many do you want (*khon njaluk piro*), Mataraman [Javanese-based

---

[47] Explanation from WIN, one of my colleagues, who is originally from Banyuwangi, 9 March 2011.

voters] and some of the Maduranese...."[48] Here we can see that Banyuwangi's multiethnic feature of Osing, Mataraman, Maduranese, becomes important to generating political support for any political leaders including Ratna Ani Lestari.

In an effort to further connect to the grassroots voters during the campaign, Ratna provided free health check-ups throughout villages, and she and her husband WS helped provide doctors and equipment. She gave money, rice and reconstructed widows' houses,[49] and ensured that news of these activities was printed in the local media to publicize her political identity as a pious, sensitive and caring woman. Ratna met with street vendors in Ketapang Port which impressed people who saw her as a leader close to the grassroots.[50] This kind of strategy, according to SF, a prominent PKB figure in Banyuwangi, became an important factor in her victory:

> ...She had a more personal door-to-door approach with all groups.... She drove her car almost every day, circling around the area (*keliling*). Even in the early morning she went to traditional markets. Other contenders did not as they merely waited for the campaign schedule to begin, which might be at 1 o'clock. Bu Ratna attended the early morning *Shubuh* [the early morning prayer for Muslims, at around 5 am]. She did not merely stick to the campaign times. So every day she went out. It can be said that attending the *Shubuh* prayer was partially intended to find women [followers].... Banyuwangi people perceive men as liking to create conflict and fights. Therefore it was an alternative to create a more peaceful nuance. That was the notion that spread in society at the time.[51]

Ratna was not only trying to approach Osing-based voters, but also was promoting her gender as a caring female leader. By doing so, she could get closer with other ethnic groups in the traditional markets, places where jobs are predominantly held by the Maduranese.

---

[48] Interview with Samsul Hadi, former regent of Banyuwangi (2000–05) and a contender against Ratna in the GPPNP convention, who is in prison for corruption (at the time of his interview with me), Banyuwangi prison, 27 July 2009.
[49] "Rumah Janda tua itupun dibangun".
[50] See "Kiat Ratna Modali Pedagang Asongan".
[51] Interview with SF, member of Banyuwangi DPRD from PKB (1999–2009) and chief of PKB in Banyuwangi DPRD (2004–09), Banyuwangi, 31 July 2009.

Manipulating Islamic Piety

As we shall see in this section, understanding that Banyuwangi was an important pocket of NU *santri*, Ratna, who did not have a strong NU background, tried to represent herself as a pious Muslim woman. One of my respondents, DS a journalist in Banyuwangi, showed me a series of photographs taken before and after Ratna became regent of Banyuwangi. The pictures vary, depicting Ratna's activities as the wife of the regent of Jembrana. In an earlier picture, on an official occasion she wore a brown batik dress. She was also depicted standing beside her husband wearing traditional Balinese clothes (an orange *kebaya*[52]) with a traditional hair style while attending a traditional commemoration, and when she attended an official activity as a member of Jembrana DPRD she also wore traditional Balinese clothes (white *kebaya*) with a traditional hair style.[53] Ratna was not wearing a veil in any of the early photographs. While prior to her nomination Ratna did not wear any Muslim clothing such as long dresses or headscarves, following her nomination she wore Muslim dress and a loose headscarf. It is clear that she was trying to embrace the idea of Islamic piety and to some extent "manipulate" the Islamic idea of piety by wearing a veil and Muslim dress as the most vivid way to represent adoption of Islamic values. I was able to interview one of Ratna's closest friends who was originally from Bondowoso. She said of Ratna's dressing style:

> Because her husband is Hindu, she did not need to be like that [wearing Muslim dress]...the freedom her husband gave her can be seen for instance when she was abroad, she never wore [the veil]. She took off her *jilbab* and wore short-sleeved shirts and a backpack together with her children and no one recognized them.[54]

Ratna's instant adoption of the veil in the lead up to the 2005 direct election was also confirmed by Samsul Hadi, former regent of Banyuwangi, who often met her before she wore the veil and was nominated as candidate for regent.[55] Ratna's effort to use and manipulate Islamic

---

[52] A long traditional batik cloth that covers a woman's arms, chest and hips.
[53] Photograph collection of DS, a local journalist in Banyuwangi, which he shared during my conversation with him, in Banyuwangi, 9 Aug. 2009.
[54] Interview with SM, prominent female radio broadcaster and good friend of Ratna Ani Lestari, Banyuwangi, 9 Aug. 2009.
[55] Interview with Samsul Hadi, 27 July 2009.

piety in the NU tradition continued in her move to produce a small booklet containing the verses of *Yaasiin* and *Tahlil* (often used by NU followers to perform collective chanting) as a media campaign as I had seen from collection of DS, local journalist of Banyuwangi. However, it provoked protest from *kyai* and NU followers because the *Yaasiin* verse had been altered from the original version.[56]

Selling an Innovative and Concrete Programme

As the only female candidate and wife of the successful regent of Jembrana, Ratna wanted to replicate her husband's successful programme of free education and health services. This also met the expectations of some of the 18 small political parties that supported Ratna. As AG from PPDI said:

> …It was not only about Bu Ratna but because of her programs. Bu Ratna's programs [free education and health services] corresponded with our [PPDI's] plan for the last 30 years especially with free education…. This is actually a national program but it has not yet been implemented; it was a smart move.[57]

Similarly, RM from PNIM further explained that it became a key strategy to promote Ratna among ordinary people, most of whom did not know her. He said:

> As for free education and health services, at the time it was new. It had never been advocated so we promoted it. Because, we saw this [program] would work, as shown by her husband's successful record in Jembrana.[58]

Ratna and her team promoted her primary programme of free education and health services through a variety of means including pamphlets. Figure 10 shows one such pamphlet urging people to choose pair number four, namely Ratna and Gus Yus, who promised to provide free education for elementary, junior and senior high school, as well as free health services.

---

[56] "Pelecehan Agama", at <http://www.gatra.com/2005-07-17/artikel.php?id=86444> [accessed 24 Dec. 2008].
[57] Interview with AG, 29 July 2006.
[58] Interview with RM, 26 July 2009.

Source: Photograph taken by author, August 2009.

Figure 10 Ratna and Gus Yus's Campaign Pamphlet

Gus MLK, son of a *kyai* in Blok Agung and a close friend of Gus Yus, affirmed that Ratna's new and clearly defined programme was an important component in generating support from undecided voters beyond PDIP's followers who wanted to see changes made in Banyuwangi.[59] Ratna, who did not have extensive women's networks to rely on, had great confidence in the effectiveness of this programme to win voters' hearts at the grassroots. Ratna said:

> Women from Muslimat, Fatayat were opposed to me. I realized that many women are often jealous. My real supporters were [members of] the community. Perhaps every time my campaign team invited me to a location, they told the story of my program. Then everybody wanted to invite me. They listened to me... [and wanted to find out] whether there would be free education and health services.[60]

---

[59] Interview with Gus MLK, one of the sons of *Kyai* Syafaat in Blok Agung and close friend of Gus Yus, Banyuwangi, 1 Aug. 2009.
[60] Interview with Ratna Ani Lestari, 29 July 2009.

When I further questioned Fatayat NU activists, they said that they did not like Ratna Ani Lestari because Ratna did not have any close engagement or organizational experiences in NU, so that it was difficult for them (NU women) to accept her.[61] Other candidates merely relied on campaigning via newspapers. For example, Soesanto Soewandi and Abdul Kadir (Golkar) had a big picture of themselves wearing dark suits and *peci*[62] with the normative slogan *"Bersama Rakyat Kita Bangun Banyuwangi Menuju ke Arah yang Lebih Baik* (With the people's support, we will develop Banyuwangi in a better direction)" displayed in *Jawa Pos* on 23 March 2005. Similarly, Ahmad Wahyudi and Eko Sukartono (PKB) also displayed a big picture of themselves in suits and *pecis* with the mere slogan *"Pemimpin Yang Mampu Menjalankan Program Kerja Yang Dibuatnya* (Leaders who are able to implement their programs)" in *Jawa Pos* on 28 March 2005. Masduki and Syafi'i (Democrat Party, PPP) rode in a mass convoy of *becaks*[63] in May 2005[64] and held a meeting with the association of street vendors and the association of local bus drivers in June 2005, after which the association eventually promised to vote for the pair.[65] Although Ali Sa'roni, a bureaucrat from Central Java and not a Banyuwangi local, was supported by some NU *kyai* and was in a partnership with Yusuf Widyatmoko, chief of the Regional Board of PDIP in Banyuwangi (2000–05), he was not able to win nationalist-based voters' hearts as they mainly favoured Ratna and Gus Yus. Generally, Ratna's campaign of promising concrete programmes in education and health was more attractive compared to the other candidates' campaigns.

Thus, the combination between Ratna and her team's strategy in approaching and winning the hearts of grassroots voters, in using networks of nationalist-based (PDIP) voters across Banyuwangi, in selling a new and clearly defined programme, in using her gender and Islamic

---

[61] Conversation with MQ, Fatayat NU activist and activist of the SBMI branch in Banyuwangi, 2 Aug. 2009.

[62] A *peci* is a traditional square hat of a dark colour, usually worn by Indonesia Muslim men in prayer. In turn, it is often worn as official attire with a suit during official occasions, either by Muslim or non-Muslim men.

[63] Traditional three-wheeled mode of transportation.

[64] See the picture under the title "Deklarasi: Pasangan Cabup Masduki Su'ud–M. Syafi'i Berkonvoi Dikawal Ratusan Becak Menuju Gedung Wanita Siang...", in *Radar Banyuwangi*, 4 May 2005.

[65] "Didukung PKL, dan Sopir Angkot", *Radar Banyuwangi*, 20 June 2005.

piety, plus the additional factor of the fragmentation of the NU elite in Banyuwangi[66] resulted in Ratna and Gus Yus's tremendous victory on Election Day on 20 June 2005. The detailed results of the 2005 direct election in Banyuwangi are depicted in Graph 4.

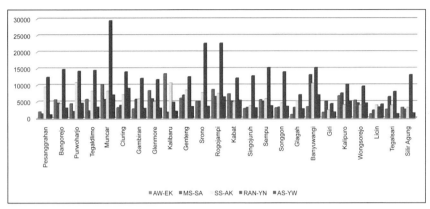

Notes: AW-EK (Achmad Wahyudi and Eko Sukartono)
MS-SA (Masduki Suud and Syafi'i Asyari)
SS-AK (Soesanto Suwandi and Abdul Kadir)
RAN-YN (Ratna Ani Lestari and Yusuf Nuris)
AS-YW (Ali Sa'roni and Yusuf Widyatmoko)

Source: Author, created based on data from Komisi Pemilihan Umum Kabupaten Banyuwangi "Rekapitulasi Hasil Penghitungan Suara Pemilihan Tingkat Kabupaten Pilkada 2005".

Graph 4 Distribution of Votes across Districts as a Result of the 2005 Direct Election in Banyuwangi

Graph 4 above shows that Ratna and Yusuf Nuris won in 20 of the 24 districts in Banyuwangi and obtained the highest number of votes in Muncar, Yusuf Nuris's home town and a Madurese pocket. The pair successfully gained the majority of votes in the primary areas of all three ethnic groups: in the southern part of Banyuwangi where the Mataraman live (Tegalsari, Tegaldlimo, Purwoharjo, Gambiran, Pesanggrahan, Silir Agung and Bangorejo), in the eastern part of Banyuwangi where mostly the Madurese live (Muncar and Glenmore), and in the centre of Banyuwangi where the Osing mainly live (Rogojampi, Singojuruh, Kabat, Glagah and Songgon). They also won the majority of votes in areas where the Mataraman and Osing intermingle such as in Cluring, Srono and

---

[66] Interview with NA, chief of *Anshor NU* in Banyuwangi, 2 Aug. 2009.

Genteng. In total, Ratna and Yusuf Nuris (GPPNP) won 311,653 votes (39.32 per cent) followed by Soesanto and Abdul Kadir (Golkar) with 150,829 votes, and Achmad Wahyudi and Eko Sukartono (PKB) in third with 120,865 votes.

Policies on Women's Issues

This section is devoted to assessing Ratna Ani Lestari's policies as a female leader, and whether she has met the normative expectation that female leaders pay more attention to women's issues and have women's perspectives in their policies.

Quite contrary to the previous two female Javanese Muslim leaders discussed in this text (Rustriningsih and Siti Qomariyah), Ratna Ani Lestari made no move to embrace various local political actors in Banyuwangi. Ratna's relatively "exclusive non-compromise" style of leadership, I believe, was a consequence of her particular journey to power. Although she comes from Banyuwangi, which has a strong NU culture, she does not have cultural roots in Banyuwangi since she never joined in any of NU's local religious activities or organizations and spent most of her youth outside Banyuwangi. She arrived in Banyuwangi just six months before the 2005 direct election and tried to break the cultural barrier by approaching NU *kyai*, as explained earlier. Although eventually she was able to get support from the coalition of 18 non-parliamentary political parties to proceed with her nomination, she remained relatively alone because they did not provide political support to ensure her victory in the 2005 direct election. Ratna said:

> They [the 18 small political parties] merely got me through the candidate nomination and registration process [in the local General Election Commission]. That was all. No, they did not give any political support (*dukungan suara*). Therefore, the next step was to secure political support by myself. We relied on the general public. We had a secretariat where someone was in charge....[67]

Understanding the political context and factions, it is understandable that Ratna seemed reluctant to embrace particular political actors and entities as she further stated, "I am accommodative, especially with

---

[67] Interview with Ratna Ani Lestari, 29 July 2009.

society, I never fight. I just persevere, as long as I'm communicative... I just persevere (*bertahan saja*)."⁶⁸ And yet her description of herself as "communicative" seems to contradict the views of some *kyai* and the Islamic community who perceived her as an uncommunicative leader.⁶⁹ Ratna appears to have been aware of the fact that she had a vice-regent from an NU background, and hence when in power, she increased the social fund for *pesantren* (with which NU followers are largely associated), for example by Rp 25,000,000 each year per *pesantren*.⁷⁰

However, Ratna did not strategically approach women's religious groups (Muslimat NU or 'Aisyiyah)⁷¹ or women's NGOs, though she would listen to and readily talk with them if any approached her.⁷² Ratna's distant relationship with local women's groups can also be seen in the negative assessment of two prominent female activists from PKB and Golkar, who were also members of Banyuwangi DPRD, and who perceived Ratna as being an emotional leader who easily got angry in response to criticism.⁷³ A former close friend of Ratna, STY said that Ratna did not have an ethical attitude, and that it caused many people to dislike her.⁷⁴ When I asked Ratna whether she felt that she represented women's needs and interests, she gave a diplomatic answer:

> In the context of government, many women's interests can be addressed though I am not always able to supervise implementation in the field due to my busyness. In this situation, I can only share my concerns with society, for instance there are some activities that can be organized by women. And yet, they do not seem to respond much....⁷⁵

---

⁶⁸ Ibid.
⁶⁹ "Bupati Banyuwangi Kurang Komunikatif", at <http://www.cmm.or.id/cmm-ind_more.php?id=A1389_0_3_0_M> [accessed 24 Dec. 2008].
⁷⁰ Interview with Gus MLK, 1 Aug. 2009.
⁷¹ Interview with NM, chief of Fatayat NU in Banyuwangi, 29 July 2009; and interview with NK, chief of 'Aisyiyah in Banyuwangi (2000–10), 30 July 2009.
⁷² Interview with Ratna Ani Lestari, 29 July 2009.
⁷³ Interview with EH, secretary of the Regional Board of PKB in Banyuwangi (1999–2004), vice-chief of PKB DPC in Banyuwangi (2004–08), and member of Banyuwangi DPRD from PKB (2004–09), 30 July 2009; and interview with YL, member of Banyuwangi DPRD from Golkar (2004–14), 31 July 2009.
⁷⁴ Interview with STY, 9 Aug. 2009.
⁷⁵ Interview with Ratna Ani Lestari, 29 July 2009.

Looking at the Local Government Mid Term Development Plan (Rencana Pembangunan Jangka Menengah Daerah, RJPDM) of Banyuwangi (2006–10), I was quite impressed that the document mentioned the effort to improve women's quality of life and to advocate women's and children's needs as one of the 11 areas of focus for development. When I further examined the document, it was clear that the local government wanted to focus on addressing four basic problems for women: violence against women and children, availability of data on gender equality, improvement of women's roles in politics, and health.[76]

Despite the fact that these topics in the document showed sensitivity towards women's needs, I was surprised to find that the document did not mention problems related to female migrant workers, given the fact that Banyuwangi is where the largest percentage of Indonesian migrant workers come from in East Java. Some important pockets of female migrant workers are located in the southern parts of Banyuwangi such as Bangorejo, Pesanggrahan, Purwoharjo and Tegaldlimo.[77] Over the last few years there were 3,429 (2006), 3,126 (2007) and 2,390 (2008) female migrant workers originally from Banyuwangi compared to 1,844 (2006), 1,143 (2007) and 558 (2008) male migrant workers from Banyuwangi, with destination countries in order of popularity being Malaysia, Brunei Darussalam, Taiwan, Hong Kong, Singapore and Saudi Arabia.[78] The high proportion of female migrant workers from Banyuwangi can be attributed to the relative lack of basic equality for women, such as in education and health.

Another important feature is prostitution. Ketapang Port is located in Banyuwangi and often creates problems as there are at least 19 illegal prostitution businesses near the port involving young girls and women mostly from outside Banyuwangi. The continuing practice of prostitution has had a negative impact, marked by an increasing number of cases of HIV/AIDS in Banyuwangi. There were 19 cases in 2005 and 105 cases in 2007, which rose to 450 cases in May 2009, where sexual activity (73 per cent) was the main method of infection. HIV/AIDS has become

---

[76] Pemerintah Kabupaten Banyuwangi, *RPJMD Kabupaten Banyuwangi 2006–2010*, p. 89.
[77] Information from conversation with SG and MQ, activists in the SBMI Branch in Banyuwangi, 2 Aug. 2009. Both are often involved in actions to advocate on behalf of female migrant workers, most of whom come from the abovementioned areas.
[78] Dinas Sosial Tenaga Kerja dan Transmigrasi, "Rencana Kebutuhan Calon TKI".

a serious threat in Banyuwangi and the local government is only now beginning to address it.[79] 'Aisyiyah, Muhammadiyah and the Islamic-based party PKS have paid attention to the ongoing problem of prostitution and its impact.[80] The Regional Board of PKS in Banyuwangi initiated a draft of a government regulation to ban prostitution in 2007.[81] Although PKS's draft gained agreement and support from Banyuwangi DPRD, Regent Ratna Ani Lestari disapproved of it so that it was not passed as a local regulation.[82] In an interview Ratna explained her rationale for not banning prostitution:

> They [the illegal prostitution businesses] existed before I came. If I stop their activities [I stop more than just them, because] one whore is interdependent with five other people. That is, one whore provides economic resources for massage services, laundry services, parking services and cigarette businesses. So, if this is multiplied by 100 that could be 500 people involved in the [prostitution business]. That was my point.[83]

While prostitution remains unresolved, in education the illiteracy rate of women in the region is higher than men: 9.28 per cent for women and only 2.83 per cent for men in 2007.[84] Women lag even further behind men when looking at the highest degree of education among the population aged above 15 years old. The lower the degree of

---

[79] Bidang Pencegahan dan Pemberantasan Penyakit Dinas Kesehatan Kabupaten Banyuwangi, "Situasi HIV-AIDS Kabupaten Banyuwangi Juni 2009", pp. 1–3. Almost all of the districts in Banyuwangi have people infected with HIV/AIDS. Therefore, while the local NGOs seriously addressed the issue in the past, nowadays the local government's Bureau of Health is coordinating efforts to overcome it. Here, *Puskesmas* (*Pusat Kesehatan Masyarakat*, Community Health Centre) are the official institutions that provide services for HIV/AIDS prevention and treatment. They have been assisted by the Global Fund (Swiss) since November 2005. Interview with Dr. JW, a staff member in charge of managing HIV/AIDS in the Bureau of Health, Banyuwangi, 7 Aug. 2009.
[80] Interview with NK, 30 July 2009.
[81] See "Rancangan Peraturan Daerah Kabupaten Banyuwangi Nomor…Tahun 2007 tentang Pelarangan Pelacuran Di Kabupaten Banyuwangi".
[82] Interview with AM, 3 Aug. 2009.
[83] Interview with Ratna Ani Lestari in the office of the regent of Banyuwangi, 29 July 2009.
[84] Badan Pusat Statistik Kabupaten Banyuwangi, *Indeks Pembangunan Manusia Kabupaten Banyuwangi 2007*, p. 30.

education the greater the percentage of women, whereas the higher the degree of education, the greater the percentage of men.[85] The health condition of women is also poor. For example the maternal mortality rate increased from six casualties per 1,000 births in 2005 to 20/1,000 births in 2006,[86] though the infant mortality rate decreased slightly from 46/1,000 births (2005) to 44/1,000 births (2006).[87] Therefore, although the local government clearly advocates the critical nature of female related problems, in practice this stance has not been supported with a strong commitment from its leader.

Conclusion

In this chapter I have shown that familial ties were a prominent factor behind Ratna Ani Lestari's political emergence. While Ratna had good individual capital due to her family business background and her educational attainments, her marital status as the wife of a powerful politician (WS, regent of Jembrana) facilitated her political career in Banyuwangi. The fact that she was wife of a successful regent increased her political acceptability for people in Banyuwangi who wanted to see a new leader. We shall underline the critical role of WS, Ratna's husband, in facilitating her initial engagement with politics, in enabling her to further pursue a political career, and in securing her victory as regent of Banyuwangi in 2005. In addition to that, her gender status as a female political leader was seen as a good selling point as it presented her as an alternative leader to breakdown domination of the established male and corrupt political elite system in the Banyuwangi region.

In laying out her political path and developing her political career, Ratna used significant male networks of a nationalist ideology from her husband's political connections with PDIP and members of the Hindu diaspora in Banyuwangi. Although Ratna's status as the wife of WS, who comes from a devout Hindu family, caused controversy to some extent, it became an important means through which to generate political support throughout the grassroots society among three ethnic groups of Osing, Mataraman and Maduranese. Ratna gained advantage from PDIP and Hindu networks and NU swing voters.

---

[85] Ibid., p. 32.
[86] Ibid., p. 81.
[87] Ibid., p. 34.

In her campaigning strategy, Ratna promoted her gender identity as *wanito Banyuwangi* and adopted Islamic norms of piety by wearing the veil in line with her effort to generate wider support from prominent NU *kyai* in Banyuwangi. While we cannot deny the significance of Ratna's new programme of free education and health services to attract mass voters, here again, gender was an important selling point rather than a hindrance to Ratna Ani Lestari's rise.

In terms of Ratna's policy stance, although the government documents state a clear desire to address local women's problems, such efforts have not yet been implemented. I suggest that this is because Ratna Ani Lestari did not closely interact with women's groups and NGOs in her past and more specifically in her quest to power. Consequently, Ratna did not actively work hand-in-hand with local female activists and groups addressing local women's problems.

Interestingly, after finishing her term in 2010, Ratna was set to face trial for an alleged corruption case on the markup of land prices in the development of a local airport in Banyuwangi that occurred during her term, as was her husband, WS, in Jembrana, Bali. However, on July 2011, WS was released without charge because the judge ruled that there was not enough evidence to convict him of corruption.[88] More recently, in February 2013, Ratna Ani Lestari was sentenced to five years in jail due to the above corruption case.[89]

Prior to this, Ratna Ani Lestari sought reelection by competing in the 2010 direct election in Banyuwangi. In the 2010 election Ratna was quite confident to compete because according to a survey she paid the Research Center for Democracy and Human Rights (Pusat Studi Demokrasi dan Ham, PusDeHAM) of Surabaya. Ratna, with her strong *abangan* background, gained quite high satisfaction ratings from non-Muslim groups such as Hindu and Christian groups mainly concentrated in the southern part of Banyuwangi, particularly Purwoharjo.[90] Initially, Ratna and Gus Yus tried to proceed with their nomination as independent candidates, but failed due to their inability to meet all the requirements.

---

[88] See coverage at "Sekkab Jadi Saksi Ratna"; "Terkait Korupsi, Mantan Bupati Jembrana Dilimpahkan ke Kejati Bali"; "Mantan Bupati Jembrana Divonis Bebas".
[89] "Ratna Ani Lestari Divonis 5 Tahun Penjara".
[90] However, the number of people in each ethnic group (Javanese, Madurese, Osing and Balinese) who were dissatisfied with Ratna Ani Lestari was higher compared to those who were satisfied. See Pusat Studi Demokrasi dan HAM (PusDeHAM), "Perilaku Memilih Warga dalam Pilkada Banyuwangi 2010".

Ratna and Gus Yus then tried to proceed with their nomination via a coalition of small political parties. However, during the process, Gus Yus withdrew from his partnership with Ratna and chose to run with the candidate for regent from the Democratic Party, H. Jalal. Ratna continued her efforts via Golkar and 15 political parties which did not have seats in Banyuwangi DPRD (APPNP, Aliansi Partai Politik non-Parlamen, Alliance of Non-Parliamentary Political Parties, which included Golkar, PPPI, P. Kedaulatan, PPD, PMB, PPDI, PDS, PKPI, PNBK, PBB, PBR, PKDI, PIS, P. Merdeka, P. Buruh).[91] Ratna recruited Pebdi Arisdiawan, the chief of Golkar in Banyuwangi, as her candidate for vice-regent. However, the Central Board of Golkar officially gave its recommendation to Abdullah Azwar Anas (PKB) and Yusuf Widyatmoko (PDIP) and asked its followers to support the pair. Pebdi did not obey the instruction, however, and continued as Ratna's partner, though the General Election Commission in Banyuwangi did not grant them approval based on failure to verify administrative issues. The commission discovered that Pebdi and Ratna did not have the support of 15 political parties (only 13; Golkar and PPPI did not support them) and Pebdi was dismissed as chief of the Regional Board of Golkar in Banyuwangi.[92] Eventually, three pairs of candidates namely Abdullah Azwar Anas and Yusuf Widyatmoko; Jalal and Yusuf Nuris; and Emilia Contesa and Zainur competed on 14 July 2011, in which Azwar Anas and Yusuf Widyatmoko won. Ratna had actually tried to interfere with the election by asking the East Java Governor to postpone it, though she failed, while her followers continued to express their disappointment through demonstrations.[93]

---

[91] Interview with SR, former chief of GPPNP, the political vehicle backing Ratna Ani Lestari in the 2005 direct election in Banyuwangi and chief of APPNP, which was intended to be the political vehicle that would support her to compete in the 2010 Banyuwangi direct election, Banyuwangi, 15 July 2010.

[92] Letter of Banyuwangi KPUD No: 234/KPU-Kab/014.329662/VII/2010, in "Penyelesaian Masalah Pencalonan dalam Pemilukada Banyuwangi"; and interview with HPR, member of Banyuwangi KPUD, 14 July 2010.

[93] "Gubernur Kawal Coblosan"; "APPNP Bakar Formulir C-6".

CHAPTER 7

Comparative Analysis and Conclusion

This chapter provides a comparative analysis of the critical factors behind the rise and victory of the three Muslim female Javanese political leaders observed, and then concludes with the findings of this study. Table 11 below summarizes the comparative analysis that follows.

Table 11 Similarities and Differences of Factors Behind the Rise and Victory of Three Muslim Female Javanese Political Leaders

SIMILARITIES	*Rustriningsih*	*Siti Qomariyah*	*Ratna Ani Lestari*
Educational background (at the time of nomination) and family origin	Bachelor's Degree Middle-class family of businessmen	Master's Degree Middle-class and honourable family	Master's Degree Middle-class family of businessmen
The role of Islam	Support from prominent NU *kyai* in Kebumen	Support from prominent NU *kyai* in Pekalongan	Support from NU *kyai* in Banyuwangi
Utilization of gender and Islamic piety	Political branding as "reformist, trusted, pious-nationalist female leader" since 2004 Used the veil in the 2008 direct governor election ("*coblos kerudunge!*")	Sold Islamic piety as a pious modern NU woman by consistently wearing the veil ("*wadon bae*" campaign)	Manipulated Islamic piety by wearing the veil to attract sympathy of NU based voters in her political campaign (*The ideal portrait of "wanita banyuwangi"*)

continued overleaf

Table 11 continued

SIMILARITIES	*Rustriningsih*	*Siti Qomariyah*	*Ratna Ani Lestari*
Gender relations	Husband is very supportive, including management of household Respected and positioned her husband as the head of the family	Husband did not posit a strict division of labour in the family Respected and positioned her husband as the head of the family	Both she and her husband were busy politicians; her husband understood her limitations in performing a role as mother Respected and positioned her husband as the head of the family
Commitment to women's issues	Passive role in addressing local women's issues	No grand design to address local women's issues, though welcoming to women's interests	Passive role in addressing local women's issues, although the local government documents state a clear desire to address local women's problems
DIFFERENCES	*Rustriningsih*	*Siti Qomariyah*	*Ratna Ani Lestari*
Social background	Originally is *abangan*; in 2004 changed into a more pious Muslim	Originally a devout *santri* (NU)	Originally from a Muslim family, but her life history made her closer to an *abangan* lifestyle
Kind of networks	Predominantly male-nationalist (PDIP) networks Penetrated women's networks by means of *nyai* (wife of *kyai*)	Intensified Islamic NU women's networks	Initially helped by women's kin networks (her aunt) Intensified male-nationalist-Hindu based networks
Familial ties	Strong familial ties (father's influence and role as politician)	No familial ties	Strong familial ties (husband's influence and role as prominent politician)

Source: Created by author based on the findings explained in Chapters 4, 5 and 6.

Similarities

As we can see from the table above, there are five points of similarity and three points of difference in the factors behind the rise and victory of female Javanese Muslim political leaders.

Firstly, I noticed a striking commonality in their educational backgrounds; all three politicians have at least a Bachelor's Degree and were raised in middle-class families, although there were differences in social background (either *santri* or *abangan*) and different levels of political experience. Their higher education served as an important element that allowed these women to persuade their electorates to vote for them. This is certainly the case with Rustriningsih, as her bachelor's degree contributed to her reputation for having exceptional individual capital; in the 1980s, it was difficult to find an educated woman within the predominantly lower-class followers of PDIP. This was also the case with Siti Qomariyah. The NU elite, especially the women's wing of NU in Pekalongan, were proud of her because she was the first NU woman in Pekalongan to gain a scholarship to study abroad for her master's degree, and thus as a smart, modern and pious NU woman she served as a good role model. Siti Qomariyah's strong individual capital became one of the important considerations for NU elite in Pekalongan when they decided to nominate her as regent candidate in the 2006 direct election. Ratna Ani Lestari's educational background allowed her to accelerate her political ambitions, which were also aided by her husband WS's education level. Their educational backgrounds proved to be crucial factors in their self-confidence and ambition to expand their roles as politicians in response to new political opportunities that arose out of the direct elections.

A second clear similarity can be seen in the strategies that Rustriningsih, Siti Qomariyah and Ratna Ani Lestari applied. Although their personal backgrounds were varied, with two being nominal Muslims (*abangan*) and the other a NU *santri*, they all strategically approached prominent Islamic religious leaders for support. In all three of these cases they approached NU *kyai*, as NU is the dominant religious orientation in Kebumen, Pekalongan and Banyuwangi. It was initially assumed that it would be difficult for women to win political positions in devout Islamic regions, where discourse on women's empowerment, let alone leadership, is considered sensitive. However, observation of NU's local standpoint on female leadership has revealed that they have provided religious support for female leadership as NU has found no religious foundation on which to oppose women's leadership as regents (*bupati*) or governors (*gubernur*). NU's local branches have also taken positions on women's leadership that are congruent with that of the NU Central Board, which has supported women's leadership since the late 1990s as I have explained in Chapter 3. While Siti Qomariyah, who has a strong NU background, had no difficulty gaining religious support, Rustriningsih and Ratna Ani Lestari, who have nationalist backgrounds, faced only minor religious opposition from some *kyai*, yet even this was largely based on political interest. In general, the three women candidates were able to make their local NU religious support into an important base through which to generate further support. This finding suggests that Islam as a belief, and religious traditions such as that of NU, have made a crucial contribution to the rise of female Javanese Muslim leaders in local politics.

Some may argue that the rise and victory of female Javanese Muslim political leaders is due to transactional politics (*politik transaksional*) and has nothing to do with Indonesian Islam's perspective on female leadership. I am aware of the phenomenon of transactional politics that have increasingly coloured direct elections, in which political candidates, either male or female, often pay political parties in order to run,[1] as well as often giving money, food and social assistance or promising social safety net programmes in exchange for votes.[2] However, as I discovered in this research, the rise and victory of female Javanese Muslim political leaders is unique and specific, and has to be explained beyond the lens of transactional politics. The importance of solid religious justification for female Muslim political leaders in local politics is real and necessary, because Indonesia is a Muslim majority country where religious belief has a significant influence on political behaviour as noted by Norris and Inglehart's research results,[3] and thus cannot be explained simply by transactional politics. As I have shown, female Javanese Muslim political leaders initially need a strong and stable religious foundation to support their nomination, especially within regions with strong Islamic bases. The three leaders studied strategically approached prominent Islamic religious leaders to gain religious suggestions, and were thus able to utilize local

---

[1] For elaboration on this phenomenon see Mietzner, "Indonesia and the Pitfalls of Low-Quality Democracy", in *Democratization in Post-Suharto Indonesia*, ed. Bunte and Ufen, p. 144.
[2] "Pengaruh Politik Uang pada Pilkada Meningkat".
[3] Norris and Inglehart, *Sacred and Secular*, p. 147.

NU religious support to generate further support. Here, there is a clear distinction between, firstly, Indonesian Islam's perspective on female leadership that clearly supports female leadership in local politics and, secondly, political praxis in how *kyai* or political parties use this religious perspective.[4] Although *kyai* support of some female candidates was due to political considerations, for example as a way to secure NU power in a region, we cannot ignore the fact that Islam as a belief and a way of life also provides a perspective that supports female leadership, especially in local politics. Political considerations in support of female leadership would be impossible if *kyai* could not find strong Islamic justification to support their political position. The significance of Indonesian Islamic support for female leadership in local politics can be seen clearly when compared with its approach to female leadership on a national level, particularly in the case of Megawati's nomination in the 1999 Presidential Election. The mounting debate over and rejection of female presidential candidates is not considered relevant in the case of local politics. The idea of a female leader as the head of state is still considered controversial, while female leadership in local politics is justified in Indonesian Islam.

Indonesian Islam's position and practices in support of female leadership in local politics are quite progressive compared with those of other countries. Religious belief (in Islam) as a determining factor for Muslim women exercising political leadership is also strong in Pakistan, as discussed by Saeeda J.A. Shah,[5] as well as in Arab societies, with Asya Al-Lamky noting that one crucial challenge for female leadership is the "'unpacking' of deeply held beliefs regarding women which are often confused with misinterpreted religious dogmas".[6] The issue of female leadership in Middle Eastern or African countries has not yet gained attention compared with other women's issues. One reason for this, according to

---

[4] AZ, a young and prominent NU leader, provided an important explanation of NU's behaviour in political practice. He said, "NU is not a political organisation, but NU cannot separate itself from politics. As NU is not a political organisation, officially NU can never give a political endorsement to a particular candidate, because [their] official endorsement is not in accordance with NU's AD/ART. However, board members of NU can indirectly give support. In this case, sometimes there are different preferences between one *kyai* and another toward one of the candidates in a direct election even though the candidate has an NU background." Email correspondence, AZ to author, Oct. 2011.
[5] Shah, "Re-thinking Educational Leadership".
[6] Al-Lamky, "Feminizing Leadership in Arab Societies", p. 64.

Pieternella Van Doorn-Harder, is that female activists in Middle Eastern or African countries are consumed with addressing issues unknown in Indonesia. For instance, in Egypt, where only the husband is legally allowed to initiate divorce, in 2000 there was controversy over the law of *khul'*, namely consensual divorce in which the wife gives her husband the monetary equivalent of the dowry or bride price in return for the freedom to leave the marriage; or in Africa, where some activists work against female genital mutilation.[7] In Saudi Arabia, women's rights activists are continuously fighting to challenge the country's ban on female drivers,[8] as well as the new system imposed in 2012 in which women are monitored by an electronic system at airports that notifies their male "guardians" when they are leaving or entering the country, an act that obviously violates their human rights and freedom; moreover Saudi women were only granted the right to vote in 2011 when King Abdullah allowed women to both vote and run in the 2015 municipal elections.[9]

Severe conditions are also prevalent in Muslim majority countries in Southeast Asia such as Malaysia, and in South Asia such as Bangladesh. Women's roles in politics in Malaysia have been relatively slow to evolve. This is related to the nature of Islamization in Malaysia. To borrow from Maznah Mohammad, Islamization in Malaysia was a "centralization" process in which the British legacy shaped the post-independence situation, where Malay elites tried to make the Islamic system and values the dominant force in building the nation, including for example allowing each state to have separate Islamic enactments and establishing the Syariah Criminal Offense Law which has authority to punish those who disobey a *fatwa*.[10] Under this centralized and conservative Islamic feature, commitment to female leadership has been relatively slow to emerge because Malaysia's official Islam is concerned with promoting Islamic beliefs and supporting the ideal norm of pious Muslim women as wives and mothers.[11] A similar thing happened in Bangladesh. Kamal Uddin Ahmed notes that the obstacles against Bangladeshi women playing greater roles in politics are due to some Islamic perspectives, which

---

[7] Van Doorn-Harder, *Women Shaping Islam*, pp. 15–6.
[8] "Saudi Woman Seeks to Put Women in the Driving Seat", *BBC NEWS Middle East*, 18 May 2011, at <http://www.bbc.co.uk/news/world-middle-east-13431562> [accessed 2 April 2013].
[9] "Saudi Arabia Accused of Tracking Women Electronically".
[10] Mohamad, "Politicization of Islam in Indonesia and Malaysia", pp. 96, 98, 106.
[11] Shuib, "Speaking with a New Voice", p. 187.

strongly oppose gender equality and women's participation in politics. For example, some *Mullah* (local religious fundamentalists) have condemned women pursuing public roles; in Kalikapur in the Madaripur district, a local *fatwa* even declared it inappropriate for women to vote.[12] By comparing the situation of Muslim women in Indonesia with those in other Muslim countries, we can see the distinguishing feature of Indonesian Islam that supports female leadership especially in local politics as somewhat progressive.

The third similarity is the three candidates' strategies to embrace, utilize or manipulate the idea of Islamic piety in combination with gender expectations to create a distinct political identity and increase their appeal to the majority of Muslim voters. For example, Rustriningsih, who was originally *abangan*, gradually embraced the Islamic norm of piety. In 2004 Rustriningsih went on the pilgrimage, adopted the *kudung*, and married. In Java, a true woman (*wanita sejati*) is one who can serve well in the home as a mother and wife, either in the kitchen or in bed,[13] which means, of course, that she must be married. Therefore, Rustriningsih's marriage in 2004 and her becoming a mother had a positive impact on her political image as a mature Javanese Muslim woman. By embracing Islam (making the pilgrimage, wearing the *kudung*) and fulfilling the religio-cultural expectation (of being married), Rustriningsih gained political confidence because she was able to fit the normative societal expectation of the ideal Javanese Muslim woman. She then gradually approached NU *kyai* and embraced NU traditions as part of her effort to create an image of a "reformist, trusted, pious-nationalist female leader". The use of the *kudung* was pertinent in the 2008 Direct Gubernatorial Election in Central Java to signify her political identity. It was evident, for instance, in the "*coblos kerudunge!*" campaign where she smartly promoted herself as the only female Javanese Muslim candidate, and one who additionally adhered to the concept of *kodrat*, which was further promoted in the "*milih wonge dhewek, milih biyunge dhewek!*" campaign aimed at attracting all voters regardless of their gender, because *biyung* (mother) is a universal position that is respected both by men and women.

The case of Siti Qomariyah, regent of Pekalongan, who has a strong NU *santri* background, is also interesting. In the initial stages of her

---

[12] Ahmed, "Women and Politics in Bangladesh", pp. 283–4.
[13] Handayani and Novianto, *Kuasa Wanita Jawa*, p. 143.

emergence, Siti often accompanied her husband to political meetings of the Regional Board of PKB in Pekalongan to show that although she was running for political office, she still respected her husband and would not disrupt the primary relationship, authority and harmony in her family. She wanted to gain public support and sympathy as a smart, modern, pious NU woman. In her political campaign, she strategically promoted her piety in combination with her gender. Thus, she confidently asked voters to *"wadon bae"* (chose a woman), and in this, she did not mean that the voters should choose an ordinary women, but her representation of the Javanese, pious, modern, NU women.

Similarly, Ratna Ani Lestari changed her style of dress by adopting the *kudung* in the lead up to the 2005 direct election in Banyuwangi, though she would take it off when she travelled outside of Banyuwangi. By wearing the *kudung*, she promoted herself as the ideal portrait of Banyuwangi women (*wanito Banyuwangi*) who cared about women-related issues (women in traditional markets, health, education), close to people, and pious. This new portrait would increase her political acceptability among the majority of NU voters, beyond her nationalist loyalist followers. An interesting note on Ratna Ani Lestari's story is that her gender was not the primary issue cited by her opponents to counter her nomination. Her private life, specifically her decision to marry WS who was Hindu, convert to Hinduism and then revert back to Islam for the sake of her political career attracted major opposition.

Behind the story of the three female Muslim politicians, there is a clear indication of the impact of the increasing engagement of Indonesian Muslims with Islamic principles and norms after 1998. We can see clearly that some aspects of private life and intimate relations, which are highly shaped by Islamic norms and are issues of concern for the majority of the Muslim community, are deliberately brought into the public sphere[14] to attract political sympathy, or are made the centre of attention by opponents to oppose an individual's political nomination. For example, Rustriningsih's private decisions to embark on the pilgrimage, where she

---

[14] Suzanne Brenner addresses the struggle between liberal and conservative Islam in Indonesia over the construction of a new moral order and symbolic control over public morality. This is done by assessing the contest between proponents of the two Islamic ideologies over the shifting boundaries and meaning of public and private spheres (through such issues as polygamy, pornography, the domestic violence bill and *sha'riah*-based law) in the newly democratic Indonesia that developed after 1998. See Brenner, "Private Moralities in the Public Sphere", pp. 479–90.

met her prospective husband and then subsequently married him, and the later decision to change her style of dress by wearing the veil, were brought into the public sphere and gained a wide public interest, which in turn contributed to her political success. Similarly, Siti Qomariyah's relationship with her husband and the way she managed it properly in accordance with Islamic norms were also brought into the public sphere, to attract political sympathy. Even more interesting is Ratna Ani Lestari's story, in that her private life and her decision to marry WS and change her religion were brought into the public sphere by her opponents, who were largely members of Muslim communities, in order to oppose her political stand. Here we can see that many aspects of private life, intimate relations and faith are brought into the public or political sphere.[15]

Of even more interest is that all three female Javanese Muslim leaders studied actively adapted to the norm of wearing the veil, which became a popular Islamic practice for the majority of Indonesian Muslim women after 1998. Although it is difficult to measure the real motive of any one woman choosing to wear the veil, we can see that ideas of Islamic piety, as evidenced by wearing the veil, were circulated and incorporated by these three female women in their political contests and in the public sphere. The decision to wear the *kudung* as an ideal Islamic act is a very personal matter. Yet there may be different dimensions of meaning found in the way the three women practised Islamic piety. So, while the basic definition of piety, as described in the work of Joy Kooi-Chin Tong and Bryan S. Turner,[16] mainly refers to self-control and bodily practices including diet, clothing and attitude, and is often associated with the transformative path into more divine life, this book suggests something beyond this. The acts of the female Javanese Muslim leaders in embracing the ideas and norms of Islamic piety, especially in their quest to power, leads me into another proposition of piety in praxis

---

[15] The situation is similar in Turkey. Under the context of countering Turkish secularism—the policies by which Turkey since the 1920s transformed itself into a secular state by instituting the gradual separation of state affairs from religion (Islam), followed Western civilization and cut links with the Islamic world—the post-1980s Islamist movement promoted "the moral control of the public sphere through the traditional practice of compelling women's modesty by veiling, limiting public encounters between the sexes...." As a result, many aspects of life, intimate relations and faith were brought into the public or political sphere. See Gole, "The Gendered Nature of the Public Sphere", pp. 70, 72; and Gole, "Islam in Public".
[16] Tong and Turner, "Women, Piety and Practice", p. 43.

politics. Perhaps in the realm of politics, it does not matter whether a candidate truly embraces Islamic piety (meaning, as their own inner personal experience of the transformative path into a more divine life), or whether they just utilize it or even manipulate it. However, their actions have surely transformed the idea of Islamic piety: from a personal act of worshipping God to a public piety in which the ideas and norms of Islamic piety become instrumental in politics in defining what I call the "common rule of conduct" for showing modesty in an increasingly Islamized society in contemporary Indonesian politics.

Okamoto Masaaki, Ota Atsushi and Ahmad Suaedy argue that one of the reasons for the electoral defeat of Islamic political parties in the general elections in the post-Suharto period was because "Islam has become less appealing as a political slogan to the voters. Parties merely selling 'Islam' cannot attract voters in an increasingly Islamized society."[17] This may be true in the case of Islamic political parties. However, based on the individual experiences and strategies of female Muslim politicians in this study, some aspects of Islam, namely the idea and norm of Islamic piety, especially as it applies to wearing the veil, are important in winning elections. Especially for those candidates who originally come from *abangan* backgrounds, it signifies their personal transformation into more pious Muslims. This piety is later used to help to define a distinct political brand for candidates, which increases their popularity in the elections of an increasingly Islamized society.

Overall, this study finds that the idea and practice of Islamic piety, in combination with gender (as an ideal Javanese Muslim woman) enabled these women to expand their political bases, gave them considerable access to more opportunities and allowed them to increase their popularity and approval rating among the majority of Muslim-based voters in the direct local elections. This book presents a new perspectives on the strategic role of gender in local politics, which contradict Satriyo's earlier findings that stated that gender was not used by female political candidates to mobilize voters.[18]

The fourth similarity is the gender relations between the women and their husbands. None of the women faced any challenges stemming from the old-fashioned normative expectation or stereotype of Javanese women as *konco wingking* (the friend in the back) or ideas about a rigid

---

[17] Okamoto, Ota and Suaedy, "Introduction", p. 5.
[18] Satriyo, "Pushing The Boundaries", p. 260.

division of labour between husband and wife. Rustriningsih, for example, in an interview said that her husband was very supportive and tolerant, was not reluctant to discuss anything including the management of the household, and allowed close relatives and a babysitter to help take care of the children.[19] Siti Qomariyah and her husband do not have a strict division of labour in the family, rather it is understood to be both their responsibilities, though Siti positions her husband as the head of the family.[20] Siti believes that the old-fashioned term *konco wingking* is no longer valid to describe the situation of Javanese women today.[21] Similarly, Ratna stated that she encountered no hurdles from the old-fashioned perspective of Javanese women as *konco wingking*. In fact, her husband allowed Ratna to perform her duty as a mother by asking for help from her mother's relatives to take care of the children while Ratna travelled frequently between Banyuwangi and Jembrana.[22] Regardless of their public roles, all three women positioned their husbands as the head of the family. Perhaps this was part of their strategy in accordance with the Javanese norm of *empan papan* (knowing one's place and situation): when a Javanese woman wants to expand her role according to her personal will, she should not disturb harmony, but should care for and serve her husband so that she can win his heart (*mengambil hati*).[23]

The fifth point of similarity is that these female politicians' policy stances on women's issues were influenced by a number of factors, such as their personal experiences, including their engagement with women's groups during their quest for power, their leadership characteristics and their personal commitments. When female leaders come from or have intense interaction with particular women's groups in their quest for power, they welcome and show more interest in women's issues, though it does not guarantee the incorporation of women's needs into their policies, as in the case of Siti Qomariyah. In contrast, when female leaders do not have intense interaction with women's groups in their quest for power, there is a smaller chance that the leader will understand the issues or work hand-in-hand with women's groups to address local women's

---

[19] Interview with Rustriningsih, office of the vice-governor of Central Java, 3 Feb. 2010.
[20] Interview with Siti Qomariyah, office of the regent of Pekalongan, 25 June 2009.
[21] Ibid.
[22] Interview with Ratna Ani Lestari, office of the regent of Banyuwangi, 29 July 2009.
[23] Handayani and Novianto, *Kuasa Wanita Jawa*, p. 44.

problems, such as in the cases of Rustriningsih and Ratna Ani Lestari. Generally, this study found that none of the three Javanese Muslim leaders incorporated women's perspectives in their policies.

The results of my study are similar to those found in Siregar's study of female members of parliament (MPs) in the national, provincial (East Java) and local (Sidoarjo) parliaments as a result of the 2004 General Election: their existence does not automatically translate to substantive representation for women.[24] Siregar cites factors about these female politicians such as their minority status, the diversity of interest among these women, the different experiences of female MPs with women's movements and the compatibility of their party platforms with regard to feminist advocacy, all of which play a part in determining whether female MPs act as substantive representation.[25]

Even on a regional scale, the phenomenon seems the same. In Thailand, Hathairat Marpraneet's study of representation of Sub-district Administration Organization (SAO) members in Kalasin Province concluded that there was no significant difference between male and female roles in government since the female leaders studied did not do things differently from male politicians.[26] However, Juree Vichit-Vadakan's research of seven female leaders in sub-districts and the Tambon Administrative Organization showed that successful female political leaders did make differences as proven by their interest in, and policies on, issues such as education, health, childcare and the elderly.[27] Vichit-Vadakan noted that these female leaders usually had strong civic engagement and became community leaders prior to entering formal politics.[28] In the Philippines, Lourdes Veneracion-Rallonza's research on the increasing number of women elected to public office (executive and legislative positions) found that women did not necessarily have a greater interest in women's issues, as they were afraid of being branded as having narrow intentions.[29] As Veneracion-Rallonza explained, this is perhaps due to

---

[24] Siregar, "Gaining Representation in Parliament", p. 193.
[25] Ibid., p. 194.
[26] Hathairat Marpraneet, "Gender Differences in Representation of Subdistrict Administration Organization (SAO) Members in Kalasin Province, Thailand", PhD dissertation, Utah State University, 2003, as cited in Vichit-Vadakan, "A Glimpse of Women Leaders in Thai Politics", p. 132.
[27] Vichit-Vadakan, "A Glimpse of Women Leaders in Thai Politics", p. 145.
[28] Ibid., p. 144.
[29] Veneracion-Rallonza, "Women and the Democracy Project", p. 229.

the fact that they successfully gained their positions not by virtue of the "women's vote" but via other factors such as political party machinery, patronage or familial/kinship ties.[30] Here we can see that the low level of commitment by female political leaders to women's issues is not exclusively an experience of Indonesian women in executive positions in local politics, but can also be found among female Indonesian parliament members on the national, provincial and regional levels, as well as in other Southeast Asian countries. My assessment corresponds with Kazuki Iwanaga's note in the introduction to the book he edited, that "the impact of women politicians may be less evident in the Asian settings than in the Nordic countries...."[31]

Differences

The first difference between these women concerns their social backgrounds, as personal backgrounds were varied, with one candidate, Siti Qomariyah, consistently maintaining herself as a *santri* (pious Muslim); and the other two candidates being nominal Muslims (*abangan*), namely Rustriningsih, who gradually changed into a pious Muslim, and Ratna Ani Lestari.

The second difference can be seen in the kinds of networks these women harnessed. While Rustriningsih and Ratna Ani Lestari relied predominantly on male networks, Siti Qomariyah worked with women's networks. Rustriningsih used the male networks available to her through the nationalist party PDIP in Kebumen and Central Java, though she also penetrated women's networks such as Muslimat NU in order to increase her political acceptability, particularly in the 2008 Central Java Gubernatorial Election. She was also assisted by networks of *nyai* connected to the wife of KH. Nashiruddin. Thus, KH. Nashiruddin was not only her vice-regent but also an important hub in Rustriningsih's network.

Similarly, Ratna Ani Lestari, who did not have a strong Islamic background and yet had to work with the significant NU base in Banyuwangi, deliberately adjusted her strategy. Ratna Ani Lestari mainly used the male networks of the nationalist party PDIP and of the Hindu diaspora, though she initially used women's networks, mainly through her aunt's connection to the wife of *Kyai* AHS in Blok Agung. In Ratna's

---

[30] Ibid.
[31] Iwanaga, "Introduction", in *Women and Politics in Thailand*, p. 6.

network, there were three important hubs, namely *Kyai* AHS in Blok Agung who had solid links to NU *kyai*, her vice-regent Gus Yus, and her husband WS with his considerable connections to the nationalists and Hindus in Banyuwangi.

Meanwhile, Siti Qomariyah was mainly assisted by the women's networks associated with NU, as shown by the role of FA, the leader of Muslimat NU in Pekalongan, and HD, the chief of Fatayat NU in Pekalongan. Both FA and HD were critical hubs in Siti's networks. Although the kinds of networks were different, each of these women shared the commonality whereby at some point each gained advantage from women's networks. Here, the agency of prominent Javanese women, in this case is Muslimat NU and *nyai* (wife of *kyai* NU) is apparent in enabling, controlling, ensuring and broadening the political loyalty of their surrounding neighbourhoods (both men and women) to support each of the three female Javanese Muslim politicians.

It is difficult to gain a clear picture of whether the kinds of networks used by female leaders is different to those of male leaders, because so far there are no detailed studies on the networks used by male leaders. While female leaders also use religious and personal networks, it seems that male candidates tend to rely on networks of bureaucrats, as in the case of Amat Antono, a contender of Siti Qomariyah in the 2006 direct election in Pekalongan. Another example is the case of Idham Samawi (networks of local newspapers, journalists and bureaucrats) who was elected regent of Bantul in 2005,[32] Ahmad Dahlan (networks of businessmen and the Malay community) who was elected mayor of Batam in 2006,[33] Syafruddin Nur (religious networks of mosques in villages and bureaucrats up to the village level) who was elected regent of Pangkep in 2005 and Andi Soetomo who was elected regent of Soppeng in 2005.[34] Here we can see that to a certain extent, the networks employed by the female Javanese Muslim leaders are quite similar to those of males. This marks an important development in Indonesian local politics: today Javanese Muslim women, though secure in their limited yet solid same-sex networks, as exemplified by Siti Qomariyah (and her Muslimat NU network), or even with no same-sex networks, as exemplified by Ratna

---

[32] Sulistiyanto, "Pilkada in Bantul District", pp. 190–206.

[33] Choi, "Batam's 2006 Mayoral Election", pp. 74–93.

[34] Buehler, "The Rising Importance of Personal Networks in Indonesian Local Politics", pp. 101–19.

Ani Lestari (because she mainly used male nationalist networks) and to some extent Rustriningsih, are gradually able to make the same moves and employ nearly the same strategies as male politicians and subsequently seize the space and power formerly dominated by men.

The third difference concerns familial ties. Based on the definition of familial ties as a strong influence, political connections and the role of a father or husband who is or was a prominent political figure, I found it was not a common factor behind the rise of the three Muslim women. Familial ties were present in the case in Rustriningsih (father's political influence) and Ratna Ani Lestari (husband's political influence), but not in the case of Siti Qomariyah. At this point, I also discovered an interesting feature beyond the common definition of familial ties. Siti Qomariyah's case shows that although neither her father nor husband were active in politics, it was her father's prominent reputation as an influential *kyai* in Pekalongan, as well as strong support from NU as an Islamic male-based organization that helped to facilitate Siti Qomariyah's political rise. So, beyond the classical understanding of the familial ties factor in Asia, we shall consider another empirical feature: that the good reputation of prominent male politicians in the family who have religious/cultural/business capital can facilitate the rise of female politicians, even though the male relatives may not be involved in formal politics. In this, we remain open to the reality that perhaps does not fit with the classical definition of familial ties, and is perhaps beyond this definition, but which has a real presence and influence.

So far, based on the three female Muslim Javanese leaders observed, familial ties were not such a pertinent factor behind the rise of female Javanese Muslim leaders in the first term of the direct elections (2005–10). Interestingly, I noticed clearly that familial ties became a strong factor in the rise of female Javanese Muslim leaders in the second term of the direct elections (2010–15). That is, female leaders were initially able to run for and win political positions because of the political positions, networks and capital of their male relatives (fathers or husbands, or, in some cases, brothers). According to the General Election Commission, there were 245 direct elections to be held in 2010/11 throughout Indonesia.[35] The second term of direct elections (2010–15) has been

---

[35] See <http://www.kpu.go.id/dmdocuments/jadwal_pilkada.pdf> [accessed 10 March 2011].

marked equally by the increasing emergence of female politicians, more than in the first term (2005–10). There were at least 45 female candidates for local government head (regents/mayors/governors) across Indonesia, consisting of 34 female candidates in Java[36] and 11 outside of

---

[36] Namely: (i) Anna Sophanah, wife of Irianto M.S. Syafiuddin, the regent of Indramayu for two periods (2000–10) as candidate for regent of Indramayu in 2010; (ii) Airin Rachmy Diany, daughter-in-law of the late Chasan Sochib, a powerful figure with a strong political dynasty in Banten, as candidate for mayor of South Tangerang in 2011; (iii) Ratu Atut Chosiyah, governor of Banten (2006–11) and another daughter of the late Chasan Sochi, as candidate for governor of Banten in 2011; (iv) Emy Susanti, wife of Win Hendarso, former regent of Sidoarjo for two periods (2000–10), as candidate for regent of Sidoarjo in 2010; (v) Yuniwati Teryana, businesswoman and wife of businessman Achmansjah Hasan, as candidate for regent of Sidoarjo in 2010; (vi) Haryanti Sutrisno, first wife of Sutrisno, former regent of Kediri for two periods (2000–10), as candidate for regent of Kediri in 2010; (vii) Nurlaila, second wife of Sutrisno, as candidate for regent of Kediri in 2010; (viii) Emilia Contessa, an artist, businesswoman and member of national legislature from PPP and originally from Banyuwangi, as candidate for regent of Banyuwangi in 2010; (ix) Sri Surya Widati, wife of Idham Samawi, who served as regent of Bantul for two periods (2000–10), as candidate for regent of Bantul in 2010; (x) Widya Kandi Susanti, wife of Hendy Boedoro, former regent of Kendal for two periods (2000–10), as candidate for regent of Kendal in 2010; (xi) Siti Nurmakesi, former vice–regent of Kendal (2005–10), as candidate for regent of Kendal in 2010; (xii) Kusdinar Untung Yuni Sukowati, daughter of Untung Wiyono, former regent of Sragen for two periods (2001–11) as candidate for regent of Sragen in 2011; (xiii) Titik Suprapti, wife of Bambang Riyanto, former regent of Sukoharjo for two periods (2000–10), as candidate for regent of Sukoharjo in 2010; (xiv) Tri Rismaharini, candidate for mayor of Surabaya in 2010; (xv) Ratih Sanggarwati, former model, as candidate for regent of Ngawi in 2010; (xvi) Siti Qomariyah, regent of Pekalongan (2006–11), as candidate for regent of Pekalongan in 2011; (xvii) Rieke Diah Pitaloka, candidate for governor of West Java in 2013; (xviii) Puput Tantriana Sari, wife of Hasan Aminuddin, former regent of Probolinggo for two periods (2002–12), as candidate for regent of Probolinggo in 2012; (xix) Idza Priyanti, former vice-regent of Brebes (2011–12), as candidate for regent of Brebes in 2012; (xx) Sri Rahayu, member of Commission IX of the People's Representative Council and wife of Sirmadji, chief of the Provincial Board of PDIP East Java, as candidate for mayor of Malang in 2013; (xxi) Heri Puji Utami, wife of Peni Suparto, chief of the Regional Board of PDIP Malang, as candidate for mayor of Malang in 2013; (xxii) Andromeda Qomariyah, former secretary of the Social Bureau of East Java, daughter of Mahmoed Zain, former regent of Mojokerto for two periods, as candidate for regent of Bojonegoro in 2012; (xxiii) Nanik Karsini, member of the General Election Commission, as candidate for regent of Magetan in 2013; (xxiv) Khofifah Indar Parawansa, as candidate for governor of East Java in 2013; (xxv) Siti Masitha Soeparno, as candidate for mayor of Tegal in 2013; (xxvi) Dewi Ratih, as candidate for mayor of Probolinggo in 2013; (xxvii) Hj. Rukmini, wife of HM Buchori, mayor of Probolinggo for two periods (2004–13), as candidate

Java,[37] in 2010–14 alone. Interestingly, there is a new trend in which most were wives, daughters, or relatives of prominent male politicians. Table 12 below presents the names of the elected female leaders, mainly with strong familial ties.

---

for mayor of Probolinggo in 2013; (xxviii) Hj. Utje Ch Hamid Suganda, wife of Aang Hamid Suganda, regent of Kuningan for two periods (2003–13), as candidate for regent of Kuningan in 2013; (xxix) Yeyet Rohaeti, as candidate for regent of Majalengka in 2013; (xxx) Iti Oktavia, daughter of Mulyadi Jayabaya, regent of Lebak (2003–13), as candidate for regency in 2013; (xxxi) Sri Heviyana Supardi, wife of Dedi Supardi, regent of Cirebon for two periods (2003–13), as candidate for regency in 2013; (xxxii) Sumiyati Mochtar Mohamad, wife of Mochtar Mohamad, mayor of Bekasi (2008–13), as candidate for mayor in 2012; (xxxiii) Neneng Hasanah Yasin, daughter of powerful Bekasi businessman Hasanan Yasin, as candidate for regent of Bekasi in 2012; (xxxiv) Hj Atty Suharti Tochija, wife of Itoch Tochija, former mayor of Cimahi for two periods (2002–12), as candidate for mayor in 2012. From these 34 female candidates, only 12 women did not have backgrounds with strong familial ties. Tri Rismaharini has an excellent background as a successful bureaucrat in Surabaya, where her husband was not a prominent politician. Rieke Diah Pitaloka has an excellent track record as a qualified PDIP cadre, and her husband is an ordinary businessman. Ratih Sanggarwati and Emilia Contessa were formerly a prominent model and an artist. Siti Qomariyah, a lecturer, was formerly regent of Pekalongan (2006–11). Yuniwati Teryana is a businesswoman and former vice president of public relations and communications with Lapindo Brantas, Inc. Nanik Karsini has experience as a staff member of the General Election Commission. Khofifah Indar Parawansa is a prominent Muslimat NU activist and a former minister of women's empowerment during Abdurrahman Wahid's Presidency. Siti Masitha Soeparno is the daughter of the former director of Garuda Indonesia Airline. Dewi Ratih, a successful businesswoman originally from Probolinggo, stays in Jakarta and has never been active in politics. Yeyet Rohaeti is a successful bureaucrat in the regency of Majalengka, and Neneng Hasanah Yasin is the daughter of a businessman in Bekasi.

[37] Namely: (i) Aida Zulaikha Nasution, wife of Ismeth Abdullah, former governor of the Riau Archipelago (2006–10), as candidate for governor in 2010; (ii) Septina Primawati Rusli, wife of Rusli Zainal, governor of Riau for two terms (2003–13), as candidate for mayor of Pekanbaru in 2011; (iii) Adlina T. Milwan, wife of Batu T. Milwan, former regent of Labuhan (2000–10), as candidate for regent of Labuhan in 2010; (iv) Ni Putu Eka Wiryastuti, daughter of Nyoman Adi Wiryatama, former regent of Tabanan (2005–10), as candidate for regent of Tabanan in 2010; (v) Rita Widyasari, daughter of Syaukani HR, former regent of Kutai Kutanegara for two terms (1999–2006), as candidate for regent in 2010 (*Gatra*, 8 September 2010); (vi) Christiany Eugenia Paruntu, successful businesswoman in South Minahasa, as candidate for regent of South Minahasa in 2010; (vii) Linneke Sjennie Watoelangkow S, politician from the Democrat Party and former vice-mayor of Tomohon (2005–10), as candidate for mayor of Tomohon in 2010; (viii) Netty Agnes Pantauw, a businesswoman who participates in politics following her husband's footsteps as a prominent

Table 12 Female Leaders Elected in Direct Elections (2010–14)

		JAVA		
No.	Name	Type of Familial Ties	Position	Party
1	Haryanti Sutrisno	Wife of Sutrisno, former regent of Kediri for two periods (2000–10)	Regent of Kediri (2010–15)	PDIP, PPP, PKNU, Golkar, Hanura
2	Sri Surya Widati	Wife of Idham Samawi, former regent of Bantul for two periods (2000–10)	Regent of Bantul (2010–15)	PDIP
3	Widya Kandi Susanti	Wife of Hendy Boedoro, former regent of Kendal for two periods (2000–10)	Regent of Kendal (2010–15)	PDIP
4	Anna Sophanah	Wife of Irianto M.S. Syafiuddin, the regent of Indramayu for two periods (2000–10)	Regent of Indramayu (2010–15)	Golkar
5	Airin Rachmy Diany	Daughter-in-law of (late) Chasan Sochib, a powerful figure with a strong political dynasty in Banten	Mayor of South Tangerang (2011–16)	PKS
6	Ratu Atut Chosiyah	Daughter of a powerful figure in Banten, (late) Chasan Sochib	Governor of Banten (2011–16)	Golkar, PDIP, Hanura, Gerindra, PKB, PAN, PBB, PPNUI, PKPB, PDS, PPD
7	Tri Rismaharini	Successful bureaucrat in Surabaya; no familial ties	Mayor of Surabaya (2010–15)	PDIP

---

politician in the Democrat Party of North Minahasa, as candidate for regent of North Minahasa in 2010; (ix) Francisca Tuwaidan, a businesswoman and politician, a member of the DPRD in North Minahasa and a candidate for regent in 2010; (x) Djeli Wisye Massie, mayor of Menado in 2010; (xi) Juliarti Djuhardi Alwi, a professional doctor and successful bureaucrat, as the director of the Bureau of Health in Sambas, who successfully won the seat of vice-regent of Sambas in the 2006 Election, and then was nominated as a candidate for the post of regent of Sambas in 2011. For a more detailed description of the profile, motivation and political process behind the candidacies of some of the female politicians from East Java and North Sulawesi, see Tim Peneliti Departemen Ilmu Politik FISIP UNAIR, *Perempun dalam Pemilukada*.

Table 12 continued

		JAVA		
No.	Name	Type of Familial Ties	Position	Party
8	Idza Priyanti	Successful businesswoman in Brebes, father is strong businessman; older brother is mayor of Tegal (2009–13); husband is middle rank policeman	Regent of Brebes (2012–17)	PDIP, PKS, Democrat, Gerindra
9	Puput Tantriana Sari	Wife of Hasan Aminuddin, former regent of Probolinggo for two periods (2002–12)	Regent of Probolinggo (2013–18)	PDIP, PKB, PKIB, PKNU, Gerindra, Hanura
10	Rukmini	Wife of HM Buchori, mayor of Probolinggo for two periods (2004–14)	Mayor of Probolinggo (2014–19)	PDIP, PKS, PAN, P. Pelopor
11	Utje Ch Hamid Suganda	Wife of Aang Hamid Suganda, regent of Kuningan for two periods (2003–13)	Regent of Kuningan (2013–18)	PDIP
12	Hj Atty Suharti Tochija	Wife of Itoch Tochija, former mayor of Cimahi two periods (2002–12)	Mayor of Cimahi (2012–17)	Golkar and PPP
13	Neneng Hasanah Yasin	Daughter of powerful businessman Hasanan Yasin in Bekasi	Regent of Bekasi (2012–17)	Golkar, Democrat, PAN
		OUTSIDE JAVA		
1	Ni Putu Eka Wiryastuti	Daughter of Nyoman Adi Wiryatama, former regent of Tabanan (2005–10)	Regent of Tabanan (2010–15)	PDIP
2	Rita Widyasari	Rita Widyasari, daughter of Syaukani HR, former regent of Kutai Kutanegara for two periods (1999–2006)	Regent of Kutai Kertanegara (2010–15)	Golkar
3	Christiany Eugenia Paruntu	Successful businesswoman in South Minahasa, father and mother are strong supporters of Golkar	Regent of South Minahasa (2010–15)	Golkar
4	Juliarti Djuhardi Alwi	Professional doctor and successful bureaucrat, career as director of Bureau of Health in Sambas, vice-regent of Sambas in 2006 election	Regent of Sambas (2011–16)	Democrat Party, PPP, PAN

Source: Created by author from various resources.

Looking at the table, we can see the names and regions of the elected female leaders in the direct elections from 2010 to 2014 in Indonesia. Looking at the political parties, PDIP is the leading political party that has nominated the most female candidates to successfully win the direct elections in Java, mainly without coalitions, such as in Bantul, Kendal, Surabaya, Kuningan, and Tabanan in outside Java. Outside Java Golkar leads the political competition in which their two female candidates won the direct elections in Kutai Kertanegara and South Minahasa. In term of religion, all of the female leaders elected in Java have been Muslim, whereas of the four female leaders elected outside Java, two are Muslim, one was Christian (Christiany Eugenia Paruntu) and the fourth Hindu (Ni Putu Eka Wiryastuti).

In regards to the primary factor behind their political success, 11 of the 13 female leaders elected in Java (Kediri, Bantul, Kendal, Indramayu, South Tangerang, Banten, Brebes, Probolinggo both in Municipal and Regency, Kuningan and Cimahi) and three outside Java (Tabanan, Kutai Kertanegara and South Minehasa) have strong familial ties, in which their fathers, fathers-in-law, husbands, brothers, were prominent politicians so that they could utilize the available resources and influences in securing political victory. Only two female leaders were elected in Java without strong familial ties, namely Tri Rismaharini and Neneng Hasanah Yasin, while outside Java there was one, namely Juliarti Djuhardi Alwi. Here, we can see clearly that the influence of familial ties was very strong in female leader victories in the second term of direct elections (2010–15).

The rise of the wives or daughters of male politicians in this term was also caused by restrictions in the regulation on direct elections. Article 58 (o) of Law No. 32/2004, the requirements for local government candidates, states that candidates must not have served as local government heads or deputy local government heads for two periods in the same position [*belum pernah menjabat sebagai kepala daerah atau wakil kepala daerah selama 2 (dua) kali masa jabatan dalam jabatan yang sama*]. Therefore, when male politicians have served as regents for two periods, they cannot run again in the next direct election for regent. In order to maintain political power in the region, these male politicians have sometimes brought in and facilitated the nomination of their wives or daughters in the second term of direct elections (2010–15). Therefore, many of the female politicians who were nominated and went on to win direct elections as regents or governors were not ordinary women, as their husbands or fathers had previously held key political positions. I can say that in the second term of direct elections, "political familial ties" had a positive impact for women, in the sense that they provided important channels for women to take on active roles in Indonesian local politics. However, we have to consider this progress carefully as it also indicates a concentration of local political power in the hands of a small group of the political elite, which hinders democratization in local politics.

Conclusion

This book began with curiosity over the widespread perception that Islam as a religion hinders women's roles and human rights. For example, drawing from the World Values Survey and the European Values Survey comprising 190 nations and 70 nations respectively,[38] Ronald Inglehart and Pippa Norris's analysis of cultural and religious attitudes concluded that "attitudes towards women vary among adherents of different religious sects and denominations; in particular, an Islamic religious heritage is one of the most powerful barriers to the rising tide of gender equality".[39] While Inglehart and Norris's conclusion, which is often cited by scholars analyzing women's political participation in Asia, including Kazuki Iwanaga's edited book,[40] may apply to orthodox Islamic states, I do not think the assessment is accurate when viewing Indonesian Islam. My research draws a conclusion contrary to Inglehart and Norris's conclusion. As I have shown in throughout this book, my research on three female political leaders indicates that mainstream Islam in Indonesia

---

[38] Including many Islamic states, such as Jordan, Iran, Algeria, Egypt, Morocco and Indonesia, which were divided into three major blocs (Roman Catholic, Muslim and Protestant), in addition to the remainder which were identified as Orthodox, Buddhist, Hindu and Jewish.
[39] Inglehart and Norris, *Rising Tide*, p. 71.
[40] Iwanaga, ed., *Women's Political Participation and Representation in Asia*, p. 13. Surprisingly, although the book tried to present a comparison of female political participation in Asia, it did not present a special chapter on women in Indonesia in spite of the rising trend of women's engagement in politics in Indonesia, the largest Muslim majority country in Asia. The book emphasized cultural factors, or in Iwanaga's words "cultural facilitators" (traditional culture, political culture or religion) by citing Inglehart and Norris (2003), who suggest that Islam is a significant barrier to women's political representation. However, in my opinion, the book fails to capture the possible contribution of Islam to the rise of Muslim women in Indonesian local politics since 2005, which is the ongoing phenomenon that my study addresses.

(exemplified by Muhammadiyah and Nahdlatul Ulama) supports promoting women's rights, especially women's leadership in local politics. The strong religious foundation that supports women's leadership is often used to support female political candidates in local politics.

This study concludes that Islamic stances on female leadership at the local level, exemplified by NU, the dominant religious organization in Java, provide a strong religious foundation for female Javanese Muslim politicians to become local political leaders. This study further concludes that for women candidates, the ability to use their gender in combination with presentations of Islamic piety, and the use of religio-political support systems and male/female-based networks, is decisive to the political rise and victory of female Javanese Muslim political leaders. While this study finds it difficult to conclude that familial ties were a common factor behind the rise and victory of female political leaders in the first term of direct elections (2005–10), including the three case studies observed, the influence of familial ties became strongly apparent in the rise and victory of female political leaders in the second term of direct elections (2010–15).

In revealing female Javanese political leaders' thoughts and actions in politics, this study discovers that the agency they hold is similar to that described by Saba Mahmood.[41] In this study, I found that female Javanese Muslim political leaders' exercised a great deal of agency, as defined by their ability as subjects to engage with the dominant cultural

---

[41] A thought-provoking study of Muslim women's piety and agency is Saba Mahmood's observation of women's mosque movements in Egypt in the mid-1990s, which were part of the Islamic Revival. She explores Egyptian Muslim women's self-cultivation practices, such as *sabr* (endurance), modesty and shyness, and sees them as practices of piety. While liberal feminist scholarship often considers these practices as acts of submissiveness embedded into a patriarchal system, Mahmood urges scholars to consider the rationale and intentions of those embracing such forms of piety within their specific cultural and historical contexts. By doing so, Mahmood challenges the liberal feminist interpretation of agency. Saba Mahmood sees "agency not as a synonym for resistance to relations of domination, but as a capacity for action...." See Mahmood, "Feminist Theory, Embodiment, and the Docile Agents", p. 203; see also Mahmood, *Politics of Piety*. Mahmood's interpretation has provoked commentary from scholars; see Turner, "Introduction: the Price of Piety", pp. 1–6; Bautista, "The Meta-Theory of Piety". Mahmood's argument has also inspired scholars to examine Muslim women's practices of piety; for example, see Haniffa, "Piety as Politics"; Frisk, *Submitting to God*.

version of gender in their quest for power without disrupting the primary relations in their Javanese families, yet at the same time using it to gain greater political space and expand the boundary of their identity in contemporary Java. In so doing, today's Javanese Muslim women are actively producing new images of the modern Muslim woman who fulfils her *kodrat*, takes on political leadership roles, actively adapts to the Islamic idea of piety and brings it into politics, and introduces new horizons into the public sphere. Finally, this study concludes that having a female leader in power does not guarantee that women's issues will be represented in their policies.

By looking at the influence of many positive factors behind the success of female Muslim political leaders in the direct elections in post-Suharto Indonesia, I suggest local politics in Indonesia has now become what I call "a critical enabler site" where Muslim women can manoeuvre comfortably within their gender, religion (Islam) and individual capital to secure leadership roles without facing as much opposition as they would receive in national politics. Local politics is an important locus for increasing female leadership in Indonesian politics. In this, the findings of this book contributes to bringing a new dimension to the discourse on gender, politics and Islam in Southeast Asia,[42] an important and contemporary theme that is highly debated in the region.[43] The findings of this book indicate that we will see more Muslim women in Indonesia continue to take political leadership roles, beginning in local politics and gradually rising to national politics, though the road contains many hurdles. This signifies a progressive future, with Muslim women's political roles actively shaping the growth and direction of democratization specifically in Indonesia, and more generally in Southeast Asia.

---

[42] Islam in Southeast Asia has a distinct historical spread and character that highly blended with local traditions. See Reid, *Charting the Shape of Early Modern Southeast Asia*; Geertz, *The Religion of Java*; Koentjaraningrat, *Javanese Culture*; Azra, *Islam Nusantara*.

[43] For the latest book addressing this contemporary change concerning gender and Islam in Southeast Asia by exploring the experiences of Muslim women in various practices related to gender relations, marriage, and social and political leadership, see *Gender and Islam in Southeast Asia*, ed. Susanne Schroter. This book provides an overview of the current intersection between Islam and gender in contemporary Southeast Asia, however, the book does not provide analysis of the rise of female Muslim political leaders in Indonesian local politics in post-Suharto Indonesia.

APPENDIX

List of Interviewees

In Jakarta

No.	Name of Interviewee	Affiliation	Date
1	Lies Luluk	Secretary General, Central Board of *Dharma Wanita* (2004–09)	25 Jan. 2010
2	Arolis	Secretary IV of the Central Board of PKK	25 Jan. 2010
3	AZ	Prominent young NU figure who is active in the Central Board of NU	Email, 28 Oct. 2011
4	EK	Female parliamentarian member from PDIP	Conversation in Jakarta, 28 Nov. 2012

In Pekalongan

No.	Name of Interviewee	Affiliation	Date
5	Siti Qomariyah	Regent of Pekalongan (2001–06)	17 June 2009 21 June 2009 25 June 2009
6	AB	Secretary of the *Tanfidz*, Regional Board of Pekalongan PKB (2002–07) and chief of Siti's campaign team	17 June 2009
7	AKH	Former friend of Siti Qomariyah in junior high school	19 June 2009
8	ZLH	Former friend of Siti Qomariyah in junior high school	19 June 2009
9	HSY	Former friend of Siti Qomariyah in junior high school	19 June 2009

Appendix continued

No.	Name of Interviewee	Affiliation	Date
10	*Kyai* SB	Chief, Pekalongan NU (2007–10)	20 June 2009
11	*Kyai* BR	Chief, Regional Board of Pekalongan PKB (2002–08)	21 June 2009
12	FA	Chief, Muslimat NU in Pekalongan (2005–10)	22 June 2009 Followed by telephone interview, 26 June 2011
13	*Kyai* MA	Vice-chief, Regional Board of PKB in Pekalongan (2002–08)	22 June 2009
14	AR	NGO activist	23 June 2009
15	KU	Prominent activist in Nasyiatul 'Aisyiyah, Pekalongan	23 June 2009
16	*Kyai* JA	Vice-chief of the Syuriah, Regional Board, Pekalongan PKB	22 June 2009
17	CS	Chief, Regional Board, Pekalongan PKS	24 June 2009
18	DRM	Vice-chief, 'Aisyiyah, Pekalongan	25 June 2009
19	SCH	Chief, Nasyiatul 'Aisyiyah, Pekalongan (2004–09)	25 June 2009
20	MM	Former Golkar candidate for Vice-regent in the 2001 regency election in Pekalongan; chief of the Small to Medium Enterprises and Cooperatives in Pekalongan	25 June 2009
21	ZFR	Secretary General, Regional Board, Pekalongan PKB	26 June 2009
22	SUR	Volunteer on Antono's campaign team	26 June 2009
23	MG	Chief, Women's Empowerment and Family Planning in Pekalongan	27 June 2009
24	TH	Amat Antono's younger sister and chief of PDIP's Regional Board in Pekalongan, (2009–14)	28 June 2009
25	AKB	Member of Siti Qomariyah's campaign team and chief of Pekalongan DPRD from PKB (2004–11)	29 June 2009

continued overleaf

Appendix continued

No.	Name of Interviewee	Affiliation	Date
26	MCH	Chief of the Regional Board of Golkar in Pekalongan (1999–2009)	30 June 2009
27	KRM	Board member of Muhammadiyah in Pekalongan, member of the Regional Board of PAN in Pekalongan, and treasurer of Antono's campaign team	2 July 2009
28	HD	Chief of Fatayat NU in Pekalongan (2000–10) and chief of PPKB (2009–14)	2 July 2009
29	CKW	Chief of Antono's campaign team in the 2006 direct local head election	3 July 2009
30	RS	Secretary of Muhammadiyah in Pekalongan	3 July 2009
31	IN	Chief, Bureau for Migrant Workers, Pekalongan	July 2009
32	Wahyudi Pontjo Nugroho	Vice-regent of Pekalongan (2001–11)	23 July 2010

In Banyuwangi

No.	Name of Interviewee	Affiliation	Date
34	Gus EN	Bustanul Makmur Pesantren, Genteng, Banyuwangi	25 July 2009
35	Gus MK	Vice-chief of the Tanfidziyah, NU in Banyuwangi	25 July 2009
36	ACW	Chief, Regional Board of Banyuwangi PKB (2002–07), member of Banyuwangi DPRD from PKB (1999–2008)	26 July 2009
37	RM	Secretary General, PNIM in Banyuwangi and lobbyist for Ratna Ani Lestari in the 2005 GPPNP Convention	26 July 2009
38	Gus Yus (Yusuf Nuris)	Vice-regent of Banyuwangi (2005–10)	27 July 2009
39	Samsul Hadi	Former regent of Banyuwangi (2000–05) and one of Ratna's contenders in the GPPNP convention in 2005. In Banyuwangi prison for corruption during interview	27 July 2009

Appendix continued

No.	Name of Interviewee	Affiliation	Date
40	SM	Secretary, Regional Board of PAN in Banyuwangi, (2005–10)	28 July 2009
41	*Kyai* DL	Chief of MUI in Banyuwangi	28 July 2009
42	Ratna Ani Lestari	Regent of Banyuwangi (2005–10)	29 July 2009
43	AG	Chief, Regional Board of PPDI in Banyuwangi; important figure on Ratna's campaign team	29 July 2009
44	AI	Chief, Regional Board of PBB in Banyuwangi (2002–09)	29 July 2009
45	UD	NGO activist in Banyuwangi	29 July 2009
46	NM	Chief of Fatayat NU in Banyuwangi	29 July 2009
47	NK	Chief of 'Aisyiyah in Banyuwangi (2000–10)	30 July 2009
48	IS	Executive secretary of Muhammadiyah in Banyuwangi and activist on the Regional Board of PAN in Banyuwangi	30 July 2009
49	EH	Secretary, Regional Board of PKB in Banyuwangi (1999–2004), vice-chief of the Regional Board of PKB in Banyuwangi (2004–08), member of Banyuwangi DPRD from PKB (2004–09)	30 July 2009
50	YW	Chief, Regional Board of PDIP in Banyuwangi, (2000–05)	30 July 2009
51	YL	Member, Banyuwangi DPRD from Golkar (2004–14)	31 July 2009
52	JL	Coordinator, Parking Service Organization in Banyuwangi	31 July 2009
53	SF	Member, Banyuwangi DPRD from PKB (1999–2009) and chief of the PKB faction in Banyuwangi DPRD (2004–09)	31 July 2009
54	*Kyai* HA	Leader of a *pesantren* in Glenmore	1 Aug. 2009
55	*Kyai* MAS	Chief of the Syuriah, Banyuwangi NU	1 Aug. 2009
56	*Kyai* AHS	Darussalam Pesantren, Blok Agung and Rais Syuriah, Regional Board of NU in Banyuwangi	1 Aug. 2009

continued overleaf

Appendix continued

No.	Name of Interviewee	Affiliation	Date
57	NW	Darussalam Pesantren, Blok Agung, Banyuwangi	1 Aug. 2009
58	Gus MLK	One of the sons of a *kyai* in Blok Agung and close friend of Gus Yus	1 Aug. 2009
59	*Kyai* SY	Mansya'ul Huda Pesantren, Tegaldlimo	2 Aug. 2009
60	NA	Chief of *GP Anshor*, NU in Banyuwangi	2 Aug. 2009
61	SG	Activist in SBMI	2 Aug. 2009
62	MQ	Activist in SBMI	2 Aug. 2009
63	AM	Chief, Regional Board, PKS in Banyuwangi (2007–10)	3 Aug. 2009
64	YD	Former chief of the Songgon sub-branch (*pengurus ranting*) of PDIP and coordinator of Ratna's campaign team	4 Aug. 2009
65	ES	Chief of Banyuwangi DPRD from Golkar (2004–09)	5 Aug. 2009
66	Dr. JW	Staff member in charge of managing HIV in the Bureau of Health in Banyuwangi	7 Aug. 2009
67	Ketut SDR	Prominent leader of Parisada Hindhu Dharma in Banyuwangi	8 Aug. 2009
68	STY	Former bureaucrat in Banyuwangi, businesswoman and former close friend of Ratna Ani Lestari	9 Aug. 2009
69	DS	Local journalist	9 Aug. 2009
70	SM	Prominent female radio broadcaster and good friend of Ratna Ani Lestari	9 Aug. 2009
71	HPR	Member of Banyuwangi KPUD	14 July 2010
72	SR	Former chief of GPPNP (2005), chief of APPNP (2010), which was expected to be Ratna Ani Lestari's political vehicle through which to compete in the 2010 direct election in Banyuwangi.	July 2010
73	WIN	One of my colleagues who originally comes from Banyuwangi	9 Mar. 2011

Appendix continued

In Kebumen

No.	Name of Interviewee	Affiliation	Date
74	RS	Rustriningsih, younger brother, chief of PDIP campaign team in the 2005 and 2008 direct elections and vice-regent of Kebumen (2008–10)	9 Feb. 2010
75	KHS	Member of Kebumen KPI	9 Feb. 2010
76	SPR	Chief, Golkar Regional Board in Kebumen, member of Kebumen DPRD (1997–2004), vice-chief of Kebumen DPRD (2004–05)	10 Feb. 2010
77	DL	*Fatayat NU, Muslimat NU*, member of Kebumen DPRD from PDIP (2004–14)	10 Feb. 2010
78	SHW	Secretary general of *'Aisyiyah* in Kebumen (2000–05)	11 Feb. 2010
79	KH. Nashiruddin Al-Mansyur	Vice-regent of Kebumen (2000–08) and regent of Kebumen (2008–10)	12 Feb. 2010
80	YC	Vice-secretary of the Regional Board of PPP in Kebumen, (1999–2000), chief of the Regional Board of PPP in Kebumen (2005–10), and member of Kebumen DPRD from PPP (1999–2014)	12 Feb. 2010
81	IS	Prominent INDIPT NGO activist	27 July 2010
82	HMR	Activist in INDIPT, a prominent NGO in Kebumen	27 July 2010
83	CA	Former correspondent for *Wawasan*, a nationalist affiliated newspaper during the New Order, close friend of KH Nashiruddin Al Mansyur and member of Kebumen KPUD (2003–09)	27 July 2010
84	SM	Chief of *Muslimat NU* in Kebumen (2005–10)	27 July 2010
85	TQ	Former parliamentarian member in Kebumen from PKB (1999–2004)	27 July 2010
86	MTJ	Director of INDIPT in Kebumen	28 July 2010
87	SW	Vice-chief of the Regional Board of PKB in Kebumen (2001–05)	28 July 2010

continued overleaf

Appendix continued

No.	Name of Interviewee	Affiliation	Date
88	HU	Former coordinator for setting up Pro-Mega PDI vice branches under Rustriningsih's instruction in Kebumen 1998, secretary of Pro-Mega PDI in Pejagon district, Kebumen (1998–99), secretary of the PDIP faction in Kebumen DPRD (1999–2004), chief of the PDIP faction in Kebumen DRPD (2004–09)	28 July 2010
89	KH. Muhammad MSKB	Chief of the Tanfidziah of NU in Kebumen (1994–2002)	28 July 2010
90	Gus TH	Chief of the Dewan Syuro of the Regional Board of PKB in Kebumen (2007–13)	28 July 2010
91	AP	Former member of the Pro Mega PDI loyalist team 9 in Kebumen	28 July 2010
92	LM	Former member of Kebumen DPRD from PPP (1997–99) and chief of *Fatayat NU* in Kebumen (1995–2005)	29 July 2010
93	*Kyai* H. ABS	Leader of Al-Hasani *Pesantren*, Jatimulyo, Alian, Kebumen	29 July 2010
94	BUS	Treasurer of the Regional Board of PDIP in Kebumen, member of Kebumen DPRD from PDIP (2004–13) and chief of Kebumen DPRD (2009–13)	20 Feb. 2010
95	PR	Chief of the Women's Empowerment and Family Planning Bureau of Kebumen	20 Feb. 2010

In Semarang

No.	Name of Interviewee	Affiliation	Date
96	FY	Chief of Central Java KPU (2003–08)	28 Jan. 2010
97	SKH	Chief of LBH APIK	29 Jan. 2010
98	FZ	Activist, Muslimat NU in Central Java and member of Bambang Sadono's campaign team (Golkar)	30 Jan. 2010
99	EV	Chief of LKJ HAM	1 Feb. 2010
100	AP	Close friend and consultant to Rustriningsih. Also a member of Central Java KPUD (2003–13)	1 Feb. 2010

Appendix continued

No.	Name of Interviewee	Affiliation	Date
101	KRS	Volunteer on Rustriningsih's campaign team during the 2008 election and businessman from Purbalingga	2 Feb. 2010
102	TY	Lecturer, Faculty of Social and Political Sciences, Diponegoro University, Central Java and former political consultant for Bambang Sadono and Muhammad Adnan (Goklar) and for Sukawi Sutrip and Sudharto (PKS, Democrat Party) in the 2008 election for governor in Central Java	Feb. 2010
103	PT	Volunteer on Rustriningsih's campaign team and former member of Central Java DPRD from PDIP (2004–09)	2 Feb. 2010
104	Rustriningsih	Regent of Kebumen (2000–08) and vice-governor of Central Java (2008–13)	3 Feb. 2010
105	Muhammad Adnan	Chief, NU in Central Java (1999–2012), and vice-gubernatorial candidate from Golkar	3 Feb. 2010
106	DW	Chief of the section on Women's Empowerment at the Women's Empowerment and Family Planning Bureau in Central Java	5 Feb. 2010
107	ML	Chief, Indonesian Women's Coalition, Central Java (2008–13)	5 Feb. 2010
108	AK	Chief, Department of Communication and Information for the Provincial Board of the PDIP in Central Java	28 Jan. 2010

GLOSSARY

'Aisyiyah	the women's wing of Muhammadiyah, founded by KH. Ahmad Dahlan in 1917
Abangan	category referring to nominal Muslims strongly influenced by the Hindu-Buddhist practices of Javanese syncretism
adat	customary or traditional law
amar ma'ruf nahi munkar	principle of doing good deeds and preventing bad or evil deeds
aurat	parts of the body which cannot be shown publicly in Islam. For a Muslim woman, all of her body is *aurat* and therefore should be covered, except for her face and the palm of her hands
bahtsul masa'il	the tradition of discussion in NU to produce *fatwa* on various problems
bahtsul masail maudu'iyyah	discussion of conceptual/thematic problems
bahtsul masail waqi'iyyah	discussion of practical/factual problems
becak	traditional three-wheeled mode of transportation
cancut tali wanda	taking the initiative to do everything necessary particularly when one's family is facing trouble
dakwah movement	the revival of Islam in Malaysia, marked by a call for the revitalization of the faith in various universities and inspired by the Islamic revivalism of the 1970s. In Malaysia it is propagated by ABIM (Angkatan Belia Islam)
dakwah	preaching, Islamic outreach
dalil	reasoning
Dewan Pembina	Supervisory Board

Dewan Syuro	Religious Advisory Council of the National Awakening Party (Partai Kebangkitan Bangsa, PKB)
Dharma Wanita	a compulsory women's organization for the wives of all civil servants, founded in 1974 in Indonesia
Fatayat NU	young women's wing of NU founded in 1950, comprised of young NU women under 40 years old
fatwa	legal decree taken as a guiding rule and given by a person with authority to do so
fiqh	legal prescription; Islamic jurisprudence
fitrah	a natural or original characteristic
fuqaha	Muslim jurists; experts in Islamic jurisprudence
hadith	sayings of the Prophet
haram	forbidden
ijtihad	independent judgment, based on recognized sources (the Qur'an and Hadith), on a legal or theological question
imam	leader, could also be a prayer leader
iman	belief in God
jalaseh	pious women's prayer meetings where they recite the Qur'an and discuss religious precepts in Iran
jarit	traditional batik sarong usually found in Java
jilbab	Muslim women's veil that covers the head, neck and shoulders
kabupaten	regency (governmental unit)
kaum	Islamic religious officials
kebaya	long traditional batik cloth covering a woman's arms, chest and hips
kecamatan	district (governmental unit)
kelurahan	administrative village (governmental unit)
kemben	traditional batik sarong made from traditional cloth which women wear to cover from their chest to their lower legs
kodrat	ability to do a particular thing, appropriateness and boundary

konco wingking	"the friend in the back", or literally in the kitchen, which is usually at the back of the house, a concept used to refer to the less than prominent position of women
Konstituante	Constitutional Assembly, the body set up to draft a permanent constitution in Indonesia after independence
kotamadya	municipality/city (governmental unit)
kudung	Muslim veil that covers the head and neck
kyai panggung	the most popular and sought-after preacher
kyai	male religious leader who often has a *pesantren*
laskar	groups or militias that support war
lurah	head of an administrative village
Mahkamah Konstitusi	the Constitutional Court
Majlis Dhikr	collective activity chanting repetitive prayers
Majlis Tarjih	Council on Law-Making and Development of Islamic Thought in Muhammadiyah, founded in 1927
Majelis Ulama Indonesia	the Indonesian Council of Ulama
makmum	followers of a collective prayer
mauluddan	celebration of the Prophet Muhammad's birthday
mubaligh	male Muslim preacher
mubalighot	female Muslim preacher
Muhammadiyah	Indonesia's modernist Islamic organization, founded by KH. Ahmad Dahlan in 1912 in Kauman, Yogyakarta
muhrim	close relative of the opposite sex, who is not to be married in Islam, such as a mother, father, sister, brother, grandmother, grandfather
mujtahid	person who carries out *ijtihad*
Muktamar	General Meeting; the highest decision making body in Muhammadiyah. A *Muktamar* is conducted once every five years
mursyid	leader of a *tarekat*
mushalla	place for praying and holding Islamic teachings, smaller than a mosque
Muslimah	Muslim women

Muslimat NU	the women's wing of NU, established in 1946
nafaka	money for living
Nasyiatul 'Aisyiyah	women youth cadre organization in Muhammadiyah founded in 1931
the New Order	political period under Suharto's regime (1966–98)
NU	Nahdlatul Ulama (Revival of the Religious Scholars); Indonesia's traditionalist Islamic organization, founded by Hasyim Asy'ari and Wahab Chasbullah in 1926
nyai	wife of a *kyai*
pamong paraja	government officials such as regents, district heads, etc.
panutan	leader
peci	traditional square hat of a dark colour, usually worn by Indonesia Muslim men in prayer. In turn, it is often worn as official office attire with a suit during official occasions either by Muslim or non-Muslim men
pengajian	religious study group
pengulu	*ulama* who were part of the palace bureaucracy and responsible for managing mosque activities
perda sha'riah	local government regulations based on Islamic teachings
pesantren	traditional Islamic boarding school, associated closely with NU
pingitan	periods of seclusion in which women were kept at home, merely obtaining instruction in religious doctrine prior to marriage. Common practice in Java around the first part of the 20th century
purdah	gender separation and restrictions on women's physical mobility, mainly present in South Asian Muslim societies
priyayi	noble upper class in Java
provinsi	province (governmental unit)
Qur'an	the holy book of Islam
Ramadhan	special month in Islam where all Muslims who have reached puberty are obliged to fast (from food and water) during daylight hours

ranting	branches of NU at the village level
Rois Syuriah NU	head of the supreme religious council of NU
sadakah	money or other material objects given for the sake of God's blessing
santri	religious students; a term for those who faithfully practice the five pillars of Islam: the commitment to the faith (belief in one God), the five daily prayers, the payment of yearly alms, the fast during Ramadhan, and the pilgrimage to Mecca
selir	co-wives
sowan	the action of visiting a *kyai*'s home
syari'ah	Islamic law
Syuriyah NU	the supreme religious council of NU, usually comprised of *ulama*
tabir	long cloth that separates men from women in meetings or in *pengajian*
tabligh	religious propagation
tafsir	interpretation, explanation, exegesis, particularly of the Qur'an
tajdid	Arabic word for renewal. It refers to the revival of Islam, in order to purify and reform society
Tanfidz	the executive board of PKB
Tanwir	a general meeting under the level of Muktamar which is held by the central board of Muhammadiyah, at least three times during the Central Board's five-year term, and usually conducted as a preliminary meeting to the Muktamar
tarbiyah movement	*gerakan tarbiyah,* an urban-based Islamic education movement
tarekat	Sufi or mystic order which provides systematic guidance and practice for individuals to get closer with God under the leadership of a *mursyid*
tasawuf	Sufism
tauhid	a basic pillar of Islam, namely the belief in one God
tudung	Muslim headscarf. Commonly used term for the veil in Malaysia

ulama	pious Muslims who acquire deep religious knowledge
umat	Islamic community
wali hakim	an Islamic authority who validates a marriage
waliyulamril al-syaukah	interim leader who wields full authority
wanita sejati	a true woman, refers to the old Javanese norm that a true woman is one who serves well in the home as both mother and wife
wanita sholehah	pious and loyal Muslim women
wilayah amanah	territory/jurisdiction under a mandate
zakat	Islamic concept of alms; the obligation for Muslims to pay a certain percentage of their wealth in alms every year
zakat fitrah	*zakat* during the month of Ramadhan

BIBLIOGRAPHY

Interviews

See Appendix for the list of interviewees.

Books, Reports, Documents and Papers

Abdullah, M. Amin. "Perlu Rekonstruksi Pembacaan Teks". In *Islam & Problem Gender: Telaah Kepemimpinan Wanita Dalam Perspektif Tarjih Muhammadiyah*, ed. Agus Purwadi, pp. 37–45. Yogyakarta: Aditya Media, 2000.

Abidin, Adi. "When the Burden is Shouldered Alone: Experiences in Autonomy at Regencies and Municipalities". In *Decentralisation and Regional Autonomy in Indonesia*, ed. Coen J.G. Holtzapper and Martin Ramstedt, pp. 59–74. Singapore: Institute for Southeast Asian Studies, 2009.

Afadlal et al. *Islam dan Radikalisme di Indonesia*, ed. Endang Turmudi and Riza Sihbudi. Jakarta: LIPI Press, 2005.

Afshar, Haleh. "Introduction: Women and Empowerment—Some Illustrative Studies". In *Women and Empowerment: Illustrations from the Third World*, ed. Haleh Afshar, pp. 1–10. Basingstoke: Macmillan Press, 1998.

Ahmed, Kamal Uddin. "Women and Politics in Bangladesh". In *Women's Political Participation and Representation in Asia*, ed. Iwanaga, pp. 276–96.

Amandemen UUD 1945 tentang Piagam Jakarta. Jakarta: Dewan Dakwah Indonesia (DDI) dan Media Dakwah, 2000.

Ananta, Aris, Evi Nurvidya Arifin and Leo Suryadinata. *Indonesian Electoral Behaviour: A Statistical Perspective*. Singapore: Institute of Southeast Asian Studies, 2004.

Andaya, Barbara Watson. *The Flaming Womb: Repositioning Women in Early Modern Southeast Asia*. Honolulu: University of Hawai'i Press, 2006.

Anderson, Benedict R.O'G. "The Idea of Power in Javanese Culture". In *Culture and Politics in Indonesia*, ed. Claire Holt et al. Ithaca: Cornell University Press, 1972.

―――. *Language and Power: Exploring Political Cultures in Indonesia*. Ithaca: Cornell University Press, 1990.

Anwar, Syamsul. "Kepemimpinan Perempuan Dalam Islam: Menggali Perspektif Syar'i Dalam Tarjih Muhammadiyah". In *Wacana Fiqh Perempuan Dalam*

Perspektif Muhammadiyah, ed. Wawan Gunawan and Evie Shofia Inayati, pp. 47–76. Jakarta: Majlis Tarjih dan Pengembangan Pemikiran Islam PP Muhammadiyah Yogyakarta, in cooperation with Universitas Muhammadiyah Prof. Dr. Hamka, 2005.

Arnez, Monika. "A Dialogue with God? Islam and Lesbian Relationships in Two Post-Suharto Narratives". In Schroter, *Gender and Islam in Southeast Asia*, pp. 73–94. Leiden: Brill, 2013.

Assyaukanie, Luthfi. *Islam and the Secular State in Indonesia*. Singapore: Institute of Southeast Asian Studies, 2009.

Aspinall, Edward and Greg Fealy. "Introduction: Decentralization, Democratization and the Rise of the Local". In Aspinall and Fealy, *Local Power and Politics in Indonesia*, pp. 1–11.

Aspinall, Edward and Greg Fealy, ed. *Local Power and Politics in Indonesia: Decentralization & Democratization*. Singapore: Institute of Southeast Asian Studies, 2003.

Azra, Azyumardi. *Islam Nusantara: Jaringan Global dan Lokal*. Bandung: Penerbit Mizan, 2002.

Badan Pemberdayaan Perempuan dan Keluarga Berencana. *Data Pilah Gender Statisik dan Analisis Kabupaten Kebumen 2008*. Kebumen: Badan Pemberdayaan Perempuan dan Keluarga Berencana, 2009.

Badan Pusat Statistik Kabupaten Banyuwangi. *Indeks Pembangunan Manusia Kabupaten Banyuwangi 2007*. Banyuwangi: Badan Pusat Statistik Kabupaten Banyuwangi, 2008.

Badan Pusat Statistik Kabupaten Kebumen. *Kebumen Dalam Angka 2008*. Kebumen: Badan Pusat Statistik Kabupaten Kebumen, 2009.

Badan Pusat Statistik Provinsi Jawa Tengah. *Statistik Sosial dan Kependudukan Jawa Tengah: Hasil Susenas 2008*. Semarang: BPS Provinsi Jawa Tengah, 2009.

Bagian Sosial Setda Kabupaten Pekalongan. *Statistik dan Analisis Gender Kabupaten Pekalongan Tahun 2007*. Pekalongan: Bagian Sosial Detda Kabupaten Pekalongan, 2008.

Bamualim, Chaider S., Cheyne Scoot, Dick van der Meij and Irfan Abubakar. *Islamic Philanthropy and Social Development in Contemporary Indonesia*. Jakarta: Center for the Study of Religion and Culture and the Ford Foundation, 2006.

Bappeda Kabupaten Banyuwangi. *Selayang Pandang Kabupaten Banyuwangi Tahun 2005*. Banyuwangi: Bappeda Kabupaten Banyuwangi, 2005.

———. *Kabupaten Banyuwangi Dalam Angka Tahun 2008*. Banyuwangi: Bappeda Kabupaten Banyuwangi, 2008.

Bappeda Kabupaten Kebumen. *Rancangan Rencana Pembangunan Jangka Menengah Daerah (RPJMD) Kabupaten Kebumen Tahun 2011–2015*. Kebumen: Bappeda Kabupaten Kebumen, 2010.

Barabasi, Albert-Laszlo. *Linked: How Everything Is Connected to Everything Else and What It Means for Business, Science, and Everyday Life*. New York: Plume, 2003.

Bayat, Asef. *Making Islam Democratic: Social Movements and the Post-Islamic Turn*. California: Stanford University Press, 2007.

Beall, Jo. "Decentralisation and Engendering Democracy: Lessons from Local Government Reforms in South Africa". Crisis States Programme, LSE, Working Papers Series No. 54, Nov. 2004.

Beatty, Andrew. *Varieties of Javanese Religion: An Anthropological Account*. Cambridge: Cambridge University Press, 1999.

Bianpoen, Carla. "Women's Political Call". In *Indonesian Women: The Journey Continues*, ed. Mayling Oey-Gardiner and Carla Bianpoen, pp. 283–302. Canberra: The Australian National University, 2000.

Bidang Pemberdayaan Perempuan. *Profil Gender Kabupaten Banyuwangi Tahun 2007*. Banyuwangi: Bidang Pemberdayaan Perempuan pada Kantor Dinas Kesejahteraan Sosial, Kesatuan Bangsa dan Perlindungan Masyarakat, 2007.

Bidang Pencegahan dan Pemberantasan Penyakit Dinas Kesehatan Kabupaten Banyuwangi. "Situasi HIV-AIDS Kabupaten Banyuwangi Juni 2009". Banyuwangi: Bidang Pencegahan dan Pemberantasan Penyakit Dinas Kesehatan Kabupaten Banyuwangi, 2009.

Biro Pusat Statistik. *Indikator Sosial Wanita Indonesia 1989*. Jakarta: Biro Pusat Statistik, 1989.

─────── . *Indikator Sosial Wanita Indonesia*. Jakarta: Biro Pusat Statistik, 1995.

Blackburn, Susan. "Gender Interest and Indonesian Democracy". In *Democracy in Indonesia 1950s and 1990s*, ed. David Bourchier and John Legge. Clayton: Centre of Southeast Asian Studies, Monash University, 1994.

─────── . *Women and the State in Modern Indonesia*. Cambridge: Cambridge University Press, 2004.

─────── . "Has Gender Analysis Been Mainstreamed in the Study of Southeast Asian Politics?". In *Gender Trends in Southeast Asia: Women Now, Women in the Future*, ed. Theresa W. Devasahayam, pp. 53–72. Singapore: Institute of Southeast Asian Studies, 2009.

Blackburn, Susan, Bianca J. Smith and Siti Syamsiyatun. "Introduction". In *Indonesian Islam in a New Era*, ed. Blackburn, Smith and Syamsiyatun, pp. 1–21.

Blackburn, Susan, Bianca J. Smith and Siti Syamsiyatun, ed. *Indonesian Islam in A New Era: How Women Negotiate Their Muslim Identities*. Clayton: Monash University Press, 2008.

Brenner, Suzanna A. "Why Women Rule the Roost: Rethinking Javanese Ideologies of Gender and Self-control". In *Bewitching Women, Pious Men: Gender and Body Politics in Southeast Asia*, ed. Aihwa Ong and Michael G. Peletz, pp. 19–50. Berkeley: University of California Press, 1995.

Buehler, Michael. "The Rising Importance of Personal Networks in Indonesian Local Politics: An Analysis of District Government Head Elections in South Sulawesi in 2005". In *Deepening Democracy in Indonesia?*, ed. Erb and Sulistiyanto, pp. 101–24.

Buku Lampiran Penyelenggaraan Pemilihan Umum Tahun 1999 di Jawa Tengah. Jawa Tengah: PPD I Jawa Tengah, 1999.

Buku Lampiran Penyelenggaraan Pemilihan Umum Tahun 1999 Kabupaten Dati II Kebumen. Kebumen: Panitia Pemilihan Daerah Tingkat II Kabupaten Kebumen, n.d.

Choi, Nankyung. "Batam's 2006 Mayoral Election: Weakened Political Parties and Intensified Power Struggle in Local Politics". In *Deepening Democracy in Indonesia?*, ed. Erb and Sulistiyanto, pp. 74–100.

Connel, R.W. *Gender and Power: Society, the Person and Sexual Politics*, 6th ed. Cambridge: Polity Press, 1987.

———. *The Men and the Boys*. Berkeley: University of California Press, 2000.

———. *Masculinities*, 2nd ed. Berkeley: University of California Press, 2005.

———. *Gender*. Cambridge: Polity Press, 2008.

Creswell, John W. *Research Design: Qualitative and Quantitative Approach*. Thousand Oaks, CA: Sage Publications, 1994.

Crouch, Harold. "The Trend to Authoritarianism: The Post-1945 Period". In *The Development of Indonesian Society*, ed. Anny Aveling. St. Lucia: University of Queensland Press, 1979.

Data Rekapitulasi Form Penilaian Calon Kepala Daerah PKB Kabupaten Pekalongan. Pekalongan: DPC Partai Kebangkitan Bangsa Kabupaten Pekalongan, 2005.

Dengel, Holk K. *Darul Islam dan Kartosuwiryo: "Angan-Angan yang Gagal"*. Jakarta: Pustaka Sinar Harapan, 1995.

Derichs, Claudia and Andrea Fleschenberg, ed. *Religious Fundamentalisms and Their Gendered Impacts in Asia*. Berlin: Friederich-Ebert-Stiftung, 2010.

Department of Information, Republic of Indonesia. *The Indonesian Women's Movement: A Chronological Survey of the Women's Movement in Indonesia.* Jakarta: Department of Information, Republic of Indonesia, 1968.

Dinas Sosial Tenaga Kerja dan Transmigrasi. "Rencana Kebutuhan Calon TKI". Banyuwangi: Dinas Sosial Tenaga Kerja dan Transmigrasi, 2009.

Dokumen Terpilih Sekitar G.30S/THE PKI, ed. Alex Dinuth. Jakarta: Penerbit Intermasa, Jakarta, 1997.

Doxey, Monika Swasti Winarnita. "Indonesian Feminist Movement: The Valued Role of 'Motherhood' as Strategically Used by 'the Voice of Concerned Mothers' (*Suara Ibu Peduli*) to Re-Politicize the Indonesian Women's Movement". Unpublished paper, n.d.

DPRD Kabupaten Kebumen. "Berita Acara Pemilihan Bupati dan Wakil Bupati Kebumen Masa Jabatan 2000–2005". 15 Mar. 2000.

DPRD Kabupaten Pekalongan. "Risalah Rapat Paripurna Khusus DPRD Kabupaten Pekalongan Dalam Rangka Pemilihan Bupati Pekalongan Masa Bhakti 2001–2006 Tahap Kedua Tanggal 23 Mei 2001".

———. "Permohonan Pengesahan Pasangan Calon Terpilih Bupati dan Wakil Bupati Pekalongan Masa Bhakti 2001–2006".

Edwards, Louise and Mina Roces, ed. *Women in Asia: Tradition, Modernity and Globalisation*. Sydney: Allen and Unwin, 2000.

Effendy, Bahtiar. "What is Political Islam? An Examination of Its Theoretical Mapping in Modern Indonesia". In *A Portrait of Contemporary Indonesian Islam*, ed. Chaider S. Bamualim. Jakarta: Pusat Bahasa dan Budaya UIN Syarif Hidayatullah Jakarta and Konrad-Adenauer-Stiftung, 2005.

Emmerson, Donald K. "The Bureaucracy in Political Context: Weakness in Strength". In *Political Power and Communications in Indonesia*, ed. Karl D. Jackson and Lucian W. Berkeley: University of California Press, 1978.

Erb, Maribeth and Priyambudi Sulistiyanto, ed. *Deepening Democracy in Indonesia? Direct Elections for Local Leaders (Pilkada)*. Singapore: Institute of Southeast Asian Studies, 2009.

Errington, Shelly. "Recasting Sex, Gender, and Power: A Theoretical and Regional Overview". In *Power and Differences: Gender in Island Southeast Asia*, ed. Jane M. Atkinson and Shelly Errington. Stanford, CA: Stanford University Press, 1990.

Forum Kajian Kitab Kuning. *Kembang Setaman Perkawinan: Analisis Kritis Kitab Uqud Al-Lujjayn*. Jakarta: Kompas, 2005.

Frisk, Sylva. *Submitting to God: Women and Islam in Urban Malaysia*. Copenhagen: NIAS Press, 2009.

Fealy, Greg and Sally White, ed. *Expressing Islam: Religious Life and Politics in Indonesia*. Singapore: Institute of Southeast Asian Studies, 2008.

Feener, R. Michael. *Muslim Legal Thought in Modern Indonesia*. Cambridge: Cambridge University Press, 2007.

Gabungan Partai-Partai Politik Non Parlemen. "Kontrak Politik Pasangan Bakal Calon Kepala Daerah dan Wakil Kepala Daerah Banyuwangi Tahun 2005–2010 dengan Gabungan Partai-Partai Politik Non Parlemen". 27 Mar. 2005.

Geertz, Clifford. *The Religion of Java*. New York: The Free Press, 1960.

———. *Peddlers and Princess: Social Change and Economic Modernization in Two Indonesian Towns*. Chicago: The University of Chicago Press, 1963.

———. *Agricultural Involution: The Process of Ecological Change in Indonesia*. Berkeley: University of California Press, 1963.

———. *The Social History of an Indonesian Town*. Cambridge: Massachusetts Institute of Technology, 1965.

Geertz, Hildred, ed. *The Javanese Family: A Study of Kinship and Socialization*. New York: The Free Press of Glencoe, 1961.

———. *Letters of a Javanese Princess: Raden Adjeng Kartini*. Lanham: University Press of America and The Asia Society, 1985.

Hadiz, Vedi R. *Localising Power in Post-Authoritarian Indonesia: A Southeast Asian Perspective*. Stanford: Stanford University Press, 2010.

Hadler, Jeffrey. *Muslims and Matriarchs: Cultural Resilience in Minangkabau through Jihad and Colonialism*. Singapore: NUS Press, 2009.

Handayani, Christina S. and Ardhian Novianto. *Kuasa Wanita Jawa*. Yogyakarta: LKiS, 2008.

Hefner, Robert W. *Civil Islam: Muslims and Democratization in Indonesia*. Princeton: Princeton University Press, 2000.

———. "Muslim Democrats and Islamist Violence in Post-Soeharto Indonesia". In *Remaking Muslim Politics: Pluralism, Contestation, Democratization*, ed. Robert W. Hefner. Princeton: Princeton University Press, 2005.

Hidayat, Syarif. "*Pilkada*, Money Politics and the Dangers of 'Informal Governance' Practices". In *Deepening Democracy in Indonesia?*, ed. Erb and Sulistiyanto, pp. 125–46.

Hilmy, Masdar. *Islamism and Democracy in Indonesia: Piety and Pragmatism*. Singapore: Institute of Southeast Asian Studies, 2010.

Holtzappel, Coen J.G. and Martin Ramstedt. *Decentralisation and Regional Autonomy in Indonesia: Implementation and Challenges*. Singapore: International Institute for Asian Studies and Institute of Southeast Asian Studies, 2009.

Howell, Julia Day. "Modulations of Active Piety: Professors and Televangelists as Promoters of Indonesian 'Sufism'". In *Expressing Islam*, ed. Fealy and White, pp. 40–62.

Hull, Valerie J. "Women in Java's Rural Middle Class: Progress or Regress?". Working Paper Series, Population Institute, Universitas Gadjah Mada, Yogyakarta, 1976.

Ida, Rachmah. "Muslim Women and Contemporary Veiling in Indonesia". In *Indonesian Islam in a New Era*, ed. Blackburn, Smith and Syamsiyatun, pp. 47–67.

Inglehart, Ronald and Pippa Norris. *Rising Tide: Gender Equality and Cultural Change Around the World*. Cambridge: Cambridge University Press, 2003.

Iwanaga, Kazuki. "Introduction: Women's Political Representation from an International Perspective". In *Women and Politics in Thailand*, ed. Iwanaga, pp. 1–26.

Iwanaga, Kazuki, ed. *Women's Political Participation and Representation in Asia: Obstacles and Challenges*. Copenhagen: NIAS Press, 2008.

———. *Women and Politics in Thailand: Continuity and Change*. Copenhagen: NIAS Press, 2008.

Jackson, Karl D. "A Bureaucratic Polity: A Theoretical Framework for the Analysis of Power and Communications in Indonesia". In *Political Power and Communications in Indonesia*, ed. Karl D. Jackson and Lucian W. Pye. Berkeley: University of California Press, 1978.

———. *Kewibawaan Tradisional, Islam dan Pemberontakan: Kasus Darul Islam Jawa Barat*. Jakarta: Graffiti, 1990.

Jaringan Perempuan dan Politik. *Tata Laksana Jaringan Perempuan dan Politik.* Jakarta: JPPOL, 2002.

Jay, Robert R. *Religion and Politics in Rural Central Java.* Cultural Report Series No. 12, Southeast Asian Studies, Yale University, 1963.

———. *Javanese Villagers: Social Relations in Rural Modjokuto.* Cambridge: MIT Press, 1969.

Kabupaten Banyuwang dalam Angka Tahun 1987. Banyuwangi: Kantor Statistik Kabupaten Banyuwangi, 1987.

Kansas, Nanoq Da. *Anak Desa Penantang Zaman: Biografi Singkat Prof. Dr. Drg. I Gede Winasa.* Jembrana, Bali: Komunitas Kertas Budaya, 2003.

———. *Menterjemahkan Otonomi Daerah Tanpa Basa-Basi (Pokok-Pokok Pikiran Prof. Dr. Drg. I Gede Winasa).* Jembrana, Bali: Komunitas Kertas Budaya, 2004.

Karim, M. Rusli. *Islam dan Konflik Politik Era Orde Baru.* Yogyakarta: PT. Media Widya Mandala, 1992.

———. *Negara dan Peminggiran Islam Politik.* Yogyakarta: PT. Tiara Wacana, 1999.

Keeler, Ward. "Speaking Gender in Java". In *Power and Difference: Gender in Island Southeast Asia*, ed. Jane M. Atkinson and Shelly Errington. Stanford, California: Stanford University Press, 1990.

Keputusan DPRD Kabupaten Kebumen No. 19/KPTS-DPRD/2000. "Peraturan Tata Tertib Pencalonan dan Pemilihan Bupati dan Wakil Bupati Kebumen Periode Tahun 2000–2005". Government document, 21 Feb. 2000.

Kimmel, Michael S. *The Gendered Society.* 2nd ed. New York: Oxford University Press, 2004.

King, Cheryl Simrell. "Sex Role Identity and Decision Making Styles: How Gender Helps Explain the Paucity of Women at the Top". In *Gender Power, Leadership and Governance*, ed. Georgia Duerst-Lahti and Rita Mae Kelly. Ann Arbor: University of Michigan Press, 1995.

Koentjaraningrat. "Javanese Terms for God and Supernatural Beings and the Idea of Power". In *Men, Meaning and History: Essays in Honour of H.G. Schulte Nordholt.* The Hague: Martinus Nijhoff, 1980.

———. *Javanese Culture.* Oxford: Oxford University Press, 1985.

Komisi Pemilihan Umum Kabupaten Banyuwangi. "Anggota Badan Perwakilan Rakyat Daerah Kabupaten Banyuwangi Masa Jabatan 1999–2004", "Anggota Badan Perwakilan Rakyat Daerah Kabupaten Banyuwangi Masa Jabatan 2004–2009", "Anggota Badan Perwakilan Rakyat Daerah Kabupaten Banyuwangi Masa Jabatan 2009–2014". Government document.

Komisi Pemilihan Umum Kabupaten Kebume. *Buku Laporan Pemilihan Bupati dan Wakil Bupati Kebumen 5 Juni 2005.* Kebumen: KPUD Kebumen, 2005.

Komisi Pemilihan Umum Kabupaten Pekalongan. "Calon Terpilih DPRD Kabupaten Pekalongan Dalam Pemilu 2009". Government document.

——— . "Dokumentasi Penyelenggaraan Pemilu Anggota DPR, DPD, dan DPRD Serta Pemilu Presiden dan Wakil Presiden Tahun 2004 Di Kabupaten Pekalongan".

Komisi Pemilihan Umum Provinsi Jawa Tengah. *Laporan Pelaksanaan Tugas KPU Provinsi Jawa Tangah Pada Pemilu Gubernur dan Wakil Gubernur Jawa Tengah 2008: Buku I*. Semarang: Komisi Pemilihan Umum Provinsi Jawa Tengah, 2008.

Koning, Juliette, Marleen Nolten, Janet Rodenburg and Ratna Saptari, ed. *Women and Households in Indonesia: Cultural Notions and Social Practices*. Richmond: Curzon Press, 2000.

KOWANI (Kongres Wanita Indonesia). *Sejarah Sentengah Abad Pergerakan Wanita Indonesia*. Jakarta: Balai Pustaka, 1978.

KPUD Banyuwangi No: 234/KPU-Kab/014.329662/VII/2010 on "Penyelesaian Masalah Pencalonan dalam Pemilukada Banyuwangi". Government document.

Lucas, Anton E. *One Soul One Struggle: Persitiwa Tiga Daerah*. Yogyakarta: Resist Books, 2004.

Maarif, A. Syafii. *Islam dan Politik Teori Belah Bambu Masa Demokrasi Terpimpin (1959–1965)*. Jakarta: Gema Insani Press, 1996.

Macaulay, Fiona. "Localities of Power: Gender, Parties and Democracy in Chile and Brazil". In *Women and Empowerment: Illustrations from the Third World*, ed. Haleh Afshar. New York: Macmillan Press, 1998.

Machrusah, Safira. "Islam and Women's Political Participation in Indonesia: Discources and Practices". In *Religious Fundamentalisms and Their Gendered Impacts in Asia*, ed. Derichs and Fleschenberg, pp. 68–87. Berlin: Friedrich-Eberth-Stiftung, 2010.

Madjid, Nurcholish. *Islam Doktrin dan Peradaban: Sebuah Telaah Kritis Tentang Masalah Keimanan, Kemanusiaan, dan Kemoderenan*. Jakarta: Yayasan Wakaf Paramadina, 1992.

Mahmood, Saba. *Politics of Piety: The Islamic Revival and the Feminist Subject*. Princeton: Princeton University Press, 2005.

Majlis Tarjih Pimpinan Pusat Muhammadiyah. *Adabul Mar'ah Fil Islam*. Yogyakarta: Majlis Tarjih Pimpinan Pusat Muhammadiyah, n.d.

Masaaki, Okamoto, Atsushi Ota and Ahmad Suaedy. "Introduction". In *Islam in Contention*, ed. Okamoto, Ota and Suaedy, pp. 1–12.

Masaaki, Okamoto, Atsushi Ota and Ahmad Suaedy, ed. *Islam in Contention: Rethinking Islam and State in Indonesia*. Jakarta: The Wahid Institute, CSEAS, CAPAS, 2010.

Masaaki, Okamoto. "The Rise of the 'Realistic' Islamist Party: PKS in Indonesia". In *Islam in Contention*, ed. Okamoto, Ota and Suaedy, pp. 219–53.

Mboi, Aloysius Benedictus. "*Pilkada Langsung*: the First Step on the Long Road to a Dualistic Provincial and District Government". In *Deepening Democracy in Indonesia?*, ed. Erb and Sulistiyanto, pp. 38–49.

McIntyre, Angus. *The Indonesian Presidency: The Shift from Personal Towards Constitutional Rule*. Oxford: Rowman & Littlefield, 2005.

Means, Gordon P. *Political Islam in Southeast Asia*. Boulder, CO: Lynne Rienner Publisher, 2009.

Memori Pengabdian DPRD Kabupaten Dati II Kebumen Masa Bhakti Tahun 1992–1997. Kebumen: DPRD Dati II Kebumen, 1997.

Ministry of Home Affairs, Republic of Indonesia. "Daftar Kepala Daerah dan Wakil Kepala Daerah Yang Telah Diterbitkan Keputusannya Presiden Republik Indonesia Hasil Pemilihan Kepala Daerah Secara Langsung Tahun 2005, 2006, 2007, dan Tahun 2008". Jakarta: Ministry of Home Affairs, Republic Indonesia, 2009.

Ministry of Social Affairs Republic of Indonesia. *Towards Social Welfare in Indonesia*. Jakarta: Ministry of Social Affairs, Republic of Indonesia, 1954.

Mir-Hosseini, Ziba. "The Construction of Gender in Islamic Legal Thought: Strategies for Reform". In *Islamic Family Law and Justice for Muslim Women*, ed. Nik Noriani Nik Badlishah. Malaysia: Sisters in Islam and the Ford Foundation, 2003.

Mietzner, Marcus. "Indonesia and the Pitfalls of Low-Quality Democracy: A Case Study of the Gubernatorial Elections in North Sulawesi". In *Democratization in Post-Suharto Indonesia*, ed. Marco Bunte and Andreas Ufen. New York: Routledge, 2009.

Mohamad, Maznah. "Politicization of Islam in Indonesia and Malaysia: Women's Rights and Inter-Religious Relations". In *Gender Trends in Southeast Asia: Women Now, Women in the Future*, ed. Theresa W. Devasahayam, pp. 95–110. Singapore: Institute of Southeast Asian Studies, 2009.

Moore, Henrietta L. *A Passion for Difference*. Cambridge: Polity Press, 1994.

Moser, Caroline. "Gender Planning in the Third World: Meeting Practical and Strategic Needs". In *Gender and International Relations*, ed. Rebecca Grant and Kathleen Newland, pp. 89–90. Suffolk: Open University Press, 1991.

Mulia, Siti Musdah. *Muslimah Reformis: Perempuan Pembaru Keagamaan*. Bandung: Mizan, 2005.

———. *Islam dan Inspirasi Kesetaraan Gender*. Yogyakarta: Kibar Press, 2007.

Mulkhan, Abdul Munir. "A New Socio-Cultural Map for Santris". In *A Portrait of Contemporary Indonesian Islam*, ed. Chaider S. Bamualim. Jakarta: Pusat Bahasa dan Budaya IAIN Syarif Hidayatullah Jakarta and Konrad Adenaur Stiftung, 2005.

Nieuwenhuis, Madelon D. "Ibuism and Priyayization: Path to Power?". In *Indonesian Women in Focus: Past and Present Notions*, ed. Elsbeth Locher-Scholten and Anke Niehof. Dordrecht: Foris Publications, 1987.

Noer, Deliar. *The Modernist Muslim Movement in Indonesia 1900–1942*. London: Oxford University Press, 1973.

———. *Partai Islam di Pentas Nasional 1945–1966*. Jakarta: Pustaka Utama Grafiti, 1987.

———. *Partai Islam Di Pentas Nasional: Kisah dan Analisis Perkembangan Politik Indonesia 1945–1965*. Bandung: Mizan, 2000.
Noerdin, Edriana et al. *Representasi Perempuan dalam Kebijakan Publik di Era Otonomi Daerah*. Jakarta: Women's Research Institute, 2005.
Norris, Pippa and Ronald Inglehart. *Sacred and Secular: Religion and Politics Worldwide*. New York: Cambridge University Press, 2004.
Norris, Pippa. "Introduction: Theories of Recruitment". In *Passage to Power: Legislative Recruitment in Advanced Democracies*, ed. Pippa Norris. Cambridge: Cambridge University Press, 1997.
Nurmila, Nina. "Negotiating Polygamy in Indonesia: Between Islamic Discourse and Women's Lived Experiences". In *Indonesian Islam in a New Era*, ed. Blackburn, Smith and Syamsiyatun, pp. 23–45.
Parawansa, Khofifah Indar. "Institution Building: An Effort to Improve Indonesian Women's Role and Status". In *Women in Indonesia: Gender, Equity and Development*, ed. Kathryn Robinson and Sharon Bessel. Singapore: Institute of Southeast Asian Studies, 2002.
Patton, Michael Quinn. *Qualitative Evaluation and Research Methods*, 2nd ed. California: Sage Publications, 1990.
PBNU. *Pendapat Alim Ulama Tentang Presiden Wanita: Keputusan Musyawarah Nasional Alim Ulama No: 004/MN-NU/11/1997 (Tanggal 16–20 Rajab 1418 H/17–21 November 1997 Di Pondok Pesantren Qomarul Huda Desa Bagu, Pringgarat Lombok Tengah Nusa Tenggara Barat) Tentang: "Kedudukan Wanita Dalam Islam"*. Jakarta: Kantor Sekreatriat PBNU, 1997.
Pemerintah Kabupaten Kebumen. *Berita Daerah Kabupaten Kebumen Nomor: 24 Tahun 2005 Seri E Nomor 21 tentang Rencana Kerja Pemerintah Daerah (RKPD) Kabupaten Kebumen Tahun 2006*. Pemerintah Kabupaten Kebumen: Kebumen, 2005.
———. *Rencana Kerja Pemerintah Daerah (RPKD) Kabupaten Kebumen Tahun 2006*. Kebumen: Pemerintah Kabupaten Kebumen, 2005.
Pemerintah Kabupaten Banyuwangi. *RPJMD Kabupaten Banyuwangi 2006–2010*. Banyuwangi: Pemerintah Kabupaten Banyuwangi, 2007.
Pemerintah Kabupaten Pekalongan. *Statistik Gender dan Analisis Kabupaten Pekalongan 2004*. Pekalongan: Pemerintah Kabupaten Pekalongan, 2005.
———. *Rencana Pembangunan Jangka Menengah (RPJM) Daerah Kabupaten Pekalongan Tahun 2006–2011*. Pekalongan: Pemerintah Kabupaten Pekalongan, 2006.
———. *Profil, Potensi, Peluang Invenstasi dan Kebijakan Pembangunan Kabupaten Pekalongan Tahun 2007*. Pekalongan: Pemerintah Kabupaten Pekalongan Kantor Pengelolaan Dara dan Informasi Telematika, 2008.
Penyelenggaran Pemilihan Umum Tahun 1992 di Jawa Tengah. Jawa Tengah: PPD I Jawa Tengah, 1992.
PKK Pusat. *Rencana Kerja Lima Tahun PKK Tahun 2005–2009*. Jakarta: Direktorat Jenderal Pemberdayaan Masyarakat dan Desa, 2005.

Platzdasch, Bernhard. *Islamism in Indonesia: Politics in the Emerging Democracy*. Singapore: Institute of Southeast Asian Studies, 2009.
PP Muhammadiyah Majlis Tarjih 'Aisyiyah. *Tuntunan Menjadi Isteri Islam Yang Berarti*. Yogyakarta: PP Muhammadiyah Majlis 'Aisyiyah, n.d.
Pratikno. "Political Parties in *Pilkada*: Some Problems for Democratic Consolidation". In *Deepening Democracy in Indonesia?*, ed. Erb and Sulistiyanto, pp. 53–73.
Purwadi, Agus. "Militerisme dan Tradisi Islam Ihwal Kepemimpinan Wanita". In *Islam & Problem Gender: Telaah Kepemimpinan Wanita Dalam Perspektif Tarjih Muhammadiyah*, ed. Agus Purwadi. Yogyakarta: Aditya Media, 2000.
Pusat Studi Demokrasi dan HAM (PusDeHAM). "Perilaku Memilih Warga dalam Pilkada Banyuwangi 2010". Surabaya: PusDeHAM, 2009.
"Rekapitulasi Hasil Penghitungan Suara Pemilihan Bupati dan Wakil Bupati Pekalongan Tahun 2006 di Tingkat Kabupaten". In *Dokumentasi Penyelenggaraan Pemilihan Bupati dan Wakil Bupati Pekalongan Tahun 2006*. Pekalongan: Komisi Pemilihan Umum Kabupaten Pekalongan, 2006.
Rais, Amien. *Moralitas Politik Mhammdiyah*. Yogyakarta: Dinamika, 1995.
――――. *Tauhid Sosial: Formula Menggempur Kesenjangan*. Bandung: Mizan, 1998.
Rangkuman Data Individu TK, RA, BA Negeri/Swasta Tingkat Kabupaten tahun Pelajaran 2008/2009 Kabupaten Pekalongan. Kajen: Dinas Pendidikan Kabupaten Pekalongan, 2009.
Rangkuman Data Taman Kanak-Kanak Negeri/Swasta Tingkat Kecamatan dan Kabupaten tahun Pelajaran 2005/2006 Kabupaten Pekalongan. Kajen: Dinas Pendidikan Kabupaten Pekalongan, 2006.
Ratnawati, Tri. "Gender and Reform in Indonesian Politics: the Case of a Javanese Women *Bupati*". In *Deepening Democracy in Indonesia?*, ed. Erb and Sulistiyanto, pp. 174–89.
Ricklefs, M.C. *A History of Modern Indonesian since c.1200*, 3rd ed. London: Palgrave, 2001.
Reid, Anthony. *Charting The Shape of Early Modern Southeast Asia*. Singapore: Institute of Southeast Asian Studies, 2000.
Robinson, Kathryn. "Indonesian Women: From *Orde Baru* to *Reformasi*". In *Women in Asia*, ed. Edwards and Roces, pp. 139–69. Sydney: Allen and Unwin, 2000.
――――. *Gender, Islam and Democracy in Indonesia*. New York: Routledge, 2009.
Roces, Mina. *Women, Power, and Kinship Politics: Female Power in Post-war Philippines*. London: Praeger, 1998.
――――. "Negotiating Modernities: Filipino Women 1970–2000". In *Women in Asia*, ed. Edwards and Roces, pp. 112–38. Sydney: Allen and Unwin, 2000.
Saefuddin, A.M. "Kiprah dan Perjuangan Perempuan Salihat". In *Menimbang Feminisme Diskursus Gender Perspektif Islam*. Surabaya: Risalah Gusti, 2000.

Saptari, Ratna. "Women, Family and Household: Tensions in Culture and Practice". In *Women and Households in Indonesia*, ed. Koning et al., pp. 10–25. Richmond: Curzon Press, 2000.

———. "Networks of Reproduction Among Cigarette Factory Women in East Java". In *Women and Households in Indonesia*, ed. Koning et al., pp. 281–98. Richmond: Curzon Press, 2000.

Saravanamuttu, Johan. "Introduction: Majority–Minority Muslim Politics and Democracy". In *Islam and Politics in Southeast Asia*, ed. Johan Saravanamuttu. London and New York: Routledge, 2010.

Satriyo, Hana A. "Decentralisation and Women in Indonesia: One Step Back, Two Steps Forward". In *Local Power and Politics in Indonesia: Decentralization & Democratization*, ed. Edward Aspinall and Greg Fealy, pp. 217–29. Singapore: Institute of Southeast Asian Studies, 2003.

———. "Pushing the Boundaries: Women in Direct Local Elections and Local Government". In *Problems of Democratisation in Indonesia: Elections, Institutions and Society*, ed. Edward Aspinall and Marcus Mietzner, pp. 246–51. Singapore: Institute of Southeast Asian Studies, 2010.

Schlegel, Alice. "Gender Meanings: General and Specific". In *Beyond the Second Sex: New Directions in the Anthropology of Gender*, ed. Peggy Reeves Sandy and Ruth Gallagher Goodenough. Philadelphia: University of Pennsylvania Press, 1990.

Schroter, Susanne. *Gender and Islam in Southeast Asia: Women's Rights Movements, Religious Resurgence and Local Traditions*. Leiden: Brill, 2013.

———. "Gender and Islam in Southeast Asia: An Overview". In *Gender and Islam in Southeast Asia*, pp. 38–42.

Schulte, Nordholt Henk and Gerry van Klinken. *Politik Lokal di Indonesia*. Jakarta: KITLV and Yayasan Obor Indonesia, 2007.

Schwarz, Adam. *A Nation in Waiting: Indonesia in the 1990s*. NSW Australia: Westview Press, 1994.

———. *A Nation in Waiting: Indonesia's Search for Stability*. Singapore: Talisman, 2004.

Sekretaris DPRD Kebumen. "Daftar Nama Anggota DPRD Kabupaten Kebumen Periode Tahun 2004–2009" dan "Daftar Anggota DPRD Masa Bakti 2009–2014".

Sekretaris Jenderal Dharma Wanita Persatuan. *Dharma Wanita: Keputusan Musyawarah Nasional Luar Biasa Dharma Wanita nomor: Kep.04/MN LUB DW/XII/1999 tentang Anggaran Dasar Dharma Wanita*, 3rd ed. Jakarta: Sekretaris Jenderal Dharma Wanita, 2001.

Sekretaris Jenderal Dharma Wanita. *Keputusan Musyawarah Nasional IV Dharma Wanita nomor: Kep 03/MN IV DW/IV/1993 tentang Penyempurnaan Anggaran Dasar Dharma Wanita*. Jakarta: Sekretaris Jenderal Dharma Wanita, 1993.

———. *Dharma Wanita Persatuan: Keputusan Musyawarah Nasional I Dharma Wanita Persatuan nomor: Kep 04/MN I DWP/XII/2004 tentang Anggaran*

Dasar Dharma Wanita Persatuan, 8th ed. Jakarta: Sekretaris Jenderal Dharma Wanita Persatuan, 2008.

Shiraishi, Takashi. *An Age in Motion: Popular Radicalism in Java 1912–1926*. Ithaca and London: Cornell University Press, 1990.

Shuib, Rashidah. "Speaking with a New Voice: Sisters in Islam in Malaysia". In *Sexuality, Gender and Rights: Exploring Theory and Practice in South and Southeast Asia*, ed. Geetanjali Misra and Radhika Chandiramani. New Delhi: Sage Publications, 2005.

Sidel, John T. "Bossism and Democracy in the Philippines, Thailand and Indonesia: Towards an Alternative Framework for the Study of 'Local Strongmen'". In *Politicising Democracy: The New Local Politics of Democratisation*, ed. John Harriss, Kristian Stokke and Olle Tornquist. London: Palgrave, 2004.

Stake, Robert E. "Case Studies". In *Handbook of Qualitative Research*, ed. Norman K. Denzin and Yvonna S. Lincoln, 2nd ed. Thousand Oaks, CA, United Kingdom, India: Sage Publications, 2000.

Stivens, Maila. "Becoming Modern in Malaysia: Women at the End of the Twentieth Century". In *Women in Asia*, ed. Edwards and Roces, pp. 16–38. Sydney: Allen and Unwin, 2000.

―――. "Family Values and Islamic Revival: Gender, Rights and State Moral Projects in Malaysia". In Schroter, *Gender and Islam in Southeast Asia*, pp. 154–9. Leiden: Brill, 2013.

Stivens, Maila, ed. *Why Gender Matters in Southeast Asian Politics*. Melbourne: Centre of Southeast Asian Studies, Monash University, 1991.

Suharyo, Widjajanti I. "Indonesia's Transition to Decentralized Governance: Evolution at the Local Level". In *Decentralisation and Regional Autonomy in Indonesia: Implementation and Challenges*, ed. Coen J.G. Holtzapper and Martin Ramstedt, pp. 75–98.

Sulistiyanto, Priyambudi. "Pilkada in Bantul District: Incumbent, Populism, and the Decline of Royal Power". In *Deepening Democracy in Indonesia?*, ed. Erb and Sulistiyanto, pp. 190–208.

Sullivan, Norma. *Masters and Managers: A Study of Gender Relations in Urban Java*. Sydney: Allen and Unwin, 1994.

Suryadinata, Leo, Evi Nurvidya Arifin and Aris Ananta. *Penduduk Indonesia: Etnis dan Agama dalam Era Perubahan Politik*. Trans. Lilis Heri Mis Cicih. Jakarta: Pustaka LP3ES, 2003.

Suryakusuma, Julia I. "The State and Sexuality in New Order Indonesia". In *Fantasizing the Feminine in Indonesia*, ed. Laurie J. Sears. Durham and London: Duke University Press, 1996.

Suryochondro, Sukanti. *Potret Pergerakan Wanita di Indonesia*. Jakarta: CV. Rajawali, 1984.

T. Huzaemah. "Konsep Wanita Menurut Qur'an, Sunah, dan Fikih". In *Wanita Islam Indonesia: Dalam Kajian Tekstual dan Kontekstual*, ed. Lies M. Marcos-Natsir and Johan Hendrik Meuleman. Jakarta: INIS, 1993.

Tilaar, Marta and Wulan Widarto. *Leadership Quotient: Perempuan Pemimpin Indonesia*. Jakarta: Grasindo, 2003.
Tim Penggerak PKK Pusat. *Hasil Rapat Kerja Nasional VI PKK Tahun 2005*. Jakarta: Direktorat Jenderal Pemberdayaan Masyarakat dan Desa, 2005.
———. *Sejarah Singkat Gerakan PKK*. Jakarta: Tim Penggerak PKK Pusat, n.d.
Tim Peneliti Depertemen Ilmu Politik FISIP UNAIR, *Perempuan dalam Pemilukada: Kajian Tentang Kandidasi Perempuan di Jawa Timur dan Sulawesi Utara*. Jakarta: Kemitraan bagi Pembaruan Tata Pemerintahan di Indonesia, 2011.
Tiwon, Sylvia. "Reconstructing Boundaries and Beyond". In *Women and Households in Indonesia*, ed. Koning et al., pp. 68–84. Richmond: Curzon Press, 2000.
"Undang-Undang Republik Indonesia No. 1/1974 tentang Perkawinan". In *Kumpulan Lengkap Undang-Undang dan Peraturan Perkawinan di Indonesia*, ed. Hasbullah Bakry. Jakarta: Penerbit Djambatan, 1978.
van Bemmelen, Sita and Mies Grijns. "What Has Become of the Slendang? Changing Images of Women and Java". In *The Java That Never Was: Academic Theories and Political Practices*, ed. Hans Antlov and Jorgen Hellman. Piscataway, NJ: Transaction Publishers, 2005.
Van Doorn-Harder, Pieternella. *Women Shaping Islam: Indonesian Women Reading the Qur'an*. Champaign, IL: University of Illinois Press, 2006.
Veneracion-Rallonza, Lourdes. "Women and the Democracy Project: A Feminist Take on Women's Political Participation in the Philippines". In *Women's Political Participation and Representation in Asia*, ed. Iwanaga, pp. 210–52.
Vichitranonda, Suteera and Maytinee Bhongsvej. "NGO Advocacy for Women in Politics in Thailand". In *Women and Politics in Thailand*, ed. Iwanaga, pp. 54–94. Copenhagen: NIAS Press, 2008.
Vichit-Vadakan, Juree. "A Glimpse of Women Leaders in Thai Politics". In *Women and Politics in Thailand*, ed. Iwanaga, pp. 125–67. Copenhagen: NIAS Press, 2008.
———. "Women in Politics and Women and Politics: A Socio-Cultural Analysis of the Thai Context". In *Women and Politics in Thailand*, ed. Iwanaga, pp. 27–53. Copenhagen: NIAS Press, 2008.
Vreede-De Stuers, Cora. *The Indonesian Woman: Struggles and Achievements*. The Hague: Mouton & Co., 1960.
Wahid, Marzuki. "Pembaruan Hukum Keluarga Islam di Indonesia Paska Orde Baru: Studi Politik Hukum atas *Counter Legal Draft* Kompilasi Hukum Islam". Paper presented at the 4th Annual Islamic Studies Postgraduate Conference, Melbourne, 17–18 Nov. 2008.
Wahid, Sinta Nuriyah Abdurrahman. "Merumuskan Kembali Agenda Perjuangan Perempuan Dalam Konteks Perubahan Sosial Budaya Islam di Indonesia". In *Jurnal Pemikiran Islam tentang Pemberdayaan Perempuan*, ed. Mursyidah Thahir. Jakarta: PP Muslimat NU and Logos, 2000.

Ward, Barbara. *Women in the New Asia: The Changing Social Roles of Men and Women in South and South-East Asia.* Netherlands: UNESCO, 1963.

Weix, G.G. "Hidden Managers at Home: Elite Javanese Women Running New Order Family Firms". In *Women and Households in Indonesia*, ed. Koning et al., pp. 299–314. Richmond: Curzon Press, 2000.

White, Sally and Maria Ulfah Anshor. "Islam and Gender in Contemporary Indonesia: Public Discourses in Duties, Rights and Morality". In *Expressing Islam*, ed. Fealy and White, pp. 137–58.

Wieringa, Saskia. "Aborted Feminisms in Indonesia: A History of Indonesian Socialist Feminism". In *Women's Struggles and Strategies*, ed. Saskia Wieringa, pp. 69–89. Farnham, Surrey: Gower Publishing Company, 1988.

⸻. *Sexual Politics in Indonesia.* New York: Palgrave Macmillan, 2002.

Winarno, Bondan. *Rumah Iklan: Upaya Matari Menjadikan Periklanan Indonesia Tuan Rumah di Negeri Sendiri.* Jakarta: Kompas, 2008.

Winarto, Yunita T. and Sri Paramita Budhi Utami. "The Persisting and Changing 'Family' in Java: Empowering Women, Changing Power Relations?". Paper presented at the international workshop, "The Making of East Asia: from Both Macro and Micro Perspectives", JSPS–NRCT 2008 CORE University Exchange Program, the Center for Southeast Asian Studies, Kyoto University, Japan, 23–24 Feb. 2009.

Winasa, Gede. *Jabatan Untuk Rakyat: Kisah Kontroversial I Gede Winasa.* Bali: Pusat Pengembangan Jembrana, 2003.

Yasuko, Kobayashi. "Ulama's Changing Perspectives on Women's Social Status: Nahdlatul Ulama's Legal Opinion". In *Islam in Contention*, ed. Okamoto, Ota and Suaedy, pp. 279–312.

Yin, Robert K. *Case Study Research: Design and Methods.* Thousand Oaks: Sage Publications, 1994.

Zainu'ddin, Alisa G. Thomson. "Kartini, Her Life, Work and Influence". In *Kartini Centenary: Indonesian Women Then and Now*, ed. Alisa G. Thomson Zainu'ddin et al. Cheltenham: Standard Commercial Printers, 1980.

Zamhari, Arif. *Rituals of Islamic Spirituality: A Study of Majlis Dhikr Groups in East Java.* Canberra: Australian National University Press, 2010.

Theses and Dissertations

Adamson, Clarissa. "Globalization, Islam and the Idea of 'Woman' in Post-New Order Java". PhD dissertation, Georgetown University, 2004.

Alfian. "Islamic Modernism in Indonesian Politics: The Muhammadijah Movement during the Dutch Colonial Period (1912–1942)". PhD dissertation, University of Wisconsin, 1969.

Basyar, M. Hamdan. "Peran Ulama Dalam Penyelesaian Kekerasan Politik Pada Pemilu Tahun 1997 dan tahun 1999 di Pekalongan". Master's thesis, University of Indonesia, 2001.

Dewi, Kurniawati Hastuti. "Women's Leadership in Muhammadiyah: 'Aisyiyah's Struggle for Equal Power Relations". Master's thesis, Australian National University, 2007.
Jatmiko, Sidik. "Kiai dan Politik Lokal: Studi Kasus Reposisi Politik Kiai NU Kebumen, Jawa Tengah Memanfaatkan Peluang Keterbukaan Partisipasi di Era Reformasi". PhD dissertation, Gadjah Mada University, 2005.
Machrusah, Safira. "Muslimat and Nahdlatul Ulama: Negotiating Gender Relations within Traditional Muslim Organisation in Indonesia". Master's thesis, Australian National University, 2005.
Nurmila, Nina. "Negotiating Polygamy in Indonesia: Between Muslim Discourse and Women's Lived Experience". PhD dissertation, University of Melbourne, 2007.
Siregar, Wahidah Zein Br. "Gaining Representation in Parliament: A Study of the Struggle of Indonesian Women to Increase their Numbers in the National, Provincial and Local Parliaments in the 2004 Elections". PhD dissertation, Australian National University, 2007.
Tjiptoatmodjo, Fransiscus Assisi Sutjipto. "Kota-Kota Pantai di Sekitar Selat Madura (Abad XVII Sampai Medio Abad XIX)". PhD dissertation, Gadjah Mada University, 1983.
Wichelen, Sonja Judith van. "Embodied Contestations: Muslim Politics and Democratization in Indonesia through the Prism of Gender". PhD dissertation, University of Amsterdam, 2007.
White, Sally Jane. "Reformist Islam, Gender and Marriage in Late Colonial Dutch East Indies, 1900–1942". PhD dissertation, Australian National University, 2004.
Zubaidah, Siti. "Strategi Pemenangan Pasangan Bibit Waluyo-Rustriningsih Dalam Pemilihan Gubernur Jawa Tengah 2008". Master's thesis, Diponegoro University, 2000.

Journal Articles

Al-Lamky, Asya. "Feminizing Leadership in Arab Societies: The Perspectives of Omani Female Leaders". *Women in Management Review* 22, 1 (2007): 64.
Al-Suwaihel, Omaymah E. "Kuwaiti Female Leaders' Perspectives: The Influence of Culture on Their Leadership". *Contemporary Issues in Education Research* 3, 3 (2010): 29–39.
Anderson, Benedict. "How Did the Generals Die?". *Indonesia* 43 (1987): 109–34.
Baswedan, Anies R. "Political Islam in Indonesia: Present and Future Trajectory". *Asian Survey* 44, 5 (Sept.–Oct. 2004): 669–90. At <http://www.jstor.org/stable/4128549> [accessed 10 Nov. 2008].
Bautista, Julius. "The Meta-Theory of Piety: Reflections on the Work of Saba Mahmood". *Contemporary Islam* 2, 1 (2008): 75–83.

Beatty, Andrew. "Adam and Eve and Vishnu: Syncretism in the Javanese Slametan". *The Journal of the Royal Anthropological Institute* 2, 2 (June 1996): 271–88.

Boeije, H. "A Purposeful Approach to the Constant Comparative Method in the Analysis of Qualitative Interviews". *Quality & Quantity* 36 (2002): 391–409.

Brenner, Suzanne. "Reconstructing Self and Society: Javanese Muslim Women and 'the Veil'". *American Ethnologist* 23, 4 (1996): 673–97.

―――. "Private Moralities in the Public Sphere: Democratization, Islam, and Gender in Indonesia". *American Anthropologist* 113, 3 (Sept. 2011): 478–90.

Brooks, Deborah Jordan. "Testing the Double Standard for Candidate Emotionality: Voters Reactions to the Tears and Anger of Male and Female Politicians". *The Journal of Politics* 73, 2 (2011): 597–615.

Bruinessen, Martin van. "Genealogies of Islamic Radicalism in Post-Suharto Indonesia". *South East Asia Research* 10, 2 (2002): 117–54.

Carlson, Matthew and Ola Listhaug. "Public Opinion on the Role of Religion in Political Leadership: A Multi-level Analysis of Sixty-three Countries". *Japanese Journal of Political Science* 7, 3 (2006): 251–71.

Davids, Tine. "The Micro Dynamics of Agency: Repetition and Subversion in a Mexican Right-Wing Female Politician's Life Story". *European Journal of Women's Studies* 18, 2 (2011): 163–4.

Dewey, Alice G. "Trade and Social Control in Java". *The Journal of The Royal Anthropological Institute of Great Britain and Ireland* 92, 2 (July–Dec. 1962): 177–90.

Dewi, Kurniawati Hastuti. "Perspective versus Practices: Women's Leadership in Muhammadiyah". *SOJOURN: Journal of Social Issues in Southeast Asia* 23 (Oct. 2008): 161–85.

―――. "Javanese Women and Islam: Identity Formation since the Twentieth Century". *Southeast Asian Studies (Tonan Ajia Kenkyu)* 1, 1 (Apr. 2012): 109–40.

Derichs, Claudia, Andrea Fleschenberg and Momoyo Hustebeck. "Gendering Moral Capital: Morality as a Political Asset and Strategy of Top Female Politicians in Asia". *Critical Asian Studies* 38, 3 (2006): 245–70.

Feillard, Andree. "The Veil and Polygamy: Current Debates on Women and Islam in Indonesia". *Moussons* 99 (1999): 5–27.

Fitzherbert, Margaret. "The Politics of Political Mothers and Wives". *Institute of Public Affairs Review* 57, 1 (2005): 39–40. At <http://wwb.ebscohost.com/ehost/delivery> [accessed 20 Jan. 2012, site no longer available].

Gidengil, Elisabeth, Alison Harell and Bonnie H. Erickson. "Network Diversity and Vote Choice: Women's Social Ties and Left Voting in Canada". *Politics & Gender* 3, 2 (2007): 151–77.

Gole, Nulifer. "The Gendered Nature of the Public Sphere". *Public Culture* 10, 1 (1997): 61–81.

———. "Islam in Public: New Visibilities and New Imaginaries". *Public Culture* 14, 1 (Winter 2002): 173–90.
Haniffa, Farzana. "Piety as Politics Amongst Muslim Women in Contemporary Sri Lanka". *Modern Asian Studies* 42, 2/3 (2008): 347–75.
Hasan, Noorhaidi. "The Making of Public Islam: Piety, Agency, and Commodification on the Landscape of the Indonesian Public Sphere". *Contemporary Islam* 3 (2009): 229–50.
Hefner, Robert. W. "Islamizing Java? Religion and Politics in Rural East Java". *The Journal of Asian Studies* 46, 3 (Aug 1987). At <http://www.jstor.org/stable/205689> [accessed 9 Nov. 2008].
Hikam, M.A.S. "Wacana Intelektualisme tentang *Civil Society* di Indonesia". *Jurnal Pemikiran Islam Paramadina* 1, 2 (1999).
Huq, Samia and Sabina Faiz Rashid. "Refashioning Islam: Elite Women and Piety in Bangladesh". *Contemporary Islam* 2, 1 (2008): 7–22.
INDIPT. "Menurunnya Komitmen Kesetaraan Gender Dalam Dokumen Pembangunan Pemerintah Kabupaten Kebumen". *SETARA*, no. 1 (May–July 2004): 7–10, 15.
Jahan, Rounaq. "Women in South Asian Politics". *Third World Quarterly* 9, 3 (July 1987): 848–70.
Jalalzai, Farida and Mona Lena Krook. "Beyond Hillary and Benazir: Women's Political Leadership Worldwide". *International Political Science Review* 31, 1 (2010): 5–21.
Josep, Suad. "Working-Class Women's Networks in a Sectarian State: A Political Paradox". *American Ethnologist* 10, 1 (1983): 1–22. At <http://www.jstor.org/stable/644701> [accessed 24 Dec. 2009].
Kahn, Joel S. "Ideology and Social Structure in Indonesia". *Comparative Studies in Society and History* 20, 1 (Jan. 1978): 103–22. At <http://www.jstor.org/stable/178323> [accessed 10 Nov. 2008].
Koentjaraningrat. Review of Hildred Geertz. *The Javanese Family: A Study of Kinship and Socialization. American Anthropologist*, new series, 64, 4 (1962): 872–4. At <http://www.jstor.org/stable/667817> [accessed 9 Nov. 2008].
Kooi-Chin Tong, Joy and Bryan S. Turner. "Women, Piety and Practice: A Study of Women and Religious Practice in Malaysia". *Contemporary Islam* 2, 1 (2008): 41–59.
Liddle, R. William and Saiful Mujani, "Leadership, Party, and Religion: Explaining Voting Behavior in Indonesia". *Comparative Political Studies* 40, 7 (July 2007): 832–57. At <http://cps.sagepub.com> [accessed 7 Nov. 2008].
Lingkaran Survey Indonesia (LSI). "Mesin Partai Dalam Pilkada: Kasus Pilkada Jawa Tengah dan Nusa Tenggara Barat". *Kajian Bulanan* 15 (July 2008).
Lont, Hotze. "More Money, More Autonomy?: Women and Credit in a Javanese Urban Community". *Indonesia* 70 (Oct. 2000): 83–100.
Lovenduski, Joni. "Gender Politics: A Breakthrough for Women". *Parliamentary Affairs* 50, 4 (1997): 708–18.

Mahmood, Saba. "Feminist Theory, Embodiment, and the Docile Agents: Some Reflections on the Egyptian Islamic Revival". *Cultural Anthropology* 16, 2 (May 2010): 202–36.

Masaaki, Okamoto and Abdul Hamid. "Jawara in Power 1999–2007". *Indonesia* 86 (Oct. 2008).

Mckay, Joanna. "Having It All? Women MPs and Motherhood in Germany and the UK". *Parliamentary Affairs* 64, 4 (2011): 714–36.

Merrit, Sharyne. "Winners and Losers: Sex Differences in Municipal Elections". *American Journal of Political Science* 21, 4 (1997): 731–43.

Means, Ingunn Norderval. "Women in Local Politics: The Norwegian Experience". *Canadian Journal of Political Science* 5, 3 (Sept. 1972): 365–88.

Molyneux, Maxine. "Mobilization Without Emancipation? Women's Interests, the State, and Revolution in Nicaragua". *Feminist Studies* 11, 2 (Summer 1985): 227–54.

Nagata, Judith. "Religious Ideology and Social Change: The Islamic Revival in Malaysia". *Pacific Affair* 53, 3 (Autumn 1980): 405–39.

Norr, Kathleen Fordham. "Factions and Kinship: The Case of a South Indian Village". *Asian Survey* 16, 12 (Dec. 1976): 1139–50. At <http://www.jstor.org/stable/2643450> [accessed 2 Apr. 2009].

Reid, Anthony. "Female Roles in Pre-Colonial Southeast Asia", *Modern Asian Studies* 22, 3 (1988): 629–45.

Reid, Robin T. "Appearances Do Matter: How Makeup and Clothes Can Affect the Outcome of Elections". *Campaigns and Elections* 25, 3 (2004): 23–4. At <http://web.ebscohost.com/ehost/detail> [accessed 22 Feb. 2012].

Richter, Linda K. "Exploring Theories of Female Leadership in South and Southeast Asia". *Pacific Affairs* 63, 4 (1990–91): 524–40.

Rinaldo, Rachel. "Muslim Women, Middle Class Habitus, and Modernity in Indonesia". *Contemporary Islam* 2, 1 (2008): 23–39.

Shah, Saeeda J.A. "Re-thinking Educational Leadership: Exploring the Impact of Cultural and Belief Systems". *International Journal of Leadership in Education* 13, 1 (2010): 27–44.

Smith-Hefner, Nancy J. "Javanese Women and the Veil in Post-Soeharto Indonesia". *The Journal of Asian Studies* 66, 2 (2007): 389–420.

Stoler, Ann. "Changing Modes of Production: Class Structure and Female Autonomy in Rural Java". *Signs* 3, 1 (Autumn 1977). At <http://www.jstor.org/stable/3173080> [accessed 14 Dec. 2008].

Syamsiyatun, Siti. "A Daughter in the Indonesian Muhammadiyah: Nasyiatul Aisyiyah Negotiates a New Status and Image". *Journal of Islamic Studies* 18, 1 (2007): 69–94.

Thompson, Mark. R. "Female Leadership of Democratic Transition in Asia". *Pacific Affairs* 75, 4 (2002–03): 535–55.

Torab, Azam, "Piety as Gendered Agency: A Study of Jalaseh Ritual Discourse in an Urban Neighbourhood in Iran". *The Journal of the Royal Anthropological Institute* 2, 2 (June 1996).

Turner, Bryan S. "Introduction: the Price of Piety: a Special Issue of Contemporary Islam on Piety, Politics and Islam". *Contemporary Islam* 2, 1 (2008).
Van Allen, Judith. "Sitting on a Man: Colonialism and the Lost Political Institutions of Igbo Women". *Canadian Journal of African Studies* 6, 2 (1972): 165–81. At <http://www.jstor.org/stable/48197> [accessed 18 Oct. 2010].
Wahid, Wawan G.A. "Kepemimpinan Perempuan dalam Kajian Majlis Tarjih Muhammadiyah (Telaah Analisis Gender)". *Jurnal Musawa* 3, 1 (2004).
Watson, C.W. "A Popular Indonesian Preacher: The Significance of Aa Gymnastiar". *The Journal of the Royal Anthropological Institute* 11, 4 (Dec. 2005): 773–92.
Wertheim, W.F. "Changes in Indonesia's Social Stratification". *Pacific Affairs* 28, 1 (Mar. 1955). At <http://www.jstor.org/stable/2753710> [accessed 14 Dec. 2008].
Woodward, Mark R. "The "Slametan": Textual Knowledge and Ritual Performance in Central Javanese Islam". *History of Religions* 28, 1 (Aug. 1988) <http://www.jstor.org/stable/1062168> [accessed 14 Dec. 2008].
Zurbriggen, Eileen L. and Aurora M. Sherman. "Race and Gender in the 2008 U.S. Presidential Election: A Content Analysis of Editorial Cartoons". *Analysis of Social Issues and Public Policy* 10, 1 (2010): 223–47.

Magazines and Newspapers

"12 PAC PBB Tetap Dukung AQUR". *Koran Wawasan*, 10 May 2006.
"2 Cabup Sampaikan Visi-Misi". *Koran Wawasan*, 4 May 2006.
"Abhisit Mengaku Kalah". *Kompas*. At <http://internasional.kompas.com/read/2011/07/04/07325610/Abhisit.Mengaku.Kalah> [accessed 8 July 2011].
"Airin-Davnie Menangkan Pilkada Ulang Tangerang Selatan". *Rima News*, 4 Mar. 2011. At <http://www.rimanews.com> [accessed 23 June 2011].
"Amien Kampanyekan Rozaq Rais". *Radar Kebumen*, 30 May 2008.
"Andalkan Rustri Rebut Suara Perempuan". *Suara Merdeka*, 6 Mar. 2008.
"Antono-Fadia Menang di 17 Kecamatan". Suara Merdeka, 7 May 2011. At <http://www.suaramerdeka.com/v1/index.php/read/cetak/2011/05/07/145708/Antono-Fadia-Menang-di-17-Kecamatan> [accessed 24 June 2011].
"APPNP Bakar Formulir C-6". *Radar Banyuwangi*, 15 July 2010.
"ARAK Tuntut Korupsi Diusut Tuntas". *Kedaulatan Rakyat*, 9 Apr. 2005.
"Beruntungnya Kebumen Peroleh Penghargaan Muri: Langkah Rustri Tutupi Kelemahan". *Wawasan*, 2 Apr. 2005.
"Bibit Minta Dukungan Mengangi Pilgub". *Suara Merdeka*, 24 Mar. 2008.
"Bibit Waluyo Diberkati". *Suara Merdeka*, 22 May 2008.
"Bibit Yakin Didukung Keluarga TNI". *Suara Merdeka*, 15 Mar. 2008.
"Bupati Banyuwangi Kurang Komunikatif". At <http://www.cmm.or.id/cmm-indmore.php?id=A1389030M?> [accessed 24 Dec. 2008, site no longer available].

"Bupati Kebumen M. Nashiruddin Al Mansyur: Kritik dan Caci Maki, Semua Kami Tampung". *Tempo*, 23 Aug. 2009.
"Bupati Samsul Kembali Kalah". *Radar Banyuwangi*, 29 Mar. 2005.
"Buyar-Djuwarni Menang Pilkada Kebumen". At <http://matanews.com/2010/06/12/buyar-djuwarni-menang-pilkada-kebumen> [accessed 13 Jan. 2011, site no longer available].
"Buyar-Djuwarni Raih Suara Terbanyak Pilkada Kebumen". *Antarajateng.com*. <http://www.antarajateng.com/detail/index.php?> [accessed 13 Jan. 2011].
"Calon Lain Pilih Dialogis". *Suara Merdeka*, 2 June 2005.
"Debat Publik Cabub-Cawabup Sepi Pengunjung". *Kedaulatan Rakyat*, 27 May 2005.
"Deklarasi Bakal Dihadiri Naga Merah". *Suara Merdeka*, 14 Mar. 2008.
"Dharma Wanita Persatuan: Wadah Istri Pegawai Negeri Sipil yang Mandiri dan Demokratis". *Media Informasi*, no. 1, 2000.
"Di Balik Pilbub Kebumen (1): Rustri Tanpa Tim, Zuhri Geleng Kepala". *Suara Merdeka*, 8 June 2005.
"Didukung PKL, dan Sopir Angkot". *Radar Banyuwangi*, 20 June 2005.
"Disodori 15 Dugaan Korupsi". *Suara Merdeka*, 8 Apr. 2005.
"Ditetapkan Hasil Pemilu Bupati dan Wakil Bupati Kebumen". At <http://kpud.kebumenkab.go.id/index.php?module=News&func=display&sid=30> [accessed 20 May 2010].
"Dra Rustriningsih M.Si: Srikandi Kabupaten Kebumen". *Tokoh Indonesia DotCom (Ensiklopedi Tokoh Indonesia)*. At <www.tokohindnesia.com/ensiklopedi/di/r/rustringingsih/index.shtml> [accessed 17 July 2008 and 20 May 2010, site no longer available].
"Dukungan ke Bibit dan Tamzil Mengalir". *Suara Merdeka*, 5 May 2008.
"Golkar Pekalongan Meradang, Mucul Calon Ganda Pilkada". At <http://www.antarjateng.com> [accessed 24 June 2011, site no longer available].
"Gubernur Kawal Coblosan". *Radar Banyuwangi*, 14 July 2010.
"Indonesia Sudah Kaja Djanda". *Harian Rakjat*, 14 Oct. 1952.
"IPNU-IPPNU Dukung Ratna". *Radar Banyuwangi*, 2 June 2005.
"Jika Terpilih Bibit Janji Keliling Desa". *Suara Merdeka*, 5 Apr. 2008.
"Kabupaten Kebumen: Dara Putih dari Kebumen". *Tempo*, 23 Aug. 2009.
"Kampanye Pilkada Disambut Dingin". *Suara Merdeka*, 25 May 2005.
"Kampanye Putaran Pertama: AQUR Gelar Rapat Terbuka". *Suara Merdeka*, 5 May 2006.
"Kampanye Qomariyah-Ponco: Massa Tertahan di Jalan Raya". *Suara Merdeka*, 12 May 2006.
"Kampanye Sasongko-Suprapto Dipadati Pendukung". *Suara Merdeka*, 2 June 2005.
"Kasus Foto Selingkuh, Goyang Qonco". *Radar Semarang*, 24 May 2006.
"Kebijaksanaan tentang Hari Ulang tahun Dharma Wanita Persatuan dan Seragam Organisasi". *Media Informasi*, no. 6 (Aug. 2001).

"Keputusan Muktamar 'Aisyiyah ke-40: Kepribadian Muhammadiyah Supaya Diamalkan Seluruh Keluarga Muhammadiyah". *Suara Muhammadiyah*, no. 14 (July 1978).
"Ketua MUI Jateng Habib M Luthfy Ali Bin Yahya: Saya Bukan Milik Salah Satu Kelompok". *Koran Wawasan*, 31 Mar. 2006.
"Kiat Ratna Modali Pedagang Asongan: Bunga Lunak, Tanpa Jaminan". *Radar Banyuwangi*, 3 June 2005.
"Kirab Peserta Pilkada Disambut Hujan Lebat". *Suara Merdeka*, 4 May 2006.
"Konstituti: Mengupayakan Demokrasi Substansial". *Kompas*, 20 Aug. 2010.
"KPU Serahkan Hasil Pilkada ke DPRD". *radar-pekalongan.com*. At <http://www.radar-pekalongan.com> [accessed 24 June 2011, site no longer available].
"Langkah Rustriningsih Setelah Gagal Dapat Rekomendasi PDIP". 8 Mar. 2013. At <http://news.detik.com/read/2013/03/08/184319/2189968/10/langkah-rustriningsih-setelah-gagal–dapat-rekomendasipdip?nd771104bcj> [accessed 21 Mar. 2013].
"Mantan Bupati Jembrana Divonis Bebas". *bali.antaranews.com*, 1 July 2011. At <http://bali.antaranews.com/berita/11942/mantan-bupati-jembrana-divonis-bebas> [accessed 29 Sept. 2011].
"Mantan Kades Siap Dukung BS-Adnan". *Seputar Indonesia*, 24 May 2008.
Majalah Detik, no. 33, 16 July 2012.
Majalah Detik, no. 93, 15 Dec. 2013.
"Masduki-Syafi'i Temui Hisyam". *Radar Banyuwangi*, 13 Apr. 2005.
"Mega Pecate Kader Mbalel". *Seputar Indonesia*, 31 Mar. 2008.
"Megawati Tagih Komitmen". *Kompas*, 17 May 2008.
"Menangkan Sukawi Akan Mendapat Sapi". *Suara Merdeka*, 22 May 2008.
"Mengenal Wakil Gubernur Jateng Terpilih Rustriningsih: Si Pendiam Yang Konsisten Jalani Dunia Politik". *Seputar Indonesia*, 24 June 2008.
"MUI keluarkan 11 fatwa". *Kompas Cyber Media*, 30 July 2005.
"Murdoko Mundur dari Bursa Cagub". *Suara Merdeka*, 21 Jan. 2008.
"Nasdem Jateng Terbentuk". At <http://nasionaldemokrat.org/articles/viewColumn WithTitle/kabar/nasdem-jateng-terbentuk> [accessed 26 Jan. 2011, site no longer available].
"Number of Candidates by Elective Positions and Gender", 13 May 2013 Elections, <http://moneypolitics.pcij.org/stories/women-candidates-a-puny-minority-in-natl-local-races/> [accessed 3 June 2013].
"Partai Gurem Bisa Usung Calon". *Jawa Pos*, 23 Mar. 2005.
"Pasangan Bibit-Rustri Dirikan Ratusan Posko". *Seputar Indonesia*, 21 May 2008.
"Pasangan Siti Qomariyah dan H Wahyudi Pontjo Nugroho MT Dapat Simpati Rakyat". *Cakrawala*, no. 247, 2–6 May 2006.
"PBB Alihkan Dukungan ke Qonco". *Suara Merdeka*, 5 May 2006.
"PDS Merapat ke PDIP". *Radar Banyumas*, 31 Mar. 2008.
"Pelecehan Agama: Kiai dan Tokoh Masyarakat akan Datangi Mapolres Banyuwangi". *Gatra News*. 17 July 2005. At <http://www.gatra.com/2005-07-17/artikel.php?id=86444> [accessed 24 Dec. 2008, site no longer available].

"Pelantikan Bupati–Wakil Bupati: Asmah Gani berhenti dari DPRD Nunukan". At <http://kaltim.tribunnews.com/2011/05/30/asmah-gani-berhenti-dari-dprd-nunukan> [accessed 21 Feb. 2012].

"Pemilukada Nunukan: Basri-Hj. Asmah Gani, Bupati-Wakil Bupati Nunukan Terpilih". *Tribun Kaltim*, 24 Feb. 2011. At <http://kaltim.tribunnews.com/2011/02/24/basri-hj-asmah-gani-bupati-wakil-bupati-nunukan-terpilih> [accessed 21 Feb. 2012].

"Pencalonan Kembali Rustriningsih: Digoyang Dugaan Korupsi". *Kompas*, 15 Apr. 2005.

"Pendukung Qonco Penuhi Lapangan Wiradesa". *Suara Merdeka*, 8 May 2006.

"Pengaruh Politik Uang pada Pilkada Meningkat". *Kompas*, 20 Oct. 2010. At <http://internasional.kompas.com/read/2010/10/20/05585546/Pengaruh.Politik.Uang.pada.Pilkada.Meningkat> [accessed 16 Sept. 2013].

"Perjalanan Panjang Bibit Waluyo: Setiap Hari Weton Selalu Menggelar Pengajian". *Suara Merdeka*, 25 June 2008.

"Pesona Perempuan di Pentas Dinastik". *Gatra*, 8 Sept. 2010.

"PKB Garap Kultur NU". *Suara Merdeka*, 6 Mar. 2008.

"Pontjo Menang Konvensi". *Radar Pekalongan*, 6 Feb. 2006.

"PPKB Alihkan Dukungan ke Qonco". *Suara Merdeka*, 3 May 2006.

"Profil" in <http://voteforwinasa.wordpress.com/profil/> [10 Feb. 2011].

"Puan: Hanya Ganjar-Heru Representasi PDIP di Pilgub Jateng". *News.detik.com*, 9 Mar. 2013. At <http://news.detik.com/read/2013/03/09/185024/2190415/10/puan-hanya-ganjar-heru-representasi-pdip-di-pilgub-jateng?nd771104bcj> [accessed 21 Mar. 2013].

"PW NU Tegaskan Netra". *Suara Merdeka*, 24 Feb. 2008.

"Qomariyah-Pontjo Resmi Berpasangan". *Radar Pekalongan*, 22 Feb. 2006.

"Qonco Digoyang Foto Selingkuh". *Radar Pekalongan*, 26 May 2006.

"Ratna Ani Lestari Divonis 5 Tahun Penjara". *Sunriseofjava.com*, 11 Feb. 2013. At <http://sunriseofjava.com/berita-306-ratna-ani-lestari-divonis-5-tahun-penjara.html> [accessed 8 Oct. 2013].

"Ratna Haul Syech Abdul Kadir Jailani". *Radar Banyuwangi*, 17 May 2005.

"Ratna Kantongi 900 Suara". *Radar Banyuwangi*, 2 Mar. 2005.

"Ribuan Orang Ikuti Istighotsah Kubro: Doakan Pilkada Aman". *Suara Merdeka*, 1 May 2006.

"Riwayat Singkat Dharma Wanita". *Dharma Wanita*, no. 19, 31 July 1981.

"Rumah Janda tua itupun dibangun". *Radar Banyuwangi*, 25 May 2005.

"Rustri Ajak Perempuan Bangkit". *Suara Merdeka*, 13 June 2008.

"Rustri Tuduh DPD 'Nyekap' Probo, Murdoko: Harus Direkomendasi DPP". *Wawasan*, 5 Apr. 2005.

"Rustriningsih Angkat Peran Perempuan". *Suara Merdeka*, 14 Mar. 2008.

"Saudi Women Seeks to Put Women in the Driving Seat". BBC NEWS Middle East, 18 May 2011. At <http://www.bbc.co.uk/news/world-middle-east-13431562> [accessed 2 Apr. 2013].

"Saudi Arabia Accused of Tracking Women Electronically as a New System Sends Men a Text If Their Wife Tries to Leave Country". *Mail Online News*, 23 Nov. 2013. At <http://www.dailymail.co.uk/news/article-2237382/Saudi-Arabian-men-sent-text-message-wives-eave-enter-country-equal-rights-campaigners-criticise-airport-system.html> [accessed 2 Apr. 2013].

"Sekjen PDIP Ingatkan Wagub Jateng yang Gabung Nasdem". *detikNews*, 24 Jan. 2011.

"Sekkab Jadi Saksi Ratna". *Radar Banyuwangi*, 9 Mar. 2010.

"Soal Rekomendasi Pencalonan Rustri-Nashir: DPD dan DPC PDIP Beda Tafsir". *Wawasan*, 5 Apr. 2005.

"Sujud Membantah Dibayar Rp 10 Jutan". *Suara Merdeka*, 15 Apr. 2005.

Suwardiman, "Banyuwangi: Pilpol Pilgub Wong Osing". *Kompas*, 25 July 2008.

"Syekh Puji Divonis Empat Tahun, Dua Istrinya Menangis". *Tempo Interaktif*, 24 Nov. 2010. At <http://www.tempointeraktif.com/hg/jogja/2010/11/24/brk,20101124-294259,id.html> [accessed 21 Dec. 2010].

"Terkait Korupsi, Mantan Bupati Jembrana Dilimpahkan ke Kejati Bali". *detikNews*, 26 Jan. 2011. At <http://us.detiknews.com/read/2011/01/26/175606/1555229/10/terkait-korupsi-mantan-bupati-jembrana-dilimpahkan-ke-kejati-bali?9911022> [accessed 26 Jan. 2011].

"Uji Kepatutan dan Kelayakan Cagub PDI-P". *Suara Merdeka*, 15 Feb. 2008.

"Updates on Women and Men in the Philippines". National Statistical Coordination Board, Makati City, the Philippines. 1 Mar. 2010.

"Usai Caesar, Nyaris Hadiri Rakerdasus Naik Ambulan". *Radar Banyumas*, 28 June 2008.

"Wanita Katholik Tantang P.P. 19 Tjela Polygamie dan Tuntut Pembrantasan Tukang2 Riba". *Harian Rakjat*, 13 Oct. 1952.

"Yingluck, PM Perempuan Pertama Thailand". *Kompas.com*, 4 July 2011. At <http://internasional.kompas.com/read/2011/07/04/10015049/Yingluck.PM.Perempuan.Pertama.Thailand> [accessed 8 July 2011].

Basyir, Ahmad Azhar. "Mekanisme Ijtihad di Kalangan Muhammadiyah". *Suara Muhammadiyah*, no. 19 (Oct. 1987).

Kartinah. "Kartini Penundjuk Djalan Kahidupan Baru". *Harian Rakjat*, 21 Apr. 1955.

Lingkaran Survey Indonesia (LSI). "Grafik 3: Tingkat Dukungan Terhadap Kandidat-Pilkada Jawa Tengah (Maret 2008-Juni 2008)". *Kajian Bulanan* 15 (Juli 2008).

⸺. "Mesin Partai Dalam Pilkada: Kasus Pilkada Jawa Tengah dan Nusa Tenggara Barat". *Kajian Bulanan* 15 (Juli 2008).

Munir, Lili Zakiyah. "Islam, Gender and Equal Rights for Women". *The Jakarta Post*, 10 Dec. 2002.

Murdoko. *Selayang Pandang PDI Perjuangan Jawa Tengah*. Semarang: DPD PDI Perjuangan Jawa Tengah, n.d.

Riza, Ali. "Di Balik Kemenangan Mantan". *Suara Merdeka*, 10 May 2011.

Si De, Tj. T vis. "Isteri Sedar Tjoekoep Oemoernja 10 Tahoen". *Keoetamaan Isteri* 6 (June 1940).
SUARA KPU, Januari 2009.

Audio

VCD of a *Mauluddan Pengajian* and Promotion of Siti Qomariyah's Nomination.
VCD Musical Media Campaign of Ratna-Gus Yus in the 2005 direct election, Banyuwangi.

INDEX

1945 Constitution, 33
1966 Coup, 34
1997 Constitution, 7
2000 Canadian Election Study, 13
2004 General Election, 18–9
2004 General Election Law, 46

Aa Gym, 48
abangan, 65, 67n7, 175, 185
    Ratna Ani Lestari, 143, 144, 151, 171, 174n11
    role in political strategies, 82, 85, 105, 179
    Rustriningsih, 67, 73, 80
Adabul Mar'ah Fil Islam, 56, 60n46
Abdullah (*kyai*), 131
Abdullah, M. Amin, 57
activists, female Muslim, 38, 41–2, 47
    relations with candidates, 77, 82, 100, 104, 154, 164, 167, 171
AD/ART. *See* Dharma Wanita: organizational platform
adat, 29, 51
Adnan, Muhammad, 89t, 91, 92, 94, 98, 99
affirmative action, 46–7
Ahmed, Kamal Uddin, 178–9
Aidha, Ida, 136
'Aisyiyah, 19–20, 30, 32, 55, 123, 132, 167, 169
    promotion of women's leadership, 58–9, 62–3
    publications, 30, 55–6

    and Rustriningsih, 82, 104
    and Siti Qomariyah, 134
AJB Bumiputera. *See* Bumi Putera Insurance Company
Ali, KH. Musyafa, 83
Alliance of Civil Society for Revision of Political Legislation (ANSIPOL), 46
Anas, Abdullah Azwar, 172
Anwar, Syamsul, 57
AQUR, 124
ARAK (Alliance of People Against Corruption), 81
Arisdiawan, Pebdi, 172
Article 59. *See* Law No. 32/2004: Article 59
Ashar, Soni Achmad Saleh, 69
Aspinall, Edward, 7
Aung San Suu Kyi, 79

Bahtsul Masa'il, 59
Banyuwangi [Regency], 18
    socio-political landscape, 141–3
Barabasi, Albert-Laszlo, 13
Basyuni, Muhammad Maftuh, 53
Bianpoen, Carla, 43
Blackburn, Susan, 1, 5, 17
Blok Agung, 150t, 153, 186
Brenner, Suzanne, 41, 180n14
Brooks, Deborah Jordan, 128
Budi Utomo, 31
Bumi Putera Insurance Company (AJB Bumiputera), 98

Bunyamin, Imam Muzani, 76t, 82, 83
bupati (regents), 79, 126, 127, 159
    female, 134, 146, 175
    See also regents
Bureau of Women's Empowerment (Central Java), 103–4
Bureau for Migrant Workers, 137

Carlson, Matthew, 10, 17
Cashuri, 138
Caucus for Women and Indonesian Politics (KPPI), 45
Center for Empowering Women in Politics (PD Politik), 45
Central Java
    2008 Direct Gubernatorial Election, 19, 85–99, 105–6, 179
child marriage, 29, 43, 48
Christian Forum (in Central Java), 98
Ciciek, Farha, 42
Coalition of Non-Parliamentary Political Parties (GPPNP), 147, 148, 149, 150, 166
Compilation of Islamic Law (KHI), 52
Concern for the Nation Functional Party (PKPB), 21–2t, 23t, 148–9, 149, 190t
Congress of Indonesian Muslims (KUI), 61
Connel, R.W., 11, 12, 13
Constitutional Court (MK), 9, 46, 147
Counter Legal Draft (CLD), 52–3

Dahlan, K.H. Ahmad, 11n40, 30, 186
dakwah movement, 38–9
darah biru, 124
Democrat Party (PD), 23t, 66t, 92, 99, 109t, 142–3, 145, 190t
    elections, 84–5, 86t, 92, 99, 138, 149, 150t, 153, 164

Department of Women's Empowerment, 137
Derichs, Claudia, 12, 79, 80
Dhanu, Umar, 97
Dharma Wanita, 36, 44
Dharma Wanita Persatuan. *See* Dharma Wanita
direct elections, 17n65, 93, 147, 176
    introduction through Law No. 32/2004, 2
    election of women through, 6–9, 21–2t, 187–93
Djamhuri, Imam, 138, 139
Djurdjani, Nyai Hj., 83
Doxey, Monika Swasti Winarnita, 43
DPRD. *See* Regional People's Representative Council
dress as political strategy
    headscarf, 69–70
    impact of non-Islamic dress, 161
    makeup, 80
    "pious" Islamic clothing, 81, 111, 161
    veil (*kudung*), 179, 180, 181
Dzuhayatin, Siti Ruhaini, 42

Effendi, H.M. Zuhri, 76t, 81, 85, 147
Engineer, Ashgar Ali, 41
Erickson, Bonnie, 13
Errington, Shelly, 5n15

Failasuf (*kyai*), 130
familial ties, 6
    among candidates profiled, 13, 15, 187–9
    and networks, 13–7
    as strategy, 19, 69–73, 105
    weak, 112–3, 144–9
family planning programmes (KB), 36, 53–4

Family Welfare Guidance (PKK), 36, 45–6
Fatayat NU
    and Ratna Ani Lestari, 144, 164
    and Siti Qomariyah, 121, 127–9, 186
fatwa, 39, 53
    on female leadership, 55, 59–63
    by NU, 59–63
    on women in public activities, 59
Fealy, Greg, 7
Feillard, Andree, 41
female leadership, 2, 4, 8, 9, 12, 13, 16, 54, 80, 133
    comparisons with male leaders, 186–7
    Muhammadiyah, 55–9
    Muslim acceptance of, 16, 176–9
    Nahdlatul Ulama (NU), 59–63, 77, 175
    rise worldwide, 14–5
Fiqh, 63
FK3. *See* Yellow Book Learning Forum
FKP/Golkar, 65–6, 142–3
Fleschenberg, Andrea, 12, 79, 80
Fourth United Nations World Conference on Women, 47
Frisk, Sylva, 39

Geertz, Clifford, 65
    categories of Javanese society, 67n7
gender, 9, 11–2, 47, 52, 85, 102
    conservative interpretations, 49
    definitions, 11–2
    and elections
        Ratna Ani Lestari, 137, 156–60, 164, 170, 171, 173t
        Rustriningsih, 64, 80, 95, 105
        Siti Qomariyah, 116, 125, 127
    and family ties, 13–6
    and Islam, 3–6, 9–11, 63
    and networks, 12–3
gender equality, 78, 101, 102, 168, 179
    acceptance of concept, 41, 45, 47, 49
    and challenge to the 1974 Marriage Law, 52
    in Islam, 9–10, 42
    Parahita Eka Praya Utama award, 104
gender identity, 5n14, 41, 127, 157, 158, 159, 171
gender ideology, 36, 43–4, 45
gender interests, 36n39
gender roles, 53, 55, 56
    Presidential Instruction No. 9/2000 on Gender Mainstreaming, 47
general elections, 2–3n6, 18–9, 60, 182
    1971 General Election, 35
    1992 General Election, 65, 108, 115
    1997 General Election, 61, 108, 115
    1999 General Election, 62, 72, 86, 86t, 109, 112, 115, 142, 143
    2004 General Election, 18, 19, 39, 46, 86, 86t, 110, 117, 142, 143, 184
    2009 General Election, 46, 65, 66, 86, 86t, 110, 143
    2014 General Election, 46
General Election Commission (KPU), 47, 72, 93, 94, 124, 149, 158, 166, 172, 187, 188
    in Banyuwangi, 149, 166, 172
    in Central Java, 93, 94
    in Kebumen, 72
    members, 104, 150t, 152
    in Pekalongan, 124

gerakan tarbiyah, 40
Gerwani (Gerakan Wanita Indonesia, Indonesian Women's Movement), 32
Gerwis, 32, 33
Gidengil, Elisabeth, 13
Golkar, 35, 44, 72, 100, 138
   in elections, 65, 66t, 72, 76t, 85–6, 92, 95, 98
      Banyuwangi, 142–3, 149–50, 154, 155, 164, 166, 172
      Pekalongan, 108–10, 113, 115, 118, 119–20, 122–3, 138–9
   female candidates, 22–3t, 24–5t, 167, 190–1t, 192
   and Muslim parties, 42, 61n50
Government Regulation No. 19/1952, 32
GPSP. *See* Movement for Educating Female Voters
Grijn, Mies, 41
gubernatorial elections
   2007, South Sulawesi, 98
   2008, Central Java, 67, 87, 88, 91, 93, 98, 105, 183
   2013, Central Java, 106, 107
Guided Democracy, 27, 33
Gus Dur (Abdurrahman Wahid), 40, 45, 47, 53, 61n50, 62, 63
Gutomo, 147

Habibie, President B.J., 7
Hadi, Samsul (former regent of Banyuwangi), 147, 153, 157, 159, 160, 161, 162
hadith, 61, 62
Hadiz, Vedi R., 4, 5, 5n14, 182
Hafidz, Wardah, 41
Hajin, H.A. Qurofi, 122, 123t, 124, 130, 132, 133

Harell, Andrea, 13
Hariri, Zuhdi (*kyai*), 130
Hasan, Riffat, 41
Hasyim, Wahid, 114
Hatta, Meutia, 46
Haz, Vice President Hamzah, 48
headscarf. *See* dress as political strategy: headscarf
Hikmah, Darul, 110
HTI. *See* Indonesian Party of Liberation
husbands, gender relations with, 182–3
Hustebeck, Momoyo, 12, 79, 80

IAIN. *See* State Islamic Institute
ibu (wives and mothers), 36, 43
ibuism, 36n38. *See also* state ibuism
ICMI. *See* Indonesian Muslim Intellectual Association
Ida, Rachmah, 47
illiteracy, 136, 169
Indonesian Council of Ulama (MUI), 61, 111, 119, 158
   fatwa against CLD, 53
Indonesian Democratic Party (PDI), 35, 105, 109t, 124, 142, 143t
   and Rustriningsih, 65–72, 74, 79, 86t
Indonesian Democrat Party of Struggle (PDIP), 91, 96, 109t, 110, 112–5, 122–3, 144, 146
   elections, 65–6, 106–7
   female candidates elected, 21–7t, 173–4t, 175, 185, 188–9t, 190–1t, 192
   Regional Board, 72, 146
   and Rustriningsih, 19, 67n7, 72–3, 75–6, 80, 84–5, 94
   2008 election, 85–93, 96–9
   and Siti Qomariyah, 131, 138, 140

and Ratna Ani Lestari, 141,
    144–7, 149, 153, 154–5,
    163–4
  See also Amat Antono,
    Rustriningsih
Indonesian Democratic Vanguard
  party (PPDI), 21t, 147, 157, 162,
  172
Indonesian Mujahedeen Council
  (MMI), 61
Indonesian Muslim Intellectual
  Association (ICMI), 42
Indonesian Party of Liberation (HTI),
  61–2
Indonesian's People Consultative
  Assembly, 45, 72
Indonesian Sports Committee
  (KONI), 118
Indonesian Survey Circle. *See*
  Lingkaran Survey Indonesia (LSI)
Indonesian Women's Association
  (PPPI), 31
Indonesian Women's Coalition (KPI),
  46, 82, 104
Indonesian Women's Commission on
  Human Rights, 48
Inglehart, Ronald, 10, 193
Institute for Gender and Human
  Rights Studies (LKJ HAM), 103
Institute for Economic and Social
  Research, Education and Analysis
  (LP3ES), 125
Iriani, Rina, 8, 18, 22t
Iskandar, Muhaimin, 143
Istiqhotsah (*istiqozah*) *Kubro*, 130
Islam and gender. *See* gender: and
  Islam
Islam and networks. *See* networks:
  Islam
Islamic feminism, 38, 41–3, 52
Islamic law, local, 48
Islamic revival, 38, 48–9
Islamic state, demands for, 48

Islamification (New Order era), 37–43
Isteri Sedar, 32–3
ijtihad, 55, 63
Iwanaga, Kazuki, 193
Izzurahman (*kyai*), 131

Jackson, Karl D., 35
Jahan, Rounaq, 14
Jalal, H., 172
Jaza, Ilyas (*kyai*), 130
Jembrana DPRD, 145, 161
jeneng and *jenang* ("popularity" and
  "money"), 29n50
JIMM. *See* Muhammadiyah
  Intellectual Youth Network
JPPOL. *See* Network for Women and
  Politics
Jurnal Perempuan, 46, 52n12
Justice Party (KS), 41

Kadir, Abdul, 149, 164, 165, 166
Karsoprayitno, Koesnanto, 76t, 82,
  83, 85
Kartini, R.A., 29, 30
Kartini schools, 29–30
Kebumen DPRD, 74, 76t, 77, 100
Kebumen Regency, 64–7
  1992 General Election, 65, 66t
  2005 direct election in, 74–85
  Rustriningsih's political rise in,
    67–74
Kholiq, Abdul, 89t, 91, 92, 99
khul' (form of divorce), 178
Kiemas, Taufik, 106
Kimmel, Michael S., 11, 12
kinship roles/politics, 6, 12, 14, 24,
  185
Kitab Kuning, 53
kodrati, 79
konco wingking (proverb), 51, 54,
  182–3

Konstituante, 33
KPI. *See* Coalition of Indonesian Women
KPPI. *See* Caucus for Women and Indonesian Politics
KS. *See* Justice Party
KUI. *See* Congress of Indonesian Muslims
kudung. See dress as political strategy: veil (*kudung*)
kulon kali (western Kebumen), 65, 80
kyai, 18, 48, 59, 173–4t, 176, 177, 179, 186, 187
 and Rustriningsih, 73, 77, 78, 82, 83, 84, 99, 100, 110
 and Siti Qomariyah, 115–9, 121–5, 129, 130, 132, 137, 140
 and Ratna Ani Lestari, 141, 149n22, 150t, 151–4, 156, 162–4, 166, 167, 171

laskar, female, 32
Law No. 1/1974 of the Marriage Code, 51–2
Law No. 2/2008 on Political Parties, 46
Law No. 2/2011 on Political Parties, 47
Law No. 5/1974, 1, 7, 8n31
Law No. 8/2012 on General Elections, 47
Law No. 10/2008 on General Elections, 46
Law No. 22/1999 on Regional Government, 1, 4, 7, 8, 112
Law No. 32/2004, 2, 4, 8, 9, 147, 192
 Article 59, 9, 147
leadership of Muslim women, 56–63
leadership style, 159
Legal Aid Foundation, Indonesian Women's Association for Justice (LBH APIK), 103

Lestari, Ratna Ani, 18, 19
 2005 direct election, 149–66
 2010 direct election, 171–2
 Banyuwangi background, 141–5
 campaign strategy, 151–75
  networks, 144–54
  piety, 161–2
  programmes, 162–6
 importance of networks
  family, 144–9
  male, 154–6
  NU *kyai*, 151–4
 Islamic piety, 161–2, 180
 on women's issues, 166–70, 183–4
 See also Banyuwangi (Regency)
Liberal Islam Network (JIL), 42
Limpo, Syahrul Yasin, 98
Lingkaran Survey Indonesia (LSI), 19, 91, 92
LKJ HAM. *See* Institute for Gender and Human Rights Studies
Local Government Development Plan (RKPD) 2006–10, 101–2
Local Government Mid-Term Development Plan (RJPDM) Banyuwangi, 169
Lutfi Ali Bin Ayahya, Habib M., 116, 118, 119, 130, 131, 140

Machrusah, Safira, 60
Madjid, Nurcholis, 40
Madrasah Aliyah Negeri, 110
Madrasah Tsanawiyah Maarif, 110
Maduranese, 142, 159, 165
Maharani, Puan, 106, 107
Mahfudh, Sahal, 63
Mahfudz, Wahib (Gus Wahib,), 77, 83
Mahmood, Saba, 194
Majlis Tarjih, 55–7, 59
makeup. *See* dress as political strategy: makeup

Malaysia, 38
  See dakwah movement
Marpraneet, Hathairat, 184
marriage law
  challenge to 1974 Marriage Law, 52
Masaaki, Okamoto, 2, 182
Masduki, Acmad, 22t, 149, 150t, 153, 164, 165
Masyhadi, Imron (*kyai*), 131
Masyumi, 34n31, 35
Mataraman, 142, 165
maternal mortality, 102, 106, 170
mauluddan, 82–4, 130
  VCD, "Pengajian *Mauluddan*", 130
Mckay, Joanna, 88
Mernissi, Fatima, 41
MIAI (Majelis Islam 'Ala Indonesia), 34n31
Mid-Term Development Plan, 102, 135
Ministry of Women's Empowerment, 46
Mohammad, Maznah, 178
Moore, Henrietta L., 11, 12
moral capital, 79
  in political rise of Siti Qomariyah, 110–4
Movement for Educating Female Voters (GPSP), 45
MPR. *See* People's Consultative Assembly
Muhammadiyah
  attitude toward female leadership, 20, 55–9, 62–3
  and Amat Antono, 123, 132
  and elections, 123
  Islamization, 40, 42, 9t, 114
  and Ratna Lestari, 147, 148, 154, 169
  and Siti Qomariyah, 132, 134, 138
  and the state, 114–5

Muhammadiyah Intellectual Youth Network (JIMM), 42
MUI. *See* Indonesian Council of Ulama
Mulia, Siti Musdah, 42
  challenge to 1974 Marriage Law, 52
Munir, Lili Zakiyah, 1, 42
Murba Party, 33
Murba Women's Union (PERWAMU), 33
Murdoko, 88, 96, 97, 106
Muritno, Dr., 113, 114
Muslimat NU, 19
  activism in, 47, 60, 62–3
  and Ratna Ani Lestari, 144, 167, 185, 186
  and Rustriningsih, 82, 94–5, 104
  and Siti Qomariyah, 111, 116–7, 119, 125, 127, 128–30, 138
Muzadi, Hasyim, 75, 114

nafaka, 51
Nahdlatul Ulama (NU), 11, 35n30, 39, 40, 114
  and Amat Antono, 123, 132
  and elections, 82, 98–9, 123t, 139, 173–4t, 176–7, 179–80, 185–7, 194
  and the state, 114–5
  and Ratna Ani Lestari, 144, 147, 148, 149t, 151–4, 156, 157, 159, 162, 164–5, 167, 169, 170–1
  and Rustriningsih, 64–6, 74, 75, 76t, 77, 78, 80, 82–3, 85, 90t, 94–5, 100
  and Siti Qomariyah, 110–40
  attitude toward female leadership, 20, 59–63
  Islamization, 40, 42, 9t, 114
  NU *kyai*. See *kyai*

NU *santri*. See *santri*
  regional differences, 18
  See also 'Aisyiyah; Fatayat NU;
    kyai; Muslimat NU;
    Pekalongan Regency; *santri*;
    Yellow Book Learning Forum
Nahdlatul Ulama Female Student
  Association (IPPNU), 154
Nahdlatul Ulama Student Association
  (IPNU), 154
NASDEM. See National Democrats
Nashiruddin Al-Mansyur, KH., 21t,
  73–4, 75, 76t, 83, 84–5
  rationale for accepting
    nomination, 78, 100
  role in 2005 election, 77, 104,
    105
Nasyi'atul Islamiyah, 83
National Awakening Party (PKB), 18,
  19, 21–2t, 23t, 74, 75, 77, 78,
  85–6, 88t, 99
  Kebuman, 65–7, 76t, 77, 78, 83,
    85, 94
  Pekalongan, 109t, 110, 112, 113
  and Ratna Ani Lestari, 140, 143t,
    147, 150t, 152, 154
  and Rustriningsih, 65–7, 76t, 77,
    100
  and Siti Qomariyah, 109t, 110,
    112–30, 132, 134
National Democrats (NASDEM), 106
National Indonesian Party-Marhaenist
  Front (PNIM), 147, 149, 155,
  162
National Mandate Party (PAN), 21t,
  23t, 76t, 85, 86t, 86, 90, 99,
  109, 113, 123t, 143t, 147, 148,
  149, 190–1t
National Ulama Awakening Party, 110
Natsir, Lies-Marcos, 42
Network for Women and Politics
  (JPPOL), 45–6

networks, 111, 118
  and family ties, 13–6, 144–9
  female, 13, 45, 104, 128–9, 134,
    163
  and *Mauluddan*, 82–5,
    128–33
  and Muslimat NU, 128, 138
  Hindu, 155, 170
  and Islam, 3–6, 9–11, 63
  male, 13, 100, 105, 154–6, 170,
    185
  military, 90, 97
  NU *kyai*, 151–4
  AJB Bumiputera, 98
  village heads, 131
networking, 12–3
New Order, 34–43
  NU alienation during, 114–5
  political role for women under,
    34–7
  stance on political Islam, 37–43
  policies on women, 53
  policy of state ibuism, 43–4, 45
  normative behaviour (for Javanese
    Muslim women), 50–5, 56
Norr, Kathleen Fordham, 14
Norris, Pippa, 8, 10, 176, 193n40
NU *santri*. See *santri*
Nugroho, Wahyudi Pontjo, 118, 119,
  122, 124, 138, 139
Nu'mang, Agus Arifin, 98
Nur Muhammad (*kyai*), 153
Nuris, Yusuf (Gus Yus), 21t, 147,
  149, 150t, 151, 152, 165, 166,
  172
Nuryani, Nyai Hj., 82
nyai, 82, 105, 128–9, 185, 186

Osing (people), 142, 159, 160, 165,
  170
Ota, Atsushi, 2, 182

PAN. *See* National Mandate Party
Parawansa, Khofifah Indar, 47
Park Geun-hye, 12, 15, 79
Parisada Hindu Dharma Indonesia, 155
Paruntu, Christiany Eugenia, 190t, 192
patron-client ties, 7
PBB. *See* Star and Crescent Party
PDI. *See* Indonesian Democratic Party
PDIP. *See* Indonesian Democrat Party of Struggle
Pekalongan Regency, 108–10
    2006 direct election in, 114–33
    Siti Qomariyah's background in, 67–74
pengajian, 118–21, 128–30
    See also Istiqhotsah Kubro
perda sha'riah, 48
pesantren, 53, 64, 65, 67n7, 73, 76t
    Al Falah, 82–3
    Asshidiqi Pesantren, 154
    At-Taqwa (KH. Nashiruddin), 73
    At-Taufiqy, 118
    Kebumen, 82, 83
    Mansya'ul Huda Pesantren, 158
    Pekalongan, 110, 111, 115, 118–9, 129
    Ratna, 144, 150t, 167
    Riadlul 'Uqul, 83
    Banyuwangi, 151–4, 158
Philippines, 7
pingitan, 29, 51n2
PKB. *See* National Awakening Party
PKI, 32, 33, 34n30
PKK. *See* Family Welfare Guidance
PKS. *See* Prosperous Justice Party
political Islam, 12–3, 34, 38, 42
political roles for women
    New Order, 37–43
    post-Suharto era, 43–9
    pre-New Order, 28–37

polygamy, 43, 48, 180n14
    as a political issue, 29
    government regulations, 32, 52
Polygamy Award, 48. *See also* Puspo Wardoyo
pondok pesantren, 115
post-Suharto era
    studies, 3–5, 17
PPP. *See* United Development Party
presidential elections, 34, 75
    1999 election, 45, 61, 62, 177
Presidential Instruction Primary Schools (SDI), 54
print culture, 30
priyayi, 65n5, 67n7
Prosperous Justice Party (PKS), 98, 148
prostitution, Lestari's policy on, 168–9
purdah, 14
Purwadi, Agus, 57
Puspo Wardoyo, 48

Qomariyah, Siti, 18
    2006 direct election, 114–33
    2011 re-election, 138–40
    kyai support, 118–22
    Pekalongan background, 108–10
    personal background, 110–2
    piety in political performance, 124–8
    political emergence, 112–4
    on women's issues, 133–7, 183
    use of women's networks, 128–31
    santri background, 110–2
    See also Muslimat NU; NU; Pekalongan
QONCO, 124
Qusyairi, A., 147

Rafiq, Fadia A., 138, 139
Rahardjo, Broto, 138

Rahma El Junisia, 29–30
Rais, Abdul Rozaq, 90, 91
Rais, Amein, 99
RAKERDASUS, 87, 88, 107
"recentralization", 8
Reform Era, 142
regents (*bupati*). *See also bupati*
Regional People's Representative
    Council (DPRD), 8, 9, 112
    Banyuwangi, 149, 150t, 156, 161,
        167, 169, 172
    Central Java, 86t, 96
    Jembrana, 145
    Kebuman, 74, 76t, 77, 100, 147
    Pekalongan, 18, 113–6, 124, 126,
        140
Reid, Robin T., 80
religious courts, 52, 60
RENSTRA. *See* Local Strategic
    Development Plan
Research Center for Democracy and
    Human Rights (PusDeHAM), 171
Richter, Linda K., 15
Riswadi, 138, 140
RKPD. *See* Local Government
    Development Plan
Roces, Mina, 6
Rosikin, H., 111
Rozaq, *Kyai* Masykur, 83
Rukmana, Siti Hardijanti, 61
Rustam, KH. Margono, 83
Rustam, *Kyai* Masrur, 83
Rustriningsih
    2005 direct election, 74–6
    2008 Direct Gubernatorial
        Election, 19, 85–99
    appropriating women networks
        through *Mauluddan*, 82–5
    and individual capital, 67–9
    Islamic piety and political
        strategy, 78–82
    family networks and political
        support, 69–74
    loss of political support in 2013,
        106–7
    policies on women's issues,
        99–104, 183–4
    rise to PDI leadership in
        Kebumen, 64–7
    See also Kebumen

Sadono, Bambang, 89t, 91, 92, 99,
    147
Sakhiyah, Nyai Hj., 82
Samawai, Idham, 180, 188t
santri
    in Banyuwangi, 161
    comparisons, 174t, 175, 179–80,
        185
    definitions, 65, 65n5–6, 67n7,
        110n4
    in Pekalongan, 110, 114, 118
    and Ratna Ani Lestari, 143, 144,
        151, 161
    and Rustriningsih, 69, 73, 74, 80,
        82, 85, 100, 105
    and Siti Qomariyah, 110, 112,
        113, 118
Sarbini (*kyai*), 153
Sa'roni, Ali, 146, 149, 150t, 153, 165
Sartika, Dewi, 29
Sasongko, Ananto Tri, 76t, 82, 85
Satriyo, 4, 5, 182
Schlegel, Alice, 11, 12
Selamat Pagi Bupati (SPB), 79
selir, 29
Semarang, 20, 22t, 24t, 30, 32, 33,
    71, 87, 89t, 91, 98, 104
Shah, Saeeda J.A., 177
Sherman, Aurora M., 69
Shiraishi, Takashi, 29
Shofwan, Akrom (*kyai*), 130
Sholohin MS, Dr., 147
SIP. *See* Voice of Concerned Mothers
Siregar, 184

slogans, 94–5, 97, 105, 126, 127, 138, 139, 140, 164
Smith, Bianca J., 17
Smith-Hefner, Nancy J., 41
Social *Fiqh* School, 63
social background as a political factor, 185
"social Islamization", 2, 3
Soendari, Siti, 30
Soetomo, Andi, 186
Soewandi, 143, 149, 150t
Soeyitno, Agus, 89, 91, 150t, 164
Star and Crescent Party, 1, 2, 3, 5, 7, 8, 124, 147, 148, 149, 172, 190t
state ibuism, 35–6, 36n38, 43–4, 45
State Islamic Institute, 49, 111
Stiven, Maila, 39
Suaedy, Ahmad, 2, 182
Sudarto, Ken, 77
Suharto, 1, 61n50, 65
    policies toward political Islam, 34–7, 41–3
    Islamification under, 37–43
Suharto, Madame Tien, 36
Sujatmoko, Heru, 107
Sukamto, 67–8, 105–6
Sukarno, 32, 33, 34, 35, 62
Sukartono, Eko, 149, 150, 153, 164, 165, 166
Sukarnoputri, Megawati, 15, 45, 61, 62, 65, 68, 70–1, 75, 87, 97, 106, 110, 177
Sulchan, KH. Muhammad Afif (Gus Afif), 77
Suprapto, 76t, 82, 85
Supriyanto, Agus, 76t, 81, 85
Surya Paloh, 106
Suryasukuna, Julia, 35–6
Sutarip, Sukawi, 89t, 91, 92
Syafaat (*kyai*), 151n25, 152
Syafi'i, 149, 153
Syamsiyatun, Siti, 17

Tanaka, Makiko, 12, 15, 79
Tandfiziah of NU, 157
tarbiyah movement, 37–8, 39, 40
    change to United Action of Indonesian Muslim Students (KAMMI), 41
Taufiq (*kyai*), 118–20
    pengajian, 119
Thailand, 7
Thompson, Mark R., 15
Tong, Kooi-Chin, 38, 181
tudung, 39
Tuntunan Menjadi Isteri Islam Yang Berarti, 55–6
Turner, Bryan S., 38, 181

Ulumul Qur'an, 41
Umar, Nasaruddin, 42
United Development Party (PPP), 21–6t, 35, 65, 66t, 68n8, 75, 77, 86t, 90t, 99, 100, 108, 109t, 110, 115, 123t, 139, 142–3t, 149, 150t, 153, 164, 190–1
Uqud Al-Lujjayn, 53
United Action of Indonesian Muslim Students (KAMMI). *See tarbiyah* movement
Utami, Sri Paramita Budhi, 54
Utomo, Imam, 146
Utomo, Muji, 87

van Bemmelen, Sita, 41
Van Doorn-Harder, Pieternella, 63, 178
veil (*kudung*). *See* dress as political strategy: veil (*kudung*)
Veneracion-Rallonza, Lourdes, 6, 184–5
Vichit-Vadakan, Juree, 184
Voice of Concerned Mothers (SIP), 43

wadon wae ("choose a woman", slogan), 126–7
Wahid, Abdurrahman. *See* Gus Dur
Wahid, Sinta Nuriyah Abdurrahmad, 53
Wahid, Wawan G.A., 57
Wahyudi, Achmad, 21t, 149, 150t, 153, 156, 164, 165, 166
Waluyo, Bibit, 19, 87, 89t, 90, 92, 97
Wan Azizah, 79
wanita sejati (a "true woman"), 51, 80, 179
wanita sholehah (a "pious woman"), 125
Widyatmoko, Yusuf, 146–7, 149, 150t, 153, 164, 165, 172
Widyastuti, Haeny Relawati Rini, 8, 18
Winarto, Yunita T., 54
Wiryastuti, Ni Putu Eka, 192
women's network. *See* networks: female
women's organizations, 31
Women's Empowerment and Family Planning Bureau, 103
Women's Parliamentary Caucus (KPP), 45
Working Group for Gender Mainstreaming, 52
   See also Counter Legal Draft (CLD)
World Values Survey, 193
WS (regent of Jembrana), 19, 164

Yaasiin and *Tahlil* (verses), 159
Yahya, Yusuf, 113, 114
Yasuko, Kobayashi, 59
Yellow Book Learning Forum (FK3), 53
Youth Cadre of Golkar (AMPG), 139

Zeehandelaar, Stella, 29
Zurbriggen, Eileen L., 69